Psychology
and
Education

THE NATIONAL SOCIETY
FOR THE STUDY OF EDUCATION

Series on Contemporary Educational Issues
Kenneth J. Rehage, Series Editor

The 1981 Titles

Psychology and Education: The State of the Union, Frank H. Farley
  and Neal J. Gordon, editors
Selected Issues in Mathematics Education, Mary Montgomery
  Lindquist, editor

The National Society for the Study of Education also publishes Year-
books which are distributed by the University of Chicago Press. Inquiries regarding all publications of the Society, as well as inquiries
about membership in the Society, may be addressed to the Secretary-
Treasurer, 5835 Kimbark Avenue, Chicago, IL 60637. Membership in
the Society is open to any who are interested in promoting the investigation and discussion of educational questions.

Psychology
and
Education

The State
of the Union

Edited by

FRANK H. FARLEY

University of Wisconsin
Madison

and

NEAL J. GORDON

University of Illinois
Chicago Circle

McCutchan Publishing Corporation
2526 Grove Street
Berkeley, California 94704

ISBN 0-8211-0506-X
Library of Congress Catalog Card Number 80-82902

© 1981 by McCutchan Publishing Corporation

Printed in the United States of America

Cover design by Terry Down, Griffin Graphics

Series Foreword

In 1977 the committee of the National Society for the Study of Education responsible for planning the series on Contemporary Educational Issues sponsored a meeting of educators from several midwestern states. The purpose of the meeting was to get suggestions for important topics that should be addressed through volumes in that series. Professor Frank Farley suggested that a publication dealing with new developments in the field of educational psychology would be a useful addition to the series. Together with Professor Neal Gordon, he subsequently submitted a proposal for such a book. The proposal was approved by the committee and became the basis for this volume, in which the editors have included papers that illustrate ways in which the field of psychology is contributing to the study of important educational problems. Several of the papers were delivered at the annual meeting of the American Educational Research Association in Boston in 1980.

The Society is most grateful to Professors Farley and Gordon and to all the contributors to this publication for their work in bringing the book to completion. We believe that a careful reading of the several chapters will be a rewarding experience for all who wish to be well informed about developments in the comparatively new disci-

pline of educational psychology and especially about the implications of those developments for educational practice. A book that
can serve this purpose is very much in keeping with the ideas that led
to the establishment in 1971 of the Society's series on Contemporary
Educational Issues.

Kenneth J. Rehage

for the Committee on the Expanded
Publication Program of the National
Society for the Study of Education

Contributors

Robbie Case, Ontario Institute for Studies in Education
Frank H. Farley, University of Wisconsin
Lawrence T. Frase, Bell Laboratories
Robert M. Gagné, Florida State University
Neal J. Gordon, University of Illinois, Chicago Circle Campus
Robert E. Grinder, Arizona State University
Guy J. Groen, McGill University
Robert J. Havighurst, University of Chicago
Philip W. Jackson, University of Chicago
David W. Johnson, University of Minnesota
Trudy Kowallis, Brigham Young University
M. David Merrill, University of Southern California
Larry Nucci, University of Illinois, Chicago Circle Campus
Joseph M. Scandura, University of Pennsylvania
Thomas J. Shuell, State University of New York at Buffalo
Kay A. Stolurow, Boston University
Lawrence M. Stolurow, University of Iowa
Sigmund Tobias, City University of New York
Herbert J. Walberg, University of Illinois, Chicago Circle Campus
Brent G. Wilson, Brigham Young University
Merlin C. Wittrock, University of California at Los Angeles

Contents

Preface: The Octogenarian

The relationship between psychology and education has been long and, we believe, mutually profitable. Psychology as a formal scientific discipline is now over a century old. Educational psychology, as a subdiscipline, is younger, with most historians tracing its origin to E.L. Thorndike (1903), whose influence is considered in several chapters of this volume. Over the past seven decades, education has been a major testing ground for the application and usefulness of psychology. In recent years, however, a trend away from the idea of *applying* psychology *to* educational contexts and a redirection toward developing significant and pervasive psychological ideas and concepts *from within* educational contexts has taken place. Educational psychology increasingly appears to be less of an applied psychology and more of a discipline with its own concepts and theories, methods and procedures. Or does it?

With the beginning of the eighth decade of life for the field of educational psychology, the time is ripe for a report on the state of the union between psychology and education: an interview with an octogenarian discipline discussing major domains of current focus, providing some perspectives on the past and making some prognoses for the future. This is the mission of the present volume. We hope you will enjoy the tour, guided by trail-hardened veterans, over much

1

of the terrain of current educational psychology from physiological models to philosophical issues, with a provocative sampling of ideas, theories, data, creativity, contention, and conclusions in between.

We have organized the book into four parts, beginning with a series of discussions relating to individual differences and achievement, continuing with considerations of development, and moving to issues of learning and instruction. The book concludes with a section on the history, current status, and future of educational psychology. The chapters reflect both an appreciation for the already established theoretical orientations upon which educational psychologists have come to rely and for current perspectives on the state of the field. These perspectives emphasize cognitive processes, student activity, life-span development, revisions of Piagetian theory, cognitive-affective interactions, individual differences, theoretical models, biological bases of individual differences, and adaptive education, learning, memory, instructional design, and teaching implications. Perspectives on behavioral models of development and instruction are also presented. Nearly every chapter incorporates empirical research, theory, and educational implications, for the book is written to appeal to a broad audience, including graduate and undergraduate students, researchers, administrators, curriculum planners, and teachers.

We caution readers who believe staunchly and exclusively in empirical data: Beware, we offer more than data here. Some of our authors present suggestions, hypotheses, models, theories—even conclusions—without conclusive empirical data. While nearly every chapter includes an obvious appreciation for empirical investigations, we have encouraged our authors to offer their own perspectives and speculations. In this fashion we have tried to reflect various unions: those of psychological and educational research; those of practice and promise; and those of specific fact and speculation. Despite these efforts, much remains disunified and unconnected; for that, too, is the state of the union. We hope that our willingness to incorporate the traditional and nontraditional will map many routes that serve to unify and connect psychology, education, research, practice, and theory.

We extend special appreciation to Herbert J. Walberg and are grateful for the efforts and comments of Harriet Talmage. In addition, we thank our authors for their outstanding scholarly contributions and fine cooperation at all stages of this work. Finally, our spouses, Sonja V. Farley and Nancy A. Gordon, have been tremendously helpful with many aspects of this volume.

PART ONE
Individual Differences

Overview

Part One addresses a fundamental question of educational psychology: What is the nature and significance of individual differences among people, and what role might these differences play in effective education? Farley's chapter introduces the section, and it focuses upon some basic assumptions concerning biological structures and functions. The chapter then proceeds to an educationally relevant theory of individual differences and individualization based upon those assumptions. Thus it is the most basic of the chapters in Part One, and in the book, from the perspective of a levels of science, reductionist, sociobiological scheme. Farley outlines a theory that allows for both treatment effects and individual differences to be commonly scalable in terms of physiological arousal processes. This theory of adaptive education proposes interactions of individual differences in arousal processes with characteristics of teachers, of instruction, and of the social and physical environment. It allows for predictions of cognitive and affective outcomes, and it has a subset of hypotheses concerning childhood disorders, such as schizophrenia and hyperactivity, and a subset of hypotheses directed at creativity and delinquency. Some tests of the theory are reported, and some untested implications are outlined.

The theory attempts to define one interface between psycho-biology and education, emphasizing that psychological processes do not exist independently of neural processes and that education cannot be maximally effective without some consideration of the biology of behavior. To some extent this chapter complements those of Tobias and Walberg in this section, both of which contain original theoretical proposals bearing upon individual differences and educa-tion. While Farley proposes "biological aptitudes" as one basis for adaptive education, Tobias proposes prior achievement as a basis, and Walberg proposes a set of primarily social-psychological variables as individual differences important for educational achievement.

In his chapter "Dimensions of Individual Differences," Shuell argues that challenges to some of the basic assumptions underlying research on individual differences characterize the current state of the field. Obviously, individual differences can be characterized in any number of ways; Shuell stresses four basic orientations. These include conceptualizations focusing on traits, abilities, performances, and types—with trait characterizations having greater frequency in recent research. Shuell recognizes the two extremes that might characterize individual differences that Gordon discusses in a later chapter on social cognition. At one extreme is the assumption that general laws apply to all individuals; while at the other extreme is the approach that assumes all individuals are unique; and general laws are, therefore, not possible. Shuell prefers an approach somewhere between these two. He argues that appropriate ways to characterize individual differences depend on the purposes one has and on certain basic assumptions regarding the nature of those differences. The major focus of the chapter is on two areas of individual differences: differences in mental abilities and in personality. It is in the discus-sion of differences in mental ability where we find a theme that is consonant with notions presented earlier in Farley's chapter and elsewhere in the book. The theme emphasizes *processes* involved in mental abilities as opposed to delineations of *how much* mental ability a given individual might have.

A change in emphasis in the literature on personality differences is also identified by Shuell. That change is in many respects an out-growth of the discovery that traits indicative of individual differences are not always consistent across time and/or situations. One strong emphasis in current research seems to focus on concern for interactions between individuals and the situations in which they find themselves. Shuell also notes a parallel in the direction of research on personality and cognitive aspects of individual differences. He points out that cognition and affectivity are merely arbitrary divisions of psychological function and that it would be a major advance for us to focus on cognitive-affective interactions. This point is also consonant with the perspectives in the Farley chapter as well as chapters in the next section by Gordon and by Nucci and Walberg.

One significant aspect of individual differences relates to how such differences aid educators in the design of education to best meet the needs of each student. The purpose of the Tobias chapter is to review educational programs that have been designed to adapt to individual differences. A review of some present versions of individualized instruction indicates that the principal type of individualization typically focuses on the rate of instruction but not on the type of instructional method. His perspective is that in a truly individualized instructional setting, both the rate of instruction and the method would be individualized. Tobias's review on the effectiveness of aptitude-treatment interactions leads to two pessimistic conclusions. The first is that the number of previous investigations leading to consistent findings is reasonably small and that one finds a considerable amount of inconsistency in these findings. The second issue concerns the lack of generality of these findings. An aptitude-treatment interaction that might be effective for one subject matter may not be effective at all for a different subject matter in a different student population. In Tobias's view there is a definite need for a classification scheme of instructional methods, on the one hand, and of characteristics of individual differences among students on the other. Tobias suggests that there is an inverse relationship between prior knowledge and amount of instructional support required to master educational objectives. His hypothesis leads to the importance of directing students' attention to various aspects of the curriculum. Tobias's chapter ends with some discussion of the practical problems involved in adaptation to individual differences. Among those problems is the need for some system for storing and retrieving information about the programs of individual students to which teachers could turn to learn where the students are in their efforts to accomplish curriculum objectives.

A fundamental assumption underlying the presentations on

individual differences has been that individualizing instruction will lead to higher student achievement. Walberg's chapter presents a psychological model of educational productivity that focuses on seven factors relevant to students' achievement. Walberg borrows from economic models of productivity to propose a model in which it is assumed that ability, motivation, quality and quantity of instruction, classroom and home environmental influences, and age affect achievement. A series of provisional hypotheses flows from the model. Applications of production theory to educational innovation and to issues of aptitude-treatment interaction are also considered. Walberg's presentation improves upon the traditional research on aptitude-treatment interaction and overcomes several of the limitations identified by Tobias.

1. Basic Process Individual Differences: A Biologically Based Theory of Individualization for Cognitive, Affective, and Creative Outcomes

Frank H. Farley

One of the most productive and promising of modern sciences is that of psychobiology, which includes research on brain behavior (such as the split-brain and hemispheric mediation paradigms), biofeedback, psychophysiology, and so on. Psychophysiology, for instance, as a formal subdiscipline, is less than fifteen years old (Sternbach 1966) but has led to such discoveries as biofeedback and autonomic self-control, which have had major implications for cardiovascular health and illness, as well as for psychosomatic illnesses of many types and for theories of cognition and of mind and body. Psychophysiology now has a rapidly developing professional society, as does biofeedback itself. Journals have proliferated, and the health sciences, clinical psychology, experimental psychology, personality psychology, and social psychology have all been profoundly influenced by this fledgling science of psychobiology. Even broader issues of the nature of human institutions and sociological thinking have been influenced by modern biological concepts, as shown for instance in the work of sociobiologists (Wilson 1975).

Educational research, however, as a contemporary social science, seems to pay minimal attention to psychobiological considerations.

Consider any recent annual program of the American Educational Research Association for example. There is a great deal of psychologically oriented research, sociologically oriented research, measurement and statistical research, evaluation research, administrative research, curriculum research but almost no research taking psychobiological ideas into account. One might conclude from the research reported at these conventions that cognition bears no relation to the nervous system; that personality, emotion, and motivation have no major bodily aspects; and that an organism could be effectively studied in complex situations without consideration of its evolutionary and biological structural and functional character, including those processes that might serve or control psychological matters.

It seems to me that there is a strong case for working with biopsychological constructs. I do not believe the attempt to explain an aspect of behavior is complete until it has been given a biological perspective, which in the long run means relating it to natural selection and evolution. All forms of behavior must depend on bodily structures (including features of the nervous system) that have appeared in the course of evolution because they contributed to the survival of the species and the individual. Taking a psychobiological perspective in our work on individual differences is desirable for a number of reasons. First, there is the potential for a more complete account of behavior as well as for the integration of the sciences. Second, such a perspective gives us a "crack" at the biggest problem of them all—the *mind/body problem*. Third, and more pragmatically, I believe this approach has been theoretically and practically fruitful, especially since the revolutionary thinking of Hebb (1949).

As far as the educational research community is concerned, however, there has been little involvement in biopsychological constructs. Aside from some genetical questions and problems of biological insult (for example, brain damage), educational researchers in recent years have pretty much tended to leave the body out of the child. In educational research the head seems to be merely the bony home of a hardworking hyphenated homunculus or information processor or schema or S-R chain gang. It is simply a place where paired associates get stuffed in and, if all goes well, pulled out intact or perhaps even elaborated. Or the head is a place to which a passage of a fixed number of words per page is presented at a fixed rate (established by the experimenter, of course), with the requirement that it indicates which one of four simple facts it has been presented. The response of the head is then noted by the experimenter. The foregoing paradigms, in various guises, prevail in much current research on learning. This may appropriately be labeled "bjark psychology." A stimulus is presented, the subject says "bjark," and the experimenter notes it down. Another stimulus is presented, another "bjark" is received and duly noted. Another stimulus is presented, another "bjark" is received, and on it goes. These bjarks (or responses) are added, multiplied, subtracted, and divided. They are analyzed by parametric and nonparametric statistics, by univariate and multivariate statistics, by metric and nonmetric methods. They are orchestrated into songs to scientific psychology and published in the journals of bjark. The paradigms of bjark are not our most ennobling inventions. In three hundred years we have progressed from the Bard to bjark, and I am worried. Grand theories of great importance to psychological understanding are reduced, in the manner of an inverted pyramid or funnel, to a simplistic empirical test paradigm. Complex mental life is tested by simple reaction time. William James long ago set us the task of comprehending the stream of mental life and the continuity and interrelatedness of psychological phenomena. We are insufficiently meeting these objectives, even though we are increasingly endorsing their centrality in the raison d'etre of psychological science. The granularity of our research paradigms is often too fine, and we make insufficient effort toward meeting James's objective of understanding the *interrelatedness* of psychologically valid paradigms, including the simultaneous study of bodily events involved in behavior. Bjark psychology, devoid of clear measures of the continuity and interrelatedness of behavior, has left us up the Jamesian stream of mental life without a paddle—or even a canoe for that matter. And we shall remain so until we bid goodbye to bjark, get our brain and body involved, and start to swim. Then perhaps we can begin to discern the meandering, meaningful course of this stream, in the real time flow of complex behavior and its source, in the upper reaches of the brain.

I must apologize for digressing. I have attempted to make the point that much research on learning and individual differences in education is a victim of bjark psychology. This problem is primarily one of measurement, of experimental paradigm, rather than of theory. More importantly, I have tried to indicate that educational-psychological research has attended insufficiently to the biological components of behavior, to the possibility of discerning the grand interrelatedness of phenomena. I have no programs for the solution to these problems. Where the oversimplification of our paradigms for research on learning is concerned, I have some hope in the outcomes of our increasing attention to research on the processing of discourse and the study of natural language behavior. Perhaps the computer may ultimately prove of value here in providing on-line, real-time interactive relationships with a stream of natural verbal behavior, with, of course, attendant and comparable indexing of biological behavior. Where the relative lack of attention in educational research to psychobiological analyses is concerned, I have hope that the strides being made in psychobiological theory and method may be increasingly adapted to our goals.

Turning to the title of this chapter two key terms, "basic" and "process," seem to me to be central to the further development of theoretically and practically useful analysis of individual differences. In my psychological vocabulary, the term *basic* refers to the classical levels-of-science model. The more basic a construct or idea is, the more it is physical and identifiable in physico-chemical structure or function. Thus, when notions about individual differences have biological referents or implications, they would be more basic than those having no such referents. The term *process* has recently emerged at or near the top of the learning researchers' charts. A major conclusion of the 1967 conference on Learning and Individual Differences was that we should be concerned with individual differences in the *processes* held to underlie attention, learning, and memory. To quote Melton's discussion of that conference, "What is necessary is that we frame our hypotheses about individual differences variables in terms of the process constructs of contemporary theories of learning and performance" (Gagné 1967, p. 239). (One might call these *process individual differences* and their measurement *process-referenced measurement*.) Since 1967 a wide array of process analyses of learning and individual differences have been offered (Farley 1974a, Hunt 1978, Snow 1978, Sternberg 1977, among others). For a review see Chapter 2 in the present volume. Glaser (1972) has referred to those process variables of relevance to individual differences as the "new aptitudes" and has presented an eloquent argument for their importance in the study of individual differences and education.

Other more physiologically referenced individual differences might lie in processes of cortical arousal, in Russian conceptualizations of strength, balance, and mobility of the nervous system (Strelau, Farley, and Gale 1981, Nebylytsyn and Gray 1972), and so on. It is such physiologically referenced process variables that are the focus of this chapter.

A few years ago I outlined a psychobiological model that seemed to have potential use in the study of education (Farley 1974a, 1974b). The present chapter reports on that model and some educationally relevant research bearing upon it. Specifically, I wish to propose one approach to basic process individual differences that I think may be fruitful for consideration where individual differences and adaptive education are concerned. It is a crude but hopeful step toward identifying a basic process individual difference that bears some theoretical implications for integrating levels of science, that puts the body into behavior, and that has useful implications for schools.

Two points are important to the discussion and theoretical perspective that follow. First, I subscribe wholeheartedly to the ancient principle of simplicity in matters of theory explication; there is a rule of art applicable to science, which is that within complexity lies simplicity. A modern version of this might be called Rutherford's dictum, after the great British physicist, Lord Rutherford, who argued that if your theory could not be understood by your local bartender, it had almost no chance of being proved true! A second introductory point is that educational research and theory concerned with individual differences, learning, and instruction should increasingly pay attention to issues outside formal education in kindergarten through grade twelve and should consider issues of learning and individual differences across the life span. Thus, a "life-span educational psychology" is needed to generalize our current work, to take into account the educational needs of an increasingly older population, and to provide theory development of more general implication. This latter view is a minority one at present, at least in aptitude-treatment interaction (ATI) research, where the current fashion is toward short-lived minor theory sharply limited by age, generation, and locale. An issue as profoundly significant for human affairs as learning and achievement cannot afford theoretical minutists or process pointillists. A search for reasonably generalizable and pervasive theory must not be abandoned. I believe painters of broad perspective and bold stroke are needed here as never before.

To get to the substance of the recent developments in our psycho-biological model of ATI let me start with an outline of the central concepts.

AROUSAL PROCESSES AND THE STIMULATION-SEEKING MOTIVE: A GENERAL THEORY

The central *biological construct* in our theory is that of physiological arousal. The central *psychological construct* is that of stimulation seeking. The construct of arousal has been part of the psychological vocabulary since the early 1950s, receiving its biggest early boost with the work of Moruzzi and Magoun (1949) on the reticular activating system (RAS) and the theoretical analyses of Lindsley (1951) and Hebb (1955). It has not, however, been much transported into research on learning and instruction or ATI. Physiological arousal is an interesting concept. It may have both dynamic and directive aspects. For heuristic purposes, it may be differentiated into cortical arousal and autonomic arousal. It may also be reasonable to talk of Arousal Process I mediated by the reticular activating system and concerned mainly with the dynamic apsects of motivation and Arousal Process II perhaps mediated by aspects of the limbic system or other as yet unspecified structures and probably concerned mainly with the directive aspects of motivation as governed by the type and range of effective reinforcements and incentives.

A nervous system differentiated for different psychological functions under normal conditions is a useful notion, as is the notion that under certain extreme conditions generalized functioning occurs. For a recent more extended discussion of arousal processes, see Farley (1981). The theory of "arousal-treatment interactions" that I have outlined elsewhere (Farley 1974a, 1974b, Farley and Sewell 1976) considers arousal as multisystem in nature. Although this theory assumes that there is more than one arousal system, for the purposes of the present chapter I shall concentrate on the "classical" arousal system, that is, the one mediated by RAS function, because most of the ATI-relevant research we have undertaken has concentrated on this system, or what I have called Arousal Process I.

The second concept in our theory, that of *stimulation seeking*, refers to a pervasive, important but little understood characteristic of human motivation, the seeking or avoiding of stimulation, sensation, and arousal. Individual differences in need for stimulation or stimulation seeking have come to be seen in recent years as a major aspect of motivation, with persons varying in their stimulation-seeking behavior and their optimal levels of stimulation (Farley 1971, Lester 1969, Zuckerman 1978). This may be a particularly *modern motive.* For example, we are in an age of stimulation—an increasingly noisy, smelly, speedy, eye-straining age. We are in the midst of a battle for our senses, and we are losing ground. The medium is the massacre. The governess of our children is a two-dimensional, 525 pointy-headed antiintellectual monster called television. Media in their many guises are taking control of our sensorium. A generation ago W. H. Auden (1946) characterized the times as the age of anxiety. But we have moved on from simple worry. We are now in the *age of arousal.* Jimmy Dorsey's dozen horns are no match for electrified rock and roll. We are an aroused citizenry but for the wrong reasons. Quietude, privacy, wee small worlds, and Walden Pond are fast fading. These may be happy days for sensation seekers, but what of their opposites, sensation reducers or avoiders? The hallways of our urban schools are drug marts and dope drops, and the medication is not for curing the aches of little tummies. Johnny may not be able to read because he is jumping up and down all the time. Many writers have argued that change is the central quality of our time, particularly change of home, change of place, locale, friends, all attributable to an unusually mobile population. Thus not only the *intensity* but also the *variety* of stimulation may be exceptional. Herman Kahn (1976) has described ours as the sensate age. If the rise of a civilization is correlated with the achievement motive (McClelland 1961), perhaps its decline is correlated with sensation seeking.

With this background to our concept of the stimulation-seeking motive, let me return to our theory. For Arousal Process I the main aspects of the theory are as follows:

1. The primary psychological motive based on arousal is the sensation-seeking motive. Sensation seeking or avoiding is the primary method to modulate Arousal Process I.
2. The sources of arousal can be categorized as intrinsic or trait arousal (being characteristic and traitlike in nature, the main individual difference term) and extrinsic (the manipulable component of arousal, for example, the effects of stimulus charac-

teristics). Sources of extrinsic arousal may be mental (such as fantasy) or behavioral (such as overt stimulation seeking).

3. The relationship between Type I arousal and performance is nonmonotonic in the form of an inverted U-shaped function. We have generalized the performance construct to include "effective psychological functioning."

4. The relationship between intrinsic arousal and the sensation-seeking motive is linear and negative. Individuals low in intrinsic arousal will seek to reduce stimulation effects (extrinsic arousal) so as to lower their overall Type I arousal to optimal levels. This modulation of stimulation effects and attempt to maintain an optimal level of arousal are significant for the survival of the organism.

A crucial part of the model for ATI research is the intrinsic arousal conceptualization; that is, the characteristic or traitlike arousal component. Intrinsic arousal may be highly heritable as well as due in part to early sensory experience.

The concept of extrinsic arousal or the variable, manipulable component of overall arousal allows for the analysis of stimulus and situation effects on overall Type I arousal, including instructional and task characteristics, environmental factors, and teacher characteristics. To the extent that any stimulus can be scaled for its arousal-eliciting value or arousal potential, it can be systematically studied in predictive analyses of ATI where A = intrinsic arousal, and T = treatable or extrinsic arousal sources. *We then have a simple, biologically based, testable theory of ATI where the aptitude and the treatment are conceptually linked, and differential predictions can be made for different levels of the A and the T variables.* The aptitude variable here can theoretically be expected to have substantial generality and stability. Intrinsic arousal level is not expected to vary greatly between sexes, cultures, races, generations, and so on. It is presumed to be not local or particularly variable, although I believe it varies somewhat with age, even less with race and gross aspects of cultures. Extrinsic arousal, the treatment variable, on the other hand, is the very subject of manipulation, of treatment, of intervention.

It should be pointed out that although arousal is used significantly in the theory, the theory could function without it. That is, we could operate solely with a dimension of stimulation seeking in which there is an optimal level of stimulation for effective performance and in which there are marked individual differences in this motive, perhaps due to early experience, learning, and so on. However, I prefer to keep arousal in the theory because of the sense it makes of some data to be discussed later and because it gives us the gambler's edge on interrelating some psychological and bodily phenomena. The physiological approach may also facilitate studies in a life-span context in that the aptitude (arousal) variable is measurable in all age groups, with minimum modification of the measurement instrument(s). The approach to treatment variables suggested by our model should allow for a comparable metric for various categories of those variables. Teacher characteristics, instructional characteristics, and environmental characteristics may be in part commonly scalable on a dimension of arousal potential (extrinsic arousal).

How can intrinsic arousal be measured? A variety of techniques can be used, including the two-flash visual threshold (Maaser and Farley 1980), the easily usable sweat-bottle technique of Strahan, Todd, and Inglis (1974), multichannel polygraph measures of skin conductance, blood volume, electroencephalograph, and so on, including basal levels and habituation rates.

The treatment variables or extrinsic arousal may have a wide range of characteristics in the model. In addition, the outcome of ATI can be cognitive-academic in nature or affective-mental health in nature, although we recognize that these domains are of course not independent. I would like to turn now to a number of implications of the general theory.

ADAPTIVE EDUCATION AND ALTERNATIVE SCHOOLING: A SPECIAL THEORY

I wish to propose that open schools, open-space classrooms, and relatively unstructured education are more arousing than traditional schools, self-contained classrooms, and structured education. The former provide more and varied stimulation, ambiguity, uncertainty, and unpredictability; more alternatives and therefore more choices and decisions. Proponents of more open and unstructured educational conditions would probably agree that these are indeed more stimulating and varied than traditional and structured educational conditions. (We know that activity levels are higher in the former than in the latter as has been reported by the Stanford project on Environments for Teaching [Lueders-Salmon 1970]). In addition to the environment for learning and teaching, instructional procedures may also be differentially arousing. Thus, lectures and expository and deductive modes would be dearousing relative to open-discussion, discovery, and inductive modes, which would be expected to be arousing. Furthermore, teachers (adults and peers) may vary in their arousal potential, although individualizing education on the basis of teacher characteristics is seldom done at any level of education.

We would predict that open and more unstructured education will be particularly suited to low-arousal, high stimulation-seeking students, while traditional and structured education will be particularly suited to high-arousal, low stimulation-seeking students. Indeed, open education may be harmful to significant numbers of high-arousal school children. I shall return to this point later. Where instructional procedures are concerned, we would predict that low-arousal children would benefit most from open discussion, discovery, and inductive procedures, while high-arousal children would benefit most from lecture, expository, and deductive procedures. Thus, school environments and instructional procedures will interact with intrinsic arousal and the stimulation-seeking (SS) motive. This proposed ATI is represented in Figure 1-1.

To summarize, the teacher, instructional, and environmental characteristics that would be expected to represent potential for high and low arousal in our theory are the following (this list is not, of course, exhaustive):

Teacher characteristics.

High-arousal potential: extrovert, lively, dramatic, loud, variable, and so forth.

Low-arousal potential: introvert, low key, ponderous, quiet and reserved, reliable, and so on.

Instructional characteristics.

High-arousal potential: discovery procedures, inductive as opposed to procedures, fast pacing, variable pacing, uncertainty, ambiguity, color media, discussion rather than lecture, and so on.

Low-arousal potential: opposite of above.

Environmental characteristics.

High-arousal potential: open-space plan, color, high activity, complexity, variety, and so forth.

Low-arousal potential: traditional self-contained classroom, opposite of above.

Our arousal-treatment model thus will allow for predictions of the separate or combined effects of teacher characteristics, task and instructional characteristics, and environmental characteristics on cognitive or affective outcomes for low-arousal versus high-arousal persons. Students in an intermediate range of intrinsic arousal are not specifically addressed by the model, as they are considered to be relatively robust with respect to the arousal potential of teachers, environments, and instruction, although presumably they should be best served by intermediate values of arousal potential in these three sources.

I mentioned above that the unstructured, open condition might be harmful to some high-arousal children. Consider, for example, an open-space school. Look in any direction and there is activity. A child can see other children in a number of other classes. In some such schools, all classes are visible from any location. Many classes move from one area to another by the moving of desks. Such activity levels and variegated intensive stimulation are clearly in contrast to the typical self-contained classroom. There may be serious long-term implications for the psychological health of the high-arousal child in such an environment. In recent years a body of research and theory has come to view overarousal as a potentially important factor in some forms of schizophrenia. Schizophrenia is a disorder of no small significance in contemporary America. One estimate of the prevalence of schizophrenia in the United States is 3 percent of the population (Reiss et al. 1977). It may be proposed that chronic overarousal generates some schizophrenic features through as yet unknown mechanisms. One characteristic often used to describe some forms of schizophrenia is social withdrawal. I would argue that this is in part an attempt of the high-arousal individual to dearouse, to reduce stimulation. (I would further suggest that the ultimate high-arousal and stimulation-reducing person is the stuporous catatonic schizophrenic, that classic still-life response to arousal.)

In addition, some characteristics of communication patterns reported for the families of schizophrenic children may serve to exacerbate an overarousal problem. For example, these might include communication vagueness, confusion, incompleteness (Friedman and Friedman 1970); fragmented, uncertain communications (Morris and

Wynne 1965); and greater "perplexity" of communications (Meyers and Goldfarb 1961). All of these characteristics may be argued to embody conflict and uncertainty, an attribute Berlyne (1960) and others have shown to be a powerful source of arousal. The uncertainty aspect of the double-bind theory of parental treatment of schizophrenic children (Bateson et al. 1956) might serve to exacerbate and prolong already high levels of intrinsic arousal. If a child is excessively high in intrinsic arousal, possibly through heritable and early sensory experience sources, then the prolonging and heightening of this hyperarousal through the environmental mechanisms noted above may lead to the social withdrawal and/or through disorder often identified in schizophrenia. Thus, extrinsic arousal might represent the environment (that is, its arousal potential) and intrinsic arousal the heritable component, that are at a minimum required for environment-heredity analyses of schizophrenia. Rosenthal (1970) and Reiss, Peterson, and O'Neill (1977), among others, have reviewed the powerful evidence supporting the hypothesis of a genetic predisposition to schizophrenia.

The contribution of open-space classrooms and more unstructured high-arousal conditions (that is, high-arousal potential features of teachers, social and physical environments, and instruction) to the general etiology of schizophrenia would lie in the chronic overarousal of already high-arousal children who are subjected to the familial factors noted above. I am not, of course, proposing intrinsic arousal and extrinsic arousal (arousal potential) as sole factors in the etiology of childhood schizophrenia. This disorder, as most psychological disorders, is surely determined by many factors, and theories are legion (Reiss et al. 1977). If our arousal theory is even in part correct, however, then the excessively high intrinsic arousal child is best served in the long haul by dearousing adaptive education. That is, education can be adaptive not only for achievement and cognitive outcomes but also for important emotional and mental health outcomes. These adaptive implications are reflected in Figure 1-1. Where childhood schizophrenia is concerned, I might go out on a limb and predict that with the increased emphasis on open space and more unstructured education in recent years, we might anticipate an increased national incidence of this disorder.

In addition to childhood schizophrenia, I believe there is reason to propose excessive chronic arousal as one factor in autism. The lack of affect and withdrawal of the autistic child may also be in part a reaction to hyperarousal, the child's attempt to dearouse. There is evidence that would support such a proposal. Hutt et al. (1965) have reported electroencephalographic data on autistic children indicating hyperarousal. If our hypothesis of arousal and autism is even in part correct, then again high-arousal-potential conditions may be expected to exacerbate this disorder, and our arousal-treatment model may be a useful source of adaptive options for these children.

I have been discussing some adaptive education and psychological implications of excessively high arousal. But such implications for excessively low arousal are considerable. The theory has specific implications for a childhood disorder of great importance in our nation's schools—that of hyperactivity or hyperkinesis. This disorder is being diagnosed in a large number of school children. I believe this to be in part a disorder of severe underarousal characterized by marked stimulation seeking. I would propose that the hyperkinetic child is chronically underaroused and is excessively low in intrinsic arousal through genetic or other perhaps early sensory experience sources. The hyperactivity is in part hyperstimulation seeking to increase the child's arousal. Thus, the treatment for hyperactivity should include the employment of arousal-inducing (high-arousal-potential) treatments. Indeed, the hypothesis would be partially confirmed if such treatments were shown to reduce hyperactivity. The child would no longer be so actively seeking stimulation to increase his or her arousal level, as stimulation would be otherwise provided.

One direct test would be in the use of stimulant drugs, which would act directly on the arousal system (Arousal Process I), raising arousal so that the function of behavioral stimulation seeking would be diminished and the child's hyperactivity would therefore be reduced. Here, paradoxically it would be predicted that a stimulant drug, rather than leading to increased activity levels, would have a calming effect on behavior. The available data suggest that stimulants may indeed be relatively effective treatments for hyperactivity. Methylphenidate, dextroamphetamine, and caffeine have all been shown to be relatively effective treatments not only for hyperactivity but also for certain learning disabilities (Conners, Eisenberg, and Barci 1967, Schnackenberg 1973). These learning disabilities may also have a significant underarousal component. By no means are all cases of hyperactivity treatable by stimulant drugs, but the incidence of success is encouraging. In a widely read cover article on troubled children, *Newsweek* magazine (April 8, 1974, p. 56) stated "Just how the stimulants have this paradoxical calming effect isn't known, but they seem to improve the child's ability to concentrate." The arousal analysis seems to account for this effect. The use of drugs in this fashion is, of course, questionable. The long-term side effects and contraindications are not well known. Some effects are loss of appetite, weight loss, and insomnia. The article in *Newsweek* notes that "As a result, children who take them for several years may not grow as tall as they might have otherwise. But the effects of the drugs can be so dramatic," they say, quoting a leading medical researcher, "that you wonder whether an extra bit of height is all that important."

Although I have heard the president of a leading educational foundation say he believes that controlled use of psychoactive drugs and related medication in education is the wave of the future and can be expected to increase, I am opposed to this development. I do not believe American education should be in the business of developing thin, stunted, junkie, sleepless children. Among other things, most of our national sports would all but disappear for want of qualified players! I have an alternative. It is an *adaptive education* alternative, rather than *adaptive medication.* I would propose that hyperkinetic children be exposed to arousing education, perhaps open-space classrooms, more unstructured conditions, discussion and discovery instructional modes, divergent creativity experiences, arousing, extraverted teachers, and so on. (See Figure 1-1.) These conditions may provide the arousal boost necessary for the hyperkinetic child to function effectively. Looking only at the environment, it would be predicted from our theory that environments with high-arousal potential would ameliorate the symptoms of hyperactivity relative to environments with low-arousal potential. Koester and Farley (1977) tested this prediction in a study of six first-grade classrooms, three of which were classified as open and three as traditional. The classroom differentiation was made using ratings based on a checklist derived from Walberg's and Thomas's (1972) "eight open education themes." It was predicted that low-arousal children would perform better over the course of the year and demonstrate diminished hyperactive symptomatology in open classrooms relative to low-arousal children in traditional classrooms and that high-arousal children would per-

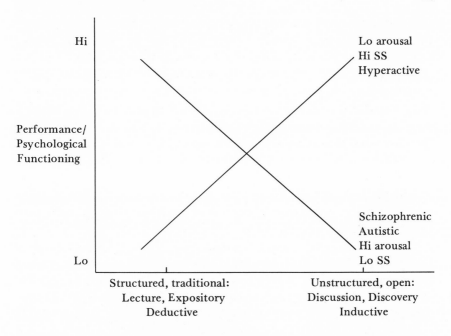

Figure 1-1

Proposed aptitude-treatment interaction

form less well in open classrooms relative to high-arousal children in traditional classrooms. Arousal was measured at the beginning of the year and again at the end, employing tonic and phasic measures of skin resistance, pulse volume, and pulse rate. Extensive indices of hyperactivity were employed, including behavior rating scales and performance measures such as perceptual-motor steadiness. Academic performance was measured by scales of the CIRCUS II battery of the Educational Testing Service. In general, the results were in accord with our arousal level-stimulation-seeking hypothesis. Given the great amount of interest in open education in recent years, these results indicate that it is the high-arousal child who appears to be ill-suited to the conditions provided by this type of schooling.

In another study of gross environment effects, Goodrick and Farley (1978) employed an affective outcome measure (rated school satisfaction) and compared students extreme on the sensation-seeking motive in two types of school, free school versus traditional school. The results indicated that, in line with the prediction, high sensation-seekers reported greater satisfaction in the free school than students low in the sensation-seeking motive, while the opposite was found in the traditional school. In a study of college students (Rautman and Farley 1975) task characteristics were varied and intrinsic arousal was measured by the two-flash threshold and a salivary index, and a questionnaire measure of the sensation-seeking motive was employed. The task manipulation involved administration of cryptograms in an example-rule (inductive) procedure versus rule-example (deductive). The results, in accord with the prediction, indicated a significant interaction between arousal and instructional method, with low-arousal and high-sensation-seeking subjects performing better under example-rule, and high-arousal and low-sensation-seeking subjects performing better under rule-example.

These studies barely scratch the surface of the research to be done on arousal-treatment interactions. Teacher effects should be studied. More than one source of extrinsic arousal should be considered in the same study. The internal versus external sensation-seeking dimension should be explored further. We have extended the general approach outlined here into research in criminal and delinquent behavior, scaling the arousal potential of the crime and the arousal/sensation-seeking level of the criminal or delinquent (Heller and Farley 1979). We have also explored areas of aesthetics (Farley and Ahn 1973), sexual behavior (Farley and Mueller 1978), creativity (Farley 1971), and so on. Clearly one is not restricted here to implications for school achievement or for child mental health. There are dozens of hypotheses awaiting empirical testing. Two areas that are of great importance to the education of children and adolescents are creativity and delinquency. These two phenomena may be connected. Our theory suggests they are.

I have proposed (Farley 1974b) that arousal and the stimulation-seeking motive are significantly predictive of creativity, that creative performance and creative personality will be in part a function of sensation seeking. The search for variety and intensity of stimulation of the low-arousal individual will lead to the openness to experience, the flexibility, risk taking, high energy level, preference for complexity, playfulness, receptivity to new and novel ideas and experiences, and so on that are held to be characteristic of the *creative person*, as well as the flexibility of performance, generation of performance variety, novelty, complexity, and so on that are often held to be important attributes of *creative performance*. Thus, the personality attributes of the creative individual, as well as the characteristics of creative performance, are seen as in part deriving from or serving the sensation-seeking motive. Elsewhere I have reviewed a substantial number of studies supporting this proposal (Farley 1974b).

Where delinquency is concerned, it has been proposed (Farley 1973, Farley and Farley 1972) that a central factor is hypersensation seeking based presumably on excessively low intrinsic arousal, as with creativity. There appears to be substantial evidence to support this view. We have found individual differences in the stimulation-seeking motive defined physiologically and by personality measurement to predict significantly such delinquent behaviors among incarcerated delinquents as disobedience and escapes, as well as blind ratings of "delinquent orientation" by counselors and social workers (Farley 1973, Farley and Farley 1972). In addition, nonincarcerated but adjudicated delinquents are significantly higher in measured stimulation seeking than matched nondelinquents (Farley and Sewell 1976). And such normal adolescent delinquency as drinking, smoking, and the taking of drugs is also significantly related to individual differences in stimulation seeking (Farley 1973). We have described delinquents as having an "arousal deficit" that is the basis for excessive stimulation seeking. It of course suggests a biological basis to some delinquency and criminality. But we believe it is treatable in the ATI model through the use of arousing treatments.

It is proposed (Farley 1974b) that creativity and delinquency have, at least in part, common origins in hyperarousal or exceptionally low intrinsic arousal levels. Or, if one is unhappy with the biology of arousal in this context, it could be said they both have, at least in part, common origins in hypersensation seeking. Certainly both creativity and delinquency seem to bear other resemblances, such as their characterization by rejection of norms, of rules, of the usual or general way of behaving, and by their unconventionality.

It is proposed that a child who is unusually strong in the stimulation-seeking motive or sensation-seeking tendencies has a high probability of becoming either a delinquent or a nondelinquent but exceptionally creative individual. What are the controlling factors? One may be the environmental provisions for stimulation. If sensation-seeking children can satisfy their stimulation needs in socially (legally) approved ways, they will become creative nondelinquents; if these needs cannot be satisfied in socially (legally) approved ways, they will become delinquents. One likely candidate, although admittedly rather molar, for a rough index of the environmental provisions for stimulation is socioeconomic status (SES). This is based on the notion that a lower SES family does not have the resources to provide sufficient socially approved stimulation to the marked stimulation seeker relative to a higher SES family, so that lower SES children will satisfy their stimulation needs in socially disapproved ways, for example, in the streets and so on, where the likelihood of running afoul of the law is greater. This elaboration of the model is summarized in Figure 1-2.

Although the model as represented in Figure 1-2 predicts that in higher SES children, stimulation seeking will be more predictive of creativity than delinquency while in lower SES children the opposite will be true, it is also predicted that as a group delinquents will be more creative than normals and highly creative individuals more delinquent than uncreative individuals. Two studies to date have direct bearing upon the foregoing predictions, significantly supporting major aspects of the model (Farley 1974b). The model suggests something positive about delinquents (creative potential) and provides clear implications for corrections. Thus, for example, traditional corrections (training in traditional trades with low-arousal potential

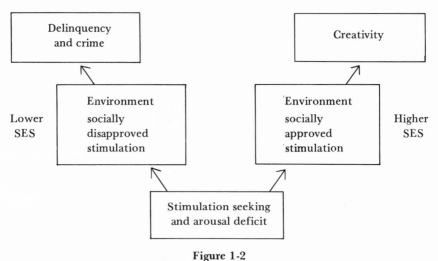

Figure 1-2

Socioeconomic status and stimulation seeking

such as carpentry and plumbing) is rejected in favor of experiences and training in pursuits with potential for high arousal such as media, art, graphics, music, and so on. It is proposed that corrections should train and, where possible, certify delinquents in the latter pursuits so that subsequent on-the-job experiences will be sufficiently stimulating, tapping creative potential, to engage and sustain the interest and commitment of the (ex) delinquent, thus hopefully reducing the usually very high levels of recidivism. Research to test these implications for corrections is needed. Aside from issues of appropriate procedures in correctional institutions, everyday crime, vandalism, and delinquency is a continuing problem in many American schools (National Institute of Education 1978a, 1978b). The present model suggests adaptive educational options (high-arousal-potential instruction, environments, and teachers) that might be considered.

CONCLUSIONS

A biologically based theory of individualization and adaptive education has been outlined in very general form, with implications for cognitive and affective outcomes being suggested. Although biologically based arousal processes and stimulation seeking are widely implicated, their contributions to differentiated behaviors depend upon differentiated environmental factors, few of which are presently understood. Some distinction should be made between the proximal and distal sources and patterning of stimulation that may influence sensation-seeking behavior. The distinction, mentioned earlier, between covert and overt sensation seeking needs further analysis, and certainly the physiological and biochemical referents for stimulation seeking require much further elaboration. Where the former is concerned, for example, it might be possible that creativity represents in part a dominance of covert over overt stimulation seeking, while delinquency might represent in part a dominance of overt over covert stimulation seeking. Although both categories of behavior represent exceptional sensation seeking, they may differ along such a covert-overt dimension.

So as not to give the impression that I am placing all my bets for a psychobiology of ATI on arousal processes, I should point out that another very fruitful approach is in the area of biological cycles (Colquhoun 1971). The likelihood that diurnal cycles may be an important variable for interaction with certain treatment parameters is a notion worth pursuing. In addition, such ideas as brain hemispheric differentiation, strength, balance, and mobility of the nervous system (Strelau, Farley, and Gale 1981, Nebylytsyn and Gray 1972) and cortical augmenting and reducing (Schooler, Buchsbaum, and Carpenter 1976) are all potential candidates for *biological aptitudes.*

The ATI concept is an important one for education, but its promise is much greater than its performance to date. A focus on process concepts will improve the situation. We must be careful, however, in the selection of process variables for study. Many information-processing and recent related cognitive psychology conceptions of learning and memory may be characterized by their short life and transient nature. Models of memory and comprehension have proliferated in recent years. Underwood (1975) recently counted some 40-50 different current psychological models of memory. The cognitive revolution has spawned, besides information processing and related approaches, a sort of experimental epistemology that transports philosophical conceptions into experimental paradigms (Shaw and Bransford 1977). This latter domain encompasses linguistics, psychology, epistemology, and logic. It provides enough conceptualizations of process in learning and cognition that have individual difference and educational possibilities to occupy ATI researchers for years to come. The process analyses of Glaser (1972), Hunt (1978), Snow (1978), Sternberg (1977), and others mentioned earlier also hold promise. The extent of process possibilities demands selectiveness in ATI efforts. I urge educational researchers to reserve a piece of the action in their fearless winnowing and sifting for that great question—the brain's relation to the mind—and the role of this relationship in the domain of individual differences, learning, and instruction.

REFERENCES

Auden, William H. *Age of Anxiety.* New York: Random House, 1946.

Bateson, Gregory; Jackson, D.D.; Haley, J.; and Weakland, J. "Toward a Theory of Schizophrenia." *Behavioral Science* 1 (October 1956): 251-64.

Berlyne, Daniel E. *Conflict, Arousal, and Curiosity.* New York: McGraw-Hill, 1960.

Colquhoun, William P., ed. *Biological Rhythms and Human Performance.* New York: Academic Press, 1971.

Conners, C. Keith; Eisenberg, Leon; and Barcai, Avner. "Effect of Dextroamphetamine on Children." *Archives of General Psychiatry* 17 (October 1967): 478-85.

Farley, Frank H. "Measures of Individual Differences in Stimulation Seeking and the Tendency toward Variety." *Journal of Consulting and Clinical Psychology* 37 (December 1971): 394-96.

————. "A Theory of Delinquency." Paper presented at the annual meeting of the American Psychological Association, Montreal, September 1973.

————. "Basic Process Individual Differences." Paper presented at the annual meeting of the American Educational Research Association, Chicago, April, 1974a.

————. "A Theoretical-Predictive Model of Creativity." Paper presented at the annual meeting of the American Psychological Association, New Orleans, August, 1974b.

————. "Physiological Arousal and Cognitive Processes: Outline of a Theory." In *Biological Foundations of Personality and Behavior*, edited by Jan Strelau, Frank H. Farley and Anthony Gale. New York: Hemisphere, 1981.

Farley, Frank H., and Ahn, Sun-hye. "Experimental Aesthetics: Visual Aesthetic Preference in Five Cultures." *Studies in Art Education* 15 (Fall 1973): 44-48.

Farley, Frank H., and Farley, Sonja V. "Stimulus-Seeking Motivation and Delinquent Behavior among Institutionalized Delinquent Girls." *Journal of Consulting Clinical Psychology* 39 (August 1972): 94-97.

Farley, Frank H., and Mueller, Carol B. "Arousal, Personality, and Assortative Mating in Marriage: Generalizability and Cross-cultural Effects." *Journal of Sex and Marital Therapy* 4 (Spring 1978): 50-53.

Farley, Frank H., and Sewell, Trevor E. "Test of a Theory of Delinquency: Stimulation-Seeking in Delinquent and Nondelinquent Black Adolescents." *Criminal Justice and Behavior* 3 (December 1976): 315-20.

Friedman, C. Jack, and Friedman, Alfred S. "Characteristics of Schizogenic Families During a Joint Story-Telling Task." *Family Process* 9 (September 1970): 333-53.

Gagné, Robert M., ed. *Learning and Individual Differences*. Columbus, Ohio: Charles E. Merrill, 1967.

Glaser, Robert. "Individuals and Learning: The New Aptitudes." *Educational Researcher* 1 (June 1972): 5-13.

Goodrick, Joann, and Farley, Frank H. "The Sensation-Seeking Motive in Free Schools versus Traditional Schools." Unpublished report, University of Wisconsin, Madison, 1978.

Hebb, Donald O. *The Organization of Behavior*. New York: John Wiley, 1949.

————. "Drives and the C.N.S. (Conceptual Nervous System)." *Psychological Review* 62 (July 1955): 243-54.

Heller, Charles H., and Farley, Frank H. "Criminal Behavior and Arousal: Test of a Theory." Unpublished report, University of Wisconsin, Madison, 1979.

Hunt, Earl. "Mechanics of Verbal ability." *Psychological Review* 85 (March 1978): 109-130.

Hutt, S.J. et al. "A Behavioral and Electroencephalographic Study of Autistic Children." *Journal of Psychiatric Research* 3 (October 1965): 181-98.

Kahn, Herman et al. *The Next Two Hundred Years.* New York: William Morrow, 1976.

Koester, Lynne S. and Farley, Frank H. "Arousal and Hyperactivity in Open and Traditional Education." Paper presented at the annual meeting of the American Psychological Association, San Francisco, August 1977.

Lester, David., ed. *Explorations in Exploration: Stimulation Seeking, an Enduring Problem in Psychology.* New York: D. Van Nostrand Co., 1969.

Lindsley, Donald B. "Emotion." In *Handbook of Experimental Psychology*, edited by Stanley S. Stevens, pp. 473-516. New York: John Wiley, 1951.

Lueders-Salmon, Erica. "Team Teaching and the Active Classroom: A Comparative Study of the Impact of Self-Contained Classrooms and Open-Space Team-Teaching Schools on Classroom 'Activity'." Technical Report. Stanford, Calif.: Stanford Center for Research and Development in Teaching, Stanford University, 1970.

Maaser, Bruce W., and Farley, Frank H. "Procedural and Statistical Methods in the Use of the Two-flash Threshold." *Bulletin of the Psychonomic Society*, 1980.

McClelland, David C. *The Achieving Society.* Princeton, N.J.: D. Van Nostrand Co., 1961.

Meyers, Donald I., and Goldfarb, William. "Studies of Perplexity in Mothers of Schizophrenic Children." *American Journal of Orthopsychiatry* 31 (July 1961): 551-64.

Morris, Gary O., and Wynne, Lyman C. "Schizophrenic Offspring and Parental Styles of Communication." *Psychiatry* 28 (February 1965): 19-44.

Moruzzi, Guiseppe, and Magoun, Horace W. "Brain Stem Reticular Formation and Activation of the EEG." *Electroencephalography and Clinical Neurophysiology* 1 (July 1949): 455-73.

National Institute of Education. *School Crime and Disruption.* Washington, D.C.: National Institute of Education, 1978.

————. *Violent Schools—Safe Schools: The Safe School Study Report to the Congress.* Vol. 1. Washington, D.C.: National Institute of Education, 1978.

Nebylytsyn, Vladimir D., and Gray, Jeffrey Alan, eds. *Biological Bases of Individual Behavior.* New York: Academic Press, 1972.

Rautman, Jenifer, and Farley, Frank H. "Arousal and Cognition: The Arousal-Treatment Interaction in a Problem-Solving Task." Unpublished report, University of Wisconsin, Madison, 1975.

Reiss, Steven et al. *Abnormality: Experimental and Clinical Approaches.* New York: Macmillan, 1977.

Reiss, Steven; Peterson, Rolf A.; and O'Neill, Patrick. "The Possible Etiologies of Schizophrenia." In *Abnormality: Experimental and Clinical Approaches*, edited by Steven Reiss et al., pp. 469-487. New York: Macmillan, 1977.

Rosenthal, David. *Genetic Theory and Abnormal Behavior.* New York: McGraw-Hill, 1970.

Schnackenberg, Robert C. "Caffeine as a Substitute for Schedule II Stimulants in Hyperkinetic Children." *American Journal of Psychiatry* 130 (July 1973): 796-98.

Schooler, Carmi; Buchsbaum, Monte S.; and Carpenter, William T. "Evoked Response and Kinesthetic Measures of Augmenting/Reducing: Replications and Extensions." *Journal of Nervous and Mental Disease* 163 (October 1976): 221-32.

Shaw, Robert, and Bransford, John, eds. *Perceiving, Acting, and Knowing: Toward an Ecological Psychology.* Hillsdale, N.J.: Erlbaum, 1977.

Snow, Richard E. "Theory and Method for Research on Aptitude Processes." *Intelligence* 2 (July-September 1978): 225-78.

Sternbach, Richard A. *Principles of Psychophysiology.* New York: Academic Press, 1966.

Sternberg, Robert J. *Intelligence, Information Processing, and Analogical Reasoning: The Componential Analysis of Human Abilities.* Hillsdale, N.J.: Lawrence Erlbaum Associates, 1977.

Strahan, R.F.; Todd, J.B.; and Inglis, G.B. "A Palmar Sweat Measure Particularly Suited for Naturalistic Research." *Psychophysiology* 11 (November 1974): 715-20.

Strelau, Jan; Farley, Frank H.; and Gale, Anthony, eds. *Biological Foundations of Personality and Behavior.* New York: Hemisphere, 1981.

Underwood, Benton J. "Individual Differences as a Crucible in Theory Construction." *American Psychologist* 30 (February 1975): 128-39.

Walberg, Herbert J., and Thomas, Susan C. "Open Education: An Operational Definition and Validation in Great Britain and United States." *American Educational Research Journal* 9 (Spring 1972): 197-208.

Wilson, Edward O. *Sociobiology: The New Synthesis.* Cambridge, Mass.: Harvard University Press, 1975.

Zuckerman, Marvin. "The Search for High Sensation." *Psychology Today* 11 (February 1978): 38-43; 46; 96-98.

2. Dimensions of Individual Differences

Thomas J. Shuell

Concern for individual differences has a long history in both education and psychology, and over the years this concern has resulted in several active areas of research. While investigators in these areas of research—for example, personality differences, developmental differences, individual differences in mental ability, and so forth—have not always shared the same purpose nor made the same basic assumptions, it is clear that during the period from approximately 1890 to 1970 research on individual differences was, for the most part, dominated by the psychometric tradition as exemplified by the mental test and by a methodology based on correlation.

During the past five or ten years, however, there have been some rather substantial changes in the way researchers conceptualize and investigate the role of individual differences. The genesis of these changes differs somewhat for the different areas mentioned above, but to some extent they seem to be headed in the same direction. In addition, it is becoming increasingly clear that some of the basic assumptions underlying traditional research on individual differences are being challenged in a manner that has very important implications both for future research on individual differences and for educational practices.

The purpose of this chapter is to outline some of the more important sources or types of individual differences among students that are relevant to education and the instructional process. Specific ways in which instructional techniques and educational programs can be adapted to various individual differences and the way these differences are related to students' achievement are discussed in the next chapter. The present chapter will focus on some of the current issues and research findings related to the identification of various dimensions along which differences among individuals can be characterized. Two problems make this task more difficult than it might appear. First, research on individual differences is currently rather diverse and somewhat fragmented; and second, the whole field is currently in a state of flux and change. To attempt an integration of the various aspects involved in studying individual differences is probably somewhat naive at the present time. Nevertheless, I shall try to portray as accurately as possible the range of dimensions with which we must deal and then discuss some of the issues that have to be addressed if an integration is ever to be achieved.

Given these difficulties, no attempt will be made here to provide an exhaustive review of the field, although I will make references to more comprehensive reviews of the literature. Rather, certain representative areas of research and certain representative studies will be discussed with an emphasis on the newer approaches to the study of individual differences. In addition, a number of theoretical and conceptual issues relevant to the general field of individual differences will also be discussed.

THE CONCEPTUALIZATION OF INDIVIDUAL DIFFERENCES

How can individual differences best be characterized? Differences among individuals are extremely obvious and virtually limitless, and there are many ways in which these differences can be defined or conceptualized. Over the years, individual differences have been defined in terms of types (a person is identified as being of one or another type), traits (an individual is characterized along several separate dimensions), abilities (a person is characterized in terms of what he or she is capable of doing), and performances on psychometric tests (a person is identified according to the score received on a mental test). These various schemes for classifying individuals have been used for purposes of simple description, prediction of future performance, and—in some cases—theoretical understanding. In recent years researchers focusing on mental abilities and on personality have both tended to think of individual differences in terms of traits; that is, characteristics of individuals that are consistent over a wide variety of tasks or situations and are reflected or measurable in terms of some form of behavioral observation. Factor analysis frequently has been used, especially in research on mental abilities, to identify various dimensions of individual differences.

This general approach proved to be quite successful over a relatively long period of time, and the basic orientation that it represents has become ingrained in our thinking. But sometimes we forget what it is we are ultimately concerned with and the arbitrary nature of our current way of thinking about the problem. The most appropriate way to characterize individual differences depends, of course, on the purpose one has for classifying individuals in the first place and on certain basic assumptions that must be made regarding the nature of those differences. In addition, we sometimes forget that individual differences, as we usually think of them, are basically just a conceptual system for representing differences *among* individuals. In a very real sense these differences do not actually exist for a single individual but merely represent how much of a particular characteristic one individual possesses relative to another individual.

Any attempt to conceptualize individual differences faces something of a dilemma. If one conceives of a continuum along which the similarity among individuals can be specified, then the problem arises as to the appropriate points or boundaries that can be used to describe reliably and validly the differences that exist among individuals. At one extreme is the possibility that all individuals are basically the same and that general laws can be discovered that apply to all individuals. This is the orientation that experimental psychologists followed for years and that we now acknowledge to be extremely shortsighted. At the other extreme is a basically idiographic orientation, which states that every individual is unique and that general laws are not possible. Any approach to developing a systematic body of knowledge about individual differences must take a position somewhere between these two extremes, but such a position is, by its very nature, rather artificial and arbitrary. Nevertheless, we must find ways to characterize differences among individuals that are useful for the research and educational purposes we are interested in pursuing. To keep these limitations in mind can only help to make that endeavor more valid and fruitful.

The remainder of this section will focus on some of the purposes one might have for classifying individuals and on some of the basic assumptions that must be made regarding the nature of those differences. In addition, several basically different ways in which individual differences are frequently characterized will be discussed.

Purposes for Classifying Individuals

There are several reasons one might have for wanting to identify differences among individuals. The following reasons for classifying people are neither exhaustive nor mutually exclusive, but they do indicate some of the different purposes people might have for wanting to identify individual differences. These reasons include: (a) to describe differences that currently exist among individuals for the purpose of identifying those persons who have a large degree—or possibly a small degree—of some characteristic, perhaps for the purpose of awarding a prize or singling people out for social or political reasons; (b) to predict performance in some future situation for purposes of selection, perhaps in order to select only those persons most qualified for a particular job or educational program or to determine which of several alternate programs might be most appropriate for a given person; (c) to diagnose a given person's strengths and/or weaknesses relative to other individuals in order to provide the most appropriate treatment for that person, e.g., remediation; (d) to identify the point along the continuum of growth or development—not necessarily in terms of chronological age—that an individual is currently at in order to determine what the most appropriate experience might be for that individual or what type of behavior one could reasonably expect to occur next; and (e) to identify the relative profile of characteristics possessed by an individual in order to determine that individual's unique distribution of strengths and weaknesses relative to some situation or task.

It is important to be aware of the substantial conceptual difference between the first three purposes listed above and the latter two. The first three all depend on a relatively strict comparison among individuals—a given individual is, for all practical purposes, assigned to a dichotomous classification relative to other individuals. In the latter two cases, however, the emphasis is more on differences that exist within a particular individual—comparison with other individuals is not forced in quite the same way as it is in the other situations. One orientation is not necessarily correct or better than the other one in any absolute sense, although the appropriateness of different approaches to the problem of how best to conceptualize individual differences may depend on the purpose involved.

Assumptions Involved in the Conceptualization of Individual Differences

The development of any conceptual system requires one to make certain assumptions, either implicitly or explicitly. The same is true when a given methodology is used to investigate a particular problem. Yet it is not at all unusual for us to forget this necessity of making assumptions; frequently we are unaware of the specific assumptions already made when someone takes a particular approach to a problem. The plausibility of various assumptions can change, as can the nature of the problem that we are trying to solve, but we seldom question the extent to which the initial assumptions are or are not appropriate for the problem we are interested in at present.

To a fairly large extent, the traditional psychometric approach to the study of individual differences is based on the Darwinian concept of survival of the fittest, usually in a preexisting and fixed environment. For example, Alfred Binet's original assignment from the French government—an assignment that led to the development of the intelligence test—was to develop a test that would predict which students would be successful and which ones would not be successful in a traditional, predefined, and fixed school environment. This approach was completely consistent with the social philosophy of that time. Physical and social environments were assumed to be givens, and individuals were either successful in adapting to a given environment or they languished due to their lack of ability to cope. The French government wanted to identify those students who would not profit from receiving an education so that they could be weeded out, and unnecessary time, money, and effort would not be spent on trying to accomplish the impossible. The set of assumptions about schooling and individual differences associated with this approach remained more or less intact until recent years. The corresponding concern for traits has reflected this orientation by focusing on how much of a particular trait, such as intelligence, an individual possesses.

While this approach may still be valid in some situations—and it certainly still has its share of adherents—it is fair to say that in recent years there has been a change in the social milieu and social assumptions that supported and helped to validate this traditional psychometric approach to the study of individual differences (Tyler 1978). The old assumptions are being questioned for a variety of reasons, some social and some scientific. There is a deemphasis on the social philosophy sometimes referred to as "Social Darwinism" that advocated rugged individualism with a heavy stress on competition and individual achievement. A different social philosophy, which emphasizes equal rights and equal opportunities for all individuals, can be seen emerging, at least in this country if not worldwide. Consequently many of the criteria used in traditional psychometric research are seen by some researchers to be no longer viable or to be viable only in a much more limited sense. A more egalitarian concept of education has developed which states that education should help facilitate the achievement of each individual to his or her maximum potential. Education and instruction, rather than being fixed and requiring individuals to make it in that system or drop out, are now being adapted to meet the needs and abilities of the individual student (Glaser 1972, 1977).

In addition, the concept or assumption that there are a limited number of traits shared by all individuals is also being questioned. Some of this questioning is related to the social issues just discussed, although part of it has clearly developed out of methodological and theoretical factors that will be discussed in later sections of this chapter. Alternatives are seriously being suggested (Bem and Allen 1974, Tyler 1978) in which the focus is on a combined profile of individual characteristics or on the possibility that traits may be differentially relevant for different individuals. Tyler (1978, p.17), for example, states that:

The question toward which the dominant trait psychology has been directed is "How much of some quality does the individual possess?" Two other questions are equally important: "Which characterictics out of the many that might have been developed does this individual show—which competencies, which interests, which motives?" And, "What shapes have these characteristics taken; which psychological structures does this person use to process experience?"

Many different assumptions are involved whenever we use a particular methodology or a particular system to help organize our thinking about some problem. These assumptions, coupled with the purpose we have for investigating or for being concerned about that problem, determine which approach is most appropriate in a given situation.

Forms of Representing Individual Differences

Several basically different formats are frequently used to represent individual differences. Unfortunately there have been very few systematic attempts to discuss the similarities and differences among these various forms. One is the traditional conceptualization discussed above in which differences among individuals are characterized in terms of traits or abilities, typically represented by scores on some kind of psychometric test. Included here would be the alternatives already mentioned, such as the various types of profiles. Another form can be referred to as group differences, since the concern here is with differences between or among predefined groups of individuals such as sex, race, and the like. A third form is related to developmental differences, in which the basic concern is for systematic changes that occur within individuals as they grow or learn.

While these various forms of characterizing differences among individuals are not necessarily mutually exclusive, a qualitative difference is usually thought to exist between developmental differences and the other types of differences. Most of this qualitative difference is reflected in whether the concern is for differences that exist among individuals at a given time or for differences that supposedly occur in each individual and can be identified only over a period of time, that is, longitudinal differences. It is important to realize that developmental differences do not merely refer to cross-sectional differences for different chronological ages—these are basically group differences; rather, they refer to sequential differences that occur within individuals as they experience different events or instructional treatments.

The distinction between group differences and individual differences also raises some issues worth considering. While both forms focus on differences among individuals, there are some very basic differences between the two. Group differences, of course, are concerned with differences that exist between or among predefined groups of individuals. Frequently the dimensions chosen for consideration and the manner in which the selected dimension is subdivided are based on some highly visible and easily defined factor such as sex, race, chronological age, and so forth. For certain types of concerns that factor may be quite appropriate, but for other types of concerns the distinction may hide more than it reveals. The purpose one has for making a distinction between groups needs to be kept clearly in mind when considering group differences. If the distinction arises out of social or political concerns, for example, then we should be extremely cautious in using that distinction as a basis for investigating individual differences in psychological processes that at best may be related in only a very remote manner to the social or political concerns that were the basis for the original distinction. It is not that those social or political concerns are not interesting and worthwhile in their own right—most of them are—or that they do not provide an appropriate context for investigating psychological issues—for most of them do provide that. The point is that many group differences are only proxy variables for those variables and those questions in which we are most interested; in these cases group differences can lead us astray. If we can focus on the similarities in psychological processes as well as on the differences that exist between groups of people defined on the basis of nonpsychological criteria, we will be closer not only to understanding the nature of the differences that exist between the groups but also to an adequate understanding of how individual differences are involved in more general processes such as learning.

So far in this chapter there has been a consideration of several general issues related to the study of individual differences. These issues help provide an appropriate context for understanding and educational research. The next two sections of the chapter will explore recent research that is investigating and helping to delineate various dimensions of individual differences

INDIVIDUAL DIFFERENCES IN MENTAL ABILITIES

The traditional study of individual differences per se is probably thought of most frequently in terms of traits representative of various mental abilities. While many different mental abilities have been studied, most of the research and theorizing has occurred within a context clearly defined in terms of intelligence and/or intelligence quotient (IQ). The various traits have nearly always been defined in terms of performance in mental tests, and the basic methodology has been correlational in nature. Statistical procedures known as factor analysis have frequently been used to help identify the various dimensions of individual differences. (See Sternberg 1977b for a general critique of the use of factor analysis in this respect.) This traditional approach to the study of individual differences in intelligence continues to occupy the interest of many investigators, and several recent reviews (Carroll and Maxwell 1979, Horn 1976, 1977, Nichols, 1978) of this research are available. One conception of intelligence that is based primarily on this psychometric approach and is currently receiving considerable attention is a hierarchical model that distinguishes between fluid intelligence and crystallized intelligence. Several different variations of hierarchical models have been suggested (Cattell 1971, Horn 1977, Snow 1978, Vernon 1971), and the present discussion will focus on the American (as contrasted with the British) version of the model.

The hierarchical model postulates several different levels of ability or intelligence. The most general level of intelligence ("g") is augmented at a somewhat less general level by fluid intelligence (G_f), crystallized intelligence (G_c), and sometimes a spatial visualization ability (G_v). Below this level in the hierarchy are various abilities of a more specific nature. The distinction between fluid and crystallized intelligence was first developed formally by Cattell (1957).

Briefly, fluid intelligence is viewed as being that aspect of general intelligence that can be diverted into almost any new activity which requires some intelligence to perform. Often there is thought to be a general decline in fluid intelligence following adolescence. Crystallized intelligence, on the other hand, is that aspect of intelligence that results from experience—certain abilities commonly acknowledged as requiring or representing intelligence appear to crystallize out of the experiences that one has during one's lifetime—and supposedly there is a general increase in crystallized intelligence throughout most of a person's lifetime. The interested reader is referred to Cattell (1971) and Horn (1977) for a more complete description of the theory.

In recent years, however, there has been a substantial shift in emphasis away from the more traditional psychometric concerns regarding mental abilities toward a concern for the psychological processes responsible for the performance we observe in various mental tests and for other behavior that we would call intelligent.

In one sense this concern for cognitive processes underlying test performance is not new (Carroll and Maxwell 1979), but the current interest is bolstered by the sophisticated methodology and theories of modern-day cognitive psychology. Two major factors are primarily responsible for the current interest in what is sometimes referred to as the "newer aptitudes." The first of these factors is the relatively recent combination of two very different methodological approaches to the study of human behavior (Cronbach 1957, Cronbach and Snow 1977). This combination of correlational and experimental methodologies has given rise to new concerns and new types of empirical questions. The other factor is the changing (often in rather subtle ways) social and philosophical milieu discussed in an earlier section of this chapter, and this changing milieu is having an influence on our educational and psychological thinking. The current concern with respect to intelligence, for example, is more in terms of ". . . what *is* it, rather than who *has* it" (Resnick 1976a, p. 4). A variety of different approaches to the study of intelligence, especially those that reflect the combination of the experimental and correlational approaches to the study of intelligence, are presented in a book edited by Resnick (1976b).

During recent years both cognitive psychologists and psychometricians have become increasingly interested in determining the relationship between performance on various psychometric tests and performance on various types of cognitive learning tasks. The perspective here is to view cognitive tasks and learning tasks as comparable to psychometric tests, in that performance in both types of situations requires the use of various cognitive processes. The main concern is to understand the cognitive processes required for performance on these tests. For example, Estes (1974) undertook to analyze various aspects of standard intelligence tests in terms of concepts from cognitive learning theory, and he discussed the results of various studies that are consistent with such an analysis. Likewise, Carroll (1976) analyzed the various psychometric tests in the Educational Testing Service's Kit of Reference Tests in terms of the cognitive processes required for performance on the various tests. While the analysis is still logical in nature, it represents a major step in trying to develop an integrated understanding of individual differences in performance.

The work of Earl Hunt and his associates (for example, Hunt,

Frost, and Lunneborg 1973, Hunt, Lunneborg, and Lewis 1975) provided the beginning of an empirical data base for this type of analysis. Hunt's general procedure was to take college students who scored high and those who scored low on an intelligence test (both verbal and quantitative tests have been used) and then see to what extent the performances of the two groups differ on a variety of different cognitive learning tasks—for the most part well-established laboratory-type tasks.

For example, a task developed by Posner and his associates (Posner et al. 1969, Posner and Mitchell 1967) has been used extensively in cognitive psychology to measure the amount of time required by subjects to access overlearned information in long-term memory. The task consists of presenting two letters to the subject, and the subject's task is to indicate whether the two letters are the same or different by pressing one of two keys. Two different types of instructions are provided to the subject on different parts of the task; precautions are taken to ensure that the subjects know on what basis they are to respond. Under the physical identity (PI) instructions, the subject is to respond "same" if the two letters presented are of the same physical configuration (for example, AA, bb) and respond "different" if they are not (for example, Aa, AB). Presumably, it is not necessary for the subject to access any verbal codes in order to perform the task. For the name-identity (NI) instructions, the subject is to respond "same" if the two letters have the same name even though they may have different physical characteristics (for example, Aa) and respond "different" if the two letters do not have the same name. In order to perform this task, the subject presumably must access the verbal code in long-term memory for the letters that are presented. Thus, the difference in the subject's reaction time on the two different tasks provides an index of how long it takes him or her to access verbal information in long-term memory.

University students who are in the lower quartile on a standard verbal intelligence test take about 40 percent longer to access this information than students in the upper quartile on the same test (Hunt, Frost, and Lunneborg 1973, Hunt, Lunneborg, and Lewis 1975). Ten-year-old children take about three times as long as the high-verbal university students, while children who are mildly retarded take about five times as long as the high-verbal university students (Hunt 1978), although in the case of mildly retarded children, at least some question can be raised as to how well the verbal labels have been learned.

Other investigators (for example, Jensen 1979, Keating and Bobbitt 1978) have also studied the relationship between reaction time and performance on intelligence tests. In general, there appears to be a reasonably strong correspondence between individual differences in reaction time and individual differences in performance on intelligence tests. The exact way in which this relationship should be interpreted is not always clear. Most psychologists would *not* interpret it in terms of physiological differences in speed of neural transmission, although that possibility cannot be ruled out. Rather, reaction time is usually taken as an index of either the number of mental operations that must be carried out in performing a task or the ease with which individuals can perform tasks of varying degrees of complexity. The use of laboratory tasks and procedures such as those described can help to clarify the nature of the cognitive processes responsible for performance on a variety of different mental tests.

A related approach for investigating the relationship between performance on psychometric tests and more complex cognitive tasks has been developed by Sternberg (1977b). This approach is known as componential analysis and involves analyzing a complex task (which might be a test item) in terms of the components involved in performing the task and the rules used for combining the components. For example, in solving the analogy $A:B::C:D$, four components might be identified. An estimate of how much time is required to perform the last component of the task is obtained by allowing an individual as much time as desired to study the $A:B::C$ part of the analogy. When the subjects indicate that they fully understand that part of the analogy, the complete analogy is presented, and the time required to give the appropriate answer is recorded. Scores representing individual differences on each component can then be related to one another and to other batteries of individual difference measures. Likewise, mathematical models of the components involved in performing a complex mental task can be compared with the obtained data in order to determine which model best fits the data. This procedure has been used to investigate both inductive analogical reasoning (Sternberg 1977a, 1977b) and deductive reasoning (Sternberg forthcoming).

While this type of analysis and investigation of the relationships between individual differences in performance on psychometric tests and on cognitive tasks is just beginning, it appears to hold considerable promise for helping us to understand the nature of individual differences better. By comparing the similarities and differences between differential performance in the two situations we may be able to ferret out and resolve theoretical issues that would otherwise escape our understanding. In addition to these theoretical and empirical advantages, it is likely that when we are able to identify the cognitive processes that result in differential performance on mental tests, we will be in a better position to interpret the scores that individuals receive and so make the appropriate educational decisions. In some cases, for example, it may be possible to provide instruction that compensates for poor performance or to improve performance through training.

INDIVIDUAL DIFFERENCES IN PERSONALITY

In many ways the traditional concern with personality has been a concern for individual differences. Personality is usually thought of in terms of relatively stable characteristics of individuals that help us to describe, and perhaps explain, why one person is, for example, shy while another person is outgoing. Although it is possible to distinguish among three rather different approaches to the study of personality—the trait model, the psychodynamic model, and the situational model (Endler and Magnusson 1976)—there is an underlying concern with factors that permit us to characterize differences among individuals in some systematic and meaningful way. While it is possible to identify methodological differences and perhaps differences in the concern for scientific rigor (see, for example, Cattell 1977) between studies of individual differences in mental abilities and in personality, the main difference may well be the type of outcomes in which the proponents of the two approaches were interested. Those who studied individual differences in mental abilities were usually interested in some form of cognitive outcome or achievement, while those who investigated personality differences were usually interested in some form of social or behavioral outcome.

In recent years, however, the general field of personality study has been going through a period of self-questioning and disarray (Phares and Lamiell 1977, Sechrest 1976). The traditional concern for traits is changing, although the change is occurring for different reasons than is the case for the changes occurring with respect to mental abilities. In the case of mental abilities, as already noted, it was realized that the combination of two different methodologies and perspectives would result in further advances than either one would by itself. In the case of personality, the change occurred primarily because it was gradually being discovered that the traits being measured were not consistent across time and/or situations (Mischel 1973). Nevertheless, the direction in which both fields seem to be headed appears very similar, namely, toward a concern for interactions between individuals and the situation they are in. Neither factor by itself is capable of adequately explaining the overall variability that is obtained. While the two concerns may be merging to some extent, the educational importance of this approach is reflected in the so-called aptitude-treatment interaction research discussed in the next chapter. The implications of the interactional approach for identifying relevant dimensions of individual differences will be discussed later in this chapter.

Cognitive Style

The concern for cognitive styles is in many ways on the borderline between mental abilities and personality. Individual differences in cognitive style are conceived to differ from individual differences in mental abilities in several notable ways (Messick 1976, Witkin et al. 1977). For the most part, mental abilities are concerned more with the content of cognition, while cognitive styles are concerned more with the manner in which an individual processes information. In addition, ability factors are usually thought to be unipolar in nature, while style factors are usually considered to be bipolar. With abilities, the more of the trait an individual has, the better the individual is able to function. With cognitive styles, however, two representative collections of individual characteristics are pitted against one another, at least in the sense that the two groupings represent opposite ends of a distribution. The distribution, however, is viewed as being continuous in nature, with individuals varying in the amount of the the two bipolar factors that they possess. This area of research presents some interesting possibilities for the eventual integration of the personality and cognitive aspects of individual differences, although

considerable effort is still required before any meaningful integration
is likely to be achieved.

Cognitive style refers to preferred ways that different individuals
have for processing and organizing information and for responding
to environmental stimuli. The research associated with five major
approaches to cognitive style—authoritarianism, dogmatism, cognitive complexity, integrative complexity, and field-dependence/
independence—has been recently reviewed in a book by Goldstein
and Blackman (1978). While each of these cognitive styles has been
reasonably well substantiated by research, field-dependence and
field-independence have been the most extensively studied and probably have the widest application to the field of education (Witkin et
al. 1977). Therefore, an examination of this would perhaps best serve
as an example of individual differences in cognitive style.

In the late 1940s and early 1950s, Witkin became interested in the
perceptual problem of how people locate the upright in space. A
rather elaborate experimental apparatus known as the rod and frame
test was used. An individual seated in a darkened room was asked to
position a rod in an upright position when a frame surrounding the
rod was tilted at some angle away from the upright. In other studies
the chair in which the person was seated was tilted, and the subject's
task was once again to position a rod in an upright position. Thus,
the person had to use conflicting cues regarding the upright position
in order to orient the rod in that position. What was observed that
had relevance for the later research on cognitive style was that there
were substantial individual differences in how persons performed this
task. For some persons, the rod was perceived to be in the upright
position whenever it was appropriately aligned with the surrounding
frame regardless of the angle to which the frame was tilted. Other
persons were more or less accurate in correctly positioning the rod in
an upright position regardless of the angle to which the frame was
tilted. The former persons seemed to see the position of the rod only
in relation to the surrounding field provided by the frame, while the
latter appeared to perceive the rod as a separate and discrete entity
from the frame of reference provided by the surrounding frame. In
addition to the rod and frame test, early research on field-dependence
and field-independence also made use of an embedded figures test
in which the individual had to locate the position of simple geometric
figures within much larger figures. Some persons could do this fairly

quickly, while other individuals required considerably more time to locate the simple figure. Performance on these two different types of tests turned out to be related. Thus, those persons who could accurately position the rod regardless of the field provided by the surrounding frame and who could also locate the simple figure fairly quickly within the larger, more complex figure appeared to perform in a manner independent of the surrounding perceptual field—hence, field-independence. Those who were heavily influenced by the surrounding frame in positioning the rod and who took longer to identify the simple figure appeared to function in a manner that was dependent on the surrounding field—hence, field-dependence.

The dimension represented by this cognitive-style variable is thus related to an individual's general mode of thinking or perceiving relative to the general field surrounding a particular stimulus event. Field-dependent persons tend to respond in a global mode with respect to the general field, while field-independent persons tend to respond in a more analytical or articulated mode. Field-dependent people are influenced by the organization of the existing field, while field-independent people tend to analyze experiences and structure them in new ways depending on the task at hand. In the bipolar tradition of cognitive styles, however, one type of style is not necessarily better than the other, as is typically the case with mental abilities, where the more intelligence a person has, the better. Whether it is better to be field-dependent or field-independent depends on the situation a person is in, both with respect to learning and with respect to vocational choice (Goodenough 1976, Witkin et al. 1977). For example, while field-dependent and field-independent persons do not appear to differ appreciably in sheer learning ability or memory, field-dependent persons are more sensitive to social information and are able to remember that type of information better than field-independent persons. Field-independent persons, on the other hand, tend to do better than field-dependent persons when it is necessary to analyze a situation in order to get relevant information or when the information must be reorganized in some way.

Locus of Control

One area of research on individual differences in personality that has been fairly active in recent years and that has been perceived as being relevant for educational purposes is locus of control. This dimension is sometimes referred to in terms of internality-externality and is based on the notion that individuals differ in the extent to which they attribute the cause of what happens to them either to internal factors (they themselves are largely responsible for what happens to them, and they have control over these various experiences) or to external factors (factors outside the individual, such as fate, are responsible for what happens to them, and they themselves have very little control over these situations). Most of the work in this area has been reviewed recently by Phares (1976b) and Lefcourt (1976). A more concise presentation is also available (Phares 1976a). The role of locus of control in a social-learning theory of personality is discussed in a paper by Rotter (1975).

Achievement Motivation

While in a general sense research on achievement motivation has reflected an underlying concern for individual differences, in a more specific sense research in this area has never really developed a systematic concern for these differences. The importance of individual differences in achievement motivation for educational concerns has long been recognized but it has not received the same type of systematic study as individual differences in mental abilities and cognitive style have. In recent years, research on achievement motivation has been related to attribution theory (Weiner 1974), which is also related to locus of control as discussed in the preceding section.

The traditional theory of achievement motivation (in which achievement motivation was viewed as a combination of motive, expectancy, and incentive) has been revised recently by Atkinson and Birch (1970) and Atkinson and Raynor (1975). Atkinson and Raynor even argue that this new theory is capable of explaining many of the traditional differences in mental ability, such as intelligence, in terms of motivational factors.

Anxiety

The role of anxiety has long been of interest to researchers concerned with learning and motivation. Concern for individual differences in anxiety—at least in a very general sense—dates back at least to the Taylor-Spence drive model and the related studies that investigated the ways in which individuals high and low in anxiety performed in various types of learning situations. More recently,

Spielberger (1972, Spielberger, Lushene, and McAdoo 1977) has distinguished between trait anxiety and state anxiety in order to deal better with the fact that even high-anxiety persons are not necessarily anxious all the time or in every situation. Trait anxiety refers to relatively stable differences among people in the range of different situations that they see as being threatening and in the extent to which a person responds to these situations with differing levels of state anxiety.

State anxiety, on the other hand, occurs in specific situations. The autonomic nervous system is activated, and consequently there are changes in such physiological responses as heart rate, blood pressure, and the like. Subjective feelings of tension, nervousness, and apprehension are consciously perceived by the individual. Most individuals respond to stressful and threatening situations with an increase in state anxiety, but there are supposedly individual differences in the intensity of this response and in the number of different situations that will elicit it. This predisposition to respond (that is, trait anxiety) remains dormant, however, until it is activated by some specific situation. Gaudry and Spielberger (1971) have studied the way in which individual differences in anxiety relate to various types of educational situations, and Sieber, O'Neil, and Tobias (1977) have reviewed much of the literature on anxiety, especially as it relates to instruction.

INTERACTIONS INVOLVING INDIVIDUAL DIFFERENCES

Research on individual differences in both mental ability and personality has been dominated by a trait conception of those differences. Traits, as we have already seen, are presumed to be dimensions of individual differences that are stable across both time and situations. It has generally been assumed that the extent to which an individual possesses a given trait determines the behavior that the individual will exhibit in any given situation—the more intelligence one has, the more one will learn in any instructional situation; the more honest a person is, the more honest the person will be in all situations. This position, the one taken by most differential psychologists, presents a sharp contrast to the position taken by most experimental psychologists, behaviorists, and social-learning theorists. These psychologists have argued that environmental factors determine the behavior that people exhibit in a particular situation.

Within the past ten years or so, however, many researchers have begun to realize that each of these extreme positions has serious limitations when considered by itself. Individual differences and situational factors interact in some important ways, and both must be considered if we are to have an adequate understanding of behavior in any given situation. This interaction position developed more or less independently in the traditional areas of differential psychology and cognitive psychology and in the traditional area of personality. The reasons for moving toward an interaction position, however, were quite different in the two areas, as we have already seen. Research in the first area has been very active in recent years under the rubric of aptitude-treatment interaction or ATI (Cronbach and Snow 1977). ATI research is discussed at length in the following chapter. In the area of personality, research on interactions is becoming increasingly active, and the present status of work in this area is discussed in a recent book by Magnusson and Endler (1977b).

Part of the difficulty with the trait approach and the problem of consistency of traits across situations may have to do with the way we typically think of traits. It is not unusual for us to think that all individuals have the same traits. Yet different traits may be relevant for different individuals (Bem and Allen 1974), and different traits may be relevant in different situations (Epstein 1977). For example, weight may be a relevant trait for being a jockey but be totally irrelevant for driving a car. In addition, consistency can occur at several different levels, and we may focus on one level at the expense of others (Magnusson and Endler 1977a). We may be unable, for example, to find consistency in behavior, but consistency might be found if we were to look instead at mediating variables—for example, motivational factors or amount of information that the individual has available—that underlie and are responsible for the overt behavior. We sometimes overlook the fact that underlying variables can often be manifested in a variety of ways. Something analogous to the distinction between genotypes and phenotypes may be involved. A good critique of why traits may still have some usefulness is available in Epstein (1977).

The term "interaction" is often used in several different ways. Thus, it is not surprising to find some differences in the various approaches that have been used for studying the relationship between individual differences and situational factors. In the case of mental abilities, where there has also been more of a concern for instructional situations, the typical procedure has been to take various types of existing mental tests, more or less off the shelf, and search for statistical interactions between these tests and various types of instructional treatments. This general approach was probably influenced by the fact that the concern with interactions developed out of the merging of two separate methodological disciplines in which the concept of traits is still fairly well accepted and the concern for statistical interactions is a natural consequence of combining the two different statistical methodologies involved.

Different approaches have been tried in the area of personality. One methodological approach that holds some promise for understanding the role of individual differences in both mental abilities and personality better has been recently developed by Bem and Funder (1978). The procedure, referred to as template matching, involves developing a template for a given situation in terms of charactertistics that describe a hypothetical, ideal "type" of person who is expected to behave in a particular way in that setting. Several such templates may be developed for a particular situation. The likelihood that any given person will behave in a certain way in a specified situation is postulated to depend on the similarity or match between the person's characteristics and the template associated with the corresponding behavior for that situation: the closer the match, the more likely it is that the behavior will occur. For example, the student who will ideally get the best grades at West High School is interested in ideas, likes sports, prefers teachers who are aloof and formal in their dealings with students, and so forth. Different templates would be associated with social success at West High School and with getting good grades at East High School. Students who have already described themselves in terms of various characteristics might then compare their characteristics with those of the template for getting good grades at West High School and determine how likely they are to get good grades in that particular setting. It is possible that one type of student would get good grades at West High School, while a different type of student might get good grades at East High School.

Concern for interactions between individual differences and various environmental situations is likely to continue and is likely to have some profound implications for the way we describe differences among both individuals and environmental situations. Our older conceptualizations may prove to be inadequate for this totally new task. One current difficulty is in finding adequate ways to characterize the environment. The template-matching system described in the preceding paragraph may prove to be appropriate for this task, although other possibilities certainly exist.

NEWER CONCEPTIONS OF INDIVIDUAL DIFFERENCES

As we have seen throughout this chapter, some of the older conceptions of individual differences are being challenged in ways that have important implications for both educational practices and psychological research. A number of important changes in emphasis have occurred since Glaser (1972) called for the development of new aptitudes that would reflect modern approaches to individual differences more realistically. Probably the biggest change has been a shift from thinking about individual differences in terms of how successful various people will be in predefined situations to a concern with how various situations and social institutions can be created in a way that meets the individual needs and requirements of each person.

This does not mean that all individuals should necessarily achieve the same level of performance or accomplish the same things. Individual diversity is still recognized. The newer aptitudes tend to focus on aspects of individual differences that will permit us to match instruction to individual students—at least to the maximum extent possible—in ways that will optimize the learning of all students. Compare this orientation with the earlier one that focused primarily on how well or how poorly a particular student is likely to perform in a predefined and largely inflexible instructional environment. This shift in orientation is characterized by the current interest in discovering or defining aptitudes relevant for learning from instruction.

Other changes can also be identified, and some of these changes are related, in varying degrees, to the shift in orientation just discussed, although other factors beyond the scope of this chapter are also involved. One of these changes is an increasing interest in the psychological processes, especially cognitive processes, that underlie individual differences in performance or in group membership (for example, sex differences). This interest in aptitude processes is evident in nearly all areas of research on individual differences. In addition to the more traditional types of psychological research already discussed, there has been substantial interest in recent years in individual differences in brain function. Much of this research has focused on individual differences in cerebral dominance or the balance of influence between the two hemispheres which are known to have somewhat different functions, although the findings are not as simple or as straightforward as is often thought. Many of these issues and their implications for education are discussed in a recent yearbook of the National Society for the Study of Education (Chall and Mirsky 1978). Another important characteristic of current research on individual differences is the concern for interactions between individual differences and environmental factors that was discussed in the preceding section. There has also been a revival of interest in understanding the role and nature of individual differences rather than just describing them or using them for simple prediction.

In general, then, there appears to be a move away from the traditional unifactor trait approach to the study of individual differences, including most of the older multifactor models that have been suggested. In their place there are attempts to identify new types of aptitudes and aptitude complexes comprised of a number of individual difference factors. One example of recent attempts to identify new aptitudes is the hierarchical models of ability discussed in an earlier section of this chapter. Another example is shown in the two aptitude complexes that Cronbach and Snow (1977, Snow 1976, 1978) have used to summarize research on aptitude-treatment interactions and that they suggest may be of interest to further research. The first complex involves intellectual factors relating to various aspects of intelligence and is referred to as the $G_c G_f G_v$ complex. It consists of fluid-analytic intelligence (G_f), crystallized-verbal intelligence (G_c), and spatial visualization ability (G_v), as described in an earlier section of this chapter. A hierarchical model is suggested, and Snow (1976, 1978) has reported several studies done within this framework. The most interesting and persisting finding at this time regarding the $G_c G_f G_v$ complex, although even this finding should be taken with a certain amount of tentativeness, has to do with the information-processing burden that a given instructional treatment places on the learner.

The second aptitude complex is concerned with personality factors that seem to be consistently related to learning. Cronbach and Snow (1977) refer to this general construct in terms of "contructive" versus "defensive" motivation. This aptitude complex, referred to as $A_i A_c A_x$, is comprised of individual differences in anxiety (A_x), achievement via independence (A_i), and achievement via conformity (A_c). Together these two complexes represent an attempt to create new aptitudes by integrating older ones in a manner that will better serve the purpose of identifying individual differences relevant to learning from instruction.

This approach certainly offers some promise for developing more useful conceptions of individual differences, although it should be realized that the specific examples described above are still dependent to a large extent on traditional methodology and use psychometric tests designed for purposes somewhat different from those inherent in some of the current concerns. Other researchers (Bem and Allen 1974, Bem and Funder 1978, Tyler 1978) have suggested more radical approaches in which individual differences are conceptualized more in terms of the individual's unique profile of capabilities—both strengths and weaknesses. This latter approach tends to downplay comparisons among individuals (one characteristic of the former approach) and focus more on the way one relates to oneself or how one compares with the characteristics of a given situation or task with little or no reference to other individuals.

The ultimate question for educational purposes may be how we can identify dimensions of individual differences relevant for instruction. A number of possibilities are discussed in this and the next chapter. Differences in the knowledge students have already acquired (Tobias 1976) may be as relevant as many of the more general processes or traits frequently used to characterize individual differences. But we should realize that the conceptual systems that will prove to be most appropriate in the future may be quite unlike the current systems that were developed for rather different purposes.

SUMMARY AND PROSPECTUS

In this chapter an attempt has been made to outline some of the various dimensions useful in characterizing the many differences among individuals. A number of the theoretical and conceptual factors that influence the way we think about individual differences have been identified, including the implicit assumptions we make and the purpose we have for wanting to differentiate among individuals.

In addition to discussing some of the research that is currently being done on various aspects of individual differences, some of the ways in which current research efforts differ from earlier ones have also been discussed. These differences include an increasing interest in the psychological processes responsible for individual differences in performance and an interest in the way different characteristics of individuals interact with characteristics of the environment or situation the individual is in—both factors must be considered in obtaining an accurate understanding of human behavior. There is also a major interest in discovering aptitudes appropriate for the task of adapting situations to the needs and requirements of each individual rather than merely determining how well an individual will function in a predefined situation.

To a large extent, research on mental abilities and research on personality seem to be moving in similar directions. If this continues, there is hope that this may be a precursor to an interest leading into an integration of the cognitive and personality aspects of individual differences. If so, then we would be on the verge of a truly major advance. Individuals are whole organisims that have both cognitive and affective factors operating at the same time; personality and mental abilities are separate only in the minds of observers. For a variety of reasons, many of which are quite appropriate, we have carved up our attempts to understand people into separate and somewhat arbitrary compartments. It is interesting and encouraging to see rather similar themes—even if they have developed for somewhat different reasons—in the two major domains. If the two could be meaningfully combined, we would have an even better understanding of individual differences and their importance for education.

But what do individual differences really mean, both for educational practices and psychological theory? Individual differences, regardless of how they are conceptualized, basically represent a taxonomy of those differences that we think are important for some purpose. In education an appropriate conception of individual differences means that we can meet the educational needs of each student better. A number of the more specific ways in which instructional programs can be adapted to individual differences will be discussed in the next chapter. With respect to psychological theory, there are a number of unanswered questions and unresolved issues, but considerable research is currently being done in this area.

The concern for individual differences and the concern for general laws are not mutually exclusive, as is often thought. Each can contribute to the other, and research in this area can serve as a crucible (Underwood 1975) for both concerns. Yet the appropriate balance between general laws and individual differences remains to be determined. This chapter has provided a sketch of what we currently know about individual differences, but much still remains a mystery, and that mystery presents an interesting challenge to those involved in this field.

REFERENCES

Atkinson, John W., and Birch, David. *The Dynamics of Action.* New York: Wiley, 1970.

Atkinson, John W., and Raynor, Joel O. *Motivation and Achievement.* Washington, D.C.: Winston, 1975.

Bem, Daryl J., and Allen, Andrea. "On Predicting Some of the People Some of the Time: The Search for Cross-Situational Consistencies in Behavior," *Psychological Review* 81 (November 1974): 506-20.

Bem, Daryl J., and Funder, David C. "Predicting More of the People More of the Time: Assessing the Personality of Situations." *Psychological Review* 85 (November 1978): 485-501.

Carroll, John B. "Psychometric Tests as Cognitive Tasks: A New Structure of Intellect." In *The Nature of Intelligence,* edited by Lauren B. Resnick, pp. 27-56. Hillsdale, N.J.: Lawrence Erlbaum Associates, 1976.

Carroll, John B., and Maxwell, Scott E. "Individual Differences in Cognitive Abilities." *Annual Review of Psychology.* Vol. 30. Edited by Mark R. Rosenzweig and Lyman W. Porter, pp. 603-40. Palo Alto, Calif.: Annual Reviews, 1979.

Cattell, Raymond B. *Personality and Motivation Structure and Measurement.* New York: Harcourt Brace Jovanovich, 1957.

————. *Abilities: Their Structure, Growth, and Action.* Boston: Houghton Mifflin, 1971.

————. "The Grammar of Science and the Evolution of Personality Theory." In *Handbook of Modern Personality Theory,* edited by Raymond B. Cattell and R.M. Dreger, pp. 3-42. New York: John Wiley, 1977.

Chall, Jeanne S., and Mirsky, Allan F., eds. *Education and the Brain.* Seventy-seventh Yearbook of the National Society for the Study of Education, Part II. Chicago: University of Chicago Press, 1978.

Cronbach, Lee J. "The Two Disciplines of Scientific Psychology." *American Psychologist* 12 (December 1957): 671-84.

Cronbach, Lee J. and Snow, Richard E. *Aptitudes and Instructional Methods.* New York: Irvington, 1977.

Endler, Norman S., and Magnusson, David. "Toward an International Psychology of Personality." *Psychological Bulletin* 83 (September 1976): 956-74.

Epstein, Seymour. "Traits are Alive and Well." In *Personality at the Crossroads: Current Issues in Interactional Psychology*, edited by David Magnusson and Norman S. Endler, pp. 83-98. Hillsdale, N.J.: Lawrence Erlbaum Associates, 1977.

Estes, William K. "Learning Theory and Intelligence." *American Psychologist* 29 (October 1974): 740-49.

Gaudry, Eric, and Spielberger, Charles D. *Anxiety and Educational Achievement.* Sydney/New York: Wiley Australasia, 1971.

Glaser, Robert. "Individuals and Learning: The New Aptitudes." *Educational Researcher* 1 (June 1972): 5-13.

———. *Adaptive Education: Individual Diversity and Learning.* New York: Holt, Rinehart and Winston, 1977.

Goldstein, Kenneth M., and Blackman, Sheldon. *Cognitive Style: Five Approaches and Relevant Research.* New York: John Wiley, 1978.

Goodenough, Donald R. "The Role of Individual Differences in Field Dependence as a Factor in Learning and Memory." *Psychological Bulletin* 83 (July 1976): 675-94.

Horn, John L. "Human Abillities: A Review of Research and Theory in the Early 1970s." *Annual Review of Psychology.* Vol. 27. Edited by Mark R. Rosenzweig and Lyman W. Porter, pp. 437-85. Palo Alto, Calif.: Annual Reviews, 1976.

———. "Personality and Ability Theory." In *Handbook of Modern Personality Theory*, edited by Raymond B. Cattell and R.M. Dreger, pp. 139-65. New York: Wiley, 1977.

Hunt, Earl. "Mechanics of Verbal Ability." *Psychological Review* 85 (March 1978): 109-30.

Hunt, Earl; Frost, N.; and Lunneborg, Clifford. "Individual Differences in Cognition: A New Approach to Intelligence." In *The Psychology of Learning and Motivation: Advances in Research and Theory.* Vol. 7. Edited by G.H. Bower, pp. 87-122. New York: Academic Press, 1973.

Hunt, Earl; Lunneborg, Clifford; and Lewis, Joe. "What Does it Mean to be High Verbal?" *Cognitive Psychology* 7 (April 1975): 194-227.

Jensen, Arthur R. "*g*: Outmoded Theory or Unconquered Frontier?" *Creative Science and Technology* 11, 3 (1979): 16-29.

Keating, Daniel P., and Bobbitt, Bruce L. "Individual and Development Difference in Cognitive-Processing Components of Mental Ability." *Child Development* 49 (March 1978): 155-67.

Lefcourt, Herbert M. *Locus of Control.* Hillsdale, N.J.: Lawrence Erlbaum Associates, 1976.

Magnusson, David, and Endler, Norman S. "Interactional Psychology: Present Status and Future Research." In *Personality at the Crossroads: Current Issues in Interactional Psychology*, edited by David Magnusson and Norman S. Endler, pp. 3-31. Hillsdale, N.J.: Lawrence Erlbaum Associates, 1977(a).

————, eds. *Personality at the Crossroads: Current Issues in Interactional Psychology*, Hillsdale, N.J.: Lawrence Erlbaum Associates, 1977(b).

Messick, Samuel. "Personality Consistencies in Cognition and Creativity." In *Individuality in Learning*, edited by Samuel Messick, pp. 4-22. San Francisco: Jossey-Bass, 1976.

Mischel, Walter. "Toward a Cognitive Social Learning Reconceptualization of Personality." *Psychological Review* 80 (July 1973): 252-83.

Nichols, Robert C. "Policy Implications of the IQ Controversy." In *Review of Research in Education*. Vol. 6. Edited by Lee S. Shulman, pp. 3-46. Itasca, Ill.: Peacock, 1978.

Phares, E. Jerry. "Locus of Control." In *Dimensions of Personality*, edited by Harvey London and John E. Exner, Jr. New York: Wiley-Interscience, 1976(a).

————. *Locus of Control in Personality*. Morristown, N.J.: General Learning Press, 1976(b).

Phares, E. Jerry, and Lamiell, James T. "Personality." *Annual Review of Psychology*. Vol. 28. Edited by Mark R. Rosenzweig and Lyman W. Porter, pp. 113-40. Palo Alto, Calif.: Annual Reviews, 1977.

Posner, Michael I., et al. "Retention of Visual and Name Codes of Single Letters." *Journal of Experimental Psychology Monographs* 79, 1, part 2 (1969).

Posner Michael I., and Mitchell, Ronald F. "Chronometric Analysis of Classification." *Psychological Review* 74 (September 1967): 392-409.

Resnick, Lauren B. "Introduction: Changing Conceptions of Intelligence." In *The Nature of Intelligence*, edited by Lauren B. Resnick, pp. 1-10. Hillsdale, N.J.: Lawrence Erlbaum Associates, 1976(a).

————, ed. *The Nature of Intelligence*. Hillsdale, N.J.: Lawrence Erlbaum Associates, 1976(b).

Rotter, Julian B. "Some Problems and Misconceptions Related to the Construct of Internal versus External Control of Reinforcement." *Journal of Consulting and Clinical Psychology* 43 (February 1975): 56-67.

Sechrest, Lee. "Personality," *Annual Review of Psychology*. Vol. 27. Edited by Mark R. Rosenzweig and Lyman W. Porter, pp. 1-27. Palo Alto, Calif.: Annual Reviews, 1976.

Sieber, Joan E., O'Neil, Jr., Harold F., and Tobias, Sigmund. *Anxiety, Learning, and Instruction*. Hillsdale, N.J.: Lawrence Erlbaum Associates, 1977.

Snow, Richard E. "Research on Aptitude for Learning: A Progress Report." In *Review of Research in Education*. Vol. 4. Edited by Lee S. Shulman, pp. 50-105. Itasca, Ill.: Peacock, 1976.

————. "Theory and Method for Research on Aptitude Processes." *Intelligence* 2 (July-September 1978): 225-78.

Spielberger, Charles D. "Anxiety As an Emotional State." In *Anxiety: Current Trends in Theory and Research*. Vol. 1. Edited by Charles D. Spielberger, pp. 23-49. New York: Academic Press, 1972.

Spielberger, Charles D.; Lushene, R.E.; and McAdoo, W.G. "Theory and Measurements of Anxiety States." In *Handbook of Modern Personality Theory*, edited by Raymond B. Cattell and R.M. Dreger, pp. 239-53. New York: John Wiley, 1977.

Sternberg, Robert J. "Component Processes in Analogical Reasoning." *Psychological Review* 84 (July 1977a): 353-78.

————. *Intelligence, Information Processing, and Analogical Reasoning: The Componential Analysis of Human Abilities.* Hillsdale, N.J.: Lawrence Erlbaum Associates, 1977(b).

————. "Components of Deductive Reasoning." In *Aptitude, Learning, and Instruction: Cognitive Process Analyses*, edited by Richard E. Snow, P-A Federico, and W.E. Montague. Hillsdale, N.J.: Lawrence Erlbaum Associates, in press.

Tobias, Sigmund. "Achievement Treatment Interactions." *Review of Educational Research* 46 (Winter 1976): 61-74.

Tyler, Leona E. *Individuality.* San Francisco: Jossey-Bass, 1978.

Underwood, Benton J. "Individual Differences as a Crucible in Theory Construction." *American Psychologist* 30 (February 1975): 128-40.

Vernon, Philip E. *The Structure of Human Abilities.* London: Methuen, 1971.

Weiner, Bernard. *Achievement Motivation and Attribution Theory.* Morristown, N.J.: General Learning Press, 1974.

Witkin, H.A. et al. "Field-Dependent and Field-Independent Cognitive Styles and Their Educational Implications." *Review of Educational Research* 47 (Winter 1977): 1-64.

3. Adaptation to Individual Differences

Sigmund Tobias

Until quite recently Mark Twain's hoary comment about the weather was probably an apt description of the state of affairs dealing with individualized instruction; that is, everyone was talking about it, but no one was doing much about it. The notion that students should be taught by an instructional method ideally suited to their interests and abilities is hardly new. A case could be made for the fact that Plato's description of Socrates' instruction of the slave boy Meno was perhaps the first recorded attempt to suit the method of instruction to the student. The interest in such individualization of instruction, then, can be traced to antiquity.

Edward L. Thorndike (1911), widely acknowledged to be the first educational psychologist, strongly endorsed individualization of instruction. He wrote:

Specialization of instruction for different pupils within one class is needed as well as specialization of the curriculum for different classes. Since human nature does not fall into sharply defined groups, we can literally never be sure of having a dozen pupils who need to be treated exactly alike. [p. 51]

In the years since then there have been numerous calls for the individualization of instruction. Teachers have been exhorted for generations to use different instructional methods for different students. Two questions related to these calls for the individualization of instruction have generally been left in an ambiguous state: (a) What student characteristics would guide the teacher in determining the type of instructional methods ideally suited to different students? (b) In what ways should the instructional methods differ? These ambiguities have generally been resolved by leaving the decision on these two matters to the teacher's art. In order to convert individualized instruction from the realm of art to science, evidence is required permitting educators to decide, for example, that students who are high on variable X should be assigned to instructional method A, and students who are low on variable X should be assigned to instructional method B. Unfortunately, such evidence did not exist in Thorndike's time, nor is it plentiful today.

One of the milestones in the attempt to provide a scientific basis for the individualization of instruction was the conference on learning and individual differences held at the University of Pittsburgh in 1965. The papers were subsequently published in 1967 (Gagné 1967). In his presentation to that conference, Cronbach (1967) suggested that in addition to individualizing the method of instruction it would also be possible to suit the outcomes of instruction to differences among students. There is little research dealing with this type of individualization.

STATISTICAL INTERACTION

In order to tailor the method of instruction to a particular student, research evidence is required relating students' standing on an individual difference variable, such as anxiety or intelligence, to differences in instructional treatments. Such interactions between aptitudes and treatments have been called "aptitude-treatment interaction" (ATI). Statistically, the type of evidence required is called interaction. Perhaps the concept of interaction can best be understood by reference to Figure 3-1.

In Figure 3-1 the X axis represents any individual difference measure such as anxiety, intelligence, and so forth. The Y axis represents instructional outcomes such as scores on posttests, tests of attitudes, and the like. The functions in the figure represent the results for two different instructional methods, A and B. Inspection of

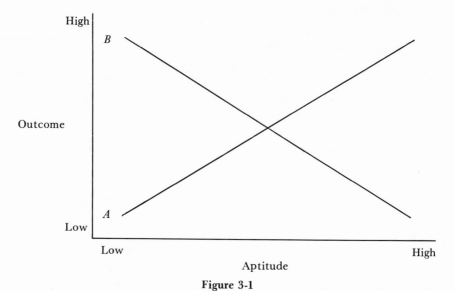

Figure 3-1

Example of disordinal interaction between aptitude and instructional method

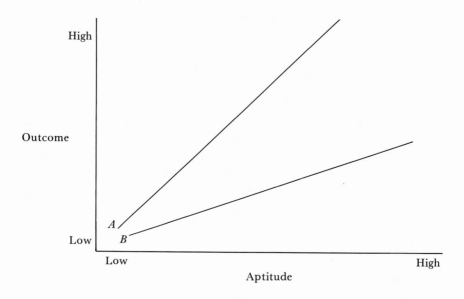

Figure 3-2

Example of an ordinal interaction between aptitude and instructional method

the figure indicates that students with low scores on the aptitude measure, let us say for example anxiety, also performed poorly on the instructional outcome measure under method A. Students with similar low scores on the individual difference measure, however, did quite well on the outcome measure when they were instructed by method B. The exact opposite is the case for students who scored high on anxiety. Those students did quite well when they utilized method A but performed poorly with method B.

The data displayed in Figure 3-1 represent a *disordinal* interaction. An interaction is described as being disordinal whenever the lines cross one another. Such disordinal interactions are the most sought after evidence in ATI research since they obviously permit assigning students to differential methods. That is, in terms of the data displayed in Figure 3-1, students whose standing on the aptitude measure is below the perpendicular dotted line should be assigned to method B so as to maximize the outcomes of instruction, whereas students whose standing on the aptitude measure is to the right of the perpendicular line should obviously be assigned to instructional method A. Were such data widely available, students would be assessed on the individual difference measure and then, depending on their scores, be assigned to either instructional method A or instructional method B.

While disordinal interactions may be the most useful for differential assignment of students to instructional methods, other types of interactions are possible. Figure 3-2 shows a somewhat different set of outcomes called an *ordinal* interaction.

In an ordinal interaction one of the outcomes is superior to the other one though the difference between the two is *not* constant. It may be easiest to understand the concept of ordinal interaction by labeling the axes in an identical manner to Figure 3-1. That is, the X axis represents an individual difference measure such as anxiety and the Y axis represents an instructional outcome such as achievement. The graph indicates that students in instructional method A do better than all students assigned to instructional method B. The difference between the methods is, however, not constant. That is, students who are high on the individual difference variable do very well utilizing method A, whereas students with low scores on the individual difference variable performed only slightly above those assigned to instructional method B. Students assigned to method B

have approximately the same instructional outcome, at least in this illustration, irrespective of their standing on the individual-difference measure.

What are the implications of research results such as those depicted in Figure 3-2? From a practical point of view it would, of course, be wisest to assign all students to method A because it always yields higher achievement. Suppose, however, that method A is twice as expensive as method B either with respect to cost or in that it takes twice as long to instruct the students. In that case, students who are high on the individual difference measure should obviously be assigned to method A, despite the extra cost, since the performance is markedly superior with that method. The performance of students who are at the lower end of the individual difference measure is, on the other hand, barely different utilizing either method A or B. Since method A is much more expensive, an instructor might opt to assign students to method B, reasoning that the trivial differences in achievement are more than made up for in the lower cost of method B. Ordinal interactions, then, have some use in making practical instructional decisions about students.

Ordinal interactions are also of some importance theoretically. Reference to Figure 3-3 may clarify this point. The solid lines in Figure 3-3 represent exactly the same data depicted in Figure 3-3. Now suppose that it were possible to recruit a sample of students whose scores on the individual difference variable were lower than those of the students in the research study. The slope of the two functions in Figure 3-3 indicates that for such students method B might lead to results superior to those obtained with method A. In other words, an ordinal interaction generally suggests that if the range of scores on the X axis could be extended, the two lines are likely to cross, and a *disordinal* interaction will result. From a research point of view, then, ordinal interaction suggests that disordinality could result if the data represented by the X axis were extended. This may be of both practical and theoretical interest. Practically, of course, students falling at the extended end of the individual difference continuum should be assigned to the method yielding higher achievement. Theoretically, ordinal interactions indicate that something about the instructional method interacts with extreme scores on the individual-difference variable. Once researchers understand what it is about the extreme scores or the instructional

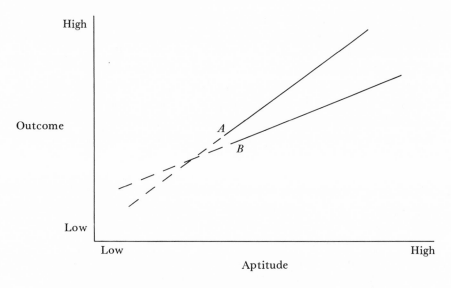

Figure 3-3

**Example of an ordinal interaction between aptitude and instructional
method with hypothetical extrapolations (shown by dotted lines)**

methods that accounts for such a relationship, it may be possible to
alter or refine the instruction in order to yield a more disordinal
interaction in the center of the individual difference continuum.

PRESENT ADAPTATIONS

Of course, quite a number of programs of individualized instruction have been implemented in different parts of the country. Baker
(1971) reviewed many of the programs that used computers in order
to assist with individualization. A number of other individualized
instructional systems have been strongly influenced by Bloom's
mastery-based learning system, which is described by Block (1974).
An equally prominent instructional methodology is Keller's (1968),
which is generally described as the Personalized System of Instruction (PSI). Block (1974) reports on the similarities and differences between Bloom's mastery-based instructional strategy and Keller's PSI.

In general, these instructional adaptations have a number of features in common. Typically, a course of instruction is arranged in a

series of relatively self-contained units. Each unit is preceded by a series of objectives that describe in specific detail the outcomes of instruction in terms of behaviors the student will be able to engage in after completing the unit. Following these, the student is directed to sets of learning materials contained either in conventional textbooks, journal articles, or on video or audio tapes, among other resources. When the students complete study of the assigned materials, they are evaluated in order to determine whether the objectives have been mastered according to satisfactory criteria, which in such instances are generally set somewhere between 75 and 90 percent. Those students who have attained the criterion are then directed to the next unit, which also contains objectives, instructional materials, posttests, and so on. Students who fail to achieve mastery are typically branched back to the same instructional resources and sometimes alternate resources, and then they are evaluated again in order to determine whether mastery has been attained.

There are differences among a variety of individualized instructional strategies. They can differ with respect to the types of evaluation used, whether a final evaluation is utilized in addition to the evaluation at the end of every unit, the degree to which computers or other forms of technology are employed, as well as differences along other dimensions. The description above is relatively accurate with respect to the underlying instructional strategy employed by most individualized instructional procedures. The type of individualization occurring in these instructional plans typically relies largely on permitting students to complete the course of instruction at their own rate. That is, students who work rapidly can complete a unit as quickly as they wish, especially if they work carefully enough not to make major errors. In that case, they will pass all of the evaluations and can move rapidly from one unit to another. Students who work slowly or encounter difficulties with the instructional materials will progress less rapidly since they are likely not to attain the criterion for mastery on the evaluation at the end of the unit and will be required to go back and work on the material again and again until mastery has been attained.

The critical point is that in instructional schemes such as those described above, individualization of the *rate* of instruction occurs but *not individualization of the instructional method*. That is, all students proceed through the instructional material in much the same way. In some mastery-based instructional modes, students who fail to attain the criterion of mastery are sometimes branched to alternate instructional sources rather than being asked to repeat the same ones they studied the first time (Block 1971). In these instances, however, the alternate instructional strategy is not assigned on the basis of research findings. Rather the assignment is made essentially on logical grounds, with a rationale that if the criterion was not attained after studying the materials the first time, little would be accomplished by asking the student to work on the same sets of material again.

In a truly individualized instruction, of course, not only would the rate at which instruction proceeds be suited to the student but the method of instruction would be individualized as well. Students would be assigned to alternate instructional strategies depending upon their scores on some individual difference variable. Such adaptation, or course, assumes the existence of well-replicated, well-documented ATIs. The specific study of such interactions is relatively new; hence there are few verified interactions permitting instructional designers to develop different teaching strategies for different learners. In the absence of these, individualization of rate is about all one can hope for. An overview of the history and present status of ATI research will highlight some of the problems in this area.

HISTORY OF ATI RESEARCH

In his presidential address to the American Psychological Association, Cronbach (1957) indicated that until then two branches of psychology had existed essentially independently. Experimental and learning psychologists in general were mainly concerned with the improvement of experimental methods. Their purpose was to develop experiments that would clearly demonstrate the superiority of one experimental or instructional method over another. When the findings invariably demonstrated that some students, in those studies utilizing human subjects, did better than others, such data tended to be dismissed as a bothersome nuisance since individual differences were seen as obscuring the essential purpose of the research. Simultaneously, another arm of psychology was devoted exclusively to the study of individual differences. Such researchers would expose individuals to a large array of tasks, expecting people to differ in the ease with which they coped with these tasks. Often the analysis concerned the relationships between students' performance on different types of tasks with little interest in which method worked best with any one task. Cronbach urged these two psychological disciplines to collaborate so that one might determine not only which method was superior but also for which type of individual that particular method was superior. In the 1965 conference on learning and individual differences mentioned above, Cronbach (1967) specifically called for research to study the interaction between individual differences on one hand and instructional methods on the other.

Bracht (1970) reviewed over a hundred studies of relevance to the ATI question. Most of these investigations had *not* been designed as ATI studies but instead compared one learning strategy or instructional method against another. In addition, researchers often had data on individual differences among the subjects. In these studies Bracht found only a handful of ordinal interactions and virtually no disordinal interactions. This led to a somewhat pessimistic conclusion regarding the future of ATIs. Cronbach and Snow (1969) published what was, until then, the most comprehensive review of ATI studies. While their review revealed a number of significant interactions, there were few findings that had been sufficiently replicated to permit confidence in the ATI approach in general or to permit instructional designers to apply these findings to the development of alternate instructional strategies. Berliner and Cahen (1973) updated reviews of this research and concluded that the development up to that time gave grounds for "cautious optimism." These writers also pointed out that ordinal interactions might hold promise for ATI research.

A major milestone occurred when Cronbach and Snow (1977) published an update of their earlier review. More recent ATI research is reviewed by Snow (1977, 1976a, 1976b). The Cronbach and Snow book is a detailed review of most of the ATI investigations prior to 1975. As such, it is of course not easily summarized. The reader interested in ATIs in any curricular area is well advised to consult this work both as a valuable review of prior research in the area and as a guide for the design and analysis of ATI investigations. A large number of significant ATIs are described in this work. While there is some cause for optimism regarding ATI research, two aspects of this compendium give grounds for pessimism, namely, the inconsistency of the findings and their lack of generality.

Inconsistency of Findings

In many of the areas reviewed by Cronbach and Snow, the number of significant ATIs tend to be balanced by an almost equal number of insignificant results. Even more troubling is the difficulty in determining specifically what attributes of students or what exact characteristics of the instructional method accounted for either the significant or insignificant findings. Failure to specify such characteristics makes it difficult to follow up leads in order to develop more consistent findings. Another aspect of the inconsistencies noted in previous results is the fact that of those studies reporting significant ATIs, few have been successfully repeated. This lack of replication can be attributed to a number of variables. First, many investigations are "one shot affairs," such as dissertations, so that it is difficult to generate a consistent body of research. More disturbing is the fact that when replications are attempted by the use of slightly different student samples, the results are frequently different from those of the initial investigation. These difficulties will be discussed more extensively below, but in any event they pose serious questions for the future of ATI research.

Lack of Generality

Another troubling aspect of ATI investigation has been the frequent finding that slight changes in the instructional method employed or in the sample of students yield markedly different ATI results. For example, I have discussed elsewhere (1972) the history of an individualized instructional program dealing with heart disease that had been used for research purposes both in a programmed-instruction format and in a format appropriate for computer-assisted instruction. In the programmed-instruction version, a number of significant interactions between the instructional strategy and the student differences in past achievement were reported. When the program was converted verbatim for presentation via computer-assisted instruction, the findings obtained with the programmed form of the materials could not be replicated. A detailed task analysis and revision of the instructional materials subsequently led to both replication and extension of the earlier findings on computer-assisted instruction (Tobias 1973). Similarly, Peterson (1977) studied the interaction between instructional method and a number of personality variables in a sample of ninth grade students. In the succeeding year, she repeated essentially the same study (Peterson 1978), using the same personality variables and instructional methods but a different subject matter and a different student population. Surprisingly, the results of the second investigation were markedly different from those of the first study.

These two investigations, among a number of others, indicate that changes in the instructional materials, the student characteristics, or the instructional methods can result in very different ATI results. This lack of robustness in the findings is a cause for grave concern to ATI researchers. If such small alterations in the characteristics of students or instructional methods can alter the results substantially, one wonders if it will ever be possible to formulate sufficiently broad generalizations about instructional methods and student characteristics for these to be useful to an instructional designer. Considerations similar to these led Cronbach (1975) to suggest that generalizations made from such research may well be limited to the particular locale in which the studies were undertaken as well as to the particular time in which they were found. Cronbach suggests that in the social sciences in general, and in ATI research in particular, findings may well shift from decade to decade rather than holding for time immemorial.

Need for Classification and Theory

The inconsistency of results and the lack of generality of many ATI findings point to an important problem: the need for a classification scheme of instructional methods on the one hand and the individual difference characteristics of students on the other. Our descriptive schemes for instructional method are vague, excessively general, and highly descriptive. For example, homogeneous-heterogeneous grouping is one of the most studied problems in education. The frequency with which this problem has been investigated has yielded few verifiable generalizations. Findley and Bryan (1971) conclude that "taking all studies [of ability grouping] into account, the balance of findings is chiefly of no strong effect either favorable or unfavorable" (p. 54). There are numerous problems in this research. Of special pertinence here is the fact that the range of abilities in one study of heterogeneous-homogeneous grouping may be very different from that represented in another study. In one study, homogeneous grouping may involve placing students with IQs from 85 to 100 in one group and those with IQs from 101 to 115 in another. Another investigation may group students with IQs between 85-115 in one class and those over 115 in another. While these are both studies of grouping, the differences in class composition may make them very different investigations. Furthermore, while two studies may both examine grouping, they may use very different instructional methods. For example, one study may employ an "open-corridor" method and another a "traditional" instructional arrangement. Clearly, given such differences it is almost impossible for this research to cumulate and lead to powerful generalizations. What is needed is a precise taxonomic scheme that allows for a thorough description of the instructional environment so that investigators can be reasonably sure of having two groups working on instructional methods that are highly similar *except* for the one variable in which they choose to have the groups differ. Indicating merely that one group was homogeneously grouped, for example, and one group was heterogeneously grouped obviously does not have sufficient precision to permit the research to build to important conclusions.

Another problem deals with the classification of student aptitudes. Let us consider the area of anxiety, for example. Most tests of anxiety tend to correlate with one another at approximately .45. That means that only about 20 percent of the variation in one of these tests is explained by the variation in the other. Hence, different studies of anxiety, an area in which there are many ATI investigations (Cronbach and Snow 1977, chap. 10; Tobias 1977), can hardly be considered to have studied the same problem if different indices of anxiety were utilized in the investigations. Similar comments can be made about studies using intelligence as the individual difference variable. Intelligence tests typically have correlations of approximately .70 with one another. This means that about 49 percent of the variation in one test can be attributed to variations in the other. Results from studies using one test of intelligence, then, may well not apply to studies varying the same instructional methods but using a different test. Clearly, a comprehensive taxonomic scheme for the classification of individual differences is required in order to permit studies to accumulate research knowledge and lead to the formulation of powerful, theoretical generalizations.

The availability of such a taxonomic scheme would make it pos-

sible to build an ATI theory regarding expected relationships between variations of individual-difference characteristics on the one
hand and different treatments on the other. The absence of such a
scheme is a major roadblock in the development of an instructional
theory that would advance research on ATIs, as well as lead to generalizations that could be implemented in practice.

PRIOR ACHIEVEMENT AND INSTRUCTIONAL SUPPORT: AN ATI GENERAL HYPOTHESIS

An attempt to integrate a number of ATI studies led to the formulation of a general hypothesis that marks one beginning step toward
an ATI theory. Tobias (1973) reviewed a number of ATI investigations dealing with programmed and computer-assisted instruction.
The findings of these studies suggested that when students had a
good deal of prior knowledge of a particular content, there were no
achievement differences among different instructional methods.
When students had little prior experience with a subject matter,
however, it was generally found that the instructional method which
gave the student the greatest amount of support generally yielded
higher achievement. The instructional support in these investigations
was in the form of eliciting student responses, providing feedback
concerning them, and organizing the material into a tight logical
sequence.

These findings (Tobias, 1976, 1977) led to the statement of a
general hypothesis proposing an inverse relationship between prior
knowledge and amount of instructional support required in order to
master educational objectives. Prior achievement is, of course, easily
defined by a student's pretest score in any subject area. Instructional
support may be defined as the assistance given to the learner in
organizing content, making provisions to maintain attention, providing feedback regarding the student's performance, and monitoring
achievement at a micro level from one unit to another. The hypothesis implies that the lower the level of prior achievement, the more
assistance the learner needs in order to master objectives. Conversely,
the higher the level of prior achievement, the less assistance needed
by students beyond finding the materials for reading in any manner
they deem most effective.

As indicated above, this hypothesis is consistent with a number of studies. Pascarella (1977) investigated the interaction between prior mathematics achievement and level of instructional support in college calculus. In that study, high instructional support consisted of learning the content in a mastery-based instructional context in which students were provided objectives for units and formative evaluation devices, and they were looped back if they had not reached mastery. The second group studied this content with a condition of lower instructional support by participating in a traditional lecture and recitation situation. Students with lower scores on the mathematics placement examination achieved more when assigned to the individualized mastery-based condition than those assigned to the lecture. At higher pretest score levels on the mathematical placement examination, there was no difference in the results obtained from the two instructional methods. This is precisely the type of ordinal interaction to be expected from the achievement formulation. Summaries of further research dealing with this hypothesis can be found elsewhere (Tobias 1973, 1976, 1977).

The prior-achievement–instruction-support hypothesis avoids a number of the problems confronting ATI research in general. Specifically, it was indicated earlier that one of the difficulties for ATI researchers dealt with the importance of classifying students appropriately due to the similarities and differences of individual-difference measures in general. Since a pretest is necessarily specific to the content to be taught, relationships with other measures become less of a problem. That is, the pretest measure is not assumed to have any generality beyond serving as an index of the degree to which a particular content has been mastered. It may very well be that pretest scores contain components other than knowledge of a specific subject matter, such as test-taking skills, general intelligence, and the like. While such more general abilities may contribute to pretest scores, in most instances these are likely to be minor components. Use of prior knowlege, then, solves a part of the problem that ATI research requires a clear-cut classification scheme for students.

The notion of instructional support may also help to clarify the problem of a taxonomy of instructional situations. While instructional support is hardly a complete classification scheme allowing researchers and practitioners to categorize a wide variety of instructional strategies, it is nevertheless a useful point of departure. One can envision a classification system dealing with at least two major categories of instructional support or assistance to the learner: (a) improving the instructional materials and (b) directing the attention of the learner and providing feedback regarding attempts to process the content. The first category could include such things as organizing the material tightly around behavioral objectives, which would reduce extraneous material; improving the vividness of the instructional input by providing pictorial illustrations, graphic displays, or lifelike illustrations and models; adding audio-visual components to an instructional sequence; and the like. It should be noted that whether any of the above actually improve achievement for *any* group of students must be determined independently by research before one can classify these as useful types of instructional support.

Directing the student's attention—the second type of instructional support—could include such procedures as eliciting overt responses in order to assure that the student's attention is fixed, monitoring the quality of these responses and providing feedback regarding them, providing behavioral objectives or advance organizers, and giving the student instruction in a variety of study skills. It should be noted that the instructional supports in this category apply mainly to the activities of students as they interact with the instructional material. A third category of instructional support would consist of some classification scheme dealing with events occurring in the classroom and/or in small groups. These events might include problem solving, drill and practice in small groups, and the like.

The hypothesis of interaction between prior achievement and instructional support is quite similar to one of the conclusions reached by Cronbach and Snow (1977) following their comprehensive review of ATI research. They suggest that any procedures which reduce the intellectual demands made on the student by the instructional method would reduce achievement differences between students of high and low intelligence. If the difference between high and low intelligence is great in the comparison instructional method, an ordinal ATI would result, much as would be expected from the prior-achievement–instructional-support hypothesis.

PRACTICAL PROBLEMS IN
THE ADAPTATION TO INDIVIDUAL DIFFERENCES

In the preceding section the theoretical and research problems standing in the way of a scientifically based adaptation of instruction to individual differences among students have been described. There are a number of other more practical problems that must be faced even if the theoretical problems are solved. These involve dealing with changes in the role of the teacher with the advent of an individualized instruction.

In a truly individualized instruction, of course, all the students in one classroom may be working at different rates, taught by different instructional methods, and working on different materials. Such an array of differences places a truly formidable task on instructors. Not only must teachers be skilled in a variety of instructional strategies, expert in providing different materials to different students in the class, but they must also possess encyclopedic and accurate memories to keep track of the student's present state. Clearly, such requirements are beyond the abilities of the average or even the master teacher. The advent of a truly individualized instruction requires that teachers be provided with two major types of assistance: (a) help with the actual delivery of instruction and (b) help in storing and retrieving information regarding the rate, content, and instructional strategy used by the student.

It is not clear at this stage what form the assistance in delivering instruction to the student will take. As indicated above, there are a large variety of individualized instructional systems presently used that rely mainly on differences in the learning rates among the students. Were one also to use individualized methods of instruction, further assistance to the teacher would be required. It is possible that such assistance might be in the form of prepackaged instructional material, or it could be that some of this assistance might be provided in the form of paraprofessional assistance to the teacher, or teachers may even use more advanced students to tutor their less advanced colleagues. Such peer tutoring has been found to be effective in a large number of instances (Allen, Feldman, and Devin-Sheehan 1976). Or, finally, some assistance may be provided by the occasional use of programmed or computer-assisted instruction. Equally likely is the possibility that some combination of the various options described above may be needed in order to implement an individualized instruction. What is certain, however, is that assistance to the teacher is certainly required in order to provide a truly individualized instruction.

The chore of keeping track of student progress, materials, and instructional strategy is equally formidable. It seems quite clear that in this area computers can be expected to make this a manageable problem for teachers. One can envision a classroom in the future in which teachers can, by the flick of a button, have students' records appear on the cathode ray screen of a computer terminal in each classroom or on one shared among several classrooms. Teachers could also enter new information on these terminals during the day, after the conclusion of the day, or assign that chore to the school secretary. The management, storage, and retrieval of such information is both a relatively trivial and inexpensive use of data processing equipment that can certainly be expected to occur in the future (Rothkopf 1973). As a matter of fact, whether a completely individualized instruction is implemented or not, it seems likely that students' records will be sorted in this manner so that the teacher can have ready access to them without the laborious keeping of paper records that are cumbersome to store and inefficient to retrieve.

INDIVIDUALIZATION OF INSTRUCTION AND STUDENT ACHIEVEMENT

An assumption underlying this chapter has been, of course, that individualizing instruction leads to higher student achievement. Recent evidence on the outcome of instruction raises some questions about the validity of this assumption. Fisher et al. (1978) have demonstrated that *any* activity that increases students' time for actively interacting with the learning material leads to gains in student achievement. In reviews of research on teaching, Rosenshine (1977, 1979) found that a number of variables called "direct instruction" lead to increments in student achievement. Direct instruction includes such activities as monitoring student's seatwork, asking directive questions, and the like.

In addition, Rosenshine (1979) reported that students working independently without adult supervision tend to achieve less than those working with such supervision, since it has been found that less of the students' studying time is spent actively engaged with the instructional material. Furthermore, Rosenshine also reports that students who have a great deal of choice about the activities they chose to pursue achieve less than those who are more actively directed by the teacher. Since many of the activities that have been found to lead to lower achievement are a part of the hallmark of individualized instruction, the effectiveness of such instruction appears open to serious question.

The implications of Rosenshine's review of this literature are challenged by Peterson (1979), who raises the question "For what educational outcomes is direct instruction most effective and for what kinds of students?" (p. 58.) She points out that there are a number of studies comparing open and traditional instruction that bear on this topic. Peterson suggests that the characteristics of direct instruction described by Rosenshine are, in general, similar to those enumerated for groups receiving traditional instruction. Peterson summarized studies reviewed by Horwitz (1979) and those she reviewed. She noted that "on the average students tended to achieve more with traditional teaching than with open-classroom teaching" (p. 61). The differences between the two approaches were very small. When the outcomes were compared with respect to students' creativity, however, results favored students taught by open instructional approaches compared to those taught by traditional methods. Furthermore, the open approaches were superior to the traditional ones with respect to students' attitudes toward school and their instructor, as well as in promoting students' independence and curiosity. Again, it should be noted that the differences between the methods were small. Finally, a number of ATI studies addressed the question of whether these approaches were better for one kind of student or another. While positive results were reported by a number of investigators, these were relatively inconsistent, and further research is required to study the interaction between these two instructional approaches and student individual-difference characteristics.

The results of recent research summarized by Rosenshine (1979) and reevaluated by Peterson and Horwitz suggest that direct instruction, like most other instructional approaches, is unlikely to be superior for all types of outcomes or for all types of students. It does not seem likely that a great deal of clarity will be achieved by gross comparisons of instructional methods. Future research should probably isolate the variables making up each of these instructional methods and determine which of these variables is most important to students of particular characteristics. For example, Rosenshine (1979) reports that, on the whole, students do best in an instructional environment in which they have little choice of materials or how rapidly they are to work or which instructional methods are to be used. Since the differences between these approaches were very small, it may well be that students with other individual-difference characteristics could profit from choice on all of these variables, even though the group as a whole did not. These findings can be summarized simply by suggesting that further ATI research is needed in order to find out which of these characteristics of instructional methods lead to optimal achievement for students with different individual-difference characteristics.

Finally, it should be remembered that, as indicated at the beginning of this chapter, there is little individualization of instructional method. The individualization of instruction that has been implemented to date allows students to proceed at their own *rate*, without necessarily individualizing the method of instruction. It is expected that suiting the method of instruction to student individual differences will improve student achievement.

SUMMARY

This chapter has described some of the problems in adapting instruction to individual differences among students. It was indicated that, in general, the types of individualized instruction implemented as this is written have varied the rate at which instruction proceeds to suit different students without individualizing the method of instruction. The latter type of adaptation requires the existence of a replicated set of interactions between student aptitudes and different instructional methods. Such research has been actively pursued only since the mid 1960s, but it has not yet produced a body of evidence that permits a scientifically based instructional adaptation to differences among students.

Among the problems faced by the research in this area has been the absence of a taxonomy of instructional events and a comparable classification scheme allowing researchers to characterize precisely the differences among students. A further problem has been the inability to replicate findings and the limited generality of some of the research data. A promising hypothesis relating student differences in prior achievement to optimal instructional method was discussed, and the convergence of this approach with others has been described. Finally, some practical problems in individualizing instruction were described, and some of the recent research reviews questioning the efficacy of individualizing instruction were discussed.

REFERENCES

Allen, Vernon L.; Feldman, Robert S.; and Devin-Sheehan, Linda. "Research on Children Tutoring Children: A Critical Review." *Review of Educational Research* 47 (Summer 1976): 355-89.

Baker, Frank B. "Computer-based Instructional Management Systems: A First Look." *Review of Educational Research* 41 (February 1971): 51-70.

Berliner, David C., and Cahen, Leonard S. "Trait-Treatment Interaction and Learning." In *Review of Research in Education.* Vol. 1. Edited by Fred N. Kerlinger, pp. 58-94. Itasca, Ill.: Peacock, 1973.

Block, James, ed. *Mastery Learning: Theory and Practice.* New York: Holt, Rinehart, and Winston, 1971.

————. *Schools, Society, and Mastery Learning.* New York: Holt, Rinehart, and Winston, 1974.

Bracht, G. H. "Experimental Factors Related to Aptitude-Treatment Interactions." *Review of Educational Research* 40 (December 1970): 627-45.

Cronbach, Lee J. "The Two Disciplines of Scientific Psychology." *American Psychologist* 12 (December 1957): 671-84.

————. "How Can Instruction Be Adapted to Individual Differences?" In *Learning and Individual Differences,* edited by Robert M. Gagné, pp. 23-39. Columbus, Ohio: Charles E. Merrill, 1967.

————. "Beyond the Two Disciplines of Scientific Psychology." *American Psychologist* 30 (February 1975): 116-27.

Cronbach, Lee J., and Snow, Richard E. *Individual Differences in Learning Ability As a Function of Instructional Variables.* Final Report, U.S. Office of Education Contract No. OEC 4-6-061269-1217, Palo Alto, Calif., 1969.

————. *Aptitudes and Instructional Methods.* New York: Irvington, 1977.

Findley, Warren G., and Bryan, M. W. *Ability Grouping, 1970: Status, Impact, and Alternatives.* Athens, Ga.: Center for Educational Improvement, 1971.

Fisher, Charles W. et al. *Teaching Behaviors, Academic Learning Time, and Student Achievement.* Final Report of Phase III-B, Beginning Teacher Evaluation Study. Technical Report VI. San Francisco: Far West Laboratory for Educational Research and Development, 1978.

Gagné, Robert M. *Learning and Individual Differences.* Columbus, Ohio: Charles E. Merrill, 1967.

Horwitz, Robert A. "Effects of the 'Open Classroom.'" In *Educational Environments and Effects: Evaluation, Policy, and Productivity,* edited by Herbert J. Walberg, pp. 275-92. Berkeley, Calif.: McCutchan, 1979.

Keller, Fred S. "Goodbye, Teacher . . . ." *Journal of Applied Behavioral Analysis* 1 (Spring 1968): 78-89.

Pascarella, Ernest T. "Aptitude-Treatment Interaction under High and Low Instructional Support Conditions." Paper presented at the annual meeting of the American Educational Research Association, New York, 1977.

Peterson, Penelope L. "Interactive Effects of Student Anxiety, Achievement Orientation, and Teacher Behavior on Student Achievement and Attitude." *Journal of Educational Psychology* 69 (December 1977): 779-92.

―――. "Aptitude by Treatment Interaction Effects of Teacher Structuring and Student Participation in College Instruction." Paper presented at the annual meeting of the American Educational Research Association, Toronto, 1978.

―――. "Direct Instruction Reconsidered." In *Research on Teaching: Concepts, Findings, and Implications,* edited by Penelope L. Peterson and Herbert J. Walberg, pp. 57-69. Berkeley, Calif.: McCutchan, 1979.

Rosenshine, Barak V. "Research on Learning from Teaching." Paper presented at the annual meeting of the American Educational Research Association, New York, 1977.

―――. "Content, Time, and Direct Instruction." In *Research on Teaching: Concepts, Findings, and Implications,* edited by Penelope L. Peterson and Herbert J. Walberg, pp. 28-56. Berkeley, Calif.: McCutchan, 1979.

Rothkopf, Ernst Z. "Course Content and Supportive Environments for Learning." *Educational Psychologist* 10 (Fall 1973): 123-28.

Snow, Richard E. "Research on Aptitude for Learning: A Progress Report." In *Review of Research in Education.* Vol. 4. Edited by Lee S. Shulman, pp. 50-105. Itasca, Ill.: Peacock, 1976(a).

―――. *Theory and Method for Research on Aptitude Processes: A Prospectus.* Technical Report No. 2, Aptitude Research Project. Palo Alto, Calif.: School of Education, Stanford University, 1976(b).

―――. "Individual Differences and Instructional Theory." *Educational Researcher* 6 (November 1977): 11-15.

Thorndike, Edward L. *Individuality.* Boston: Houghton Mifflin, 1911.

Tobias, Sigmund. "A History of an Individualized Instructional Program of Varying Familiarity to College Students." Unpublished report, CAI Center, Florida State University, 1972.

―――. "Review of the Response Mode Issue." *Review of Educational Research* 43 (Spring 1973): 193-204.

―――. "Achievement-Treatment Interactions." *Review of Educational Research* 46 (Winter 1976): 61-74.

―――. "Anxiety-Treatment Interactions: A Review of Research." In *Anxiety, Learning, and Instruction,* edited by Joan E. Sieber, Harold F. O'Neil, Jr., and Sigmund Tobias, pp. 86-116. Hillsdale, N.J.: Lawrence Erlbaum Associates, 1977.

4. A Psychological Theory of Educational Productivity

Herbert J. Walberg

Two perennial questions in education are: "What are the ends of education?" and "Do the educational means, that is, the manipulations of the environment, justify the ends?" These philosophical questions concern values, morality, and ethics. Modern psychology and social science raise additional points: "Can the ends and means of education be measured?" and "Do the presumed means in fact cause the ends? If so, to what extent or with what degree of productivity?"

Although all these questions are important and incompletely settled, the last two concerning causality and productivity are of major concern here. In this area, education follows medicine, agriculture, and engineering: the physician wants to know the cure rates

Previous versions of this paper were presented at the American Psychological Association and Georgia Educational Research Association annual meetings, the University of Michigan, and the University of Wisconsin, and at symposia at the American Educational Research Association annual meeting and at the Institute of Research on Teaching at Michigan State University. The research was supported by the National Institute of Education and the National Science Foundation; the points of view and opinions stated do not necessarily reflect the official position or policy of either agency.

of groups of patients subjected to different drugs or treatments and possibly a no-treatment control condition; the agronomist estimates the yield responses to various amounts of fertilizer and rainfall; and process engineers find the effect of control settings on output. After these estimates of causal relation have been made, policy can be specified within an explicit, objective, rational framework, and the feasible treatment or combination of treatments that maximizes outputs can be recommended. Or, if costs of the treatments and the level of the outcome are known, the least expensive feasible treatment or combination can be identified. Judging from the accumulated research, however, such causal relations and most efficient policies are not easily identified in education.

To determine educational policy and practice requires not only the valuing of certain ends but also the assumption that the means employed do indeed bring about the ends in question. Experiments with random assignments to treatments are ideally suited to prove or assess causality, but in a recent review Gilbert, Light, and Mosteller (1975) were only able to find what they considered to be two well-executed field experiments in education. Although the stringency of their criteria might be relaxed to include more experiments, it seems that experiments are difficult to implement in the natural settings of education. Two alternatives, quasi-experiments and path analysis, also present difficulties in establishing causation. In practice quasi-experiments usually only control for one or two rival causes rather than for a reasonably complete list of the known correlates of educational achievement; and path analysis or structural equations as employed in behavioral research usually beg causal questions by assuming rather than probing their answers. Thus, educational researchers who wish to base policy on creditable causality are faced with the dilemma of choosing among experiments that are difficult to implement and quasi-experiments and path assumptions that are difficult to defend. A promising way to resolve this dilemma, it is argued here, is to include in both experimental and nonexperimental research the chief known correlates of educational achievement: age or developmental level; ability, including prior achievement; the social environment for learning; and the home environment.

A PROPOSED THEORY OF EDUCATIONAL PRODUCTIVITY

Psychological Production Functions

Many psychological theories can be subsumed by Lewin's (1963) general formulation of behavior as a function of personality and environment

$$B = f(P,E).$$

Educational researchers have implicitly or explicitly adopted a similar general equation:

$$L = f(A,T).$$

In this formulation learning is a function of individual aptitude and instructional treatment. Some have preferred to include environment in the equation,

$$L = f(A,T,E),$$

since in natural settings of education, nonmanipulated factors often seem to carry more weight in producing learning than deliberate instruction does (Walberg 1976), and since observational research (without treatment randomization) requires all determining factors in the equation of causal inference.

The problems of these general equations in educational and psychological research are: agreeing on a list of the parts of each of the constructs; operationally defining and measuring each part; stating the rules for adding up the measurements for an overall estimate of each construct, if required; specifying the form of the equation; and estimating its coefficients. The discussion here touches all of these problems but is mainly concerned with specifying the form of the equation and applying it to the explanation of several educational production problems. Operational measurement issues are treated in the references cited.

For simplifying the discussion in this subsection, consider that instructional treatment is a part of the environment in the last equation so that learning can be considered a function of individual and environmental factors. For further simplification, consider that the parts of each have been optimally defined, measured, and summarized to provide overall indexes of the two constructs

$$L = f(A,E).$$

The usual form of the regression equation (of which t and analysis of variance and covariance are special cases) for estimating learning is

$$L = a + bA + cE,$$

where a is a constant and b and c are coefficients or regression weights for the aptitude and environment terms. In normal science, the estimated coefficients would explain, account for, or predict the amount of learning. For example, assuming linearity and causality, weight c would estimate how much increased learning would take place by increasing the environmental factor by one unit. Such equations are usually unreplicated because different combinations of constructs and measures are used in each study and the estimated weights are often unreported.

A possible problem of the equation itself, however, is that it does not allow for the possible "interaction" of aptitude and environment (Lindquist 1951, Cronbach 1957). For example, a student with high visual aptitude may benefit more than others from instruction making use of pictures. Such interactions may be tested by adding an arithmetic product term (not to be confused with educational or economic product) AE to the regression

$$L = a + bA + cE + dAE.$$

Although such interactions seem educationally sensible, they are also generally found weak and difficult to replicate not only because of the variation in constructs and measures but also because the high correlations of aptitude and environment with their product result in large errors in estimating the weights (Bracht 1970, Walberg 1976). Moreover, the extra product term is scientifically and practically unparsimonious unless it is clearly needed. A different kind of interaction seems required.

Economic Production Functions

The notion of interactions of aptitudes and environments may yet bear fruit; part of the problem may be in the form of the equation. Econometric production functions incorporate interactions parsimoniously and also suggest other analogs worth attempting to apply in education. Econometricians often assume that output production, nationally or at the factory level, is a function of capital and labor (subsuming land under capital for simplicity of illustration):

$$O = f(K,L).$$

This simple specification often serves to account extremely well for economic processes that are known to be highly complex. Samuelson (1962) showed "how we can sometimes predict exactly how certain quite complicated heterogeneous capital models will behave by treating them *as if* they had come from a simple generating production function" (p. 194). In a discussion of economic growth, Solow (1956) commented: "The art of successful theorizing is to make the inevitable simplifying assumptions in such a way that the final results are not very sensitive" (p. 65).

The most celebrated form of the production function in economics is attributed to Cobb and Douglas (1928), although Wicksell and Wicksteed put it forward before the turn of the century (Jones 1976) and were clearly cited by Cobb and Douglas. Douglas's replication of its coefficients in various countries and time periods led to its widespread use. Other more complicated production functions by Arrow, Leontief, and others (discussed by Jones) may eventually prove superior, but they presently lack the long record of successful empirical verification of the Cobb-Douglas form and are beyond the scope of the present treatment (see Bosworth 1976 and Jones 1976 for recent comparisons of functions applied to various industries and firms).

The classical Cobb-Douglas function may be written

$$O = aK^b L^c,$$

where a is a constant and b and c are the coefficients for capital and labor. The coefficients may be conveniently estimated in linear regression by simply taking natural logarithms of all the variables:

$$\log O' = \log a + b \log K + c \log L.$$

Following Wonnacott and Wonnacott (1970, pp. 91-98) and Jones (1976, pp. 23-35), the function incorporates several valuable properties.

1. Positive marginal returns: The marginal products of capital and labor are both positive, that is, adding either more labor or more capital increases output (at least up to a point). For example, adding more or better machines, or more workers, or overtime, as measured by amounts or costs, increases output. Thus b and c are both positive.

2. Diminishing marginal returns: Successive equal increments in either capital or labor, without increasing the other factor, results in smaller and smaller increments in output (although such diminishing returns may not set in immediately). For example, doubling the work force of a farm, factory, or nation will less than double output if capital (including land) remains constant. Thus b and c are both less than one.

3. No input, no output: If either no capital or no labor are used, no production can ensue. A value of zero for either K or L or both results in a value of zero for output in the equation since any number multiplied by zero equals zero.

4. Constant returns to function: Increasing both capital and labor by any factor or percent increases output by the same factor or percent. For example, doubling both K and L doubles O. The sum b and c is assumed and often is found to equal approximately one.

5. Changing substitutability between labor and capital: Additional labor can substitute or trade off for diminished capital, but more and more labor must be added to compensate for each unit reduction in capital, and vice versa. Thus the function is multiplicative or interactive rather than additive. The productivity of labor (or O/L, output per hour or worker) increases as the capital-labor ratio (K/L) increases, but decreases with increases in labor alone (the diminishing returns case).

6. A measure of effect: Taking logarithms of output means that the regression weights are estimated percentage increases in output with a one-unit increase in the respective independent variable. Taking logarithms of the independent variables means that they are also being expressed as percentages. Thus the

original Cobb-Douglas (1928, p. 151) time-series regression estimates of the coefficients

$$O = 1.01 \, L^{.75} \, K^{.25}$$

for the United States economy 1899 through 1922 mean that .75 and .25 percent increases in output are associated respectively with one percent increases in labor and capital ($R = .97$).

7. Developmental effects: Although the production function proved useful in fitting both longitudinal data for single nations, industries, and factories and also cross-sectional comparisons of samples of these units, Solow, Samuelson, Hicks, Kuznets, and others point out that the increasing efficiency of industry beyond that which can be explained by increases in capital and labor inputs suggests that a third factor must be added to the equation. This factor is the technological progress brought about by education, science, engineering, and management (Jones 1976). While labor and capital can be calculated fairly conveniently from national corporate statistics, technology cannot: so time is used as a proxy in the general formula

$$P = f(L,K,t).$$

In the neoclassical Cobb-Douglas form, time may be entered as an exponent t

$$P = aK^b L^c e^t,$$

where e is the base of the natural logarithm 2.71 . . . .

Points 1 through 3 are illustrated in Figure 4-1. Increases in capital alone or labor alone increase output but at a diminishing rate. When a factor is zero, no output ensues.

Similarly, Figure 4-2 illustrates points 4 and 5. Increasing both factors by the same amount produces the same amount of gain in output from A to A^1. One factor can substitute for the other but at decreasing returns to the factor and increasing costs.

Figure 4-3 illustrates points 6 and 7. The purpose of the production function is to explain change in output per unit of time, beyond that attributable to natural technological growth with time, as a function of changes in amounts of capital and labor.

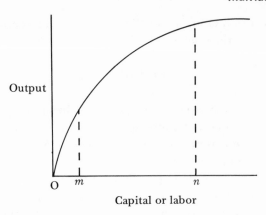

Figure 4-1

Diminishing marginal returns

Note: The effect of increasing one factor of production, capital or labor, while holding the other fixed is diminishing marginal returns; that is, smaller and smaller increases in output are produced by equal increases in the factor.

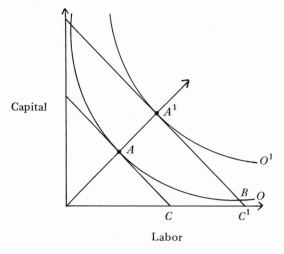

Figure 4-2

Equal-product and equal-cost lines

Note: Line O represents the various combinations of labor and capital required to produce a given, equal amount of output. Line C represents the combinations of labor and capital of given costs. A is the point of lowest cost for a given output O since any other point, for example, B, requires higher costs. A^1 indicates the minimum cost for a higher quantity of output O^1 brought about by increasing capital and labor by the same amount, assuming their costs are equal for purposes of illustration rather than either one excessively.

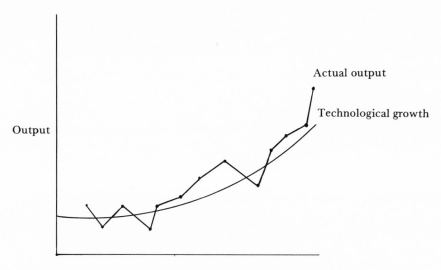

Figure 4-3

Technological growth and actual output

Production in Education

Economists are blessed with such a strong model of production. Even if it can be shown to be clearly wrong, it is explicit and testable. Given only three or four variables that are reasonably well defined and measured and an explicit form of the equation with only a few coefficients, the estimates of the function can be repeated and possibly replicated. As a matter of academic interest or policy decisions, the results and forecasts from them can be expressed as easily understood percentage changes, notwithstanding differences in metrics and units.

Perhaps Lewin's formulation (1963) of behavior as a function of personality and environment comes as close to the general production equation as any other in psychology. If transitional processes such as perception are set aside, Lewin's split of forces within and outside the individual seems reasonable. But psychology has reached little consensus on the list of parts of each construct, their definition, measurement, and scoring, and the specific explicit form of the equation.

If the problem is narrowed, however, from behavior in general to academic achievement on standard tests, then a preliminary list of the production factors can be drawn up on the basis of their reason-

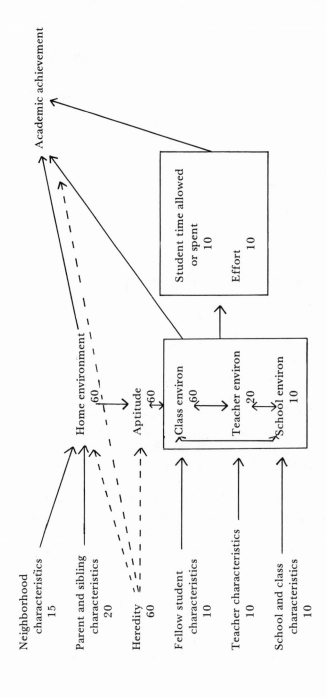

Figure 4-4

Production factors in school learning

Note: The figures for each factor are representative estimates of the percentage of accounted-for variance in learning.

able consistency in predicting variance in achievement (Figure 4-4). Such estimates of variance accounted for (Walberg 1971, 1976) undoubtedly have large margins of error depending on: sampling, unreliability of the measures; the level of aggregation (for example, individual, class, or school); the lack of variance of some factors, which prevents the detection of their covariance with achievement; the limited range of achievement tests themselves; and the possibility of nonlinear covariations. Nevertheless, these estimates may serve provisionally to prune the many variables that might enter equations.

There are plausible theoretical rationales and empirical evidence on the significance of the relations shown in Figure 4-4 in the published literature from which the estimates have been drawn (Berliner 1979, Bloom 1976, Rosenshine 1979, Walberg 1971, 1976, and Walberg and Marjoribanks 1976). A problem within the research in this literature is that the variables are often studied in isolation rather than in concert because of the division of psychology and sociology, subdivisions within these fields, and specialized individual research interests.

It is possible to prune the list further, and the variables in the left-hand column may be tentatively deleted. First, heredity cannot be directly measured; it and the other variables in the column seem reasonably well mediated by those in the second column. For example, the quality and quantity of adult supervision in the home environment are much more closely related to achievement and achievement gain than is an index of parental education and income and number of siblings in the home (Walberg and Marjoribanks 1976). Similarly, it seems that teacher age, sex, experience, and even personality are superfluous once the teacher's action or the environmental press on the student is taken into account (Rosenshine 1979).

Rearranging the production factors, specifying some in measurable policy detail, and adding age yields Figure 4-5. Two or three factors would be more parsimonious, but seven seem required because of their plausible and empirical correlations with achievement. Indeed, in some applications it may be desirable to disaggregate the variables more finely; research on instructional quality may include each of the five to fifteen teaching variables thought to promote student achievement (Rosenshine 1979), rather than an overall weighted index.

There is still considerable redundancy or colinearity among the seven independent variables. For example, measures of cognitive aptitude and home environment each account for about 60 percent of

92 Individual Differences

Constructs   Aptitude   Environment   Age

Instruction

Variables	Ability (Abl)	Motivation (Mot)	Quality (Qul)	Quantity (Qun)	Class (Cls)	Home (Hom)	Age (Age)
Reliability	.85	.75	.60	.60	.80	.80	.90
Achievement variance	60	10	15	15	60	40	.80
Cost	5	10	30	30	10	100	2

Figure 4-5

Seven constructs related to school learning

Note: The reliability of each factor, the variance in achievement it accounts for, and the dollar cost per student to obtain the measurement are very rough estimates.

the variance of achievement, but together they account for about 80 percent. (Note that these percentages of variance and those in Figure 4-4 are the squares of the correlations between the factors and achievement, not the more desirable percentage forecasts from multiple logarithmic regression such as in the Cobb-Douglas function.) Similarly, cognitive aptitude and student perceptions of the class environment account for about 90 percent (Walberg 1971, 1976). Generally a student high on any variable, except age, is more likely to be high on the other variables. But a planned sample should produce enough exceptions to hold down the correlations among the independent variables sufficiently relative to the multiple correlation. Thus, despite redundancy, variables in a complete equation are expected to carry significant weight in achievement regressions; that is, they should each explain unique variance in achievement provided they are reasonably well measured and vary over a moderate range.

In my opinion, the best equation—the one that would allow the best basis of causal inference and estimates of effects—would include all seven constructs (see Figure 4-5) in the following Cobb-Douglas form:

$$Ach = a(Abl)^b (Mot)^c (Qul)^d (Qun)^f (Cls)^g (Hom)^h (Age)^i$$

The coefficients for the equation are conveniently estimable in a linear regression by taking logarithms

$$\log (\text{Ach}) = \log a + b \log (\text{Abl}) + c \log (\text{Mot})$$

By analogy to the earlier points, the following provisional hypotheses can be put forth.

1. Increasing any production factor (as distinct from the age factor, a proxy for growth processes) increases achievement; coefficients b through h are positive (see however the note to Figure 4-1).

2. Increasing any factor while holding the others fixed produces diminishing marginal returns; b through h are each less than one (Figure 4-6).

3. A direct extension of the economic production function is that any factor equal to zero results in zero achievement. Unlike capital and labor, however, the educational production factors may not have validly measurable zero points. Thus, it is more reasonable to hypothesize that when any factor is near minimum, it is unlikely that achievement will be high unless the other factors are near their maximum levels.

4. Increasing all the factors by a given amount raises achievement by the same amount. The sum of coefficients b through h approximates one.

5. The factors substitute or trade off for one another but at diminishing rates of return.

6. The coefficients b through h are estimates of the percentage increase in achievement associates or, if causality is imputed, are determined by a 1 percent increase in the corresponding factor. It would be possible to plot a profile of the factors for diagnosis and forecasting of achievement production for each student. Those achieving productively will have high and flat profiles. Unproductive students will have low, uneven profiles; and raising the lowest factor would produce the greatest returns, although it may be costly, difficult, and beyond the control of educators.

7. Just as time serves as a proxy for technological progress in the neoclassical function, so age serves as an index of maturation (Piaget 1954) or "spontaneous schooling" (Stephens 1968)

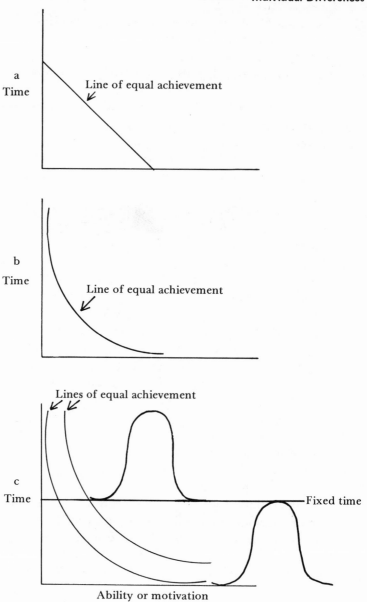

Figure 4-6

Acceleration and enrichment as functions of aptitude and time

Note: The trade-off lines indicate equal amounts of achievement at each point on the line with compensating amounts of aptitude and time.

that seems to occur inexplicably, incidentally, and unintentionally with increasing age, apparently independent of the known production factors. Given a wide span of age and a wide-range measure of achievement, the growth curve may turn out to be linear, exponential, or logistic. Presumably if the production factors were constant, the age term would generate the growth curve. Varying the other factors would result in accelerations and decelerations around it. It may be further hypothesized that steady application of the factors produces more growth than fits and starts do.

The seven variables in the function are known to correlate with academic achievement (Berliner 1979, Bloom 1976, Rosenshine 1979, Walberg 1976, Walberg and Marjoribanks 1976). It may seem educationally plausible to impute causality to them, although it would be more defensible to do so after they are analyzed in full concert or, one might say, in competition with each other because one or more may be sufficiently redundant with the others to delete. Moreover, if true experiments cannot be done, with random manipulation of the factors, then the best possible hope for causal inference is to include all possible causes in a regression.

Some of the factors, however, may partially mediate each other: a supportive home environment, for example, may lead to better motivation and the perception of a productive social environment in the class; and capable students may stimulate more teaching of higher quality. In samples that are nearly homogeneous in age, such as those from a single grade level, age can be ignored. Thus, incomplete regressions may be of some value. Moreover, feedback mechanisms, such as higher achievement producing better motivation and classroom perceptions, should be considered. Such possibilities can be investigated using advanced econometric analyses (Jones 1976, Wonnacott and Wonnacott 1970). Simultaneously analyzed panel data, collected on many individuals over multiple time periods, will be most valuable for detecting such complex mechanisms. If the simplifying assumptions of the function are reasonable, even incomplete or partially defective data should generally and replicably fit the function better than the usual linear and multiplicative functions.

APPLICATIONS OF PRODUCTION THEORY

Educational Innovation

The theory of educational productivity as formulated above appears capable of subsuming a number of educational models, principles, and empirical regularities. Before illustrating these applications, it may be of interest to return to the discouraging methodological problem mentioned in the opening section of this chapter and use the theory to explain the apparent lack of effects of educational innovation. Many federal- and state-supported educational innovations that have been evaluated in the last few decades are attempts to change the quality of instruction or teaching in order to raise measured achievement. Since quality of instruction is only one of the six production factors, and the other five may remain unchanged, diminishing marginal returns would ensue (see Figure 4-1), or the other factors may vary systematically. In either case or both, any one of the following points could explain the apparent lack of dependency of outcome with the innovative instruction:

1. Volunteers who have already nearly maximized their teaching effectiveness participate, and the increased returns (past point n in Figure 4-1) are therefore too small to be detectable.

2. Untransformed linear terms are used to fit curved, logarithmic relations.

3. The sample is drawn from a single school district that is relatively homogeneous in quality, even after the innovation. Therefore, the increment in achievement with respect to a small change in quality is undetectable.

4. The other five production factors are unmeasured and are not brought into the equation. Therefore, any point on the smooth curve (Figure 4-1) is given five large random shocks, resulting in a scatter of points that make the true returns to quality undetectable.

5. Two large random shocks due to error in measurement of achievement and quality of instruction to any data point obscure the relation of achievement and quality.

6. Only ability and quality are included in the analysis. Quality adds only 3 percent to the 60 percent of the achievement variance explained by aptitude; the variance-increment approach underestimates the true returns to teacher quality.

7. The innovation and control groups overlap substantially in teaching quality. A nominal two-group categorization rather than a continuous measure of implemented quality is made.

8. The "noninnovating" control teachers compete with the innovators by assigning a greater quantity of time to instruction in the subject unit.

9. Students in the "noninnovating" control group compete by doing more homework.

10. The quality-of-teaching index contains a mix of elements, most of which have not been shown by previous research to be productive of achievement.

These points are overlapping and concern design, measurement, and specification problems that in various combinations are sufficient to vitiate the field-evaluation research. A more reasonable evaluation of innovations, and probe of the production theory, would include reasonably complete representations of the production factors, valid measures of each, sufficient variation in instructional quality (and the other factors), and logarithmic transformations in accordance with the hypothesized function to account for the diminishing marginal-returns curvature and the multiplicative substitution, trade-off, or compensation.

Quantity of Instruction

The time scheduled, allowed, or assigned for a given instructional unit by the teacher or, better yet, the fraction of this time the student actually spends in learning the unit content is turning out to be a moderately consistent though apparently weak correlate of academic achievement (Karweit 1976, Rosenshine and Berliner 1978). The usual problems of operational definition, measurement, and lack of factor variation may account for the small correlations; but the production function suggests that misspecification may also be a problem. Bringing more of the production factors into the equation, finding data in which time varies over a greater range, and taking logarithms may help considerably. More specifically, the form of the production function suggests nonlinear relations among time and the other factors that seem more conceptually defensible than the linear assumptions that pervade the research.

Consider the concepts of acceleration and enrichment as consequences of the presumed linear trade-off of time and aptitude

(Figure 4-6a), where aptitude is motivation or cognitive ability or a weighted combination. For a given criterion amount of achievement or "mastery" in acceleration models of school learning, it seems reasonable to say that, other factors being equal, moderate-aptitude students require relatively moderate amounts of time and that the brighter students require correspondingly less and the less bright correspondingly more. Extrapolating such linear reasoning to extremes, however, produces the absurd conclusion that geniuses learn instantaneously and the the least bright require just a little more time than the subnormal. Figure 4-6b shows a more plausible trade-off: aptitude and time compensate for one another, other things being equal, at diminishing rates of marginal returns. Ever larger amounts of time, approaching a poorly measured asymptote at infinity, are required to substitute for equal decrements of aptitude. Thus, to attain the highest performance levels will require at least a small amount of time for a genius, and an immense, possibly prohibitive, amount will be required by the least bright.

While acceleration models, in principle, hold the dependent variable of achievement at a constant "mastery" level and allow time to "substitute" for aptitude, enrichment holds time constant and allows achievement to vary with aptitude (Walberg 1971). Thus, as indicated in Figure 4-6c, achievement would be purely a function of aptitude if other production factors are held constant. If aptitude is normally distributed, achievement would be also, and the achievement ranking of students after instruction would approximate the aptitude ranking before instruction.

The instructional theories of Carroll (1963) and Bloom (1976) may be interpreted as acceleration models within the production-theory framework. Carroll's formulation is

$$\text{degree of learning} = f\left(\frac{\text{time actually spent}}{\text{time needed}}\right)$$

where "the numerator of this fraction will be equal to the *smallest* of the following three qualities: (a) opportunity—the time allowed for learning; (b) perseverance—the amount of time the learner is willing to engage actively in learning; and (c)—the amount of time needed to learn, increased by whatever amount is necessary in view of the poor quality of instruction and lack of ability to understand less than optimal instruction. This last quantity (time needed to learn after adjustment for quality of instruction and ability to understand instruction) is also the denominator of the fraction" (Carroll 1963, p. 730). Recast in the production function: (a) opportunity becomes quantity of instruction, that is, time allowed including self-instructional time; (b) perseverance becomes motivation (although an observer rating the percentage of engaged time is a reasonable proxy or even a more direct though expensive measure); (c) time needed becomes unadjusted ability; and (d) quality of instruction explicitly enters the equation rather than adjusting ability. Thus, rather than redefining all the independent variables in terms of time, the production function would assess the direct effect of each measured factor (including student age, the home environment, and the social environment of the class, because of their known connections with achievement) in an explicit equation form.

Bloom's (1976) adaption of the Carroll model may be written

$$\begin{pmatrix} \text{level of achievement,} \\ \text{affective outcomes,} \\ \text{rate of learning} \end{pmatrix} = F \begin{pmatrix} \text{quality of instruction,} \\ \text{cognitive entry behaviors,} \\ \text{affective entry behaviors} \end{pmatrix}$$

In the production function, affective outcomes would be considered a particular type of achievement possibly involved in a feedback loop with motivation for subsequent achievement. Instead of measuring time to reach a criterion or gain in achievement divided by time to obtain a rate, time would enter the equation directly as an independent variable, quantity of instruction. The other variables have obvious correspondences in the production function. Thus, the sets of redefined variables in the Carroll and Bloom theories may be hypothesized to show substitutability and diminishing returns of the function.

In connection with time, a methodological point can be made. Bloom estimates that the slowest 10 percent of the students may need five to six times as much time to learn as the most rapid 10 percent do. Rarely are such large ratios encountered for variables in educational research. In a typical class, for example, the highest and lowest IQs might be 120 and 80, and the extreme scores on a fifty-item achievement test might be 45 and 30; both ratios are 1.5 to 1. As emphasized in the earlier section on growth, educational measurements are severely limited in range and reliability. Even so, when achievement is related to time, the regression most often turns out to be logarithmic both in studies of school attendance—hours per day, and days per year (Karweit 1976)—and computer-assisted instruction (Suppes and Morningstar 1972, Atkinson 1972). Similarly in swimming, Arthur (1977) shows that at "1,000 yards a day one reaches 75 percent of the maximum training effort and at 2,000 yards, 85 percent. In order to reach 95 percent of maximum, one needs to go 10,000 yards a day in training, and to get 99 percent to 100 percent, one would need to go 16,000 yards a day" (p. 2), which would take perhaps four hours. (My calculation of the variance accounted for by a logarithmic regression is .96 in contrast to .87 for the linear equation; nearly all the variance might be accounted for by bringing other production factors into the equation.) Although such things as performance in ballet, music, chess, science, and writing cannot be measured so precisely, they appear to show diminishing returns relative to time: good or even excellent performance by the usual standards may only require a half hour to an hour a day of concentrated effort; but national rankings or one's best may require, among other things, three to ten hours of instruction and practice. (Pushing past an uncertain point, of course, may produce not only diminishing but negative returns.)

Diminishing marginal returns to time can be well fitted by logarithmic transformations and can only be crudely approximated in the usual linear regression if the variation or reliability or both are minimal. On the other hand, to make a good estimate of the effect of any production factor, such as time, would require reasonably wide and reliable variation of the factor as well as achievement. Moreover, interpolation within such data can be made more confidently than extrapolating beyond the range of narrow, collinear factors. A rival hypothesis to diminishing achievement returns, however, which requires investigation with wide-ranging tests, is that more and more students peak out on the conventional test's low ceiling as time goes by; that is, the test is incapable of detecting true linear returns at the upper range.

Aptitude-Treatment Interaction

The production function assumes that the factors interact by substituting for one another with diminishing returns. This trade-off differs from the way that interactions are usually conceived by educational researchers, which is that students of type A achieve more using instructional method A, and students of type B achieve more using method B, as discussed earlier. Among the problems of such usual conceptions, are: (a) the plethora of constructs and measures of aptitudes and characterizations of instructional treatment that are used in a multitude of combinations by various investigators; (b) the usual reduction of complexes of continuous variables to a few dichotomies, thereby eliminating much precious reliable information in the data; (c) the obscure interpretations that are required of such interactions; (d) the extra degrees of freedom for estimations; and (e) the conclusions that such interactions apparently turn up no more often than chance (Bracht 1970) and are rarely replicated (Cronbach and Snow 1977, Walberg 1976). As noted earlier, these interactions are scientifically unparsimonious and would be difficult to implement in an ordinary classroom.

In contrast, the production function approach has the following features. First, it narrows the selection of constructs and measures to those seven with a causally plausible and empirically verified ("main-effect") connection with achievement (the references cited above describe operational measures). Second, the continuous variation of the measure of each construct is brought into the equation (although, for more specific clues to the best improvements that might be made it will be useful to disaggregate the parts of constructs such as quality of instruction and the classroom environment in some equations in addition to using overall indexes). Third, the interpretation of effect coefficients and policy forecasts are direct and straightforward; for example, increasing the instructional time or quality by 1 percent increases achievement .2 percent. Fourth, the seven factors and the constant require eight degrees of freedom for the coefficients estimated in contrast to twenty-eight for the conventional approach with main effects and first-order interactions. Fifth, the correlations of achievement with the production factors replicate to varying degrees—ability, class, home environment, and age most strongly and stably; motivation, quality and quantity of instruction less so. But rarely have more than two or three been simultaneously analyzed in production form. Thus, given the possible advantages of the production function over the older method of analyzing interactions and the required presence of all causal variables in analyses that seek causal inference from nonrandomly manipulated factors, it seems worthwhile trying to estimate the production coefficients in concert and to probe the validity of the functional form.

On the other hand, the original approach to aptitude-treatment interactions requires more research (Cronbach and Snow 1977). In these cases, the aptitude, quality, and their interactions would be brought into the production function as linear terms. The other production factors would then serve to increase the overall variance in achievement accounted for and so, too, the precision of estimation of the interaction effects. Moreover, in the frequent case of nonrandomized treatments, the presence of all the production factors in the regression will make causal inferences about the interactions more defensible.

Compensatory Education

During the 1960s some policy makers and educational practitioners appeared to believe that increased instructional advantages can compensate for social and family disadvantages in the determination of achievement. Although this conception was somewhat vague, it often seemed to amount to the hypothesis of a linear trade-off between family and instructional environments. Such expectations resulted in frustration because the returns in achievement to real increases in educational expenditures and apparent improvements in schooling seemed by no means linear. Some even concluded that the marginal returns might be zero (see, for example, the references in the opening paragraph of this chapter). By the standards of the production function, adequate evidence and analyses of the returns are unavailable. Home environment was indicated by socioeconomic status, family size, ethnicity, objects in the home, and other sociological, anthropological, or psychological variables rather than the more educationally relevant amount and intensity of adult-child interaction that accounts for several times as much variance in achievement (Walberg and Marjoribanks 1976). In addition, the reviews of Rosenshine (1979) and others on productive factors in teaching that indicate predictively valid constructs and measures of instruction had not yet been completed. Because of poor measurement and the lack of evidence on the other production factors, the returns to compensatory programs are very poorly estimated.

Moreover the returns to quality, although expected to be positive,

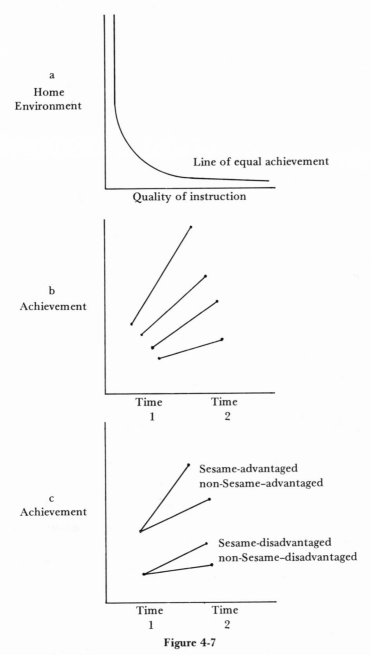

Figure 4-7

Problems of compensatory education

are expected to be diminishing, as shown in Figure 4-7a, rather than linear. Aside from the a priori postulate of the production function that calls for such returns, evidence on the achievement "fan-spread" of individuals and "increasing gap" of groups over time supports the hypothesized relation. Cook and Campbell (1976) show that in educational programs for the disadvantaged, the relatively rich often get richer (Figure 4-7b); that is, the higher the score of a student on a pretest, the higher will be that student's posttest score and the greater the student's absolute and relative gain, even though the program is designed for students scoring lower on pretests. Similarly, the "Sesame Street" television series conferred a greater achievement benefit to advantaged groups than to those for whom it was intended and thereby increased rather than reduced the gap (Cook and Campbell 1976). The production function predicts precisely such phenomena: the higher any factor becomes for all students, the smaller the marginal returns (say, at about point n in Figure 4-1) and the greater the weight and relative determination of achievement by the other factors. Conversely, the lower the relative level (say, about point m in Figure 4-1) of a production factor, the greater its marginal returns and the more promising it would be to change, provided that budgets and other social and political forces allow for it.

The fact that measures of home environment account for about 60 percent of the variance in achievement suggests that many students (not just lower-income or minority ones) would achieve considerably more if the amount and intensity of intellectual stimulation in their home environments were increased. Indeed, the two field studies of school programs that were designed to help parents in highly disadvantaged neighborhoods stimulate their children at home show that achievement gains can be doubled over comparable control students at least over periods of six to twelve months (Smith 1958, Walberg, Bole, and Waxman (1977). The two programs cost very little and were met with enthusiasm by parents. Further investigation of such programs over longer periods using the production approach may bear out the promise of the initial field studies.

A CAVEAT

The educational production-function theory appears to explain some important phenomena concerning the relation of test achievement to production factors. The best probe or validation of the function would require longitudinal data on all seven factors and a wide-range achievement test that reflects the curriculum content. Data at only one or two time points on only some of the factors or on proxy or somewhat unreliable rather than optimal measures may prove valuable in partially testing the function. Should the production-function theory survive such tests, replicated values of the coefficients might be used to stimulate and forecast the effects of changes. Given cost estimates and acceptability of such changes, the best strategy for reaching achievement goals could then be chosen.

Even so, production economics also offers caution in attempting to maximize only one output. Despite the numerous ability and achievement tests available, they tend to measure only one major factor, verbal-educational accomplishment—an important aspect of human quality surely, but by no means the only one. Performance on such tests predicts subsequent grades and performance on similar tests. For samples of adults that have attained the same amount of education, however, neither test scores nor grades predict indicators of success in later life such as income, participation in community activities, self-concept, supervisor- and peer-related effectiveness, and number of prizes, written works, patents, and other accomplishments. Rather, engagement in independent, self-sustained ventures and extracurricular activities during the high school and college years forecasts adult success (see reviews by Erickson 1977, Jennings and Nathan 1977, and Walberg 1976).

How much effort should be given to the production of test achievement? The "law of increasing relative costs" in economics states that to produce equal additional amounts of one good, other things being equal, larger and larger amounts of other goods must be sacrificed (Samuelson 1970, p. 26). Thus in setting achievement goals on the usual tests and the earliest or most effective, cost-efficient or rapid means of attaining them, educators, parents, and students should consider the extent to which other goals, opportunities, and experiences—valuable for the present or future—must be sacrificed. The causal mechanisms and the costs and benefits of other goals and their trade-offs with test achievement cannot be accurately estimated. However, measures of student perceptions of the social environment of their classroom experience in terms of its cohesiveness, democracy, goal direction, and other sociopsychological properties not only provide demonstrably valid indicators of a production factor for achievement but also possible educational process goals in their own right as a balance against test scores alone (Walberg 1976). Additional productivity research on these variables is obviously in order and might contribute much to educational wisdom.

Given the caveat concerning the diversity of educational goals and the limitations of outcome measures, economics and psychology have a lot to gain in joining forces to improve educational productivity. Psychologists have contributed much to establishing the consistent, strong correlates of educational achievement, but they have tended to examine the relation of achievement to only one or two production factors at a time in isolation from the others. Economists provide comprehensive frameworks for the study and improvement of productivity; but in applying production models to education, they have accepted weak proxies such as student social class, school racial composition, and teacher salaries for the more direct and potent determinants of outcomes such as aptitude, quality of instruction, and home environment. Combining the best of both disciplines is likely to be most fruitful.

REFERENCES

Arthur, R. J. "Masters Swimming Program Stimulates Fitness Motivation." *Swim-Master* 6 (1977): 1-2.

Atkinson, Richard C. "Ingredients for a Theory of Instruction." *American Psychologist* 27 (October 1972): 921-31.

Berliner, David C. "Tempus Educare." In *Research on Teaching*, edited by Penelope L. Peterson and Herbert J. Walberg, pp. 120-35. Berkeley, Calif.: McCutchan, 1979.

Bloom, Benjamin S. *Human Characteristics and School Learning*. New York: McGraw-Hill, 1976.

Bosworth, D. L. *Production Functions*. Lexington, Mass.: D. C. Heath, 1976.

Bracht, Glenn H. "Experimental Factors Related to Aptitude-Treatment Interactions." *Review of Educational Research* 40 (December 1970): 627-45.

Carroll, John B. "A Model of School Learning." *Teachers College Record* 64 (May 1963): 732-33.

Cobb, Charles W., and Douglas, Paul H. "A Theory of Production." *American Economic Review* 18, Supplement (March 1928): 139-65.

Cook, Thomas C., and Campbell, Donald T. "The Design and Conduct of Quasi-Experiments and True Experiments in Field Settings." In *Handbook of Industrial and Organizational Psychology*, edited by Marvin D. Dunnette, pp. 223-326. Chicago: Rand McNally, 1976.

Cronbach, Lee J. "The Two Disciplines of Scientific Psychology." *American Psychologist* 12 (December 1957): 671-84.

Cronbach, Lee J., and Snow, Richard E. *Aptitudes and Instructional Methods: A Handbook for Research on Interactions.* New York: Irving, 1977.

Erickson, Donald A. "An Overdue Paradigm Shift in Educational Administration." In *Educational Administration: The Developing Decades,* edited by L. L. Cunningham et al., pp. 119-43. Berkeley, Calif.: McCutchan, 1977.

Gilbert, John P.; Light, Richard J.; and Mosteller, Frederick. "Assessing Social Innovations: An Empirical Base for Policy." In *Some Critical Issues in Assessing Social Program Evaluation,* edited by Arthur A. Lumsdaine and Carl A. Bennett, pp. 34-193. New York: Academic Press, 1975.

Jennings, Wayne, and Nathan, Joe. "Startling/Disturbing Research on School Program Effectiveness." *Phi Delta Kappan* 58 (March 1977): 568-72.

Jones, H. G. *An Introduction to Modern Theories of Economic Growth.* New York: McGraw-Hill, 1976.

Karweit, Nancy. "A Reanalysis of the Effect of Quantity of Schooling on Achievement." *Sociology of Education* 49 (July 1976): 236-46.

Lewin, Kurt. *Field Theory in Social Science.* London: Tavistock, 1963.

Lindquist, E. F. *Design and Analysis of Experiments in Psychology and Education.* Boston: Houghton Mifflin Co., 1951.

Meade, J. E. *A Neoclassical Theory of Economic Growth.* London: Allen and Unwin, 1961.

Piaget, Jean. *The Construction of Reality in the Child.* New York: Ballantine, 1954.

Rosenshine, Barak V. "Content, Time, and Direct Instruction." In *Research on Teaching,* edited by Penelope L. Peterson and Herbert J. Walberg, pp. 28-56. Berkeley, Calif.: McCutchan, 1979.

Rosenshine, Barak V., and Berliner, David C. "Academic Engaged Time." *British Journal of Teacher Education* 4 (1978): 3-16.

Samuelson, Paul A. "Parable and Realism in Capital Theory: The Surrogate Production Function." *Review of Economic Studies* 29 (June 1962): 193-206.

———. *Economics.* New York: McGraw Hill, 1970.

Smith, Mildred B. "School and Home: Focus on Achievement." In *Developing Programs for the Educationally Disadvantaged,* edited by A. Harry Passow, pp. 87-107. New York: Teachers College Press, 1958.

Solow, Robert M. "A Contribution to the Theory of Economic Growth." *Quarterly Journal of Economics* 29 (February 1956): 65-94.

Stephens, J. M. *The Process of Schooling: A Psychological Examination.* New York: Holt, Rinehart, and Winston, 1968.

Suppes, Patrick, and Morningstar, Mona. *Computer-Assisted Instruction at Stanford, 1966-68: Data, Models, and Evaluation of Arithmetic Programs.* New York: Academic Press, 1972.

Walberg, Herbert J. "Models for Optimizing and Individualizing School Learning." *Interchange* 2, 3 (1971): 15-27.

———. "Psychology of Learning Environments: Structural, Behavioral, or Perceptual?" In *Review of Research in Education.* Vol. 4. Edited by Lee S. Shulman, pp. 142-78. Itasca, Ill.: Peacock, 1976.

Walberg, Herbert J.; Bole, R.; and Waxman, H. "School-based Family Socialization and Reading Achievement in the Inner City." Chicago: Office of Evaluation Research, University of Illinois at Chicago Circle, 1977.

Walberg, Herbert J., and Marjoribanks, Kevin. "Family Environment and Cognitive Development: Twelve Analytic Models." *Review of Educational Research* 46 (Fall 1976): 527-552.

Wonnacott, R. J., and Wonnacott, T. H. *Econometrics.* New York: John Wiley, 1970.

PART TWO
Development

Overview

The four chapters in the section on development and educational psychology reflect an appreciation for various models that psychology has to offer educators. Gordon focuses on issues of social and emotional development. His chapter begins with a series of definitions of social cognition, indicating their comprehensiveness and their focus on aspects of human behavior in which the subject of knowledge is another person's thoughts, feelings, intentions, perspectives, or personality. He notes that a review of data in social cognition reveals an emphasis on cognitive-developmental or Piagetian theoretical assumptions. In addition the research reveals the complexities involved in understanding the behavior of others, the methodological difficulties associated with research on social cognition, the focus on descriptive studies of developmental change, the importance of the years six through nine, and the difficult issues of stage definition. Gordon offers three perspectives that psychologists have taken in explaining the behavior of others. In the core-tendency perspective, the assumption is that all individuals behave to fulfill the demands of certain fundamental needs. In the unique-characteristics perspective, the assumption is that each individual is distinctive, special, and different, thereby making it imperative that one assume no set of commonalities among all people. In the personality-types perspective, the assumption is that there are basic types of individuals with commonalities among types but not across groupings. Gordon reviews the three perspectives and then identifies similarities among them. Despite difficulties in these respects, all three perspectives emphasize the importance of affective phenomena, physiological and survival needs, the self, and the search for understanding. The chapter concludes with educational implications underlining the importance of social interactions within classrooms, the essential linking of cognitive and affective processes, and the importance of feelings.

While Gordon has suggested a perspective on social and emotional development, Case reviews intellectual development. He begins from a Piagetian perspective and then reinterprets Piaget's theory using an information-processing framework. After outlining several limitations of Piaget's theory, Case emphasizes the need for a new theoretical perspective. He then presents developmental changes in executive strategies, or cognitive operations, at each of the four Piagetian phases of cognitive development. Case suggests that each stage of cognitive development can be represented as a series of executive strategies with one additional "loop" added at each substage. The loops may be characterized as outgrowths of the individual's actions toward either problem solving, exploration, or observation. They also reflect changes in short-term memory storage. The hypothesis is that when a new cognitive operation is first assembled, its execution takes virtually the entire central processing space, with very little space left for short-term storage. However with time, execution of cognitive operations becomes more efficient, and more space becomes available for short-term storage. Case's presentation relies upon familiarity with physiological processes, information processes, and cognitive developmental orientations (Piaget's theory). His emphasis on short-term storage and attention span suggests the educational importance of developing attentional processes in children. In terms of educational implications, he also suggests that educators identify strategies that children use to process cognitive tasks, that they rework the curriculum to highlight the inadequacies of students' current processes, that they design instructional procedures to keep short-term storage demands to a bare minimum, and that they arrange the sequence of tasks so that cognitive development progresses in reasonably small steps, with sufficient practice at each step to allow the procedure to become as automatic as possible.

Both Case and Gordon emphasize development in the childhood and adolescent years and neglect the importance of development over the life span. Havighurst, on the other hand, focuses on life-span development and educational psychology. Since life-span developmental psychology might be less familiar to readers than developmental psychology, Havighurst begins by focusing on the work of two pioneers in the field, Buehler and Erikson. He then considers the adult learner and underscores the notion that adult behavior is continuous and changing throughout the adult life span. He argues that the assumption of decreases in learning ability during adulthood is a myth, and he discusses differences between fluid and crystallized intelligence across the life span. In his presentation of the developmental tasks of middle age and late adulthood, he discusses the importance of adjusting to physiological changes, to retirement, to reduced income, and to the death of a spouse. He emphasizes the needs of older adults to become explicitly affiliated with the late adulthood age group and to establish satisfactory living arrangements. This chapter concludes with a discussion of how to maximize the options available to individuals throughout the life span.

The final chapter in the section on development and educational psychology presents various models of educational growth. Nucci and Walberg begin with Dewey's emphasis on growth as the goal of education, and they contend that researchers have made small and fitful progress in defining and measuring educational growth. They then review two major sets of models available from psychology for potentially assessing educational growth. The first type—the psychometric model—is identified with the work of behaviorists and psychometricians. This model has several identifiable problems, among them the emphasis on grade- or age-group means and the dearth of longitudinal studies. The second type of model—the stage model—is differentiated from a psychometric model in that cognitive and affective growth are portrayed as series of qualitative transformations rather than quantitative additions. Three types of stage models are reviewed: the functional descriptive, psychoanalytic, and cognitive developmental. Each of these variants is assessed in terms of strengths and limitations, with none of the orientations seen by the authors as providing a sufficiently comprehensive perspective on educational growth. The functional-descriptive models fail to explain the relationships of events in one stage to another or why certain events appear together at certain ages or how movement from stage to stage occurs. The psychoanalytic model is criticized for the sexist aspects of its orientation and the methodological difficulties of assessing psychoanalytic growth. Finally, the authors find the Piagetian orientation to have internal inconsistencies in the Piagetian stages and the nature of stage change. The Nucci-Walberg chapter concludes with reference to recent and promising attempts by Gagné, Scandura, and Case to bridge the differences between psychometric growth models and Piagetian stage theory.

One finishes the developmental chapters with the feeling that at this point in the state of the union between education and psychology there is a willingness to look critically at the available theoretical orientations and to offer possibilities for correcting limitations. Suggestions for improvement focus on the importance of recognizing that development progresses throughout the life span, that development can and should be closely associated with educational growth, that cognitive and affective development are closely intertwined, and that it is possible to merge neobehavioral informational processing and cognitive developmental orientations toward development.

5. Social Cognition

Neal J. Gordon

Clearly, educational psychologists have interests in the development of cognitive processes, for much of schooling focuses on improving students' abilities to learn, remember, think, and create. Concurrent with this interest in cognitive development there has been a less intense but nevertheless present interest in the development of social and emotional processes. Although it is well known that most school curricula predominantly emphasize cognitive processes and devote less attention to the affective components of students' lives, there have been those who emphasize the importance of focusing on students' feelings. Their writings (Jones 1970, Lyon 1971, Miller 1976) have provided educators with a series of curriculum suggestions in the affective domain. In addition, developmental researchers have investigated numerous components associated with social and emotional development. An area of specialization within developmental psychology has grown enormously, especially within the past ten to fifteen years. That area, referred to as social cognition, incorporates many of the components previously associated with the concepts of social and emotional development. In this chapter, some of the recent research on social cognition and theory is reviewed, conceptual frameworks for organizing that material are suggested, and the relevance of social cognition to educational psychology is indicated. We begin by reviewing some of the available definitions of social cognition.

DEFINITIONS OF SOCIAL COGNITION

One of the most thorough reviews of social cognition was prepared by Shantz (1975), who indicated that in the ten years preceding her review, a great deal of attention had been devoted to the study of the development of social cognition. Her review focuses on "how children conceptualize other people and how they come to understand the thoughts, emotions, intentions, and viewpoints of others" (p. 1). Research areas, such as role taking, person perception, empathy, and egocentrism, are included. For her purposes, social cognition "refers to the child's intuitive or logical representations of others, that is, how he characterizes others and makes inferences about their covert, inner psychological experiences" (p. 1). Her presentation is organized around five questions: what another person might see, how another person might feel, what the other thinks, what the intentions of others are, and, finally, what the other person is like. In the second section of this chapter, I, too, will follow that organization.

The definition Shantz offers, however, has been expanded by other investigators; Damon (1978) and Youniss (1975) include information on moral judgment, conceptions of interpersonal relationships (such as friendships), the self, nonmoral social regulations, and conceptions of social institutions. For Glick (1978) and Flavell (1979), social cognition is also broadly defined, for it includes all the processes involved in knowing others. According to Flavell, social cognition

includes our conceptions ("naive theories"), knowledge, inferences, and observations concerning our own and other peoples' feelings, perceptions, motives, intentions, thoughts, personality traits, social interaction, moral and other norms (social, legal), and numerous other contents of our social world. [p. 43.]

Finally, the recent edition of the *Nebraska Symposium on Motivation,* focusing on social cognitive development, includes chapters on communication skills, visual perception, social convention, self-development, empathy, intentionality, motives, interpersonal awareness, and social attributions.

In each of the definitions, an enormous amount of research and
theory is incorporated. In fact, the 1977 *Nebraska Symposium on
Motivation* was an attempt to integrate the literature in social cognition and thereby overcome a tendency for research in some areas to
proliferate without a concurrent integration of material. The chapters of the *Nebraska Symposium* are in their own ways very good
integrations of the separate topics in social cognition. It is still
necessary for us, however, to have an overall integration. For at least
two reasons it seems that the arrival of that integration is still well in
the future. For one thing, research in social cognition is relatively
new. It has far less history than does research in the cognitive
processes associated with understanding nonsocial or physical phenomena. Second, an integration of the diverse areas associated with
understanding others is unlikely in the near future, for understandings
of others are extraordinarily complex. Bromley (1979) points this
out when he asks us to reflect on how difficult it is to understand
one's self. Bromley's research on "the self" leads him to conclude
that our "self-conception is not a single idea but rather a complex
system of ideas, feelings, and desires, not necessarily well articulated
or coherent" (1979, p. 164). Much the same may be said about an
understanding of others.

In short, definitions of social cognition have been various and
broad and incorporate enormously complex processes. Other reviewers have expressed the same view (Broughton 1978, Forbes 1978).
Cooney and Selman (1978) may have said it best when they wrote,
"there may be as many ways to map social cognition as there are
map makers" (p. 26).

Just how complex the area is and whether we might ever move
toward an understanding of that complexity is debatable. Glick expresses a point of view that I share:

We have thus far built an argument that seems to indicate that social knowledge
in fully rational form is most likely unattainable, dealing as it does with a shifting and subtle object in an informationally rich and unanalyzable world. Locked
in a world of this complexity, we seem to have no choice but to indulge in social
fantasizing. [1978, p. 5.]

Although I believe that a complete understanding of others is unlikely in the near future, it is essential for at least three reasons that educational psychologists (among others) become familiar with what is known about social cognition and its development. First, students are affected by their own feelings and emotions. Knowing more about the affective components of students' lives enables us to work better with students. Second, students are affected by their peers and learn much from them. By knowing more about how students interpret the feelings, thoughts, and intentions of others, we can better understand the dynamics of peer influences. We also need to know more about how students perceive others. What are their conceptualizations of others, and why do they think others do what they do? Third, there is every reason to believe that social cognition interacts with processes of physical cognition. We may design better curricula if we consider not only the cognitive demands associated with understanding mathematics, for example, but also the feelings students have about mathematics. For those reaons at least, social cognition is relevant to educational psychology.

Since the topic area is so broad and diverse and since there have been previous reviews in the area (Forbes 1978, Hoffman 1977, Livesley and Bromley 1973, and Shantz 1975), I have decided to review some of the material in a selective fashion in the next section. Relying heavily on the previous and very recent reviews, I shall try to discuss what is known. After those descriptions have been presented, I shall turn in the third section toward a framework that might be useful for integrating and conceptualizing research in social cognition.

SELECTIVE REVIEW OF SOCIAL COGNITION RESEARCH

Although the history of research in social cognition is relatively brief, there are numerous investigations and several tentative conclusions already available. To assist in remembering and organizing the material, I offer six considerations. First, methodological concerns loom heavily in research on social cognition. Attempting to design investigations that will capture the complexity of social behavior is extremely difficult, and a variety of methods have been employed, including interviews, observations, videotaped presentations, slide and graphic displays. Since videotaped presentations of social interaction have become more accessible, there is likely to be increased usage of that format. This makes sense, for capturing the complexity of social understanding is more likely when the presentation of materials reflects the naturalistic complexity of our social world. While some investigators have used filmed or videotaped presentations (Chandler, Greenspan, and Barenboim 1973, Flapan 1968, Gollin 1958, Gordon 1976, Rothenberg 1970), the number of researchers using videotapes has been relatively small. This is not to suggest that videotaped presentations are the only means to arrive at accurate understandings of the development of social cognition. It does suggest, however, that as more studies incorporate videotaped presentations, it is increasingly likely that our understandings will reflect the complexity of the naturalistic social world. Methodological concerns are also apparent in the questions asked of subjects and the reliance on verbal responses. Subjects may have quite refined abilities to understand others but are not yet able to verbalize those thoughts. Therefore, the consequent data may underestimate the child's abilities.

Second, the social world is extraordinarily complex. One has to understand both generalized and particular others. Some of these understandings are the result of stereotypical judgments; others result from detailed personal experiences with friends, parents, or employees. The knowledge base differs and so, too, do the consequent understandings. Some people may assume that all others operate from the same general motives; others may assume that motives are as individualistic as the number of people involved; and still others may assume that there are several types of people, and that each type is principally motivated by a particular cluster of motives. All these complexities can enter into our understandings of others. The more one thinks about social cognition, the more complex the area becomes. Researchers may attempt to cut through the complexity by studying separately any of the numerous components of social cognition (for example, visual perspective taking, role taking, understanding feelings of others, person perception, intentionality), but a complete understanding of social cognition involves all these areas and more. The differentiations in subject areas are merely artificial conveniences to provide some taxonomy of our understandings.

Third, most of the research is descriptive. It focuses on *what* children and adolescents are able to do at various developmental levels. Questions relating to the processes involved in understanding others have generally not been asked.

Fourth, the descriptions reveal that children's abilities to understand others change, particularly between ages six and nine. Usually the changes reflect movement from reliance on external features of others (such as appearance and behavior) to reliance on internal factors (such as motives, traits, and dispositions). The children become less egocentric, more able to take the perspective of others.

Fifth, most of the research in social cognition has been associated with the cognitive developmental, or Piagetian, theoretical perspective. This orientation assumes that individuals develop as a result of their interactions with the environment. The cognitive developmentalists do not assume that individuals develop simply as a result of maturation, nor do they make the assumption of behaviorists, such as Skinner (1971, p. 16), that behavior is shaped and maintained by its environmental consequences. The interactional assumption that they do make suggests that individuals' understandings of the social world derive not only from maturational and environmental components but also from the individuals' interactions. These interactions are social; consequently, social cognition is broadly defined.

The sixth point to keep in mind also relates to the cognitive-developmental perspective. The issue is whether social cognition can be described in terms of developmental stages. Many of the studies have presented stages in social-cognitive understanding in much the same manner as the Piagetian stages of cognitive development. Each of these stage conceptualizations has attempted to mirror the characteristics of stages as defined by Piaget (1970). These characteristics indicate that stages are hierarchically arranged, qualitatively different, structured wholes—invariant and universal across cultures. In only one area of research on social cognition, moral development, has there been the same thorough analysis of the stages in a variety of cultural settings that we find in studies of cognitive development.

Role taking has also been one of the areas more thoroughly explored, although somewhat less so than the area of moral development. Both the concept of stages and the issues of role taking loom heavily in research on social cognition. One may well wonder whether social cognition and its various aspects can be accurately described in terms of stages of development. In addition, there has been some questioning lately of whether there are stages of role-taking development. As we review some of the topic areas within social cognition, it is important to keep in mind questions concerning the appropriateness of stage descriptions and the appropriate functions of role taking.

What Is the Other Seeing?

In the investigations focusing on what the other is seeing, the central issue is the identification of whether or not children recognize that the same physical object looks different when viewed from differing perspectives. The research flows from Piaget's and Inhelder's (1956) study of spatial representation. Three stages of understanding what the other might be seeing were described. In the first stage, there is an inability to recognize that the perspective of another differs from one's own. In the second stage, there is some understanding that perspectives may differ, but the specification of these differences is occasionally made in error. In the third stage, the differences in perspective are clearly and accurately described. Again, since the research from this point of view flows from a cognitive developmental and interactional perspective, the ages associated with these three stages are approximate. It appears, however, that stage one occurs in children four to six years of age, stage two in children from six to seven, and stage three in children between seven and nine years of age. The developmental progression and understanding of other's visual perspectives moves from a sequence of correctly stating that the other does see something to a description of what it is that the other sees and, finally, to how what is seen appears to the other (Shantz 1975, p. 19).

In a recent review of research on the development of knowledge about visual perception, Flavell (1979) indicated that recent investigations suggest that children can accurately infer another's view of a visual display at a younger age than had previously been believed, "provided that the display is sufficiently simple (for example, composed of one object rather than three) and the child's task is communicated to him very clearly" (p. 45). This recent finding occurs as a result of a modification in the method used to assess visual perception. In the first level, children understand that others see objects, and they can correctly infer what objects the other sees if they are provided with adequate cues. The second level describes children who not only understand that people see objects, "but also that they can have differing visual experiences while seeing the same object; most notably, they can have different spatial perspectival views of it when looking at it from different positions" (p. 74). At level two, in other words, the child recognizes that if the other changes perspectives, the things that the other sees look different as well. That recognition does not occur in the child who is at level one.

The large number of investigations in the area of visual perspective-taking has done much to increase our understanding of the developmental sequence involved in knowing that things look different to others if their spatial location differs from our own. Several of those investigations are reviewed in detail in the Flavell paper (1979), and the interested reader is referred to that paper for more detailed analysis of those studies. For present purposes, however, three points from the Flavell review are important. First, methodological concerns, such as the questions asked of the subjects and the materials presented to them, play important roles in the results that are presented. Second, the development of the idea that another's perspective differs from one's own appears to occur with relatively young children (about four years of age). Third, Flavell himself raises the possibility that the two sequences or "levels" of knowledge about visual perception may not reflect two qualitatively different stages (p. 71). The fact that Flavell questions whether the levels are qualitatively different reflects back to our earlier comments concerning the appropriate viewpoint to take on the role-taking literature. Whether role taking is accurately described as a strategy for understanding others or as a series of qualitatively different structures for conceptualizing understandings of others remains debatable.

What Is the Other Feeling?

A related aspect of research on social cognition focuses on investigations designed to understand the developmental processes involved in recognizing feelings in others. This research has often been associated with work on empathy (see Hoffman 1979). It is also associated with the role-taking work, for one is interested, in part at least, in understanding how the subject is able to put himself into the role of another. Again, Shantz provides a comprehensive review of this material and concludes that children "as young as three years of age can recognize reliably that certain familiar situations typically elicit certain emotions such as happiness and fear" (p. 25). Shantz continues that children are more easily able to identify another's feeling state if the children are familiar with the situation of the other and if the children perceive themselves as similar to the other person. Recognitions of feeling states in adults, especially adults participating in nonfamiliar situations, are more difficult for children. At about the time children are eight or nine years old, they can better recognize emotions expressed in people dissimilar to themselves or in nonfamiliar situations.

The research concerned with identifying feeling states in others has taken various methodological approaches. Nearly all of the investigations have focused on a few emotions such as happiness, fear, anger, and sadness. In addition, most of these studies have assumed that there is an accurate identification that the subjects might make. For example, Flapan (1968) had judges score on a three-point scale the comments that six-, nine-, and twelve-year-old girls offered to a filmed presentation. In my own research, using the same film, I found that subjects ages six, seven and a half, nine, twelve, and fifteen years responded in a variety of ways to the question, "How does the actor feel at a certain point in the movie?" Results from that study (Gordon 1976) indicate that young children respond to questions about feelings of others with reference to relatively global states, such as happy, sad, angry, and afraid. These responses are typical of six- and seven-and-a-half-year-old subjects. In the interval between seven and a half and nine years of age, however, the identifications of emotional states in others become more specific and include references to such feelings as jealous, worried, upset, nervous, and disgusted. At twelve years of age, one finds identifications that not only include references to these more specific emotional states, but also reflect upon the thoughts and intentions of the filmed actor. For example, in response to a question asking how an actor feels, the twelve-year-olds like to respond, "He feels worried and was wondering whether he should have done that." This tendency toward incorporating more references to intentions and moral judgments in responses to questions about the feelings of others increases with development. There is a corresponding decrease in the frequency of responses focusing only on the emotional states of the actor, for adolescents and adults respond to questions asking for how another feels with a heavy mixture of references to feelings, thoughts, and intentions of the other.

What Does the Other Think?

As is evident from the review of research on what others feel, neat differentiations between perceptions of another's thoughts and perceptions of another's feelings are difficult to make. For present purposes, however, research within the area of what another is thinking basically incorporates the role-taking investigations. Previous reviews by Glucksberg, Krauss, and Higgins (1975) and Looft (1972) should also be considered by the interested reader. In general, research in role taking enables us to be better aware of *what* inferences children are able to make about another person's thoughts, but it provides little information on *how* children are able to make those inferences (Shantz 1975).

Selman (1973, Selman and Byrne 1974, Selman 1976) has provided a theoretical model of role-taking development. According to this model, children younger than about age six are principally egocentric, thereby signifying an inability to differentiate their own perspectives from those of others. Children younger than six could be aware that the other holds a differing thought, but they are unable to specify how those thoughts might compare. Between six and ten years of age, as we have already seen, children become able to recognize the thoughts, intentions, and feelings of others. Mutual role taking occurs around ten or eleven years of age when children understand that they might take another person's thought at the same time that the other is taking their perspective. At around twelve years of age, young adolescents are able to take the perspective of "generalized others." Finally, in adolescence, one finds individuals capable of assessing the dynamics of role taking. Other investigators (DeVries 1970, Feffer 1970, Flavell 1974, and Kuhn 1972) provide data that substantiate the description offered by Selman.

Recently, Turiel (1978a, 1978b, 1979) has questioned the advisability of conceptualizing these role-taking changes in terms of stage definitions. Turiel's argument is that stage conceptualizations should possess characteristics of cross-cultural universality, structured wholes, hierarchical arrangement, and qualitative differences. He believes that the developmental changes described in the role-taking research do not reflect those characteristics; instead they represent quantitative differences occurring with age. This is to say that children are able to do quantitatively more things to understand how others feel as they develop, but their additional capabilities are not differences in kind. Turiel substantiates his proposition that role taking is a method one uses to understand others rather than a conceptual area which undergoes qualitative developmental changes by noting that the findings in a number of role-taking studies reveal inconsistent patterns of change from egocentrism to role taking. These inconsistencies principally occur at the ages when children are able to make inferences concerning another's thoughts. Turiel believes that the inconsistencies can be explained, in part, because the "so-called role-taking tasks entail *both* role-taking activities and conceptual activities on the part of the subject" (1979, p. 105). In order to understand what another is thinking, children must first have concepts about the internal psychological states of another.

For children to take the perspective of another's thoughts or feelings, they must first have stable concepts of thinking and emotion (part of the psychological domain). In the absence of such concepts on the part of the subject, it becomes trivial to say that the subject does not take the perspective of the other: it is as if there were no person (in the psychological sense) there. [1979, p. 106]

Without a stable concept of the other person, the child will rely on the only information available, information about the self or the situation. Dependence on that information is likely to lead to the age differences in role-taking skills.

Turiel's contention that the development of role taking does not consist of qualitative stage transformations comes as part of a larger theoretical orientation which suggests that there are three domains of social-cognitive development and four methods of information-gathering strategy. The domains are moral, societal, and psychological. The methods of gathering social information include such activities as observation, communication, imitation, and role taking. The methods do not undergo structural changes with development, although there are structural changes within the domains. Methods also operate across domains. Turiel and others (Nucci 1977, Nucci and Nucci 1979, Nucci and Turiel 1978) have provided convincing data for the existence of separate developmental domains, differentiating moral judgments from conventional and psychological judgments. Whether the Turiel position that role taking is best described with quantitative changes in development as opposed to the qualitative changes described by Selman and others remains for future investigations. At this point, it appears that questions of how best to view role taking appropriately will be central in research on social cognition.

In a review of recent research on children's social cognition, Forbes (1978) focuses on the role-taking research. He proposes that role taking can be classified into three types: taking the role of specific persons in context, taking the role of unusual persons, and taking the role of the generalized other (p. 126). Forbes also follows the distinction previously presented by Flavell (1968), which differentiated studies of accuracy in role taking from studies focusing on the activity of role taking. After reviewing the research, Forbes concludes that the role-taking literature has become diverse and that it is now appropriate to move toward a comprehensive synthesis of that material. He also believes that Turiel's research and theoretical orientation offer the promise of synthesizing findings. The need for such a synthesis has also been expressed by the authors in the *Nebraska Symposium* (1979) and by Kurdek (1978). In the third section of this chapter, I shall offer three perspectives that might be used to integrate and synthesize the literature on social cognition. Prior to turning to those suggestions, however, I will briefly review studies on what the other intends and investigations of what the other is like.

What Is the Other Intending?

Our review of the literature on what the other is seeing, feeling, and thinking has suggested that developmental differences do occur with age. In addition, we have seen that various methodological procedures have been employed and that results of research focus more on description than they do on an understanding of the processes involved in social cognition. Much the same pattern of findings is identifiable in studies of what the other intends. For example, methodological problems in studying intentionality have been noted (Hebble 1971, King 1977, Shantz 1975, Turiel 1966).

The research on intentionality indicates that by age six children are clearly capable of differentiating between intended and accidental actions, although the differentiations might vary depending on whether the consequences are positive or negative (Shantz 1975). In addition, methodological concerns focusing on the medium of presentation to the subject have also been expressed by Chandler, Greenspan, and Barenboim (1973). In these respects, research on what the other is intending again provides us with the expected descriptions of development and the suspected questions about the effects of methodology on the findings. In another respect, the question of understanding the development of children's abilities to recognize intentions in others has been associated with research on attribution theory (Heider 1958, Jones and Davis 1965, Kelley 1967, 1973). This research refers to the processes of explaining the behaviors of self and others. Guttentag and Longfellow (1979) differentiate research on social attribution from that on social cognition in that the former focuses on how differences in the *object* of thought affect one's understanding of behavior. For example, the sex, age, and race of the persons being observed may significantly influence how one thinks about or knows those persons (p. 305).

Although research on social attribution almost always has focused on work with adults, Guttentag and Longfellow review the research on children's attributional processes. Their review points to the years between six and nine as times when significant developmental changes occur in coordinating information on the possible causes of another's behavior. This research is conceptualized in terms of two dimensions: whether the behavior of another may be explained in terms of internal factors (such as ability or effort) or whether it might be classified with reference to external factors (such as the difficulty of the task or luck). Ability and task difficulty are considered to be stable factors; effort and luck are variable factors.

The review of the literature and the empirical data generated by Guttentag and Longfellow substantiate the notion that not only do levels of cognitive development provide a dimension in understanding children's social attributions, but so, too, do variations in the social-psychological influences (sex of the perceiver, sex of the perceived, peer-group influences, classroom characteristics). In short, the picture one has of research in understanding the intentions of another is extraordinarily complex, incorporating investigations not only in social cognition but also in social attributions.

That complexity is also reflected in an excellent review of children's developing awareness and usage of intentionality and motives (Keasey 1979). Keasey points out that only relatively recently has there been a differentiation between researchers investigating intentionality and those investigating motives. He organizes a review of theoretical and empirical work on the development of intentionality and motives by differentiating the two topic areas. Keasey's review emphasizes that a number of methodological issues need to be considered when assessing developmental patterns in understanding intentionality and motives. In that respect, he also confirms a conclusion that we have offered throughout our review of these topic areas.

What Is the Other Like?

The final topic area for review focuses on the developing awareness of abilities to conceptualize other people. This area is sometimes
referred to as "person perception." Livesley and Bromley (1973)
present a thorough review of this literature. A more recent review,
comparing the literature on person perception with that on self-
perception, is available in the 1977 *Nebraska Symposium* (Bromley
1979). Much of the research in person perception flows from Werner's
(1948) developmental theory suggesting that with development one
finds increasing differentiations and hierarchical integrations of
thoughts about others. In this area one again finds developmental
differences, particularly in the age range between seven and eight
(Shantz 1975). Developmental patterns seem to suggest that younger
children focus on the external qualities of others (such as their appearance), then move to the older children's focus on internal infer-
ential concepts, such as the values, beliefs, and dispositions of others.

Again, the research in person perception reveals the enormous importance of dealing with methodological issues. For example, several
of the investigations employ free-description techniques whereby
subjects are to describe in their own words what one of their friends
is like. There are questions concerning the strengths and weaknesses
of the free-description method; these questions focus on the students' interpretations of the instructions (Shantz 1975).

Research on person perception has been associated more recently
with self-perceptions as well. Bromley (1979) is interested in comparing the way we describe ourselves with the way we describe others.
His work responds to the question of whether self-understandings are
similar to understandings of others by focusing on descriptions in
ordinary (as opposed to psychological) language. He finds that, in
general, developmental changes in self descriptions are similar to
those in descriptions of others. Much as we found in other areas, the
conclusions that Bromley offers about self-conceptualizations reveal
that they are extraordinarily complex, not necessarily well articulated
or coherent (p. 164).

Another approach to self-systems is offered by Nucci (1977), who
attempted to investigate whether children's and adolescents' conceptualizations of moral, societal, and psychological issues develop in a
similar fashion and represent a single conceptual framework or
whether they reflect differing developmental domains. Nucci's

research substantiates the Turiel claim that development in the three areas (societal, psychological, moral) follows different patterns and reflects distinct developmental conceptualizations. He argues, in other words, that it is erroneous to assume that societal, psychological, and moral conceptualizations develop as a single unit. In this respect, the Nucci research also substantiates the Bromley contention that social cognition is an extraordinarily complex area.

EXPLAINING OTHERS: THREE PERSPECTIVES

Earlier I reviewed various definitions of social cognition and noted how comprehensive and inclusive they were. I referred to Glick's comment concerning the necessity for indulging in social fantasizing when thinking about the complex nature of social knowledge. I now offer three perspectives from which such "social fantasizing" may be viewed. The first perspective assumes that when trying to conceptualize social cognition one should turn to core or common explanations. The second assumes that each person behaves in a unique fashion. The third recognizes that although persons are unique, there are still some general types of people. These types differ in fundamental ways; how one explains one type differs from how one explains another, even though there is commonality among the people in each type grouping.

The Core-Tendency Perspective

Some theorists believe that all people do things for a few reasons. These reasons might be, as suggested by Freud, to live out sexual and aggressive instincts. All of the theorists listed in Table 5-1 believe that, when trying to explain behavior, it is preferable to refer to core tendencies common to all people. For Glasser (1975) behavior is explained by noting that individuals want to be loved and to achieve self-worth. Maslow's (1955, 1962) well-known five motivational explanations are also presented in Table 5-1. In his perspective, people do what they do because of the need to survive physiologically, then for safety, then for belonging, then for self-esteem, and finally for self-actualization. Erikson's (1950) eight well-known stages also reflect the core-tendency perspective. Behavior has also been explained with reference to needs to relate, to be separate from others, to belong, to have an identity, to have a frame of reference,

Table 5-1

Core tendencies for explaining behavior

Freud (1925)	Sex, aggression, life
Glasser (1975)	Love, self-worth
Maslow (1962)	Physiological, safety, belonging, self-esteem, self-actualization
Erikson (1950)	Trust/mistrust; autonomy versus shame and doubt; initiative and responsibility versus guilt; industry versus inferiority; identity versus role confusion; intimacy versus isolation; generativity versus stagnation; ego identity versus despair
Sullivan (1947)	Power, the desire for physical closeness, oral dynamism, lust dynamism, self dynamism (avoiding insecurity of disapproval)
White (1959)	To achieve competence
Fromm (1947)	Need for relatedness, transcendence (to be separate from people and things), belongingness, identity, frame of reference (to have a stable way of perceiving and comprehending the world)
Kelly (1955)	The attempt to predict and control the events one experiences
Loevinger (1976)	Presocial, impulsive, self-protective, conformist, conscientious-conformist, conscientious, individualistic, autonomous, integrated

and to hold stable ways of perceiving the world (Fromm 1947, 1956). Kelly's (1955) personal-construct theory suggests people behave so as to predict and control the events that they experience. Loevinger's (1976) stages of ego development are also presented in Table 5-1. Common to each of these orientations is the underlying tendency to assume that there are one, two, three, four, five, or, as in Erikson's case, eight reasons why all people do what they do.

The Unique-Characteristics Perspective

Another perspective assumes that people are unique, different, and special. Consequently there are a variety of reasons to explain behavior. This perspective suggests that the things that motivate *A* are different from those that motivate *B*. It also assumes that *A* can be

Table 5-2

Some suggested explanations (among many) for behavior

1. Particular motives, traits, dispositions, labels: He does it because he is selfish. She does that because she is smart. He does it because he is always looking for approval. She does those things because she likes to be different.

2. Resolutions of feelings (includes wants): She did it because she was sad. He wanted to be happy and he thought that would make him happy, so he did it.

3. Sociological, cultural, ethnic, conventional, and familial reasons: He does those things because of his background; that is what all middle-class guys do. She plays up to him because she has to; it is expected behavior in that place. He does those things because he is looking for the love that he didn't get in his family, especially from his father.

4. Moral: She did it because she thought it was right. She felt that she had to be true to her principles.

5. Biological and physiological reasons: He does that because he has some physical problem, and it affects his behavior. She acts like that because she was born that way. He does it to survive.

6. Interaction with and imitations of significant others: She acts like that because she hangs around with the right people, and they have influenced her. He models himself after her.

7. Chance and situationalism: He happened to be in the right place at the right time. She saw what was going on and realized that it was best for her to speak up in that situation.

8. Logical necessity and responsibility: When she works, she does her best because she feels she has to keep her position. He works that way because he knows what his responsibilities are.

Note: This model has a potentially infinite number of explanations for behavior. These eight are suggested examples and are partially based on the work of Heider (1958), partially on intuitive appeal, and partially on their relevance for organizing the social-cognition literature.

motivated by different causes at various points in A's life. Each person is unique, with a distinctive and individual motivational hierarchy. Table 5-2 provides some explanations for behavior. As is apparent from Table 5-2, *at least* eight explanations are possible. Sometimes the behavior of others is explained with reference to particular traits, motives, and dispositions. For example, we may say A works hard because she is conscientious or B asks for opinions because he is looking for approval. A second set of reasons to explain the behavior of another flows from feelings. When the feelings of another are not the way the person would like them to be, he acts. For example, if he is not happy, he does things to become happy. If she does not understand and feels uncertain, she acts to resolve the uncertainty. A third set of reasons flows from sociological, familial, or conventional concerns. For example, it is conventional for students to come to class wearing what they do. Another example is to explain *A*'s behavior by saying it is typical for someone of that social background. Explanations relying on issues of morality (justice and fairness) provide a fourth explanatory set of reasons for the behavior of others. A fifth set focuses on issues of biological survival (for example, "he had to do that to stay healthy"), while a sixth set emphasizes behavior resulting from imitations of, or interactions with, significant others. Chance, luck, and situationalism provide a seventh set of explanations, for people sometimes do things simply by chance or by being in the right situation at the right time. Finally, people act for reasons of logical necessity and responsibility (for example, "She knew that if she was to get the position, she had to perform to the best of her ability").

In offering these eight sets of reasons I am suggesting that there are several explanations for behavior. Those explanations may be as different and as unique as the people who are discussed, but they also may vary for the same individual at different points in that person's life.

The Personality-Type Perspective

A third perspective from which to view the behavior of others focuses on personality types, recognizing that while specific manifestations of a person may differ and are probably unique, there are nevertheless groups or clusters or types of people. Assuming that the theorists in Table 5-1 have devoted considerable attention to the question of why people do what they do, I examined the reasons they have offered to see if there are commonalities among them. Table 5-3 identifies those commonalities in terms of seven personality types. As is apparent from Table 5-3, the behavior of others may be explained with reference to issues of: (a) survival, safety, and security; (b) personal satisfaction and the avoidance of displeasure; (c) sexuality, love, and lust; (d) the need to control, exercise power, and display competence; and (g) the need to achieve understanding and self-actualization.

Table 5-3

Seven possible personality types

---

1. *Survival, safety, and security*
   Freud
   Maslow

2. *Satisfaction*
   Skinner
   Thorndike

3. *Sexuality, love, lust*
   Freud
   Glasser
   Erikson (intimacy versus isolation)
   Sullivan (lust dynamism)

4. *Belonging*
   Maslow
   Sullivan—physical closeness
   Fromm—relatedness, belongingness
   Loevinger—conformist, conscientious-conformist

5. *Self-worth, identity*
   Glasser—self-worth
   Maslow—self-esteem
   Erikson—shame and doubt, initiative and responsibility versus guilt;
        identity versus role confusion; generativity versus stagnation; ego
        integrity versus despair
   White—competence motivation
   Fromm—identity, transcendence (to be separate from people and things)
   Loevinger—self-protective, conscientious, individualistic, autonomous,
        integrated
   Sullivan—self-dynamism

6. *Aggression, power, competence*
   Freud—aggression   Erikson—industry versus inferiority
   Adler—power   White—competence
   Sullivan—power motive   Loevinger—conscientious

7. *Understanding and self-actualization*
   Kelly—attempts to predict and control events one experiences
   Fromm—frame of reference (having a stable way of perceiving and
        comprehending the world)
   Piaget—equilibration
   Maslow—self-actualization

Two Benefits of the Three Perspectives

The three perspectives serve as useful organizations of the diverse literature on social cognition, for underlying all the research is a common attempt to describe and explain the development of knowledge about others. We have seen that the available research is focused on descriptions; attention to the explanations of the behavior of others has been less intense. Each of these perspectives emphasizes explanations of behavior but also provides a heuristic framework for incorporating the available descriptive research as well.

The core-tendency perspective has an extensive history and has been well researched (see Maddi 1968). The personality-type perspective is an outgrowth of the core-tendency position, for the personality types were formulated after reviewing the various core tendencies emphasized by the leading theorists. Consequently, that perspective also has considerable empirical support. The unique-features perspective has the least empirical support. The eight proposed reasons to explain the behaviors of others were generated as heuristic and suggestive examples of the causes of behavior. They have relevance to the work of Heider (1958), and they have an intuitive appeal. Whether they are substantiated after empirical investigations is as yet uncertain. With this in mind, we turn to a discussion of the heuristic and organizational features of the perspectives, emphasizing the commonalities among them.

First, all three incorporate an emphasis on feelings. Obviously, there are an enormous number of feelings that individuals may experience, but relatively few have been particularly emphasized in the three perspectives. These include feelings of love, self-worth, trust, guilt, inferiority, intimacy, despair, aggression, power, and lust. Some of these feelings have been extensively researched; others are relatively neglected. Since they apparently are of such extraordinary importance in an understanding of behavior, it seems we would be well advised to investigate each feeling. The educational implications associated with feelings of despair, self-worth, inferiority, power, trust, and (even) love are great. As educators, we would do well to know more about the dynamics of these affective states.

Second, each perspective emphasizes the self. Whether the focus is on self-understanding, self-worth, or self-actualization, the primary importance of the self is evident. There has been a long history of research on the self (see Wylie 1968, 1974), and the area has enormous methodological complexity. Nevertheless, it seems as if we would do well to continue our efforts to understand "the self" better.

Third, each perspective emphasizes the importance of "understanding." Perhaps the best way to express this is with reference to the Piagetian concept of equilibration. It appears that harmony, understanding, prediction, competence, and awareness of logical necessity are essential elements of human functioning. It is not mere projection for a psychologist, such as myself, to argue that people seek to understand and make sense of the world. All the literature on social cognition is concerned in one way or another with how people make sense of other people.

Finally, each perspective emphasizes physiological processes, including security and survival skills. While these emphases may be placed lower in the hierarchy of social cognition and are often neglected in psychological research, it appears that people strive to survive and to be secure. Additional research on how these goals affect individual behavior certainly seems in order. In short, these commonalities suggest areas where additional empirical attention may very well be directed. As educators know more about how feelings, self-conceptualizations, the search for understanding, and survival objectives affect students' behavior, they may arrive at more comprehensive, effective curricula and teaching methods.

In addition to suggesting research directions, one of the perspectives in particular provides a taxonomy for organizing the diverse literature of social cognition. Table 5-4 suggests how the numerous separate research areas referred to as social cognition are incorporated within the perspective of unique characteristics. Nearly all the research areas are included, but as Table 5-4 indicates, that perspective does not incorporate the research on communication, role taking, and visual perception. Despite these limitations, which may be explained by agreeing with Turiel that role taking and communication are methods of social cognition rather than content areas, the key strength of this perspective is that it not only incorporates eight sets of reasons to explain the behavior of others, but it also helps organize the literature on social cognition.

I realize that each of the three perspectives is limited and does not reflect fully the complexity of understanding others that we have identified earlier in this chapter. They do suggest, however, that we have available routes toward organizing the diverse literatures of social cognition.

Table 5-4

The unique-characteristics perspective:
A taxonomy of social-cognition literature

Incorporates literature on:

1. Particular motives, traits, dispositions, and labels — Person perception, intentionality, psychological causality, empathy, motives, gender identity, self

2. Resolutions of feelings — Affective development

3. Sociological, cultural, ethnic, conventional, and familial reasons — Social conventions, social class affects sex role development

4. Moral — Moral judgment

5. Biological and physiological — Social behavior resulting from the resolution of biological needs

6. Interactions with and imitations of significant others — Imitation, modeling

7. Chance and situationalism — Attribution process, situationalism

8. Logical necessity and responsibility — Logic, cognitive development, principled level of moral judgment

EDUCATIONAL IMPLICATIONS OF SOCIAL COGNITION

The cognitive-developmental assumption that development results from the activity of individuals as they interact with others leads directly to an educational implication of primary importance: "The social climate of the classroom should be such as to encourage students to interact with one another, to ask questions freely, and to challenge each other's ideas and explanations" (Nucci and Gordon 1979, p. 94). The research in social cognition emphasizes how children and adolescents interpret the behavior of others. Their interpretations presumably affect their interactions. As we learn more about the development of those interpretations, we can design better opportunities for more effective student-student interactions.

A second educational implication focuses on the importance of recognizing the interactions between cognition and affectivity. The social-cognition literature focuses on cognitions concerning social (and frequently affective) phenomena. Numerous interactions between cognition and affectivity are identified in the literature. In psychological works the distinction often made between cognitive and social emotional processes is a simplistic convenience not in accord with actual psychological functioning (Kohlberg 1969, Nucci and Gordon 1979). This point was noted by Piaget (1967) as he discussed the inseparability of cognition and affectivity. He suggested that affectivity provides the energetic component to cognitive processes. The message behind this material is clear: the prudent educator is interested not only in cognitive processes but also in affectivity.

Feelings were identified as key components in interpretations of the behavior of others. The three perspectives also underscore the importance of feelings. One may well argue that feelings provide the rudder underlying the direction of human activity. Thus, in terms of educational implications, additional attention should be directed toward giving students opportunities to discuss, share, and learn about their own feelings and the feelings of others. Failure to provide this focus reflects only a partial approach to the complexity of human behavior. In short, the educational implications of the literature on social cognition emphasize the importance of incorporating affective components and social activity in educational environments.

Summary

This chapter began with various definitions of social cognition and noted the diverse sets of research literature incorporated within what used to be called social and emotional development. I suggested that it is unlikely that we will have a complete understanding of the disparate and complex processes involved in social cognition in the near future and that we may have to rely on what Glick (1978) refers to as social fantasizing. We then reviewed the recent literature in social cognition, following the organizational framework proposed by Shantz (1975). Methodological difficulties, descriptive and cognitive-developmental emphases, stage definitions, complexities of understanding others, and developmental changes in the years between six and nine were discussed. Three perspectives from which to view and explain behavior were then presented. One (the core tendency) assumes all people do things for the same reasons; the second (unique characteristics) assumes people are different, unique, and special; and the third (personality types) assumes there are types or clusters of people, each having their own separate, explanatory concepts. The perspective of unique characteristics is favored, for it recognizes that behavior results from interactions between the individual's thoughts, intentions, desires, and feelings on the one hand and the restraints, demand characteristics, and the particularities of the social setting in which the individual operates on the other. Together these features provide extraordinarily complex sets of influences on behavior, leading to the conclusion that one simplifies behavior by explaining it with reference to a few underlying commonalities. The chapter concludes with educational implications, stressing the importance of supplementing an emphasis on cognition within schools by attending to feelings, emotions, and social interactions as well.

REFERENCES

Bromley, David B. "Natural Language and the Development of the Self." In *Nebraska Symposium on Motivation, 1977*, edited by Charles B. Keasey, pp. 117-67. Lincoln, Neb.: University of Nebraska Press, 1979.

Broughton, John. "Development of Concepts of Self, Mind, Reality, and Knowledge." In *Social Cognition*, edited by William Damon, New Directions for Child Development, No. 1, pp. 75-100. San Francisco: Jossey-Bass, 1978.

Chandler, Michael J.; Greenspan, Stephen; and Barenboim, Carl. "Judgments on Intentionality in Response to Videotaped and Verbally Presented Moral Dilemmas: The Medium Is the Message." *Child Development* 44 (June 1973): 311-20.

Cooney, Ellen W., and Selman, Robert L. "Children's Use of Social Conceptions: Toward a Dynamic Model of Social Cognition." In *Social Cognition*, edited by William Damon, New Directions for Child Development, No. 1, pp. 23-44. San Francisco: Jossey-Bass, 1978.

Damon, William, ed. *Social Cognition*, New Directions for Child Development, No. 1. San Francisco: Jossey-Bass, 1978.

DeVries, Rheta. "The Development of Role-Taking As Reflected by the Behavior of Bright, Average, and Retarded Children in a Social Guessing Game." *Child Development* 41 (September 1970): 759-70.

Erikson, Erik H. *Childhood and Society*. New York: Norton, 1950.

Feffer, Melvin. "Developmental Analysis of Interpersonal Behavior." *Psychological Review* 77 (May 1970): 191-214.

Flapan, Dorothy. *Children's Understandings of Social Interaction*. New York: Teachers College, Columbia University Press, 1968.

Flavell, John H. *The Development of Role-Taking and Communications Skills in Children*. New York: John Wiley, 1968.

————. "The Development of Inferences about Others." In *Understanding Other Persons*, edited by Theodore Mischel, pp. 66-116. Oxford: Blackwell, Basil, Mott, 1974.

————. "The Development of Knowledge about Visual Perception." In *Nebraska Symposium on Motivation, 1977*, edited by Charles B. Keasey, pp. 43-76. Lincoln, Neb.: University of Nebraska Press, 1979.

Forbes, David. "Recent Research on Children's Social Cognition: A Brief Review." In *Social Cognition*, edited by William Damon, New Directions for Child Development, No. 1, pp. 123-39. San Francisco: Jossey-Bass, 1978.

Freud, Sigmund. "Instincts and Their Vicissitudes." In *Collected Papers*. Vol. 4, pp. 60-83. London: Institute for Psychoanalysis and Hogarth Press, 1925.

————. "Some Character Types Met with in Psychoanalytic Work." In *Collected Papers*. Vol. 4, pp. 318-44. London: Institute for Psychoanalysis and Hogarth Press, 1925.

Fromm, Eric. *Man for Himself*. New York: Holt, Rinehart and Winston, 1947.

————. *The Art of Loving*. New York: Harper, 1956.

Glasser, William. *Reality Therapy: A New Approach to Psychiatry*. New York: Harper & Row, 1975.

Glick, Joseph. "Cognition and Social Cognition: An Introduction." In *The Development of Social Understanding*, edited by Joseph Glick and Alison Clarke-Stewart, pp. 1-10. New York: Gardner, 1978.

Glucksberg, Sam; Krauss, Robert M.; and Higgins, E. Tory. "The Development of Communication Skills in Children." In *Review of Child Development Research*. Vol. 4. Edited by Frances Horowitz, chap. 6. Chicago: University of Chicago Press, 1975.

Gollin, Eugene S. "Organizational Characteristics of Social Judgments: A Developmental Investigation." *Journal of Personality* 26 (June 1958): 139-54.

Gordon, Neal J. "Children's Recognitions and Conceptualizations of Emotions in Videotaped Presentations." Ph.D. dissertation, Harvard University, 1976.

Guttentag, Marcia, and Longfellow, Cynthia. "Children's Social Attributions: Development and Change." In *Nebraska Symposium on Motivation, 1977*, edited by Charles B. Keasey, pp. 304-41. Lincoln, Neb.: University of Nebraska Press, 1979.

Hebble, Peter W. "The Development of Elementary School Children's Judgment of Intent." *Child Development* 42 (October 1971): 1203-15.

Heider, Fritz. *The Psychology of Interpersonal Relations*. New York: John Wiley, 1958.

Hoffman, Martin L. "Personality and Social Development." *Annual Review of Psychology*. Vol. 28. Edited by Mark R. Rosenzweig and Lyman W. Porter, pp. 295-321. Palo Alto, Calif.: Annual Reviews, 1977.

————. "Empathy: Its Development and Prosocial Implications." In *Nebraska Symposium on Motivation, 1977*, edited by Charles B. Keasey, pp. 169-217. Lincoln, Neb.: University of Nebraska Press, 1979.

Jones, Richard M. *Fantasy and Feeling in Education*. New York: Harper & Row, 1970.

Jones, Edward E., and Davis, Keith E. "From Acts to Dispositions: The Attribution Process in Person Perception." In *Advances in Experimental Social Psychology, 2*, edited by Leonard Berkowitz, pp. 219-66. New York: Academic Press, 1965.

Keasey, Charles B. "Children's Developing Awareness and Usage of Intentionality and Motives." In *Nebraska Symposium on Motivation, 1977*, edited by Charles B. Keasey, pp. 219-60. Lincoln, Neb.: University of Nebraska Press, 1979.

Kelley, Harold H. "Attribution Theory in Social Psychology." In *Nebraska Symposium on Motivation,* edited by David Levine. Lincoln, Neb.: University of Nebraska Press, 1967.

————. "The Processes of Causal Attribution." *American Psychologist* 28 (February 1973): 107-128.

Kelly, George A. *The Psychology of Personal Constructs.* New York: Norton, 1955.

King, Michael. "The Development of Some Intention Concepts in Young Children." *Child Development* 42 (October 1977): 1145-52.

Kohlberg, Lawrence. "Stage and Sequence: The Cognitive-Developmental Approach to Socialization." In *Handbook of Socialization Theory and Research,* edited by David Goslin, pp. 347-480. New York: Rand McNally, 1969.

Kuhn, Diane. "The Development of Role-Taking Ability." Unpublished. New York: Columbia University, 1972.

Kurdek, Lawrence A. "Perspective Taking as the Cognitive Basis of Children's Moral Development: A Review of the Literature." *Merrill-Palmer Quarterly* 24 (January 1978): 3-28.

Livesley, William J., and Bromley, David B. *Person Perception in Childhood and Adolescence.* London: Wiley, 1973.

Loevinger, Jane. *Ego Development: Conceptions and Theories.* San Francisco: Jossey-Bass, 1976.

Looft, William R. "Egocentrism and Social Interactions Across the Life Span." *Psychological Bulletin* 78 (August 1972): 73-92.

Lyon, Harold C. *Learning to Feel—Feeling to Learn: Humanistic Education for the Whole Man.* Columbus, Ohio: Charles E. Merrill, 1971.

Maddi, Salvatore R. *Personality Theories: A Comparative Analysis.* Homewood, Ill.: Dorsey Press, 1968.

Maslow, Abraham H. "Deficiency Motivation and Growth Motivation." In *Nebraska Symposium on Motivation,* edited by Martha R. Jones, pp. 1-30. Lincoln, Neb.: University of Nebraska Press, 1955.

————. *Toward a Psychology of Being.* New York: D. Van Nostrand Co., 1962.

Miller, John P. *Humanizing the Classroom: Models of Teaching in Affective Education.* New York: Praeger, 1976.

Nucci, Larry P. "Social Development: Personal, Conventional and Moral Concepts." Ph.D. dissertation, University of California, Santa Cruz, 1977.

Nucci, Larry P., and Gordon, Neal J. "Educating Adolescents from a Piagetian Perspective." *Journal of Education* 161 (Winter 1979): 87-101.

Nucci, Larry P., and Nucci, Maria S. "Social Interactions and the Development of Moral and Societal Concepts." Paper presented at the meeting of the Society for Research in Child Development, San Francisco, March 1979.

Nucci, Larry P., and Turiel, Elliot. "Social Interactions and the Development of Social Concepts in Preschool Children." *Child Development* 49 (June 1978): 400-407.

Piaget, Jean. *Six Psychological Studies.* New York: Random House, 1967.

————. "Piaget's Theory." In *Carmichael's Manual of Child Psychology.* Vol. 2. Edited by Paul H. Mussen, pp. 703-32. New York: John Wiley, 1970.

Piaget, Jean, and Inhelder, Bärbel. *The Child's Conception of Space.* London: Routledge and Kegan-Paul, 1956.

Rothenberg, Barbara B. "Children's Social Sensitivity and the Relationship to Interpersonal Competence, Intrapersonal Comfort, and Intellectual Level." *Developmental Psychology* 2 (May 1970): 335-50.

Selman, Robert L. "A Structural Analysis of the Ability to Take Another's Social Perspective: Stages in the Development of Role-Taking Ability." Paper presented at the meeting of the Society for Research in Child Development, Philadelphia, 1973.

————. "Social Cognitive Understanding: A Guide to Educational and Clinical Practice." In *Moral Development and Behavior: Theory, Research, and Social Issues,* edited by Thomas Lickona, pp. 299-316. New York: Holt, Rinehart and Winston, 1976.

Selman, Robert L., and Byrne, Diane F. "A Structural-Developmental Analysis of Levels of Role Taking in Middle Childhood." *Child Development* 45 (September 1974): 803-806.

Shantz, Carolyn U. "The Development of Social Cognition." In *Review of Child Development Research.* Vol. 5. Edited by E. Mavis Hetherington, chap. 5. Chicago: University of Chicago Press, 1975.

Skinner, Burris F. *Beyond Freedom and Dignity.* New York: Bantam Books, 1971.

Sullivan, Harry S. *Conceptions of Modern Psychology.* Washington, D.C.: William Alanson White Psychiatric Foundation, 1947.

————. *The Interpersonal Theory of Psychiatry.* New York: Norton, 1953.

Turiel, Elliot. "An Experimental Test of the Sequentiality of Developmental Stages in the Child's Moral Judgments." *Journal of Personality and Social Psychology* 3 (June 1966): 611-18.

————. "The Development of Concepts of Social Structure: Social Convention." In *The Development of Social Understanding,* edited by Joseph Glick and Alison Clarke-Stewart, pp. 25-108. New York: Gardner, 1978(a).

————. "Social Regulations and Domains of Social Concepts." In *Social Cognition,* edited by William Damon, New Directions for Child Development, No. 1, pp. 45-74. San Francisco: Jossey-Bass, 1978(b).

————. "Distinct Conceptual and Developmental Domains: Social Convention and Morality." In *Nebraska Symposium on Motivation, 1977,* edited by Charles B. Keasey, pp. 77-116. Lincoln, Neb.: Univ. of Nebraska Press, 1979.

Werner, Heinz. *Comparative Psychology of Mental Development.* New York: International Universities Press, 1948.

White, Robert W. "Motivation Reconsidered: The Concept of Competence." *Psychological Review* 66 (September 1959): 297-333.

Wylie, Ruth C. "The Present Status of Self Theory." In *Handbook of Personality Theory and Research,* edited by Edgar F. Borgatta and William W. Lambert, pp. 728-87. Chicago: Rand McNally, 1968.

————. *The Self-Concept.* Rev. ed. Lincoln, Neb.: University of Nebraska Press, 1974.

Youniss, James. "Another Perspective on Social Cognition." In *Minnesota Symposia on Child Development.* Vol. 9. Edited by Anne D. Peck, pp. 173-93. Minneapolis: University of Minnesota Press, 1975.

6. Intellectual Development: A Systematic Reinterpretation

Robbie Case

THE NEED FOR A NEW THEORETICAL PERSPECTIVE ON INTELLECTUAL DEVELOPMENT

When Piaget's theory was introduced to North America in the early 1960s (see Hunt 1961, Flavell 1963), the result was a dramatic shift in the direction of research in developmental and educational psychology. The content of Piaget's theory is by now well known (see Flavell 1963, Ginsberg and Opper 1969, Piaget 1970). According to this theory, children pass through four qualitatively distinct stages in the course of their intellectual development: the sensorimotor stage (birth to two years), the representational or preoperational stage (two to seven years), the concrete operational stage (seven to twelve years), and the formal operational stage (twelve to eighteen years). During each stage, children's thinking has a characteristic logical form or "structure." It is by applying their current form of thought to their experience that children learn about the world. And

The work reported in this chapter was supported by grants from the Canadian Social Sciences and Humanities Research Council, the Canada Council, the Spencer Foundation, the United States National Institutes of Mental Health and Child Development, and the United States National Institute of Education.

142

it is by wrestling with the inconsistencies that result from applying lower-order forms of thought that children gradually evolve higher-order forms of thought.

A number of features of Piaget's theory made it attractive to North American psychologists: First, it offered an explanation for the fact that tasks with very different surface content are all passed at the same age. The explanation was that these tasks all require the application of the same underlying logical form of thought. Then the theory offered an explanation for the invariant sequences of development that had been discovered but not explained by previous psychologists. The explanation was that higher-order forms of thought—being assembled out of lower-order forms by the process of conflict elimination or "equilibration"—could not possibly emerge before lower-order forms. Consequently, tasks requiring the application of higher-order forms of thought could not possibly be mastered before tasks requiring the application of lower-order forms of thought.

Third, the theory offered an explanation for the phenomenon of "readiness." The explanation was that until children had acquired the appropriate form of thought, they could not possibly profit from certain kinds of experience, since they would have no internal mechanism for assimilating that experience. Finally, and perhaps most importantly, the theory offered a coherent and systematic account of human mental processes that did justice to their power, complexity, and organization. In sharp contrast to the other prevailing theories of the day, the theory focused on the difference between adult human thought and lower forms of thought and on the endogenous rather than exogenous factors that affect its development. As a consequence, the theory served as a focus for the reaction to behaviorism that was forming in North America at the time.

In spite of these powerful strengths, by the late 1960s it had become apparent that Piaget's theory had a number of serious weaknesses as well: First, the theory failed to account for the wide difference (decalage) in the age of acquisition of certain tasks that supposedly require the same logical form of thought (see Pinard and Laurendeau 1969). Second, the theory failed to account for the low age-partialled intercorrelation among tasks that do not show any decalage, that is, tasks requiring the same form of thought and mastered at the same age (see Beilin 1971).

Third, it failed to account for those instances in which instruction was successful in bringing children who were not even on the verge of acquiring a particular logical form of thought to complete mastery of tasks that supposedly required that form of thought (see Gelman 1969, Lefebvre and Pinard 1972, Case 1974). Finally, and again perhaps most importantly, the theory failed to provide definitions of each of the four types of thought, or of the stage-transition process, which could easily be made operational. Nor did it specify the experiential, maturational, or "equilibrative" factors that were presumed to affect the stage-transition process. As a consequence, precise hypothesis testing or even precise documentation of internal changes proved to be difficult.

Given the strengths and weaknesses of Piaget's theory, a major challenge developmental psychology has been faced with is to develop a new theory of intellectual growth. The requirements that this theory must meet are quite clear: (a) it must account for the data already explained by Piaget's theory (cross-content age norms, universal sequences, and readiness); (b) it must do so in a fashion that is nonreductionist, systematic, and coherent; (c) it must account for the data not easily explained by Piaget's theory (decalage, low age-partialled correlations, strong training effects); (d) it must do so in a fashion that will lead to novel and testable empirical hypotheses.

In this chapter, I will present a theory developed in response to this challenge. After describing the theory, I shall summarize and test the adequacy of the empirical research completed or under way. Finally, I shall consider the relationship of the new theory to Piaget's theory and attempt to show that it meets all four of the above requirements.

A NEW THEORY OF INTELLECTUAL DEVELOPMENT

In the theory I have developed, two of the central postulates of Piaget's theory are preserved. These are (a) that there are four different types or levels of basic intellectual operation and (b) that an operation at any given level is assembled from the components consolidated at the previous level. In addition, a number of postulates are introduced that derive from other cognitive theories. The most important of these are (a) that the intellectual structures into which basic operations are organized can be modeled as sets of executive strategies (Simon 1962); (b) that the acquisition and application of any executive strategy requires a specifiable amount of short-term storage space (Newell, Shaw, and Simon 1958); (c) that the size of short-term storage space increases with age (McLaughlin 1963, Case 1968, Pascual-Leone 1969, Halford 1970); (d) that the more efficient an operation becomes with time, the less attention it requires for execution and the more attention becomes available for short-term storage as a consequence (Solomons and Stein 1896, Schneider and Shiffrin 1977; and (e) that developmental changes in operational efficiency are at least partially under the control of maturational changes in neural functioning (Luria 1973).

In and of themselves none of these postulates is particularly novel. The overall picture that emerges when these postulates are combined, however, is both novel and productive. The clearest view of the theory can probably be had by considering a few concrete examples of the changes that occur in children's repertories of intellectual strategies as they proceed through each of the four stages of development.

Developmental Changes in Executive Strategies

Changes During the Stage of Sensorimotor Operations. From birth to age one and one half, children pass through a series of substages in which their motor strategies become increasingly complex and powerful. Consider, for example, the changes that occur during this period in children's strategies for performing a directed action with their hands (Piaget's "means-ends" scheme).

Substage 1: Operational Consolidation (one to four months). Somewhere between one and four months, children become capable of executing a directed rather than a reflexive manual action. Although children gain basic control over the movement of their hands during this substage, they cannot yet relate this movement to the movement of some other object.

Substage 2: Operational Coordination (four to eight months). During the second substage, children become capable of centering not just on one action of their own but on the relationship between this action and some consequence in the external world. For example, if children happen to strike a mobile in a way that produces a particularly interesting movement, they will repeat that striking action again and again, delighted with the result produced.

Substage 3: Birelational Coordination (eight to twelve months).

During the third substage, children become capable of executing actions that only indirectly produce interesting results. For example, they become capable of striking a barrier and producing a movement that permits them to obtain the real object of their interest.

Substage 4: Reciprocal Coordination (twelve to eighteen months). During the fourth substage, children become capable of coordinating two actions while they oscillate their attention between two objects. For example, they can combine the actions of pulling on and swiping with a stick in order to produce a movement that will allow them to attain an object that is out of reach.

The most salient characteristic of this sequence is that each successive strategy is a modified and more powerful version of the previous one. That is, although the basic type of operation (hand movement and monitoring of external movement) remains the same, each successive strategy into which this type of operation is embedded contains one additional element. As is indicated in Table 6-1, the sequence may therefore be represented as a series of executive strategies with one extra routine, or "loop," added at each substage.

Table 6-1

Major strategies (and their components) at each substage of means-end development

Sub-stage	Strategy observed	Component of strategy for which an independent subroutine is required
1	Hand directed to given point under voluntary rather than reflexive control	(1) Direct action of hand to A
2	Hand used to produce a desired visual or auditory event	(1) Direct action of hand to A (2) Monitor reaction of environment at A
3	Hand used to eliminate a barrier to obtaining an object	(1) Direct action of hand to A (2) Monitor environment at A (3) Monitor environment at B*
4	Hand used in novel fashion to obtain distant object	(1) Direct (or anticipate) action X of hand (2) Direct (or anticipate) action Y of hand (3) Monitor (or anticipate) movement at A (4) Monitor (or anticipate) movement at B

*Once object at B is available, it is obtained by recursive application of subroutine 1.

Given that this sort of "loop addition" constitutes an adequate characterization of the nature of the developmental change that takes place as the infant proceeds from substage to substage, the question as to how this addition occurs naturally arises. It seems to me that the addition could actually occur in a variety of different ways.

1. The child might be executing an existing routine (reaching) and discover that the expected goal (attaining an object) was not reached. After searching for the reason the expectation was violated, the child might experiment with possible ways to deal with whatever feature was seen as being problematic. This could occur prior to being placed in a Piagetian task situation, or it could occur in the actual course of confronting a Piagetian task. In either case, the process could be characterized as one of active *problem solving*.

2. The child might be executing some existing routine (swiping at a nearby object) and discover that it had an unanticipated consequence (making a more distant object attainable). The next time this newly noticed consequence was desired as a goal state, the previously unrelated routine would be incorporated into the strategy for attaining it. In effect, then, the new strategy would be a natural consequence of *exploration*.

3. Finally, the child might notice that some feature of the environment changed in some way on its own and that an interesting consequence resulted. For example, after seeing a barrier fall over, the child might observe that another object was now easily in reach. Alternatively, the child might see someone else remove a barrier to attain another object. When next in a similar situation, the child would attempt to produce the same sort of sequence. In effect, then, the new strategy would be a natural consequence of *observation*.

Regardless of which of these processes is responsible for producing the addition of a new component to a previously existing strategy, it seems clear that the infant's active attention would have to be involved. Stated differently, it seems clear that the components to be assembled into a new strategy would have to be present in the infant's central processing space simultaneously (Hebb 1949, Pascual-Leone 1977). This being the case, it becomes possible to suggest a number of factors, both general and specific, that could exert an effect on the process.

Strategic Evolution: The General Developmental Hypothesis

If the execution of a visual scanning operation wiped out any trace of a previous swiping operation, an infant clearly could not progress from substage 1 to substage 2, no matter what sort of experience was encountered. Similarly, if focusing on and reaching for a barrier took up a child's entire attention and wiped out any trace of having previously focused on the goal object, it would be difficult for that child to progress from substage 2 to substage 3. Yet young infants' short-term storage space (STS) reveals precisely this sort of limitation (Watson 1967). One factor that might exert an effect on the pace of infants' development, then, is the rate of growth in their capacity for short-term storage (Watson 1967, Bruner 1968, Bower 1974, Pascual-Leone personal communication). On the basis of detailed analysis of some seven to eight tasks, my hypothesis is that infants are capable of storing the trace of only one sensorimotor operation in the age range from one to four months, but that they can store two in the age range from four to eight months, three in the age range from eight to twelve months, and four in the age range from twelve to eighteen months. Stated differently, my hypothesis is that infants' sensorimotor STS is one at one to four months, two at four to eight months, three at eight to twelve months, and four at twelve to eighteen months (Case 1979). For present purposes, the exact values are not important. What is important is the notion that specific changes in children's sensorimotor strategies are dependent on the prior occurrence of a very general change, namely, a change in the infants' capacity for short-term storage.

Strategic Evolution: The Specific Experiential Hypothesis

The existence of a short-term storage space of two is obviously not sufficient for an infant to discover that swiping at a mobile produces interesting visual results. Nor is the existence of a short-term storage space of three sufficient for an infant to discover that swiping at a barrier produces a spatial reaction that then permits the object behind it to be reached. In addition to the prerequisite short-term storage space, the infant must have some experience with the task in question. Since experience can only have an effect insofar as it relates to schemes or strategies already in the infants' repertory, however, and insofar as these schemes are actively attended to, at least three different sorts of experiential influence can be isolated.

The first source of experiential influence is the match between the task to which the child is exposed and the child's current level of development. In an extremely disorganized environment, the arrangement of tasks is left to chance, with very few tasks matching the child's current level of functioning and with no easy pattern of progression being possible from one task to the next. In an extremely organized environment, such as a school, the arrangement of these tasks is geared to the child's existing level and is arranged in ascending order of difficulty.

The second source of experiential influence is the frequency with which the type of task in question occurs in the infant's environment. The higher this frequency, the greater the probability that the infant will go through one of the above-mentioned processes (problem solving, exploration, observation). Furthermore, the greater the frequency of the experience, the greater the probability the child will attend to the appropriate elements, make the appropriate connection between or among them, and consolidate this connection.

The third source of experiential influence is the emotional, perceptual, or habitually acquired salience of the cues in the task situation to which the child is exposed. For example, children will be more likely to acquire a strategy for barrier removal (a) if the goal object is highly desirable, (b) if it is plainly visible behind the barrier, and (c) if the barrier is of the same size and shape as objects that they have already learned to swipe at (or had seen others swipe at).

Changes During the Stage of Representational Operations. During the years from one to five, children pass through another series of substages in which their strategies become more complex and powerful. The operations employed in these strategies differ fundamentally from those of the earlier strategies. In Piagetian terms, they tend to be symbolic or "representational" rather than sensorimotor. In spite of this obvious difference, however, there is a remarkable similarity in both the sequence of substages and in the type of process that must be postulated in order to explain the transition from one substage to the next. Consider, for example, how children's performance changes on the task of communicating with adults via speech.

Substage 1: Operational Consolidation (one to one and one-half years). Somewhere soon after their first birthday, children begin to consolidate their first linguistic operations. They begin to isolate frequently heard and pragmatically relevant words from the stream of language to which they are exposed and repeat them. They also begin to use these words to request objects or actions they enjoy or to draw other's attention to events they find interesting. As yet, however, they show no indication of combining words into phrases or sentences.

Substage 2: Operational Coordination (one and one-half to two years). As they approach their second birthday, children enter the "two-word" substage. If they are asked to repeat pairs of words, such as "Daddy come," they can do so. In generating requests or comments, they speak in similar sentences. As yet, however, they neither generate nor can repeat sentences with subject, verb, and object.

Substage 3: Birelational Coordination (2 years). The two-word substage does not last long. Children soon master more differentiated patterns or "frames" that refer to objects or actions ("the little boy," "wanna go"). They also combine these into sentences involving a subject, verb, and object. As Bever (1970) has pointed out, this is also the age when children start misinterpreting more complex sentences by imposing a subject-verb-object pattern on them.

Substage 4: Reciprocal Coordination (four to five years). During the fourth substage, children can encode and repeat sentences having several fully differentiated linguistic frames arranged in the conventional subject-verb-object pattern, even those with a modifier frame attached. A sentence repetition item that appears on the Stanford Binet, for example, is "Jack likes to feed the little puppies in the barn." Children also speak in sentences of similar complexity.

There is a clear parallel between the above sequence of substages and that observed during infancy. The basic type of operation (linguistic encoding or decoding) remains the same. At each successive substage, however, the child becomes capable of using this type of operation in a linguistic performance that takes account of some new cognitive element and incorporates a new linguistic "loop" for dealing with it. The parallel in the loop sequence is illustrated in Table 6-2. Given the parallel in the sequence of underlying strategies, it seems likely that there is a parallel in the underlying factors that regulate the child's progress through the sequence. That is, it seems likely that the more complex structures are built up by some combination of problem solving, exploration, and observation, and that both general-

Table 6-2

Major strategies (and their components) at
each substage of linguistic development

Sub-stage	Strategy	Components of strategy for which an independent subroutine or "loop" is required
1	Label object (or action) of greatest interest	(1) Generate appropriate vocalization for object (or action)
2	Label object and action of interest	(1) Generate vocalization for action (2) Generate vocalization for object
3	Label object, action, actor of interest	(1) Generate vocalization for actor (2) Generate vocalization for action (3) Generate vocalization for object
4	Label object, action, subject, and modifier	(1) Generate vocalization for actor (2) Generate vocalization for action (3) Generate vocalization for object (4) Generate vocalization for modifier or indirect object

developmental and specific-experiential factors regulate the rate of development.

On the general-developmental side, as a number of psycholinguists have noted, further growth of short-term memory is very probably a prerequisite for discovering and utilizing each of the linguistic constructions appearing in this period (Bates 1976, Slobin 1973). Although there is no standard procedure for segmenting sentences and counting their memory demands, segmentation may proceed according to the frame analysis proposed by Halliday and utilized by Winograd in his computer simulation of natural language comprehension (Winograd 1972). If this is the case, and if one unit of short-term memory is necessary to store each frame, then the absolute numerical progression across substages is also the same as on the means-ends task. The demand for segmenting and reproducing at the first level is one; at the second level it is two; at the third level it is three; and at the fourth level it is four.

Given that the required short-term memory is available, the children's development of any given representational structure should still depend on the specific experience to which they are exposed.

Once again, one would expect that the amount of exposure to the particular structure, the salience value of the relevant cues (emotional, perceptual, habitual), and the match of tasks to current developmental level would all exert an effect on the sequence and the pace of the children's development.

Changes During the Stage of Concrete Operations. During the age range from four to eleven, children again go through a number of qualitatively distinct substages in which their thinking becomes increasingly complex and powerful. The operations that their intellectual strategies entail are fundamentally different from those entailed in simply generating or responding to speech. In spite of this obvious difference, however, there is once again a remarkable similarity both in the observed sequence of substages and in the type of process that presumably underlies this sequence. Consider, for example, how children's strategies change on a task designed by Noelting (1975). In Noelting's task, children are shown two large pitchers, *A* and *B*. The experimenter explains that he is going to dump several tumblers of orange juice and several tumblers of water into each. The children's task is to predict which pitcher will taste more strongly of orange juice.

Substage 1: Operational Consolidation (three to four years). By the age of three or four, children are usually capable of counting a small array of objects. However, they do not use this capability in Noelting's task to compare the two arrays. Instead, they evaluate each array in isolation, noticing only the presence or absence of juice (or occasionally "how much," if either side has a very large number).

Substage 2: Operational Coordination (four and one-half to six years). During the second substage, children notice not only the presence or absence of juice on each side but also the precise quantity of juice. That is, they begin to use their counting routine for comparing the amount of juice on each side. Their strategy is to pick the side with the greater number of juice tumblers and say it will taste more strongly of juice.

Substage 3: Birelational Coordination (seven to eight years). At the next substage, children notice the number of water tumblers on each side as well as the number of juice tumblers. If the number of orange juice tumblers is equal, they count the number of water tumblers on each side and pick the side having less water. If both sides have an equal number of water tumblers they base their decision on the amount of juice.

Substage 4: Reciprocal Coordination (nine to ten years). By age nine, children notice the extent of the excess or deficit of juice over water on each side and make their decision on this basis. They therefore succeed on any item where the correct answer may be obtained by determining which side has the greater excess of juice over water. They continue to fail, however, on all other items.

Once again, there would appear to be a definite parallel between the sequence of substages in Noelting's task and the sequence of substages in the sentence-generation and means-ends tasks. The basic type of operation at each substage remains the same (counting). However, each successive strategy into which this operation is embedded takes account of some additional feature of the array of tumblers and incorporates some additional procedure for dealing with it. In short, as is illustrated in Table 6-3, each successive strategy incorporates one additional "loop."

Table 6-3

Major strategies (and their components) at each substage of concrete development on Noelting's task

Sub-stage	Strategy	Components of strategy for which an independent subroutine or "loop" is required
1	Count number of orange juice tumblers in isolation	(1) Count orange juice A
2	Compare quantity of orange juice in array A to quantity in array B	(1) Count orange juice A (2) Count orange juice B
3	Compare quantity of water in array A to quantity in array B, providing quantity of orange juice on each side is equal	(1) Note equality of orange juice A and orange juice B* (2) Count water A (3) Count water B
4	Compare quantity of orange juice in A to quantity in B, do same for quantity of water; make decision on basis of most salient difference	(1) Count orange juice A (2) Count orange juice B (3) Count water A (4) Count water B

*While this was actually being computed, two subroutines would be necessary (if arrays were large). Once computed, it could be stored as single unit.

Given the parallel in sequence, there is very probably a parallel in the underlying process that propels children through the sequence. It seems likely that higher-order strategies are assembled by active attention in the course of problem solving, exploration, or observation to the elements from which they are composed. It also seems likely that children's progress is influenced by the same general-developmental and specific-experiential factors.

On the general-developmental side, if one counts the number of items that must be held in memory to execute Noelting's strategies, one notices the same progression as during previous stages. For the simplest strategy, the operation of counting can be executed in isolation. For the second strategy, the product of one counting operation must be stored while a second is executed. For the third strategy, two items must be stored; while the subject is counting the number of orange juice tumblers in B, she must store both the number of water tumblers in B and some information regarding the relative amounts of each substance in A. Finally, for the fourth strategy, an additional item must be stored, namely the exact quantity of the difference between orange juice and water in A (Case 1978a).

Changes During the Stage of Formal Operations. The nature of the development that occurs during the stage of formal operations is probably less well understood than that which occurs during any other stage. Nevertheless, if Noelting's task is at all representative, it seems likely that children may once again go through a series of distinct substages in which the type of operation is qualitatively different but in which the underlying process is the same. Consider the strategies observed in Noelting's juice-making task in the age range from nine to eighteen.

Substage 1: Operational Consolidation (nine to ten years). By the age of nine or ten, children in Western societies are normally capable of understanding and computing a simple ratio. They do not, however, use this newly consolidated operation to compare side A with side B. Instead, they consider each side in isolation and classify each side as having more, less, or the same amount of juice as water (see substage 4, concrete operations).

Substage 2: Operational Coordination (eleven to twelve years). During the second substage, children do use their understanding of ratio to compare side A with side B. If the two ratios are equal, they respond that both sides will taste the same. If the two ratios are clearly unequal (2/4 versus 3/4, or 1/4 versus 1/3), they also respond appropriately. If the two ratios are not directly comparable (1/3 versus 4/9), they fall back on the most sophisticated concrete operational strategy, namely, computing the difference between the number of juice and water tumblers on each side.

Substage 3: Birelational Coordination (thirteen to fifteen years). During the third substage, children take the relationship between the two denominators into account as well. Thus, if the two ratios are not directly comparable, they compute the factorial relationship between them and use this factor to put the two ratios in a comparable form. For example, if the two original ratios are 1/3 and 4/6, they notice that 6 = 3 x 2, and they convert the 1/3 to 2/6. They then compare 2/6 with 4/6 and answer appropriately.

Substage 4: Reciprocal Coordination (fifteen to eighteen years). At the final substage, children become capable of solving the problem even when the relationship between the two denominators is not a simple factorial one. First, they multiply the first ratio by the denominator of the second ratio, thus generating a new fraction as in the previous substage. They then repeat this operation in reverse, multiplying the second ratio by the denominator of the first ratio and obtaining a second new fraction. Finally, they compare the two new fractions and respond accordingly.

The sequence of strategies children employ is listed in outline form in Table 6-4. As may be seen, the basic operation at each substage remains the same (ratio). At each successive substage, however, children take account of some additional feature of the problem and incorporate a new step or set of steps for dealing with it. Given this fact, it seems likely that the incorporation of new elements must again be mediated by attention (via problem solving, exploration, and observation) and that a growth in the span of attention (that is, short-term storage space) as well as specific experience with ratio problems influences the child's rate of progress through the stages.

So far, I have analyzed a task from each of Piaget's stages to make four simple yet central points: (a) as children progress through each stage, they pass through a sequence of substages in which the basic operations of which they are capable become embedded in strategies of increasing complexity; (b) the addition of a new element or "loop" to a strategy requires the active mediation of the child's attention; (c) a general requirement for substage transition is an increase in the

Table 6-4

Major strategies (and their components) at each
substage of formal development on Noelting's task

Sub-stage	Strategy	Major components for which an independent subroutine or "loop" is required
1	Compute ratio of array only in isolation	(1) Compute ratio: A/B
2	Compare ratio of orange juice to water in A, with that of orange juice to water in B (if possible)	(1) Compute ratio orange juice A/water A (2) Compare ratio orange juice B/water B
3	Convert ratio in B to simplest form; compare to ratio in A	(1) Compute ratio orange juice A/water A (2) Compute ratio orange juice B/water B (3) Convert ratio orange juice B/water B to comparable form (which requires computing ratio water A/water B)
4	Convert ratio to lowest common denominator (LCD); compare	(1) Compute ratio orange juice A/water A (2) Compute ratio orange juice B/water B (3) Convert ratio A to LCD (which requires multiplying by water B) (4) Convert ratio B to LCD (which requires multiplying by water A)

span of attention or short-term storage space; (d) a specific requirement for stage transition is exposure to the situation, with the rate
of transition being affected by the frequency, cue salience, and developmental match of the task to the child's current level.

I turn now to a consideration of two further points: how it is that
short-term memory increases within any given stage and how it is
that children make the transition from one major stage to the next.

Developmental Changes in Short-term Memory

As the reader will no doubt have noted, I have proposed four
different short-term memory scales, each of which shows a similar
growth curve and each of which is presumed to exert a similar influence on strategic development. A question as to what underlying
process is responsible for this pattern of cyclic growth naturally
arises. My explanation is as follows. The total processing space that a
subject has available at any one time may be divided into two com-

ponents: space that must be devoted to executing basic operations and space that is available for short-term storage. Symbolically, this may be represented as follows:

$$TPS = OPS + STS$$

where TPS equals total central processing space or total attentional resources; OPS equals the space required for executing basic operations (operating space); and STS equals the space left over for storing the products of these operations for short periods of time (short-term storage space).

My working hypothesis is that the total processing space does not change with age. What changes is the amount of that space required for operating and, consequently, the amount that is left over for short-term storage. When any new operation is first assembled, whether it be reaching, verbal labeling, counting, or calculating ratios, its execution takes virtually the entire processing space the subject has available. As a consequence, very little space is left over for short-term storage. With time, the execution of this operation becomes more efficient, and more space becomes available for short-term storage as a result.

To say that total processing space does not change with age is not to belie the importance of the changes in STS that do take place. It is simply to push the chain of explanation back one step. Just as the increasing sophistication of children's executive strategies within any stage may be partially explained by postulating an increasing STS, so the increasing STS may be partially explained by postulating a decreasing demand on OPS due to increased operational efficiency.

As soon as one postulates that the underlying mechanism of STS development is a gradual change in operational efficiency, two further questions naturally arise. The first is whether this change is due to the same type of reorganization as that occurring with higher-order strategies. The second is whether the change is due to maturation or experience. With regard to the first question, my belief is that changes in operational efficiency are not due to the same type of reorganization that may be observed in executive strategies. Unlike changes in executive strategies, changes in operational efficiency yield smooth growth curves within individual subjects (Kurland in preparation). Every month there is a tiny but measurable change.

By contrast, strategic efficiency stays relatively constant for long periods of time and then undergoes a relatively rapid change as some new component is added or rearranged. It thus seems unlikely that any of the reorganizational processes that have been proposed to explain strategic change (Neches and Hayes 1978) can be invoked to explain changes in operational efficiency.

With regard to the second question, I believe that, whatever the underlying basis of operational change, the change is dependent primarily on maturation; that is, it is relatively independent of any specific experience. I believe that gradual neurological changes produce gradual changes in the maximum efficiency with which basic operations can be executed. A certain amount of practice is then necessary to insure maximum utilization of this potential. Even massive practice, however, will not enable the system to transcend this potential. One possible neurological factor that might be responsible for producing content-free changes in operational efficiency is the amount of myelin surrounding the neurons in the brain. As children mature, a fatty sheath, referred to as myelin, accumulates around these neurons. The build-up of this sheath affects the conductance properties of the nervous tissue. Transmission occurs more rapidly and in a more insulated fashion (Tasaki 1953). The increased insulation presumably causes a decrease in interference with the (electrochemical) record of previous transmission, thus producing an increase in the effective short-term storage capacity of the system. At the same time, it produces an increase in operational speed.

A gradual change in the degree of myelinization is not necessarily the only neurological change that would produce a concomitant change in both operational efficiency and measured STS. Nevertheless, it is clearly one such change, and the fact that it occurs relatively independently of experience serves to lend plausibility to the hypothesis that biologically regulated changes set a limit on the rate of intellectual growth by regulating the rate of change in operational efficiency.

Developmental Changes in Basic Operations

So far I have spoken primarily of developmental changes *within* stages. What about developmental changes *across* stages? Several questions are of interest with regard to cross-stage development. The first is how best to characterize the qualitative difference among the four types of basic operations. The second is how to account for the fact that the sequence of these operations is invariant. The third is how to account for the fact that the approximate timing of operational emergence is relatively invariant across cultures (at least for the first three classes of operation).

Qualitative Differences in Basic Operations. In discussing the achievements of each stage, I have spoken as though the differences between the underlying operations (sensorimotor, representational, concrete operational, and formal operational) were obvious. In fact, although their labels represent rather "natural" categories, they suffer from the same disadvantage as all such terms. The entities they represent are relatively easy to recognize but not to define and not even to discriminate once the examples are not prototypic. For the moment, the best definition I can offer is that a sensorimotor operation is one whose releasing component is some sort of sensory input and whose effecting component is a physical movement, such as reaching. A representational operation is one whose releasing component is a set of sensory inputs and physical movements and whose effecting component is a symbol, such as a word. A "concrete" operation is one whose releasing component is a set of sensory inputs, physical movements, and symbols and whose effecting component is a second-order symbol, such as a number. Finally, a formal operation is one whose releasing component is a set of sensory inputs, movements, and first- and second-order symbols and whose effecting component is a third-order symbol, such as a fraction. Note that these definitions imply a hierarchical relationship of the same sort as postulated by Piaget. It is this relationship that provides an answer to the question concerning the invariant sequence of operational emergence.

The Sequence of Operational Emergence. Given that the basic operations of one level are built on the basic operations of the previous level, it is clear that their emergence cannot begin until the previous operations are established. If $A \supset B$, then A cannot possibly emerge before B for purely logical reasons. The hierarchical organization of basic operations does not, however, explain the timing of their emergence. The first sensorimotor operations are observed at one to four months, yet the first representational operations are not observed until twelve to eighteen months, and the first concrete operations not until four years. Why is this so? An answer to this question depends on examining the specific antecedents of each class of operation and the constraints on the assembly process.

The Timing of Operational Emergence. Bates (1976) has suggested what sorts of prior understanding may be necessary for the emergence of the first verbal-representational operations. She contends that the first use of a word to accomplish an end (that is, the imperative use) depends on the realization that one object can be used to obtain another, which is not attained until the final substage of the sensorimotor period. Translating this suggestion into the sort of terminology used in the first section, one could say that the infant would have to coordinate a set of sensorimotor schemes such as the following in order to master the imperative use of language: (a) a scheme representing the desired object; (b) a scheme representing the desired instrument (the adult); (c) a scheme representing the desired action; and (d) a scheme representing the vocalization which will produce that action. Since the capacity to coordinate four sensorimotor schemes does not emerge until the age of twelve to eighteen months, one would not expect the first use of the imperative until that time.

A similar sort of hypothesis may be advanced with regard to the assembly of the first concrete operations. Consider the basic operation underlying the concrete strategies in Noelting's task—counting. Granted that even two-year-olds have some understanding of counting (Gelman 1978), a certain functional storage space may still be necessary for counting in adult fashion. One unit of space may be required to monitor the set of objects just counted, one to monitor the next object to be counted, one to monitor the number just said, and one to monitor the number about to be said. Since a functional storage space of four units is not attained during the representational period until age four or five, this might help to explain why accurate counting is rarely observed prior to this age. It might also explain why children do not progress through Noelting's series of strategies until that time.

Finally, a similar sort of contingency may be present at the transition point from concrete to formal operations. In order to understand or compute a simple ratio (6/2 = 3/1), children might have to be able to compute and store each of the terms involved in some concrete situation. For example, they might have to be able to count out six apples and count out three people. They might then have to note that when the apples are divided among the people, each person receives two apples. This would presumably require a short-term storage of at least three and probably four. Since a short-term storage space of this size is not normally available while executing a counting operation until the age of nine or ten, this would help explain why the teaching of the ratio operation is not normally successful until grades four or five and the teaching of strategies requiring ratio comparison not until grades six or seven.

In summary, then, if one assumes that higher-order operations are constructed from the products of lower-order operations and, further, that the assembly process entails the coordination of these products in STS, one can explain both the invariant sequence and the timing of operational development. The pace of both changes is regulated by the same sort of slowly occurring operational change, namely, a change in operational efficiency. The only possible difference is that the efficiency of each level of operation may well be controlled by maturational changes in a distinct functional system of the brain. Transition to the next level in a normal fashion may then depend *both* on sufficient maturation of the lower-order system and on the onset of maturation in the higher-order system.

My exposition of the basic postulates of my theory is now complete. In summary, I have proposed (a) that children pass through a series of four general stages, each of which is characterized by the emergence of a different type of operation; (b) that within each stage, children's strategies for using the type of operation in question become increasingly complex; (c) that the major prerequisite for this increase in strategic complexity is the children's active attention to the events in their environment (via problem solving, exploration, or observation); (d) that as a consequence, any specific factor that affects the frequency, salience, or developmental match of event sequences will affect the rate of strategic development; (e) that, as a further consequence, any general factor which affects the span of attention (short-term storage) will also affect the rate of strategic development; (f) that one such general change is a change in operational efficiency; (g) that the emergence of high-level operations is dependent on the emergence both of lower-level operations and of the processing space necessary for coordinating several of these operations simultaneously. I turn now to a review of the empirical data bearing on each of these postulates.

REVIEW OF RELEVANT EMPIRICAL EVIDENCE

Four Basic Types of Operation

From a sociological point of view, there is little disagreement that children's growth can be divided into four stages. Cultures around the world acknowledge the existence of a major transition in development at about the age of five (White 1970), as well as the more obvious transitions that occur with the acquisition of language and the onset of puberty. Neuropsychological data are also congruent with this assertion. They show that sensorimotor, representational, and higher-order processes involve different functional neural systems and that lesions which disturb one system do not necessarily disturb the others. They also show that the major biological change in each system occurs during a different developmental period (Luria 1973, Yakovlev and Lecours 1967). Finally, although the evidence is by no means strong, data on the growth of intelligence are at least congruent with this assertion as well. They show a gradual increase with age in the correlation of child intelligence and adult intelligence, with the increase appearing to occur in steps. The breaks in the curves appear to occur at approximately ages one and one half, five, and eleven (Bloom 1964). Although the available evidence is by no means conclusive, it is broadly compatible with the hypothesis. There appear to be at least three and perhaps four classes of intellectual operations that emerge in an invariant developmental sequence and that permit the development of a similar number of distinct classes of intellectual strategy.

Before proceeding, it is worthwhile to mention two kinds of evidence *not* directly relevant to the first postulate. The first is evidence that children do not acquire all the operations of a given period at exactly the same time (Brainerd 1973). The second is evidence that developmental precursors of any given operation can be found at much earlier ages than the normally cited age of emergence (Gelman 1972, 1978). While these data are difficult to reconcile with the sort of extreme stage hypothesis often imputed to Piaget, they are completely compatible with the form of stage hypothesis advanced in the present theory. In fact, with the development of appropriate measurement techniques, the present theory should be able to predict decalage in operational emergence (due to differences in operational efficiency and/or difficulty), as well as the age of mastery of developmental precursors of any operation (due to reductions in the STS demand of the assembly process).

Increasing Within-Stage Complexity of Intellectual Strategies

Data on strategic development are not yet available for all the major stages mentioned above. At least for the concrete operational stage, however, the validity of the second postulate seems undeniable. Siegler has now conducted detailed investigations of about ten different Piagetian tasks. For each of these, he has hypothesized the existence of an underlying sequence of strategies such as that described by Noelting. For each task, he has also invented a new set of problems to test the hypothesis. Finally, for each of the problem sets, he has found that the predictions are strongly confirmed (Siegler 1978). One of the merits of Siegler's approach is that it permits predictions to be made not only about developmental progressions but also about developmental regressions as well.

Equivalence of Different Attentional Processes in Producing Strategic Development

As mentioned in the introduction, the concept of "equilibration" is not easy to make operational. Nevertheless, to the extent that it is possible to distinguish activities that involve equilibration from those that do not, it appears that such activities are not superior as a developmental process to the various other forms of activity in which attention is actively involved. First, during the years of most rapid intellectual development, children spend a relatively small proportion of their time in any active form of problem solving. The greatest proportion of their time is spent in simply staring at or listening to the events in their environment (B. White 1975). Second, when laboratory studies have been designed to accelerate development by inducing equilibration, they have not produced any higher incidence of development than techniques such as modeling (Zimmerman and Rosenthal 1974), cue highlighting (Gelman 1969), or direct instruction (Case 1974, 1977a). Third, studies on the development of academic skills have repeatedly failed to show an advantage of discovery methods over other methods, whereas studies have shown a consistent and strong effect due to the amount of time spent in active attention (Jackson 1968).

Role of Experience in Fostering Appropriate Attentional Processes

Three sorts of experiential variables were proposed earlier as being relevant to children's attentional processes and consequently to the rate of their strategic development. These were (a) the naturally occurring frequency of the task in question in the child's environment, (b) the extent to which the relevant cues and responses are made salient when the child is engaged in the task, and (c) the match of the task to the child's current developmental level.

From studies that have included a control for the effect of repeated testing it is apparent that repeated exposure to a task, in and of itself, can have an influence on the level of strategic sophistication a child develops. For sensorimotor, representational, concrete-operational, and formal tasks alike, there is an increase in the percentage of subjects who employ a high-level strategy simply as a function of repeated exposure to the test paradigm (Jackson, Campos, and Fischer 1978, Fowler and Swenson 1979, Strauss and Langer 1970, Case 1974). The importance of frequency as a factor is also borne out by studies that have examined the relationship between ecological event frequency and age of spontaneous strategy acquisition (Price-Williams, Gordon, and Ramirez 1969).

Two sorts of data bear on the role of cue and response salience. First, training studies that have explicitly directed children's attention to task dimensions of relevance or have produced explicit models of how to respond to these cues have tended to have higher success rates than studies not focusing on this dimension (Lefebvre and Pinard 1972, Gelman 1969, Zimmerman and Rosenthal 1974). Second, in one study where cue salience was varied directly, there was an increasing percentage of successes across the treatments that made the relevant dimensions increasingly salient (Case 1977a).

Finally, three sorts of evidence are of relevance to the hypothesis that the match of the task presented to the child's current developmental level is important. First, training studies that have included an assessment of children's initial level of functioning have almost invariably found a relationship between this level and the children's responsiveness to instruction (Strauss and Langer 1970, Inhelder, Sinclair, and Bovet 1974). Second, studies that have geared the treatment to the level of the subject have produced strong results. In one such study, Siegler worked with a group of subjects who had not yet come to focus on the relevant dimension of a particular task. He found that if training in the strategy was preceded by training in focusing on the relevant dimension, the subjects developed the strategy. However, when such training was not included, they did not develop the strategy. For subjects who were already focusing on the relevant dimensions, Siegler also found that the preliminary training was not necessary (Siegler 1978). A third source of evidence comes from the literature on instruction. For some time, instructional theorists have stressed the importance of assessing a child's initial level and of carefully sequencing and grading the tasks presented (Gagné 1970). Studies that have compared this approach to less carefully planned approaches have invariably shown a larger and significant difference (Case 1978b). While other experiential variables might also be of relevance, it would appear that event frequency, cue and response salience, and developmental match all constitute important sources of influence on the rate and course of a child's strategic development.

Importance of STS in Limiting the Effectiveness of Experience

Three types of evidence indicate that STS growth plays a role in limiting the extent to which children can make use of the specific experience to which they are exposed. Tests designed to measure STS growth show the same norms as revealed by the task analysis. The first of these tests to be developed was a visually presented task in which a set of simple stimuli had to be detected in a compound stimulus (Pascual-Leone 1970). This test was criticized on both theoretical and methodological grounds (Trabasso and Foellinger 1977). However, subsequent versions of the test, which eliminated the methodological difficulties, revealed essentially the same norms (Pulos 1979). In addition, a model of the test that had greater intuitive validity suggested the same STS values (Case and Serlin 1979). Since the original development of the test, seven other STS tests have been developed using different content and different but equally difficult operations. The norms they reveal are essentially the same as Pascual-Leone originally hypothesized (Case 1972, Burtis 1974, Biemiller, Boychuck, and Rochford 1979, DeAvila and Havassy 1974, Diaz 1974, Case and Kurland 1978).

The tests of STS mentioned above have been administered together with Piagetian tasks, and they show substantial correlations with them, even with the effects of age partialled out statistically

(Parkinson 1976, Case 1977b, Lawson 1976, Pulos 1979).

Children who are at strategy level X and who are exposed to the opportunity for learning strategy X + 1 tend to make the transition only if they have the requisite STS (Case 1972, 1974, 1977a). Again this is true even when age is equated across groups.

In spite of the original criticism (or indeed, perhaps because of it), the evidence with regard to this postulate appears to be strong and compelling. The one caveat to be entered is that the evidence as yet relates only to the concrete operational period. While we have recently begun similar sorts of investigations for the representational period and while the general pattern of results appears to be the same (Case and Kurland in press, Daneman 1977, Case 1979), a fully informed decision on the postulate's validity must await empirical investigation in all four of the hypothesized stages.

Role of Operational Efficiency in Development

Two recent studies are relevant to the operational-efficiency hypothesis. In one, children's counting efficiency, as indexed by counting speed, was correlated with their performance in a digit-span paradigm, where counting was the operation by which the digits were input. The results showed a virtually perfect linear relationship between the development of speed and span. Furthermore, when adults' operational efficiency was reduced to that of six-year-olds, by being forced to count in a foreign language, their span was also reduced to that of six-year-olds (Case, Kurland, and Daneman 1979). A formally parallel study has been conducted using younger children and simple word span. Again, the growth of operational efficiency (as indexed by speed of word repetition) and span were virtually perfectly correlated. And when the efficiency of older subjects was reduced to that of three-year-olds, their span was also reduced to that level (Case, Kurland, and Daneman 1979). Both of these studies strongly support the hypothesis of a causal connection between the growth of STS and the growth of operational efficiency.

Role of Maturation in Limiting the Growth of Operational Efficiency

The role of maturation in limiting the growth of operational efficiency can only be established by indirect means, given our current understanding of the biological underpinnings of its development. Nevertheless, the indirect evidence is of considerable interest. First, when the growth of counting efficiency is examined across different cultural contexts, it is found that the growth curves are virtually identical (Kurland in preparation). Either the amount of practice subjects receive in counting is remarkably constant across cultures, or the increase in operational efficiency is under maturational control.

In a study designed to test which of these two possibilities was correct, Kurland (in preparation) exposed a group of first-grade children to massive practice in counting. The children counted one hundred arrays of dots every school day for two consecutive months, while a matched control group received no special practice of this sort. At the end of that period, the speed of children's counting was only marginally greater than it had been at the beginning of the period and no greater than that of the control group. By contrast, adults exposed to comparable conditions in a foreign language showed dramatic improvements in counting speed.

Finally, in a study already cited, Yakovlev and Lecours examined the myelinization of different parts of the brain at different points in development. They found that the parts of the brain most likely to be implicated in a process such as counting showed their period of most rapid myelinization during the same period in which counting shows its most rapid improvement and that myelinization is completed at the same time that counting speed reaches its asymptote.

While again not conclusive, the evidence does appear to favor a maturational interpretation. If for some reason a population has not been exposed to any experience with a given operation (adults in a foreign language), then practice can produce relatively rapid improvement. The extent of the improvement will be limited, however, by the maturational ceiling associated with the functional system of the brain that is responsible for controlling the particular operation in question.

Hierarchical Organization of Operations

Luria (1973) has presented clear neuropsychological evidence of hierarchical organization in human intellectual functioning. The form of the evidence is as follows: if children suffer damage in a lower-order neural system, their higher-order systems fail to develop appropriately. If adults suffer the same sort of damage, however, the functioning of their higher-order systems is not impaired. Unfortunately, while extremely impressive, this sort of evidence cannot be mapped directly onto the present hypothesis, since the sorts of operations that Luria tested are not identical with (although they are similar to) those suggested by the present theory. For the moment, the safest conclusion is that the final hypothesis remains unproven. Indeed, it seems likely that before it can be tested adequately, the nature of the operational components and their growth will require further theoretical and empirical clarification.

As I mentioned in the introduction, a major challenge facing developmental psychology in the 1970s has been to evolve a theoretical structure that retains the most important strengths of Piaget's theory, while eliminating its weaknesses. Before turning to a consideration of the educational implications of the theory I have proposed, therefore, I would like to reconsider these strengths and weaknesses.

RELATIONSHIP OF THE NEW THEORY TO PIAGET'S THEORY

Consider first the explanation the theory offers for those aspects of development that Piaget's theory can already explain with reasonable adequacy. The invariant sequence in intellectual development is accounted for in my theory in exactly the same way as it is in Piaget's theory. Operations are presumed to build on each other in a hierarchical fashion, with the result that an invariant developmental sequence is a logical necessity. The similarity of age norms across different content areas is accounted for in my theory in a fashion similar to Piaget's at a formal level but different at the level of the psychological mechanism that is proposed. Piaget believes that tasks passed at a particular age all share certain common logical properties and that the children who pass them all share a common logical structure. I believe that tasks passed at the same age tend to share a similar set of information-processing requirements and that children who pass them tend to share a common information-processing capacity.

Finally, the phenomenon of readiness is accounted for in my theory in a fashion again quite similar to Piaget's at a formal level but different at the level of the psychological mechanism proposed. Piaget believes that children are not ready to master a particular task until the appropriate general logical structure is at least in the process of formation. I believe that children are not ready to master a particular task if the simplest form in which this task could possibly be presented still demands a greater short-term storage space than the children have available (or could be made to have available, with sufficient pretraining on the component operations).

Consider next the aspects of development for which Piaget's theory does not offer a satisfactory explanation. The existence of low correlations among logically similar tasks is difficult to account for within the context of Piaget's theory. Within my theory, the explanation is simple. Although a certain minimum information-processing capacity is a necessary requirement for acquiring a particular competency, it is by no means sufficient. In addition, children need to have a good deal of relevant experience, under affective and perceptual conditions, that encourage them to focus on the aspects of that experience relevant to whatever strategy is being assessed. Given that children vary widely in these other factors, one would not expect the correlations across task domains to be high, even though the age norms (obtained by averaging across subjects) are quite similar.

The existence of wide separations in the age of accession on logically similar tasks (that is, decalage) is difficult to account for within Piaget's theory. Within the context of my theory, several explanations are possible. The tasks that share common logical properties might differ (a) in the load they place on the short-term storage system, (b) in the frequency with which they are encountered in the natural environment, or (c) in the inherent difficulty of the basic operations they employ. Any one of these factors would be expected to produce a reliable decalage across tasks of equivalent logical complexity.

The existence of strong learning effects (that is, learning prior to any evidence of the underlying logical structure) is difficult to explain in the context of Piaget's theory. According to my theory, such learning may be expected under two types of circumstances; (a) where the child has developed the required short-term storage space but has not previously been exposed to the requisite prior experience, or (b) where some way is found of reducing the short-term storage demands of the learning process.

Finally, as I mentioned in the introduction, Piagetian researchers have had difficulty in making the notion of a logical structure operational. They have also had difficulty in specifying in any sort of detail what sort of experiential and maturational factors might affect the course of development or how these factors might interact with the child's equilibrative activity. In my theory, all these difficulties are much less severe. First, the notion of an intellectual strategy, which plays the same formal role as does the logical structure in Piaget's theory, is much easier to specify analytically. It is also much easier to make operational and assess, as the recent work of Siegler (1978) has made clear. Second, in my theory the process of equilibration is relieved of the burden of being the sole developmental mechanism of stage transition. Several possible processes are specified, which share in common only one requirement, namely, that attention be actively employed. It is also much easier to specify what experiential and maturational factors might affect the rate of development. In fact, as mentioned in the previous section, a number of studies have already been conducted in which the interaction of the factors has been specified and successful predictions about their interaction have been generated (Case 1972, 1974, 1977a, 1977b). While not actively at variance with Piagetian theory, these predictions could not have been made on the basis of it.

My theory shares one problem with Piaget's theory, as has been pointed out by Lawson (1976) and Flavell (1978), among others—that of task analysis. Within the context of Piaget's theory, no rules are provided for the logical analysis of tasks. It is thus difficult if not impossible to determine the "logical structure" of a task other than one that has already been analyzed by Piaget. Within the context of my theory, a number of explicit guidelines for task analysis are proposed (Case 1978b). Nevertheless, it is certainly not the case that any two investigators who apply these heuristics will arrive at the same analysis.

On the surface, this is a disadvantage. It means that the analyses presented in the first section of this paper, for example, could be disputed, as could the more detailed and rigorously conducted analyses on which they were based (Case 1979). At a deeper level, however, this is actually an advantage, since I make no claims that these analyses are dependent purely on the logical structure of the task or are in any sense necessarily valid. What any so-called task analysis actually represents is a model of how subjects approach a task. Thus, the strategies proposed, the segmentation of these strategies into steps, and the computation of the minimum number of units that have to be coordinated at any step are actually hypotheses inviting empirical exploration.

I believe that the analyses I have presented provide a reasonable fit to existing empirical data. I also believe, however, that they will have to be modified and refined as further data are gathered. One of the most exciting developments of modern cognitive psychology, in my opinion, has been the development of a technology for precisely this sort of fine-grained empirical investigation. Using appropriate task construction and an analysis of error patterns, decisions can almost invariably be made as to which of several possible strategies a subject is using (Siegler 1978). Using appropriate task construction and reaction time, decisions can also be made as to which of two sequences of steps most adequately model the inner workings of a strategy and what components are involved in these steps (Sternberg 1977). I turn now to a consideration of the educational implications of the theory I have outlined.

IMPLICATIONS FOR INSTRUCTION

Of the various postulates in the theory, the three that have received the most extensive empirical documentation are (a) that children often approach complex intellectual tasks with strategies that are reasonable but oversimplified, (b) that repeated exposure to a task can be helpful in enabling children to use more sophisticated strategies (especially if the experience is matched to their current strategic level and renders salient the aspects of the task they have ignored), and (c) that a major factor limiting children's ability to profit from such experience is the limited capacity of their short-term storage system.

In modern industrial society, school is of course one of the primary life situations in which children encounter complex intellectual tasks. Furthermore, one of the explicit objectives of most school curricula is to provide children with sophisticated strategies for dealing with these tasks. It follows, therefore, that in cases where these objectives are not being met, one of the possible reasons is that children's level of intellectual development has not been adequately taken into account. That is, it follows that, due to the low STS of the subjects in question, they may be approaching the task with an oversimplified strategy, which the curriculum has not been designed to take into account. In situations where this is the case, it also follows that the curriculum can very likely be improved by means of the following four steps.

1. Identify the most common oversimplified strategy utilized by children who are failing the task.
2. Rework the curriculum so that it highlights (a) the inadequacy of this strategy, (b) the features of the task that children are ignoring, and (c) the appropriate procedure for taking these features into account.
3. In designing the instruction, keep the short-term storage demands to a bare minimum.
4. In arranging the sequence of tasks, keep the step size reasonably small, and provide sufficient practice at each step so that the understanding and/or procedure in question can become as automatic as is possible.

I have suggested elsewhere a detailed set of procedures that can be used for accomplishing each of these steps (Case 1978b). I have also summarized the research conducted to date on the effectiveness of these procedures. Like the research related to the developmental theory I have presented, the evidence is by no means complete. Nevertheless, when compared against the curricula currently in force, curricula designed according to the set of procedures I have described have tended to produce rather dramatic improvements in learning. On the average, the success rates have been 70 to 80 percent as opposed to 20 to 30 percent for the conventional curricula. These differences raise the possibility that a developmental approach to instruction might be fruitful, even in areas where current methods appear to be reasonably successful already. The core of such an approach would be to examine children's responses across grade levels for evidence of a developmental progression such as that described in the Noelting juice problem. If such a sequence were identified, then instruction might be improved by making this progression explicit in the curriculum and bringing children up through it. A start toward this sort of approach in the area of reading has already been made by Marsh and his colleagues (Marsh et al. in press).

SUMMARY AND CONCLUSION

In summary, it seems reasonable to conclude that progress is being made in solving the theoretical problems posed by Piaget's theory without sacrificing the advantages offered by its breadth and comprehensiveness. It also seems reasonable to conclude that, as these problems are solved, the potential relevance of developmental psychology to education will become increasingly apparent. Presumably the next decade will bring a considerable improvement both in our theoretical understanding of intellectual development and in our practical understanding of how to make children's learning optimal at each stage. Hopefully, researchers in each area will follow each other's progress closely, so that cross fertilization will occur and progress in all areas will be as rapid and fruitful as possible.

REFERENCES

Bates, Elizabeth. *Language and Context: The Acquisition of Pragmatics.* New York: Academic Press, 1976.

Beilin, Harry. "Developmental Stages and Developmental Processes." In *Measurement and Piaget,* edited by Donald R. Green, Marguerite P. Ford, and George B. Flamer, pp. 172-89. New York: McGraw-Hill, 1971.

Bever, Thomas G. "The Cognitive Basis for Linguistic Structures." In *Cognition and the Development of Language,* edited by John R. Hayes, pp. 279-362. New York: John Wiley, 1970.

Biemiller, Andrew; Boychuk, Linda; and Rochford, M. "A New Measure of M-Space." Unpublished manuscript, University of Toronto, Institute of Child Study, 1979.

Bloom, Benjamin S. *Stability and Change in Human Characteristics.* New York: John Wiley, 1964.

Bower, Thomas G. R. *Development in Infancy.* San Francisco: W.H. Freeman, 1974.

Brainerd, Charles J. "Neo-Piagetian Training Experiments Revisited: Is There Any Support for the Cognitive-Developmental Stage Hypothesis?" *Cognition* 2, 3(1973): 349-70.

Bruner, Jerome S. *Processes of Growth: Infancy.* Worcester, Mass: Clark University Press, 1968.

Burtis, P.J. "Two Applications of Measurement Theory in Developmental Psychology." Unpublished manuscript, York University, 1974.

Case, Robbie. "Difficulties Encountered by Disadvantaged Children in Solving a Visually Represented Problem." Master's thesis, University of Toronto, 1968.

―――. "Validation of a Neo-Piagetian Mental Capacity Construct." *Journal of Experimental Child Psychology* 14 (October 1972): 287-302.

―――. "Structures and Strictures: Some Functional Limitations on the Course of Cognitive Growth." *Cognitive Psychology* 6 (October 1974): 544-73.

―――. "The Process of Stage Transition in Cognitive Development." Final Report, Project #R01HD09148-01 NIMHCD, 1977(a).

―――. "Responsiveness to Conservation Training as a Function of Induced Subjective Uncertainty, *M*-Space, and Cognitive Style." *Canadian Journal of Behavioural Science* 9 (January 1977b): 12-26.

————. "Intellectual Development from Birth to Adulthood: A Neo-Piagetian Interpretation." In *Children's Thinking: What Develops?* edited by Robert Siegler, pp. 37-71. Hillsdale, N.J.: Lawrence Erlbaum Associates, 1978(a).

————. "A Developmentally Based Theory and Technology of Instruction." *Review of Educational Research* 48 (Summer 1978b): 439-63.

————. "The Development of Sensorimotor Strategies in Infancy." Unpublished manuscript, Ontario Institute for Studies in Education, 1979.

Case, Robbie, and Kurland, D. Midian. "Construction and Validation of a New Test of Children's M-Space." Unpublished manuscript, Ontario Institute for Studies in Education, 1978.

————. "A New Measure for Determining Children's Subjective Organization of Speech." *Journal of Experimental Child Psychology*, in press.

Case, Robbie et al. "Operational Efficiency and the Growth of M-Space." Paper presented at the Biennial Meeting of the Society for Research in Child Development, San Francisco, 1979.

Case, Robbie, and Serlin, Ronald. "A New Processing Model for Predicting Performance on Pascual-Leone's Test of M-Space." *Cognitive Psychology* 11 (July 1979): 308-26.

Daneman, Meredyth. "An Experimental Paradigm to Explore the Cognitive Prerequisitions, both Semantic and Formal, for the Development of Language." Master's thesis, University of Toronto, 1977.

DeAvila, Edward A., and Havassy, B. *Intelligence of Mexican-American Children.* Austin, Texas: Dissemination Center for Bilingual and Bicultural Education, 1974.

Diaz, S. *Cucui Scale: Technical Manual. Multilingual Assessment Program.* Stockton, Calif: Stockton Unified School District, 1974.

Flavell, John H. *The Developmental Psychology of Jean Piaget.* Princeton, N.J.: D. Van Nostrand Co., 1963.

————. "Comments on Case's Paper." In *Children's Thinking: What Develops?* edited by Robert S. Siegler, pp. 99-102. Hillsdale, N.J.: Lawrence Erlbaum Associates, 1978.

Fowler, William, and Swenson, Amy. "The Influence of Early Language Stimulation on Development: Four Studies." *Genetic Psychology Monographs* 100 (August 1979): 73-109.

Gagné, Robert M. *The Conditions of Learning.* 2d ed. New York: Holt, Rinehart and Winston, 1970.

Gelman, Rochel. "Conservation Acquisition: A Problem of Learning to Attend to Relevant Attributes." *Journal of Experimental Child Psychology* 7 (April, 1969): 167-87.

————. "Logical Capacity of Very Young Children: Number Invariance Rules." *Child Development* 43 (March 1972): 75-90.

————. "Counting in the Preschooler: An Analysis of What Does and Does Not Develop." In *Children's Thinking: What Develops?* edited by Robert S. Siegler, pp. 213-241. Hillsdale, N.J.: Lawrence Erlbaum Associates, 1978.

Ginsburg, Herbert, and Opper, Sylvia. *Piaget's Theory of Intellectual Development.* Englewood Cliffs, N.J.: Prentice Hall, 1969.

Halford, Graeme S. "A Theory of the Acquisition of Conservation." *Psychological Review* 77 (July 1970): 302-332.

Hebb, Donald O. *The Organization of Behavior: A Neuropsychological Theory.* New York: John Wiley, 1949.

Hunt, J. McVicker. *Intelligence and Experience.* New York: Ronald Press, 1961.

Inhelder, Bärbel; Sinclair, Hermine; and Bovet, Magali. *Learning and the Development of Cognition.* Cambridge, Mass.: Harvard University Press, 1974.

Jackson, E.; Campos, J.J.; and Fischer, Kurt W. "The Question of Decalage between Object Permanence and Person Permanence." Unpublished manuscript, University of Denver, 1978.

Jackson, Philip W. *Life in Classrooms.* New York: Holt, Rinehart and Winston, 1968.

Kurland, D. Midian. "Operational Efficiency, Automization, and the Development of M-Space." Ph.D. dissertation, University of Toronto, in preparation.

Lawson, Anton E. "M-Space: Is it a Constraint on Conservation Reasoning Ability?" *Journal of Experimental Child Psychology* 22 (August 1976): 40-49.

Lefebvre, Monique, and Pinard, Adrien. *"Apprentissage de la Conservation des Quantites par une Méthode de Conflict Cognitif."* Canadian Journal of Behavioral Science 4 (January 1972): 1-12.

Luria, Alexander R. *The Working Brain.* London: Penguin Books, 1973.

McLaughlin, G. Harry. "Psycho-logic: A Possible Alternative to Piaget's Formulation." *British Journal of Educational Psychology* 33 (February 1963): 61-67.

Marsh, George et al. "A Cognitive Developmental Theory of Reading Acquisition." In *Reading Research: Advances in Theory and Practice.* Vol. 2. Edited by T. Gary Waller and G. E. McKinnon. New York: Academic Press, forthcoming.

Neches, Robert, and Hayes, John R. "Progress towards a Taxonomy of Strategy Transformations." In *Cognitive Psychology and Instruction,* edited by Alan M. Lesgold, James W. Pelligrino, Sipke D. Fokkema, and Robert Glaser, pp. 253-67. New York: Plenum Press, 1978.

Newell, Allen; Shaw, J.C.; and Simon, Herbert A. "Elements of a Theory of Human Problem Solving." *Psychological Review* 65 (January 1958): 151-66.

Noelting, Gerald. "Stages and Mechanisms in the Development of the Concept of Proportion in the Child and Adolescent." Paper presented at the Fifth Interdisciplinary Seminar on Piagetian Theory and its Implications for the Helping Professions, Los Angeles, University of Southern California, 1975.

Parkinson, Glennys M. "The Limits of Learning: A Quantitative Developmental Investigation of Intelligence." Ph.D. dissertation, York University, 1976.

Pascual-Leone, Juan. "Cognitive Development and Cognitive Style." Ph.D. dissertation, University of Geneva, 1969.

―――. "A Mathematical Model for the Transition Rule in Piaget's Developmental Stages." *Acta Psychologica* 32 (August 1970): 301-345.

―――. "A Theory of Constructive Operators, a Neo-Piagetian Model of Conservation, and the Problem of Horizontal Decalages." Unpublished manuscript, York University, 1977.

Piaget, Jean. "Piaget's Theory." In *Carmichael's Manual of Child Psychology.* Vol. 2 Edited by Paul H. Mussen, pp. 709-733. New York: John Wiley, 1970.

Pinard, Adrien, and Laurendeau, Monique. "Stage in Piaget's Cognitive-Developmental Theory: Exegesis of a Concept." In *Studies in Cognitive Development: Essays in Honor of Jean Piaget,* edited by David Elkind and John H. Flavell, pp. 121-70. New York: Oxford University Press, 1969.

Price-Williams, Douglas; Gordon, William; and Ramirez III, Manuel. "Skill and Conservation: A Study of Pottery-making Children." *Developmental Psychology* 1 (November 1969): 769.

Pulos, Steven. "Developmental Cognitive Constraints on Structural Learning" Ph.D. dissertation, York University, 1979.

Rich, Susan. "The Development of Information Processing Speed and Span in Normal and Retarded Children." Master's thesis, University of Toronto, 1979.

Schneider, Walter, and Shiffrin, Richard M. "Controlled and Automatic Human Information Processing: I. Detection, Search, and Attention." *Psychological Review* 84 (January 1977): 1-66.

Siegler, Robert S. "The Origins of Scientific Reasoning." In *Children's Thinking: What Develops?* edited by Robert S. Siegler, pp. 109-149. Hillsdale, N.J.: Lawrence Erlbaum Associates, 1978.

Simon, Herbert A. "An Information Processing Theory of Intellectual Development." In *Thought in the Young Child,* edited by William Kessen and Clementina Kuhlman, *Monographs of the Society for Research in Child Development* 27, 2 (1962): 150-55. Serial No. 83.

Slobin, Dan I. "Cognitive Prerequisites for the Development of Grammar." In *Studies of Child Language Development,* edited by Charles A. Ferguson and Dan I. Slobin, pp. 175-208. New York: Holt, Rinehart and Winston, 1973.

Solomons, Leon M., and Stein, Gertrude. "Normal Motor Automatism," *Psychological Review* 3 (September 1896): 492-512.

Sternberg, Robert J. *Intelligence, Information Processing, and Analogical Reasoning.* Hillsdale, N.J.: Lawrence Erlbaum Associates, 1977.

Strauss, Sidney, and Langer, Jonas. "Operational Thought Inducement." *Child Development* 41 (March 1970) 163-75.

Tasaki, Ichiyi. *Nervous Transmission.* Springfield, Ill.: Charles C. Thomas, 1953.

Trabasso, Tom, and Foellinger, David B. "Seeing, Hearing, and Doing: A Developmental Study of Memory for Actions." *Child Development* 48 (December 1977): 1482-89.

Watson, John S. "Memory and Contingency Analysis in Infant Learning." *Merrill-Palmer Quarterly* 13 (January 1967): 55-76.

White, Burton L. *The First Three Years of Life.* New York: Englewood Cliffs, N.J.: Prentice-Hall, 1975.

White, Sheldon H. "Some General Outlines of the Matrix of Developmental Changes between Five and Seven Years." *Bulletin of the Orton Society* 20 (1970): 41-57.

Winograd, Terry. *Understanding Natural Language.* New York: Academic Press, 1972.

Yakovlev, Paul, and Lecours, A.R. "The Myelogenetic Cycles of Regional Maturation of the Brain." In *Regional Development of the Brain in Early Life*, edited by Alexandre Minkowski, pp. 3-70. Oxford: Basil Blackwell and Mott 1967.

Zimmerman, Barry J., and Rosenthal, Ted L. "Observational Learning of Rule-Governed Behavior by Children." *Psychological Bulletin* 81 (January 1974): 29-42.

7. Life-Span Development and Educational Psychology

Robert J. Havighurst

The decade of the 1970s has seen a major growth of interest and work in the field of "life-span developmental psychology." To psychologists, the field known as "developmental psychology" in 1970 and earlier generally meant the study of child and adolescent development carried up to the age of eighteen or twenty. Now the study of human development through the life cycle is bound to require attention to the third decade of life and beyond; developmental psychology must pay attention to the adult years. This chapter will describe the work that is being done on the adult segment of the life span. A relatively small but rapidly growing number of scholars and teachers now work in this area. One group consists of those working in the field of adult or continuing education. Another consists of men and women who have chosen to carry on research in the area of adulthood and aging. Both of these groups were lonesome pioneers in the 1940s.

The American Psychological Association demonstrated interest in the area of adult development in several ways during the 1970s. Division 20 of the Association, concerned with "maturity and old age," has grown substantially. A conference sponsored by the association in Washington, D.C., in 1972 resulted in a publication entitled *The Psychology of Adult Development and Aging,* edited by Carl Eisdorfer and M. Powell Lawton.

Societal Change

By midcentury American society was losing its "accent on youth" and was beginning to discover and to stress the possibilities and problems of middle age and aging. The proportion of the population over sixty-five was increasing, as was the segment of the population aged twenty to sixty-four. There would be some basic changes in the structure of American society that would require adaptation and adjustment by adults during the final quarter of the twentieth century.

In 1900 more than 60 percent of the American working population was engaged in the extraction of goods, through agriculture, mining, fishing, and forestry—a condition that still obtains for pre-industrial societies in most of the world. After 1900 the United States became an industrial society, a goods-producing society in which machines, feeding upon energy and designed and directed by men, do most of the work. In 1950 approximately 50 percent of American workers were engaged in the production of goods, including 33 percent in manufacturing, leaving a much smaller group in farming, mining, and fishing. The fact was that most of the energy used to keep the machines working and the wheels going came from cheap petroleum, thus enabling industrialists, merchants, and workers to increase their real income substantially compared with that at the beginning of the century. This situation was simply accepted as though it would continue indefinitely.

Daniel Bell, professor of sociology at Harvard University, and other analysts of contemporary society say that we are now emerging from an industrial society into a postindustrial society in which most workers will be providing services rather than producing goods. Bell (1973) predicted that by 1980 70 percent of employed persons would be engaged in service occupations. The balance between the number of producers of goods and providers of service during the remainder of this century will be determined partly by the cost of the energy needed to run machines compared with the cost of the services provided by men and women. The occupations claiming a growing proportion of the labor force today are professional, technical, managerial, clerical, and sales. Factory workers, transport workers, and skilled craftsmen are barely holding their own, and farming now claims only 5 percent of the labor force.

These developments point clearly to the increasing centrality of education in the formation of a white-collar, middle-class society. Bell and others say that in the postindustrial society it is education rather than inheritance of property that provides access to status and income. The educational system was growing rapidly in the 1960s and 1970s, with 75 percent of an age cohort graduating from high school in 1975, 45 percent entering college, and about 25 percent finishing college with a bachelor's degree.

The major social goals of the coming two decades will require serious and concentrated study and action by the adults of this period. We will simply mention three major problem areas to indicate the challenge that confronts us: 1. *The energy crisis:* Our economy has grown rich on the basis of cheap energy coming from cheap petroleum. We have become addicted to petroleum, and now we see that the world supply of petroleum and natural gas will be exhausted by the year 2000, greatly reducing available energy unless we find and exploit major kinds of replaceable energy (Commoner 1976). 2. *The population explosion:* World population continues to grow so fast that famine for large numbers will occur unless the growth rate of population is reduced and food production is brought within sight of food needs. 3. *World cooperation:* Countries at various levels of economic and social development must work out a system of peaceful cooperation.

LIFE-SPAN DEVELOPMENTAL PSYCHOLOGY

According to Goulet and Baltes (1970), human life-span developmental psychology "is concerned with the description and explication of ontogenetic (age-related) behavioral change from birth to death" (p. 12). A number of books now deal in broad detail with the adult segment of the life span. Among them are *Life-Span Developmental Psychology: Research and Theory,* edited by Goulet and Baltes (1970); *Life-Span Developmental Psychology: Personality and Socialization,* edited by Baltes and Schaie (1973); *Life-Span Developmental Psychology: Introduction to Research Methods,* edited by Baltes, Reese, and Nesselroade (1977); *Handbook of the Psychology of Aging,* edited by Birren and Schaie (1977); and the volume by Eisdorfer and Lawton (1973) already mentioned.

Pioneer Work. Two people, working first in Europe and later in the United States, opened up the field for American psychologists. Charlotte Buehler, working in Vienna with her students, began to collect life histories from elderly persons. On the basis of these data, she postulated five "basic life tendencies": need satisfaction, adaptive self-limitation (adjustment), creative expansion, establishment of inner order, self-fulfillment. These tendencies are acting to some extent at all ages, but they have periods of dominance at various points in the life cycle. For instance, Buehler saw the age period from eighteen to twenty-five as dominated by the young person's tentative self-determination of an adult occupational role, in response to the need for adaptive self-limitation. This is followed in the twenty years from age twenty-five to forty-five by self-realization in occupation, marriage, and family development, in response to the need for creative expansion. The drive for establishment of inner order takes the form of critical self-assessment in the mature years of forty-five to sixty-five, and the need for self-fulfillment is normally fairly well met in the period of well-earned rest and retirement after about age sixty-five.

The next great step was taken by Erikson (1963) with his conception of growth through the life span as a process of meeting and achieving a series of eight "psychological tasks," each of which dominates the development of the individual at a certain stage. These eight major tasks with their approximate modal age periods are: basic trust versus mistrust (infancy); autonomy versus shame and doubt (early childhood); initiative versus guilt (prepuberty); industry versus inferiority (puberty); identity versus role confusion (adolescence); intimacy versus isolation (early adulthood); generativity versus stagnation (middle adulthood); integrity versus despair (later adulthood). In Erikson's view, the failure to achieve a successful resolution of one or another of these tasks results in persistent problems in the later periods of life.

The Kansas City Study of Adult Life, conducted by the Committee on Human Development of the University of Chicago between 1951 and 1964, was focused on a representative sample of men and women between the ages of forty and seventy-five. Drawing upon this work, Neugarten (1977) placed special emphasis on the timing of events such as reaching a peak of occupational competence, having grown-up children leave home, retiring from one's principal occupation, adjusting to the death of a spouse. If these events occur "on time," they can be taken as matters to be expected by the individual and the society and can be met in a very satisfactory way.

Throughout research on adult behavior and development, there is always the question of whether or not changes are maturational, that is, based on a kind of biological time clock, as is the menopause or the reduction of elasticity of the lens of the eye. Some changes are of this type, while others are caused by the social environment or by social experience. The growing proportion of middle-aged women who are employed outside the home is an example of environmentally induced change, as is the reduction in the 1960s of the average age of retirement for men.

There is also the question of personality change related to age. Studies of adults aged forty to eighty confirm the broad hypothesis that human personality does change in visible ways as people grow older. These changes in personality are not *caused* by the passage of time, but the various biological and social events that occur with the passage of time are the causes of personality development. Growing through early and middle age to old age is a process of adaptation in which personality is the key element. Given a reasonably supportive environment the individual will choose a life style that offers the greatest ego involvement and life satisfaction.

Table 7-1 provides an overview of changes in personality and in social adjustment during the adult life span and shows significant differences between men and women in behavior and in the development of social personality.

The Adult Learner

Life-span developmental psychology has become an attractive field for study and research on the basis of what may be called the principle of continuity and change: *adult behavior is continuous and changing throughout the adult life span.* The terrain of adulthood has hills and valleys; it is not a plateau that people traverse and fall off of into old age when they reach the edge. Consequently, in order to be successful, adults must be alert to meet the new tasks and challenges that they encounter at various points.

The most profound educational change of this century is a change of attitude toward education, which is no longer regarded as merely essentially preparatory but rather as a way to meet the demands and aspirations of the present period of one's life. Thus education has

Table 7-1

The life cycle

20	25	30	35	40	45	50	55	60	65	70	75
	Time to build and achieve							Time left to live			
								Time left to live is finite. Must plan to get some important things accomplished. Death must be expected and is nothing to dread provided it comes more or less "on time."			
	Active mastery of outer world. Social personality is established around career development, family life, homemaking; one takes the initiative in coping with life				*Reexamination of self.* Introspection, stock taking, planning ahead, normal events are not crises if timing is appropriate.			*Passive mastery.* Introversion. Preoccupation with inner self.			
Female		Last child to school			Last child leaves home; not a significant crisis; increased freedom and home satisfaction.			Women become more dominant, more instrumental, and more accepting of their aggressive impulses.			
			40 percent of women work		*55 percent of women work*						
Male	Men take the lead in economic, civic, and social activities. They gain competence and autonomy. They are self-confident. They become stabilized for the period of middle age.						Men grow more nurturant and more affiliative.				

uses in every stage of the life cycle, not just during childhood and adolescence. Every stage of the life cycle in modern society requires people to learn new things if they are to live up to their own aspirations and the expectations that others have of them.

As the twentieth century draws to a close, the educational activity of adults, and especially that of older adults, will increase. The level of formal schooling is more closely related to participation in continuing education than any other socioeconomic factor. If present trends continue, that level will increase dramatically. According to census data, the median number of school years completed by those sixty-five and over in the United States in 1950 was 8.1. In 1970 the median had risen to only 8.7, but it is estimated that by 1990 the median will have jumped to 11.9, or just short of a high school education.

In 1976 Congress passed the Lifelong Learning Act, which had been sponsored by Senator Walter Mondale. This act authorized federal government support for (a) research and analysis, (b) demonstration and dissemination, and (c) state-level programs. Lifelong learning was given a very broad definition in the preamble:

Lifelong learning includes, but is not limited to, adult basic education, continuing education, independent study, agricultural education, business education, labor education, occupational education, preretirement education, education for older and retired people, remedial education, special educational programs for groups or for individuals with special needs, and also educational activities designed to upgrade occupational and professional skills, to assist business, public agencies, and other organizations in the use of innovation and research results, and to serve family needs and personal development.

The National Center for Education Statistics reported that 17 million adults were participating in some form of structured learning in 1975. These were not "regular" college students, but 6.6 million were working toward college degrees; another 1.3 million were working for other forms of credit; and fully half were taking noncredit courses. This latter group was vaguely defined and probably included informal programs offered by senior centers as well as compulsory literacy courses for welfare recipients.

There can be little doubt that the number of post-college-age people who are interested in continuing education will increase during the 1980s and will become very important to the financing of college and university programs, since the number of traditional college students will decline due to low birthrates. In recognition of this situation, the annual conference of the American Association for Higher Education in 1978 included papers dealing with the adult learner. In one of these papers Cross (1978) described the characteristics of adult learners, stating that adults who have had some success in their past education develop an insatiable appetite for further learning. She described two contrasting approaches to the organization of a program for adults: "instruction of adults," a traditional, didactic, and formal procedure; and "facilitation of learning by adults," which relies on the initiative and interest of the adult students and provides the resources that will best serve them.

In another paper given at the conference, Tough (1978) reported on his study of self-initiated learning projects. He defined a learning project as "a deliberate effort to gain a defined area of knowledge or a skill. To be included in this definition, a series of learning sessions must add up to at least seven hours." Examples might be planning and arranging a summer tour of England, making a systematic survey of the work of contemporary painters in a large city, reading systematically on the growing use of solar energy. Tough found that the average person engages in five such learning projects in a year.

Lifelong Learning for the Over-Fifties. There are two broad categories of educational programs for adults. One is concerned with career development or improvement in some other service role, such as homemaker, parent, consumer, or citizen. This we may call "instrumental" learning, or learning for a purpose or goal that lies outside and beyond the learning experience. The second type of program operates to improve or enhance the quality of life. This we may call "expressive" learning, where the goal lies within the act of learning or is so closely related to it that the act of learning appears to be the goal. The reward for this kind of learning is immediate—one does not have to wait until the learning becomes useful. To take an extreme example, some may study mathematics for the pleasure of learning about numbers, while most people will study mathematics instrumentally to prepare for a job of some kind or to be promoted to the next level in school.

Learning Ability of Senior Citizens. Any new educative experience requires some ability to learn, and many people have the notion that ability to learn, which is another expression of intelligence, decreases during adulthood so that people over fifty or sixty cannot learn very much. This is a myth. Practically everybody who was educable at age fifteen can learn quite well at sixty-five or at seventy-five (Botwinick 1970, Baltes and Labouvie 1973, Schaie 1970).

Research on the relation of aging to learning during the past twenty years has found that there are two broad categories of intelligence, one of which increases during adulthood, while the other decreases. "Crystallized intelligence" consists of abilities that are learned as part of the culture in which one lives. Vocabulary and the use of numbers (mathematical skills) are parts of this broad factor. So is general information about the present and the past. Although some of this kind of intelligence may be lost through disuse, people who "keep in touch" with the world around them grow in this kind of intelligence as long as they are in reasonably good physical and mental health.

"Fluid intelligence" tends to decrease after about the age of fifty. These abilities have a physiological basis and probably decrease due to changes in the nervous system that are not visible through the microscope. For instance, the speed of reaction to a touch on the back or to a light signal decreases. Abilities that depend on space perception also decrease. It would be an oversimplification to say that fluid intelligence depends only on psychomotor speed. There must be other biological variables that decrease with age after maturity and that affect performance on an intelligence test. For instance, the state of nutrition of the body or the presence in the body of certain medicines or drugs may influence alertness.

The performance of adults of various ages over about fifty on a battery of some thirty tests of mental ability has been studied by Horn (1970) and by Horn and Cattell (1966, 1967). They found one set of skills or abilities that did not decline with age in the fifty to seventy-five age range, another set that decreased with age, and other groups or abilities that did not fit either of these two categories but depended on such variables as visual and auditory acuity. The abilities that they categorized as crystallized intelligence included verbal comprehension, mechanical knowledge, arithmetic ability, fluency of ideas, experiential evaluation, and general information. The abilities categorized as fluid intelligence included inductive reasoning, figure matching, memory span for numbers or nonsense syllables, and perceptual speed.

In more general language, crystallized intelligence is the collective intelligence of a society that is passed on from one generation to the next by means of schooling, the parental word, personal example or instruction, or is learned through experience. This kind of intelligence grows rapidly during childhood and adolescence and continues to grow more slowly during the adult years. It varies among persons of equal potential for learning in relation to the amount and quality of their learning experience. After about age sixty, crystallized intelligence only increases in people who are intellectually active.

Fluid intelligence consists of the abilities that depend most directly on the physiological structure of the organism, and especially upon the central nervous system. The neural structures of that system grow during infancy and childhood and thereafter may decline due to injuries. The decline becomes marked after about fifty years of age.

Changing Life Styles of Women. Postindustrial society will probably bring more change in the life styles of women than in those of men. We know that the proportions of women in college and graduate school have increased relative to men during the 1970s. Family life is changing; there are fewer families in which the wife keeps house and the husband is the breadwinner. In almost half of all husband-wife households, both parties are now in the labor force. About 40 percent of children under age eighteen live in families with both mother and father employed outside the home. In 1977 over half of the women aged forty-five to fifty-four were employed. It appears that midlife women will increasingly want a balance of work and family responsibility. They will want to maximize their options, and they will want to try new kinds of work and new types of community service. Increasing use of educational facilities appears to be an inevitable outcome of these changing life styles.

DEVELOPMENTAL TASKS OF THE ADULT YEARS

Developmental psychology has made use of the concept of "developmental tasks" for more than twenty-five years in the study of the growth and development of children and adolescents. My volume entitled *Developmental Tasks and Education* (1972) has been used especially in the training of teachers as a supplement to a text in educational psychology. In that volume I included chapters showing how the concept of the developmental task can easily be applied to the adult years—early adulthood, middle age, and later maturity. I shall summarize the argument here briefly in such a way as to suggest the implications for continuing education, for counseling, and especially for services to the elderly.

The tasks the individual must learn—the developmental tasks of life—are those things that constitute healthy and satisfactory growth in our society. They are the things a person must learn if one is to be judged and to judge oneself to be a reasonably happy and successful person. *A developmental task is a task that arises at or about a certain period in the life of the individual, successful achievement of which leads to happiness and to success with later tasks, while failure leads to unhappiness in the individual, disapproval by the society, and difficulty with later tasks.*

Developmental tasks originate from forces inside and outside the individual. Internal forces are primarily biological and are seen most clearly in the early years of human growth. The infant's legs grow larger and stronger, so that the task of walking can be achieved. As the nervous system grows more complex, the child is able to reason more subtly and to understand the complexities of subjects such as arithmetic. At puberty the sex glands develop rapidly and pour sex hormones into the bloodstream, making young adolescents more aware of their sexuality and more interested in the opposite sex.

Other tasks arise primarily from the cultural pressure of society, such as learning to read (for a child) and learning to participate as a socially responsible citizen in society (for a young adult). There is a third source of developmental tasks, namely, the personal values and aspirations of the individual that are a part of one's personality or self. The personality or self emerges from the interaction of organic and environmental forces. As the self evolves, it becomes increasingly a force in its own right in the subsequent development of the individual. Already by the age of three or four, the individual's self is effective in defining and accomplishing the developmental tasks of that age.

Thus, developmental tasks may arise from physical maturation; from the pressure of the surrounding society upon the individual; or from the desires, aspirations, and values of the emerging personality. In most cases, they arise from combinations of these factors acting together. During early and middle adulthood the social demands and personal aspirations dominate in setting and defining developmental tasks, with the biological changes of late middle age asserting a major force in the years after fifty.

Developmental Tasks Related to Erikson and Buehler

The concept of the developmental task is a useful mental tool for the work of analyzing and evaluating progress through the human life span. Something like this is necessary for a person who is stimulated by Buehler or by Erikson to make a practical application of their broad and integrative concepts of development. Buehler divides life after about age eighteen into four periods, each of which is dominated by a reigning "life tendency." Erikson also divides the same age span into four periods, each of which is dominated by a reigning "psychosocial task."

The analysis of developmental tasks gets down to earth by making use of the concept of social role and by searching for empirical data to define and evaluate a person's performance in the various social roles that are acted out in response to a life tendency or a psychosocial task. The social roles most generally relevant are: worker, parent, spouse, homemaker, citizen, association member, friend.

Descriptions of Developmental Tasks

In thinking about human development through the adult part of the life span (Havighurst 1976), we can divide this broad period into the following three stages: early adulthood (ages twenty to thirty-five); middle age (ages thirty-five to sixty); later maturity (age sixty and over).

Developmental Tasks of Early Adulthood. The tasks of early adulthood are simply listed here in order to give more attention to middle age and later maturity. These tasks include selecting a mate and getting married, learning to live with a marriage partner, starting a family and rearing children, getting started in one's occupation, taking on civic responsibility, and finding a congenial social group.

Developmental Tasks of Middle Age. Middle adulthood, for most people, is likely to be the fullest and most creative season of the life cycle. People are more sure of themselves and more sure that they can rely on their decisions to be rational and free from some of their former illusions. The developmental tasks of the middle years arise from changes within the organism, from environmental pressures, and above all from demands or obligations arising from the individual's own values and aspirations. Since most middle-aged people are members of families with teen-age children, it is useful to look at the tasks of husband, wife, and children as these people live and grow in relation to one another. Each family goes through a process of evolution, from its beginning as a newly married couple through the bearing and rearing and launching of children into adulthood, with the original young couple finally becoming heads of a three-generation family.

1. *Achieving mature social civic responsibility:* Erikson identified the major psychosocial task of middle age as that of *generativity*, by which he means generating and passing on a fair world to the next generation. This is done within the family by helping children in various ways. It is also done in the broader society by assuming greater civic and social responsibility.

The obligations of citizenship lie most heavily upon middle-aged people. Since they are at their peak of influence and still possessed of great energy, they are the natural leaders in the civic life of the community. Men often find this task irksome because they are so engrossed in making money or seeking professional success that they have no time for civic responsibilities, or they may have the attitude that "politics is rotten" and that government is hopelessly monopolized by incompetent and irresponsible individuals. On the other hand, many men find real pleasure in working for the civic welfare. They enjoy keeping up to date on economic and political events and are glad to spend the necessary time studying and working with other people.

For women whose children are growing up and leaving the home, the development of new social and civic interests at this time of life fills the void left by disappearing children. Thus, an increasing number of women become active in civic organizations and in movements for civic reform and give time to the serious study of foreign affairs.

2. *Assisting teenage children to become responsible and happy adults:* Just as adolescence is a time for boys and girls to become emotionally independent of their parents and to become emotionally mature people, middle age is a time for parents to cooperate with adolescent children in this task. Perhaps the most useful and important thing a father or mother can do is to provide a worthy pattern for the adolescent to follow—a pattern of the good father or mother, the good husband or wife, the good homemaker, and the good

citizen. Adolescents are still going to follow the example of their parents, through the ingrained and unconscious habit of imitating them, a habit which was formed as a young child.

Parents should also get enough insight into their own emotional reactions to their children to be able to give their children the freedom as well as the guidance they need. The mother should understand herself well enough to avoid projecting the problems of her own adolescence onto her daughter and therefore being oversolicitous or overpunitive, and similarly with the father in relation to his son.

3. *Reaching and maintaining satisfactory performance in one's occupational career:* During the middle adult years most men attain the highest status and income of their careers. Women do likewise, if they have been employed all their adult lives. But many women return to the labor force after a considerable absence. They are not likely to seek prestige and income as much as to seek the satisfaction of working effectively and thus using their time productively. Also, a number of men change their jobs between the ages of forty and sixty, and therefore they have to start almost from the beginning on a new career. This is true of men whose work requires the greatest physical skill and energy, such as professional athletes, as well as policemen, firemen, and army officers. Such work requires a level of physical strength and skill that some cannot maintain after about age fifty-five. And then certain types of work are eliminated from the labor market because of changes in technology.

There are also men and women who have held more or less routine jobs and deliberately make a change in search of work that is more interesting or more rewarding to them in other ways. At present it appears that approximately 53 percent of women aged forty to fifty-nine are in the American labor force, many of them having sought jobs after raising a family. Also, approximately 10 percent of men change the nature of their work between the ages of forty and sixty, either of their own volition or because their jobs disappear through no act of their own. Thus the career task for many people is not so much that of reaching and maintaining their peak of prestige and income as it is the task of achieving a flexible work role that is interesting, productive, and financially satisfactory. Changes in the worker role during the middle years often require some retraining that can be obtained in public or private school systems and universities. Additionally, some large employers in public service and private enterprise make provision for change of jobs with related training to serve those employees who wish to change or whose jobs are discontinued.

4. *Learning to accept and adjust to the physiological changes of middle age:* For men and women there is a decline in physical capacity, and for women there is a profound physiological change during the middle years. All must adjust their ways of living to these changes and accept them with as good grace as possible. Aging of the body tissues has been going on, mostly unnoticed, since early adulthood. Muscular strength has been diminishing, neuromuscular skills have been fading, and the body has been slowing down. Some of the physical symptoms of aging are: growth of stiff hair in the nose, ears, and eyelashes of men, growth of hair on the upper lip of women, drying and wrinkling of the skin, deposition of fat around the middle, and presbyopia—loss of accommodative power of the lens in the eye. The elasticity of the lens decreases steadily from childhood to old age, and by the age of seventy-five, the lens is ordinarily completely inelastic, making it impossible for the eye to adjust itself unaided to the task of focusing on objects at varying distances. Between ages forty and fifty, accommodative power usually ceases to suffice for ordinary close work, and bifocals or reading glasses become necessary.

The menopause occurs in women over a period of several years, usually between the ages of forty-five and fifty-five. With the cessation of ovarian activity, the delicate balance of the endocrine system is disturbed. Physical symptoms may take the form of hot and cold flashes, dizziness, sweating, insomnia, and excitability. It was formerly thought that the menopause tended to bring on a period of psychological depression. This is not necessarily true. Neugarten's (1968) research with middle-aged women indicates that those who have been competent with their developmental tasks of early adulthood seldom experience anything other than mild physical discomfort for a brief period around the menopause.

For the men, adjustment to the physical changes of middle age is usually smooth enough. There may be a few flurries, such as an argument with the doctor about giving up physical exertion, or a period of denying the manifest need for reading glasses, but generally a man slows down on the more strenuous forms of physical activity, conserves his energy if he is a manual worker, and counts on experience and skill to enable him to hold his own with younger, more active men. Sexual activity and interest decrease slowly in men but continue far into the period of old age.

To a limited extent, knowledge about the physiology of aging would probably help people adjust to the changes that their bodies are undergoing. Therefore this topic might be treated in courses for adults. More important, as far as education is concerned, is the task of assisting middle-aged people to develop the new interests and activities that are appropriate to their biological and psychological capacities. This means the development of courses dealing with civic and political problems and instruction in arts and crafts, gardening, dramatics, and other leisure-time activities that will survive as the person grows older.

5. *Adapting to aging parents:* During middle age, a person is usually a member of a three-generation family. The older generation is from sixty-five to eighty-five years old, while the middle generation is forty to sixty years old, and the younger generation is five to twenty-five. Thus, as the children grow to maturity and leave the home, the grandparents become older and may become a charge on the home. The aging parents may need financial help or physical care. They may be passing through a crisis of loss of employment and reduced income. The death of one of the older couple may leave the other to adjust to the breakup of long-standing partnership.

In spite of the general feeling of obligation on the part of grown-up children for their aging parents, it often happens that neither generation wants to live with the other. Yet there may be real advantages for a couple with growing children in having grandparents live with them. The grandparents can look after the children if the parents want to leave home for a while. When domestic help is hard to get, the grandparents may be invaluable aides to their married children.

When neither generation wants to live with the other, it is partly due to a desire for privacy and to avoid overcrowding, but very often there is an added factor of a not altogether satisfactory parent-child relationship which one or the other generation does not wish to revive.

Developmental Tasks of Late Adulthood. We have deliberately described the period of middle age as ending at about sixty, but we know that when Americans aged sixty to seventy are asked to name the age group to which they belong, with choices among young, middle-aged, elderly, and old, the great majority call themselves "middle-aged." Furthermore, at age sixty the average person will live to be almost eighty. These individuals are not likely to think of themselves as "old" until they are past seventy-five. With a moderate improvement in the prevention of mortality from heart disease, life expectancy for a sixty-year-old person in the year 2000 may be twenty years or even a little more.

These considerations lead to the idea that it is useful to make a division in the elderly population between the "young-old" and the "old-old" with the line between the two phases at about seventy-five to eighty years of age. With this in mind, we may describe the developmental tasks of later maturity with a focus on the period of the young-old, that is, from about sixty to seventy-five years of age.

1. *Adjusting to decreasing physical strength and health:* The human body does age in almost every one of its cells and cellular systems. The cells accumulate useless or poisonous materials that they cannot get rid of. They gradually slow down in their nutritional processes, and they gradually lose their self-repairing properties. Most people, however, are fairly active and vigorous until they reach the age of seventy-five, and many maintain this state of health well beyond that age. If persons have been spared from the diseases or accidents that might take their lives at any age, their bodies will eventually wear out and give way.

2. *Adjustment to retirement and reduced income:* In American society a job is the axis of life for most men and for an increasing number of women. Often when the occupation goes, the individual no longer feels like a worthy member of society. Yet the occupation must be abandoned by the great majority of people, whether they are professional or manual workers, sometime between ages sixty and seventy. Some people fill the vacuum created by retirement in their lives with a useful and interesting leisure-time activity. Others find part-time jobs that keep them busy and happy, but too many fret and mope over the forced inactivity.

In America we are watching with great interest a major social experiment that started in Sweden in 1975, when a new law went into effect allowing people between ages sixty and seventy to retire from full-time employment, take part-time employment, and supplement their salaries with a fraction of a full state-supported old-age pension. This fraction would increase to a full pension as the fraction of full-time work decreased to zero. Such a system allows the work life to be based primarily on one's interests and on the positive nonfinancial rewards of work to the individual.

3. *Adjusting to death of spouse:* After a man and woman have lived together for many years, it is hard for one to get along without the other. Yet death ultimately separates every married man and woman. Women lose their husbands more often than men lose their wives because women are longer lived than men. There are about twice as many widows as widowers in the average community. By their late sixties as many women are widows as are living with their husbands. Among women eighty-five years of age and over, 85 percent are widows.

If a woman loses her husband, she may have to move from her house to a smaller place, she may have to learn about business matters, and above all she has to learn to be alone. A man has the same adjustment to make to loneliness, and he may have to learn to cook, to keep house, and to keep his clothes in order, if he did not do these things as a married adult.

4. *Becoming explicitly affiliated with the late-adulthood age group:* Many people "fight" the recognition that they are among the elders or the senior citizens. They grimly hold on to their middle-adulthood associations. But the time comes when they feel more comfortable as members of a senior age group. Prestige positions are available to them in organizations of older people where the tempo is slower. They may participate in political action groups and in social or recreational groups. For thirty or forty years the individual, now growing old, has participated in occupational, social, and religious groups in which age grading was at a minimum and status was achieved on the basis of social position, economic power, talent, and other things largely independent of age. The aging person must now learn once more to participate in an age-graded group. The ease or difficulty of this task depends on the relative magnitudes of the rewards and punishments that have been suggested above.

5. *Establishing satisfactory physical living arrangements:* Nearly all people have to change their living arrangements after age sixty-five. An elderly couple may move to a smaller house or apartment. And loss of a spouse forces increasing numbers to live alone or with an adult child. At present, approximately 35 percent of the women aged sixty-five and over and 15 percent of the men are living alone in apartments or houses. During the past twenty years there has been a

definite trend among older couples to move to places where the climate is warm—Florida, Arizona, California, Oregon, and Washington in the United States. A growing number of such people also move into communities or subcommunities where older people predominate. While the proportion of the older population who choose this kind of living arrangement may not become very large, it seems clear that older people who can afford the cost will try out a variety of climates and housing during the coming years.

On the other hand, as more people live on into their eighties and nineties, it seems likely that more of these older old people will have to find congregate living arrangements that provide physical care for them as they become less able to care for themselves. Thus there will be a good deal of experimentation with residential arrangements, such as old people's homes and nursing homes. There will also be an extension of homemaking services through housekeepers who can provide meals and other services needed by elderly people who wish to live as independently as they can.

MAXIMIZING THE OPTIONS

Studying the adult segment of the life span with the methods and interests of a psychologist or sociologist brings out the fact that these are years of growth and development when the individual exercises many options. The goal of the individual is to use these options successfully. The objective of a good society is to facilitate the person's exercise of options. One function of the psychologist is to study the performance of people as they seek to exercise these options. Another function is to counsel people so as to help them do a good job with their options.

There are three areas of activity outside the home and family that offer opportunity: employment, education, and volunteer activity. For young adults and middle-aged people, employment and education are the principal theaters. But for people past fifty, volunteer work also becomes an attractive option.

The Over-Fifty Age Group

People beyond age fifty have either settled into an occupational career and do not seek options in the employment area or have not been encouraged to look for new and different kinds of work, although women do seek new careers at this time. The schools and colleges have not yet seen this age group as a promising one for extended education, but events and trends of the 1970s seem to promise some changes and offer a challenge to educational institutions and to society as a whole to open up new options.

Employment. Between 1950 and 1970 the proportion of men aged sixty and over who were in the labor force decreased drastically, while the proportion of employed women in this age group increased sharply. Then, during the 1970s—a time of growing unemployment in the labor force as a whole—there were a number of changes in the employment status of people over fifty that have provided more options for them. Congress passed a law raising the age at which mandatory retirement is permissible from sixty-five to seventy, as well as a law that expanded and stabilized pension programs in private companies.

A program for matching people with jobs was given a thorough trial in Portland, Maine. Koyl (1974) selected a set of seven tests of ability and physical fitness, called GULHEMP (from the first letters in the test titles). These tests are given to persons who may feel maladjusted in their present jobs or may want help in selecting new jobs. The profile of a person's scores on the test battery can be compared with the profiles indicating fitness for various jobs. Thus persons may be able to transfer to jobs with a present employer for which they are better suited. They may also learn what kinds of jobs to apply for when entering the labor market.

Education. Until very recently, the presence of people past fifty years of age in college classes was rare. The Harris Poll of 1974 found 5 percent of people aged fifty-five to sixty-four enrolled in educational programs. This does not include a large and growing number of mature people who belong to Senior Centers and take part in a variety of quasi-educational activities that are not labeled "educational."

As noted earlier, 17 million adults participated in some form of structured learning in 1975. The majority of these people were under fifty years of age, but it is clear that more and more people beyond fifty will involve themselves in lifelong learning as the proportion in this age group with completed high school education increases during the next decade. There will be a growing number of attractive options in the field of adult education.

Volunteer Service. Unpaid voluntary service is a popular activity with people who have extra time. The Harris Poll of 1974 found that 22 percent of people over sixty-five were doing volunteer work, and 10 percent more would like this kind of activity. Volunteer services were being provided by 33 percent of those in the age-group from fifty-five to sixty-four. The most frequent services were: teaching at various levels and various types of institutions; service in hospitals and clinics; providing automobile transportation to the ill, aged, handicapped; civic affairs—lobbying and voter registration.

Government-Funded Programs for the Over Fifties

Men and women of this age group who are in the labor force are, of course, employed by private or public employers or are self-employed. As they move through their fifties and sixties, they exercise the options we have described in order to make a satisfactory use of their time. A relatively small but interesting group find their way into government-funded programs aimed at meeting a variety of societal needs that the system of private enterprise does not meet. The government pays the cost of administering these programs and also pays relatively small amounts to some people with low incomes. Table 7-2 provides information on these programs. The only one that involves substantial payments to fairly large numbers of elderly people is CETA (Title II of the Comprehensive Employment and Training Act), which is aimed at helping the "structurally unemployed" group consisting largely of disadvantaged people, minority groups, women, the elderly, the handicapped, and jobless youth. To enhance their employability, the structural programs provide skill training along with on-the-job experience and subsidized employment in the public sector.

CONCLUSION

The field of educational psychology has added to itself a concern with the description and explication of age-related behavioral change during the adult segment of the human life span. This carries with it an increasing amount of research and the application of research findings. The major developments in this field have taken place during the decade of the 1970s, and the coming decades of the 1980s and 1990s will certainly expand this kind of activity, related to the development of postindustrial society.

Table 7-2

Government-funded programs for the over fifties

Program	Numbers	Volunteer or paid
SCORE: Service Corps of Retired Executives	12,500	Volunteer
RSVP: Retired Senior Volunteers	250,000	Volunteer
FGP: Foster Grandparents	16,500	Part-time, small payment
SCP: Senior Companions	3,100	Part-time, small payment
Senior Community Service Employment Program (for age 55–plus)	40,000	Minimum wage rate
Teacher Corps (age 50–plus)	Small	Variable
Peace Corps (age 50–plus)	500	Subsistence
VISTA (age 50–plus)	500	Subsistence
Comprehensive Employment and Training Act (CETA)—structural public service employment	Varies	About $8,000

REFERENCES

Baltes, Paul B., and Labouvie, Gisela V. "Adult Development of Intellectual Performance: Description, Explanation, and Modification." In *The Psychology of Adult Development and Aging,* edited by Carl Eisdorfer and M. Powell Lawton, pp. 157-219. Washington, D.C.: American Psychological Association, 1973.

Baltes, Paul B.; Reese, Hayne W.; and Nesselroade, John R. *Life-Span Developmental Psychology: Introduction to Research Methods.* Monterey, Calif.: Brooks/Cole, 1977.

Baltes, Paul B., and Schaie, K. Warner, *Life-Span Developmental Psychology: Personality and Socialization.* New York: Academic Press, 1973.

Bell, Daniel. *The Coming of the Post-Industrial Society.* New York: Basic Books, 1973.

Birren, James E., and Schaie, K. Warner, eds. *Handbook of the Psychology of Aging.* New York: D. Van Nostrand Co., 1977.

Botwinick, Jack. "Learning in Children and in Older Adults." In *Life-Span Developmental Psychology: Research and Theory,* edited by L. R. Goulet and Paul B. Baltes, pp. 257-84. New York: Academic Press, 1970.

Commoner, Barry. *The Poverty of Power: Energy and the Economic Crisis.* New York: Knopf, 1976.

Cross, R. Patricia. "The Adult Learner." In *Current Issues in Higher Education,* 1978 National Conference Series, pp. 1-8. Washington, D.C.: American Association for Higher Education, 1978.

Eisdorfer, Carl, and Lawton, M. Powell, eds. *The Psychology of Adult Development and Aging.* Washington, D.C.: American Psychological Association, 1973.

Erikson, Erik. *Childhood and Society.* New York: Norton, 1963.

Goulet, L.R., and Baltes, Paul B., eds. *Life-Span Developmental Psychology: Research and Theory.* New York: Academic Press, 1970.

Havighurst, Robert J. *Developmental Tasks and Education.* 3d ed. New York: David McKay, 1972.

————. "Education through the Adult Life Span." *Educational Gerontology* 1 (January-March, 1976): 41-51.

Horn, John L. "Organization of Data on Life-Span Development of Human Abilities." In *Life-Span Developmental Psychology: Research and Theory,* edited by L.R. Goulet and Paul B. Baltes, pp. 423-66. New York: Academic Press, 1970.

Horn, John L., and Cattell, Raymond B. "Refinement and Test of the Theory of Fluid and Crystallized General Intelligences." *Journal of Educational Psychology* 57 (October 1966): 253-70.

————. "Age Differences in Fluid and Crystallized Intelligence." *Acta Psychologica* 26 (March 1967): 107-129.

Koyl, Leon F. *Employing the Older Worker: Matching the Employee to the Job.* Washington, D.C.: National Council on the Aging, 1974.

National Council on the Aging. *The Myth and Reality of Aging in America.* Washington, D.C.: the Council, 1974.

Neugarten, Bernice L. "Personality and Aging." In *Handbook of the Psychology of Aging,* edited by James E. Birren and K. Warner Schaie, pp. 626-49. New York: D. Van Nostrand Co., 1977.

Neugarten, Bernice L.; Wood, Vivian; Kraines, Ruth; and Loomis, Barbara. "Women's Attitude toward the Menopause." In *Middle Age and Aging,* edited by Bernice Neugarten, pp. 195-200. Chicago: University of Chicago Press, 1968.

Schaie, K. Warner. "A Reinterpretation of Age Related Changes in Cognitive Structure and Functioning." In *Life-Span Developmental Psychology: Research and Theory,* edited by L. R. Goulet and Paul B. Baltes, pp. 485-507. New York: Academic Press, 1970.

Tough, Allen. "Major Learning Efforts: Recent Research and Future Directions." In *Current Issues in Higher Education,* 1978 National Conference Series, pp. 9-18. Washington, D.C.: American Association for Higher Education, 1978.

8. Psychological Models of Educational Growth

Larry P. Nucci and *Herbert J. Walberg*

John Dewey emphasized growth as the goal of education, and most educators today would support the value of promoting it. Yet researchers have made small and fitful progress in defining and measuring growth and in plotting its trajectory during the school years. Only by having reliable absolute measures calibrated for growth and a clear picture of the normal course of individual growth in a given environment is it possible to estimate the dependencies of accelerations in growth on given processes of teaching.

One major obstacle impeding the definition of educational growth is the current status of the science of education in what has been referred to as a transition period (Kuhn 1972). In its present transitional state, education is without a predominant paradigm. Instead, several paradigms (borrowed from psychology and epistemology), existing side by side, attempt to explain the same or related phenomena, each with its own set of assumptions and concomitant definitions of growth. In this chapter we discuss those models of intellectual and affective growth with greatest relevance to education, point out the relative strengths and weaknesses of each model, and describe some recent attempts to formulate general growth paradigms that treat prior models as special cases.

Many of the twentieth-century views of educational growth discussed here were clearly anticipated by Plato and Aristotle, were rediscovered and amplified by many western philosophers and psychologists, and deserve at least brief mention for historical perspective. For a more detailed discussion, see Riegel (1972) on the historical evolution of psychological conceptions of growth and development and Walberg (1975) on the educational applications of developmental theories.

The continental European tradition of psychological structuralism includes Descartes, Leibnitz, Hegel, Rousseau, Kant, Pestalozzi, Froebel, Montessori, Freud, Spranger, and Piaget and derives from Socrates and Plato, whose dualistic mind-matter theory of education portrays the teacher as a "midwife of ideas" inherent in the child's mind. The tradition emphasizes the uniqueness of the child and the qualitative stages of psychic growth. It has often led to educational applications that are child centered or child directed in varying degrees and forms. Rousseau's romantic idea of the child's inherent savage nobility is one extreme of this tradition. From the continental perspective, the child's educational progress is not so much a function of individual needs and innately determined development; rather, the structuring, integration, and stage-wise transformation of knowledge (rather than the accumulation of discrete elements) are stressed.

The Anglo-American tradition includes Hobbes, Locke, Darwin, Spencer, Sumner, Pearson, Galton, Hall, Thorndike, Gesell, and Terman and derives from Aristotle's notion of learning as the association of discrete ideas. Atomism, both mental and behavioral, is a dominant psychological idea in England, the United States, and other English-speaking nations. The Anglo-American model of mental growth assumes the steady amassing of knowledge rather than stage-wise reorganizations. As represented in the work of Thorndike and Terman, educational applications of atomistic theory include curricular materials divided into units and discrete elements and continuous indexes of growth indicated by sums of items correctly answered on multiple-choice, psychometric tests. The Anglo-American educational psychologist characteristically employs statistical analysis of cross-sectional psychometric data on large numbers of students or of closely manipulated, controlled experiments, whereas continental psychologists typically employ intensive, longitudinal case studies of one or a few children.

The division of psychology by the English Channel is obviously oversimplified; both continental and Anglo-American psychologists are aware of the two traditions and draw on both of them. Nonetheless, the intellectual gap between them in its philosophical, scientific, and pedagogical aspects persists and causes misunderstandings among educational theorists and practitioners. Our discussion of twentieth-century research starts with the atomistic tradition because it is more familiar, but more attention will be given to stage models because they currently offer an interesting challenge to American psychologists and educators. In the last section, we present several recent models that attempt to bridge the gap between the two traditions.

PSYCHOMETRIC MODELS

Empirical research on educational effects since 1950 has been based primarily on the two mainstreams of educational psychology—behaviorism and psychometrics—which have been characterized as atheoretical by two of their leading proponents (Skinner 1950, Lumsden 1976), although many others would not agree. Behaviorism carries with it a characteristic methodological concern with experimental isolation of short-term discrete observables rather than long-term developmental processes in natural settings. In the cognitive domain, psychometrics in education usually involves atomistic items of verbal knowledge as revealed by internally consistent, multiple-choice, paper-and-pencil tests. Thus, much of the research on teaching effects is an attempt to correlate student gains on multiple-choice tests of knowledge with observed and counted acts of teaching.

Few psychometric studies have been conducted on children tested repeatedly throughout the school years. In the main, those studies have been concerned with vocabulary, general verbal intelligence, and special abilities rather than achievement in the usual school subjects. Nearly all suffer from one or more methodological problems arising from cross-sectional data; small, unrepresentative samples; unreliable measures; and limitations in analysis. Nevertheless, it is far easier to criticize such studies than it is to do them well; moreover, there is much to learn from them, and they may anticipate what will be found with more adequate research methods.

It may be recalled that Binet and Simon (1916), turn-of-the-century French founders of mental measurement, sought to devise and select intelligence test items for a given age upon which about half the children would succeed. Items with either near zero or near complete success have little power to discriminate among students, and—being out of the appropriate age range—would be too easy or too difficult for efficient measurement of individual differences. Since Binet, educational measurement as it is taught and used concerns such normative or relative comparisons of individuals of the same age or grade rather than the absolute growth of single individuals over time. The pervasive technique may be likened to using a different and relative scale to measure height at each year of age. This would encourage statements such as, "Tom was at the sixty-fifth percentile at age ten and at the fifty-fifth at age thirteen," instead of concrete expressions of absolute growth such as, "Tom grew two inches in three years" or of metric relations such as, "an average protein deficiency of 40 grams per day is associated with growth deficit of .15 meter in height over a given age range."

Normative or relative measurement is seldom used in the natural sciences; and one of the main impediments to behavioral theory and research in natural settings is the lack of absolute measures. Coaching and physical training offer the best examples of teaching most feasible for productivity research because absolute measures, such as time and distance, can be used. Thus it is possible to observe in the coaching of competitive swimming that many laps at a moderate rate lead to fast times for endurance swims such as the 1500 meter, and moderate numbers of fast laps with short rests lead to fast sprint times (Counsilman 1968). Gains in academic teaching efficiency since 1900 might be difficult to prove, but coaching for athletic competition has made steady progress in breaking records decade after decade, partially due, no doubt, to the availability of absolute measures of independent and dependent variables, even without true experimentation. Random manipulation of the independent variables in coaching many sports eventually permits the accurate forecasts of the multiple outcomes of a given regimen for an individual. The analytic work of Thurstone (1929), Bock (1975), and Wright (1977) on absolute psychometric scaling holds out the possibility of comparable precision in the area of academic growth.

Investigators have estimated vocabulary growth more often than any other cognitive measures (Dale 1965), perhaps because the number of words can be estimated and because most aptitude and achievement tests are saturated, that is, correlate highly, with vocabulary. Nonetheless, the estimation of vocabulary is fraught with methodological difficulty (Lorge and Chall 1963). Estimates of vocabulary for a given grade or age group can vary by a factor of ten depending on the sample, what is meant by knowing a word (for example, pronouncing it, selecting the correct definition from a list, or recalling it from memory), whether multiple meanings of words are considered, and other factors.

Smith's (1941) study, one of the most extensive in the literature, produced smoothed estimates of vocabulary for grades two through twelve. Her estimates of the twenty-fifth, fiftieth, and seventy-fifth quartiles suggest decelerated growth in grades three through six and acceleration after ninth grade. However, dropouts in the high school years leave a more select group in school, which may account for the late acceleration in these cross-sectional data. Dale (1965) estimates that children on the average finish first grade with a vocabulary of three thousand words and add linearly one thousand words a year through the fourth year of college. Smith's and Dale's estimates of twelfth-grade vocabulary (sixty thousand versus fourteen thousand words) and projections of the growth curve (reaccelerating versus linear) differ sharply. The discrepancies may be attributable to cross-sectional, aggregate data.

Thurstone's (1929) cross-sectional estimates of Binet intelligence of 4,208 children ages three through seventeen cover a wider span than most vocabulary studies and suggest accelerating growth from birth through age twelve and rapid deceleration thereafter. Bayley's analysis of longitudinal data from three studies, however, suggests rapid linear growth in intelligence from birth through the school years until about age nineteen and slow growth thereafter. Thus even the best estimates of cognitive growth seem indecisive.

One problem with all the estimates of cognitive growth discussed thus far is that they are based on grade- or age-group means. As Bock (1975) points out, biologists have long known from physical growth studies that means obscure the actual growth curve of individuals. The plot of height by month of a single individual during adolescence usually shows a sharp growth spurt at a certain period. But the onset of that period will vary considerably among individuals, and a plot of means of age groups will be far more regular and gradual than for an individual (Batschelet 1971). Bock's analysis of longitudinal growth in verbal ability of thirty-six boys and twenty-eight girls in a laboratory school during the three years from grade eight to grade eleven shows that only linear growth can be detected for any individual. Yet a decelerating trend of means by grade is highly significant. Thus the precision and regularity of averaging reveals the decelerating trend, but the tests—though technically good by the usual standards and reliable for measuring differences among individuals and linear and quadratic growth of the group—are too unreliable to measure any curvature or other departure from linear growth for a single individual. Indeed, in a recent interview, Linn and Slinde (1977) conclude that even difference scores for individuals from a pretest to a postest are too unreliable to warrant calculation and interpretation.

If agronomists had been unable to relate yield or value added to amount of irrigation, rainfall, and fertilizer, agricultural productivity would be far lower than it is. Before considering stage models of growth, the limitations and the important possibilities of the psychometric tradition should be considered.

Unlike biology and economics, educational research has no widely agreed-upon theory of growth; and despite three-quarters of a century of effort, cognitive measures are insufficiently reliable to trace accurately the growth trajectory of vocabulary, general intelligence, special abilities, and school achievement among individuals. Only by having reliable absolute measures throughout the school years and a clear picture of the normal course of individual growth in a given environment will it be possible to estimate the departures from natural growth curves replicably and accurately or, more specifically, the dependencies of acceleration in growth on given educational processes.

Successfully or not, school staffs in recent decades have attempted to tailor instruction to individual needs rather than using the compromise of factors that would presumably suit the hypothetical median student. Wright (1977) suggests several ways that testing might also be tailored in this way. For example, a booklet of test items of ordered difficulty can be designed so that the students can rapidly find the sequence of moderately challenging items which provide the most reliable estimate of their ability in a minimum amount of time. Extensions of the Rasch model permit the accurate calibration of items and tests for reliable measurement of individual growth. Moreover, Bock (1975) has adapted the mathematical theory of logistic biological growth for educational research and has shown how to estimate cognitive growth of individuals from their responses to items of heterogeneous difficulty.

To conclude this section, it may be speculated that one precondition for a warranted theory of educational productivity is an adequate theory and measure of cognitive growth. Such a contention follows from analogous historical reasoning in biology and economics. The theoretical development underlying applications from those fields to agriculture and investment required explicit models of growth and measures of increased yield. The same contention may also be argued on the grounds of operational definition: if the theory of education must specify the quantitative constants of the dependencies of learning on educational processes, then reliable measures of absolute growth and its acceleration are required to estimate the constants accurately and replicably. Biology provides growth curves and equations that seem good bets for probing in educational research. It seems that such probing is prevented more by our ingrained habits of normative conception and measurement than by actual theoretical or technological obstacles.

STAGE MODELS

Unlike the psychometric models that assume steady growth, a number of accounts of cognitive and affective growth portray development as a series of qualitative transformations or stages. Common to all stage models is the assumption that each stage represents a point of discontinuity with past ways of organizing information or interacting with the environment. Another assumption common to these models is that the sequence of transformations of growth stages is invariant in the sense that more advanced levels can never precede more primitive levels. Beyond these points of commonality, however, stage models can be divided into different types by considering (a) their assumptions regarding the mechanism of stage change and (b) their definitions of the structure and content of the growth sequence. In this review we will look at three types of stage models: functional-descriptive, psychoanalytic, and cognitive-developmental. Throughout our discussion we will refer to Table 8-1, which presents a sketch of the stage sequences offered by the various growth models.

Table 8-1

Stages of development defined by Havighurst, Freud, Erikson, Piaget, and Kohlberg

Approximate ages	Functionalist: Havighurst (1964) Stages of vocational dev.	Psychoanalytic: Erikson (1950) Ego stages	Psychoanalytic: Freud (1953) Psychosexual stages	Cognitive-Developmental: Piaget (1970) Cognitive dev.	Cognitive-Developmental: Kohlberg (1975) Moral dev.
0–2 years		Trust versus mistrust	Oral stage	Sensorimotor	
2–4		Autonomy versus doubt	Anal stage	Preoperational stage / Preconceptual phase	Level I Preconventional / Stage 1 – Heteronomous morality
4–6	Identification with a worker	Initiative versus guilt	Phallic stage	Intuitive phase	
10	Acquiring the basic habits of industry	Industry versus inferiority	Latency period	Concrete operations	Stage 2 – Instrumental hedonistic morality
12		Identity versus role confusion	Genital stage	Formal operations	Level II Conventional / Stage 3 – Interpersonal concordance "good-boy" morality
15	Acquiring identity as a worker		To adulthood	To adulthood	
18–25		Intimacy versus isolation			Stage 4 – Social system law-and-order morality
Adulthood	Becoming a productive person	Generativity versus stagnation			Level III Postconventional principled / Stage 5 – Social-contract morality
Old age		Integrity versus despair			

Functional-Descriptive Growth Models

We classify as functional-descriptive growth models those systems that focus on the definition of what is typical of a person at a given age, and/or the nature of the developmental tasks associated with a given age, with less concern for the mechanisms or processes that underlie the transformations from one point in development to another. Two such models have had important influences on educational practice in this century and thus deserve our attention: Gesell's growth stages and Havighurst's sequence of developmental tasks.

Gesell's Sequential Levels. The notion of sequential levels of growth as an important idea for educators first gained prominence when proposed by Gesell in the 1920s. By observing and recording a wide range of physical and behavioral features at successive ages, Gesell (1928) defined a sequence of age norms that he generalized as a set of universal stages (Bayley 1970). Each stage, which is equivalent to the characteristics of a given age, is believed to represent the child as a total organism. Such descriptions as the "terrible twos," and the "terrific threes" sprang from this proposal.

Gesell's approach has been criticized in recent years for the circularity of ascribing behavior to a stage merely because the behavior typically appears at a given age (Achenbach 1978) and for failing to demonstrate the interrelationship among the various aspects presumed to define a given stage (Ginsburg and Opper 1969). Nonetheless, Gesell's notion of the sequential emergence of various competencies has had great influence on notions of school readiness. Recently researchers at the Gesell Institute (Ilg and Ames 1965, Ames and Ilg 1964) have reestablished the age norms and proffer a set of school-readiness tests intended to determine overall readiness rather than a single index of intellectual development, such as the IQ. Kaufman and Kaufman (1972) determined that the battery of Gesell measures taken at kindergarten correlated moderately with first-grade achievement ($r = .56$ to $.64$ as measured with the Stanford Achievement Test). This predictive validity was higher than that for a standardized group intelligence test. The utility of the proposed "whole organism" view of growth is challenged, however, by findings of near zero predictive validity of general maturational growth measures such as teething. A possibility (unresolved by the Kaufman and Kaufman study) is that the success of the Gesell Institute battery as a measure of school readiness may well be mediated by the kinds of cognitive changes described by Piaget. We will discuss Piaget's model later in this chapter.

Havighurst's Developmental Tasks. A second functional-descriptive model that has had an impact on educational practice is Havighurst's (1948, 1953) sequence of developmental tasks. In Havighurst's model, individual development is defined as a series of developmental tasks each of which must be dealt with successfully at the proper time in order for later developmental tasks to be achieved. Examples of developmental tasks at the elementary grade level include such things as learning to get along with age mates, learning an appropriate masculine or feminine role, developing fundamental skills in reading, writing, and calculating. At the secondary grade level the tasks include achieving emotional independence of parents and other adults, selecting and preparing for an occupation, and preparing for marriage and family life. Accordingly, Havighurst asserts that the purpose of education is to help the student achieve his or her developmental tasks in a personally and socially satisfactory way. Consistent with this aim, Havighurst integrates his view of the developmental task with the notion of "the teachable moment" or the critical period in which the learning of the role or task achievement should occur. For example, he proposes (1964) that adolescence is the really critical period for vocational decision making (see Table 8-1).

Havighurst's developmental progression offers an insightful descriptive analysis of age-typical events. His emphasis is upon the normal and his integration of social and emotional growth with both intellectual attainment and practical life-task skills have made his description particularly appealing to educators put off by the overtones of pathology in psychoanalytic accounts and the abstract nature of Piagetian descriptions of logical forms. Havighurst's model is seriously limited, however, as a measure of educational growth. First, the assumption of critical periods of development can be questioned. For example, recent research (McLaughlin 1977, Snow and Hoefnagle-Hohle 1978, Walberg et al. 1978) in the area of second-language acquisition, long thought to be a facility that diminishes with age (Lenneburg 1967), has indicated that there is no critical period for learning a second language. Second, Havighurst's model catalogs a series of sociocultural tasks that are, by definition, normative descriptions of age-related behaviors of a particular historical period for members of a given social class, sex, ethnic group, or culture. Thus,

Havighurst's progression cannot serve as an absolute measure of educational growth.

In summary, functional-descriptive models offer educators a clear set of descriptions of age-typical behaviors that can be used as bench marks of the student's progress toward maturity. Because of the lack of emphasis on theory, however, these models do not adequately explain (a) how events in one stage are related to occurrences in later stages, (b) why certain things appear together at given ages, and (c) how movement from one stage to the next occurs. Thus, it becomes difficult for the educator to plan strategies that will insure that growth will occur. A final limit of many functional-descriptive models (as evidenced in Havighurst's approach) is the description of growth in terms of sociocultural achievements, thus limiting the utility of a given model to a particular cultural group or historical period.

Psychoanalytic Stage Theories of Freud and Erikson

Freud's Psychosexual Stages. Development according to Freud is a progression of psychosexual stages in which movement from one level to the next is dictated by biological factors that regulate the shift of libidinal energy from one region of the body to another. Each shift results in a novel set of interactions with the environment made necessary by the individual's needs to find acceptable ways to reduce the psychic tension associated with the libidinal urges of a given stage. As each stage is encountered, concomitant personality structures are formed (see Table 8-1). The form that the resolution of the problems of a given stage takes is greatly affected by environmental circumstance. Thus, although the sequence of stages is determined by maturation, the structure of the individual's psyche is unique.

The process of development and the universal struggles attributed to each level are presumed to be responsible for qualitative shifts in the type of intellectual activity associated with various ages. Anna Freud (1966) links intellectual creativity or fervor with various periods of psychosexual development. Preschool children, she writes, display a number of brilliant and creative intellectual achievements as a result of prohibitions against their inquiries into the mysteries of sex, which cause them to redirect their questioning into other areas. Similarly, the adolescent seems brighter than younger children essentially owing to the enormous surge of libido at puberty. Like a forest ranger who becomes more sharp sighted when he hears that there might be a fire in the area, his ego, responding to the increased instinctual pressures, expands its powers of rationality. According to Freud, during the period of latency in the elementary school years, children not only dare not indulge in abstract thought; they may have no need to do so. Infancy and puberty are periods of instinctual danger, and the intelligence that characterizes them serves at least in part to assist the individual to surmount that danger. In latency and adult life, the ego is relatively strong and can without detriment to the individual "relax its efforts to intellectualize the instinctual process" (p. 164).

Though attempting to explain a set of assumed age-related intellectual characteristics in terms of psychosexual development, Anna Freud does not offer any objective data of her own to support such a contention. For the most part, Freudian educational psychologists focus their attention upon the relationship between the school environment and the psychodynamics of each stage as they relate to ego functioning and the development of the healthy personality. Educational productivity is viewed as a function of sublimated libidinal needs channeled through the reality function of the ego. Since maturation determines the sequence of developmental events, the role of the environment (hence education) is to foster the "healthy" or successful resolution of the problems presented at each age (Bettelheim 1948, Ekstein and Motto 1966, A. Freud 1969).

Freud's account of development offers a positive contribution to education in that it moves the question of achievement away from the predominant emphasis upon cognitive mechanisms and brings the relationship between emotional development and the overall aims of education into focus. Second, the Freudian model offers education an absolute set of age-related variables with which to assess growth and development and upon which to base intervention strategies. The emphasis on maturation makes it difficult, however, to see how education can alter the rate of development or movement through disruptive periods.

Major criticisms of the theory attack the sexist aspects of the explanation of growth that define female psychosexual development in terms of lacks in male characteristics rather than in terms of female attributes. This particular criticism is important if such definitional flaws result in an inaccurate assessment of female growth. While a number of contemporary analysts (Barglow 1977) have attempted to address this issue, it is not clear that they have succeeded in demonstrating the efficacy of Freudian typology for assessing female psychosexual maturity.

A second set of criticisms focuses on problems in measuring growth in terms of psychosexual level. One aspect of this problem is the vagueness and complexity of psychoanalytic interpretations that make assessment of an individual's growth largely unreliable even among experts (Anastasi 1976). Another measurement problem stems from the definition of growth stages in terms of a sequence of qualitatively differing attributes without defining the structural relationship between later stages and the outcome of earlier stages. Thus, as Loevinger (1966) points out, the measurement of psychosexual level means measurement of a whole series of things, at least one for each level, each to be measured in terms of muchness. Referring to Blum (1949), Loevinger reminds us that such judgments are notoriously difficult to make. A third and perhaps damning criticism is the contention that Freudian theory, with its emphasis upon unobservable intrapsychic events and post hoc explanatory devices for observed behaviors (for example, reaction formation: you say you don't agree with me because you do agree with me, but you don't want to admit to yourself that you do agree), renders itself untestable and hence not within the realm of scientific investigation.

Erikson's Psychosocial Stages. While adhering to the basic tenets of Freudian doctrine, Erikson (1950) takes exception to Freud's accounts of ego development. Basing his position on Hartmann's (1939) notions of "conflict-free ego," Erikson set out to study transformations of the ego as attempts, through the "reality" or cognitive functions, to place the self within a societal context while maintaining a sense of personal continuity or individual identity. Erikson's account of ego development may be viewed as relevant to attempts to chart the course of educational growth in two ways. First, the bipolar sequence of transformations in ego structure (see Table 8-1) may be viewed as a description of potential socioemotional achievements that education may wish to foster. Second, the stages indicate potential periods of psychological stress that may portend periods of disruption in the course of academic achievement.

Recent research within the Eriksonian framework has demonstrated that the stages proposed are age related (Ciaccio 1971) and has

offered measures that can differentiate among the different forms of
development at Stage 5—identity versus role diffusion (Constantinople
1969, Dignan 1963, Marcia 1966). Use of these scales has demonstrated changes in ego-identity status over time (Marcia 1976, Waterman
and Goldman 1976) and has shown relationships between ego-
identity status and various behavioral and personality variables
(Marcia 1975, Marcia and Friedman, 1970, Orlofsky et al. 1973,
Waterman and Goldman 1976). These studies lend support to Erikson's proposals of the stages as developmental and offer the prospect
that one may identify individual developments with some precision.

Criticisms of Erikson's theory are centered, as was the case with
criticism of Freud, upon the discrepancies between male and female
development. The most disturbing of the observed discrepancies with
regard to the veracity of Erikson's model are recent studies indicating
that within the constraints of traditional American society, the stage
of identity versus role diffusion works only for male adolescents.
Women either display types of identity formation inconsistent with
the theory (Marcia and Friedman 1970), skip the stage entirely by
proceeding directly from industry versus inferiority to the stage of
intimacy versus isolation, or display the stage of identity versus role
confusions after first going through the period of intimacy (Douvan
and Adelson 1966). In her cogent analysis of these inconsistencies,
Gallatin (1975) concludes that the strongly biological orientation of
the theory regarding the identity issue creates a problem for the
theory as a whole. From her point of view, history rather than
anatomy is probably the central factor. She suggests that Erikson's
description of the moratorium period is something of an ideal—a
notion with acceptance in the twentieth century. Consistent with
Gallatin's analysis are findings of a recent study (O'Connell 1976) indicating that contemporary career women, who do not disrupt their
careers when they have children, develop identity statuses essentially
like men. These findings offer strong support for the contention that
Erikson's stages represent a series of sociocultural adjustments rather
than a maturationally determined sequence. As such, Erikson's
model may best be understood as a sequence of age-typical, culturally
relative developmental tasks much like the model proposed by Havighurst. Such a conclusion has been reached by Broughton (1975),
Haan (1977), Kohlberg (1973), and Loevinger (1966). As a model of
educational growth, Erikson's approach may thus suffer the same

limitation as that we have attributed to the functional-descriptive growth sequences.

Piaget's Cognitive-Developmental Stage Theory

Most recent research on the relationship between developmental variables and education focuses upon or refers to cognitive-developmental theory. The cognitive-developmental approach presented by Piaget shares a number of features in common with the stage theories already presented. That is, Piaget views intellectual growth as proceeding through an invariant sequence of qualitative transformations in cognitive function organized as stages, rather than by the accumulation of knowledge or incremental quantitative shifts in intellectual capacity characterized by the psychometric approach discussed in the first section.

Too much can be made, however, of the commonalities between Piagetian and other stage theories. While recognizing the role of genetic and environmental factors in the process of intellectual growth, Piaget's approach attributes the emergence of cognitive structure to the individual's construction of meaning as a result of interacting with the environment rather than to the predetermined unfolding of cognitive structure as a process of maturation, or the acquisition of mental structures isomorphic to those of the culture. Piaget's four-point definition of developmental stages summarizes his view: (a) Stages imply distinct or qualitative differences in person's modes of thinking or of solving the same problem. (b) These different modes of thought form an invariant sequence, order, or succession in individual development. While cultural factors may speed up, slow down, or stop development, they do not change its sequence. (c) Each of these different and sequential modes of thought form a "structural whole." A given stage-response on a task does not represent a specific response determined by knowledge and familiarity with that task or tasks similar to it; rather it represents an underlying thought orientation. (d) Cognitive stages are hierarchical integrations. Succeeding stages reintegrate the structure of previous stages into increasingly differentiated and integrated forms of reasoning (Piaget 1960). Four stages of development are defined. These are included in Table 8-1, along with their approximate ages of appearance.

The results of research examining Piaget's description of cognitive development, while largely supportive, have been mixed. Results from a series of cross-cultural studies (Dasen 1977) are consistent with the proposition that the sequence of stages is universal. In concert with those results, a series of training studies (for example, Inhelder et al. 1974, Kamii and Derman 1971, Smedslund 1961) provided evidence that movement from one stage to the next does not occur as a simple function of direct instruction. (For more complete reviews, see Modgil 1976, Strauss 1972, 1975). Studies by Kuhn (1972), Strauss and Liberman (1975), Strauss et al. (1977), and Turiel (1966, 1974) have provided empirical support for the proposal that structural regressions do not occur, thus supporting the proposal that stages progress unidirectionally through a process of transformation and reorganization. Finally, the proposal that development occurs through a series of discrete qualitative transformations rather than through an incremental, cumulative process is supported by a recent study demonstrating that qualitative shifts in problem-solving strategy are associated with marked rather than incremental changes in the quantity (bits) of information obtained (Neimark 1975).

Challenges to Piaget's theory come from several sources. (See Brown and Desforges 1977 for a thorough discussion). Two issues, however, are of central concern: (a) the internal consistency of stages and (b) the nature of stage change. With regard to the first issue, a number of studies have reported moderate correlations between an individual's performance on separate tasks said to measure the same cognitive operation. Typically, these correlations are about .40 (Brown and Desforges 1977). Piagetians explain these findings as illustrating the existence of "horizontal decalage" (temporal lag in the ability to generalize a given form of logic from one task to another, for example, the ability to conserve quantity but not amount). It is necessary, however, that the extent of decalage not overwhelm the examples of internal consistency if the stage notion is to have any utility. In offering a clarification of his notion of structure, Piaget (1968) has raised a number of interesting possibilities. In sum, he has made clear that his notion of structure is not intended to suggest that everything is connected with everything else but rather that knowledge is constructed within "partial structures," which interact with one another to form one's total system of thought. This hypothesis has received expression in recent research and theory in social cognition (Nucci 1977, Nucci and Turiel 1978, Turiel 1978), indicating that various aspects of social reasoning are constructed within distinct conceptual and developmental domains. (See Chapter 5 in this volume for further discussion.) In addition, recent work on formal reasoning (Piaget's fourth stage) may be viewed as attempts to define partial structures by means of factor analysis (Bart 1971) and through more general correlational approaches (Neimark 1970, 1975). While this research offers a possible resolution of the problems associated with defining cognitive structure, the possibility also exists that the research will demonstrate instead that the "cognitive pie" can be divided up any number of ways, thus refuting the notion of cognitive structures and the concomitant stage theory.

The second major issue, the nature of stage change, is equally controversial. A main strength of Piagetian theory as a model of intellectual growth is its inclusion of an explanation by which earlier stages are transformed by the individual into more advanced ways of thinking. One limit to the ready acceptance of Piaget's paradigm as a model of intellectual growth, however, is the apparent lack of specificity regarding the steps individuals take in moving from one level to the next. Recognizing this deficiency, researchers in Geneva (for example, Cellérier 1972) have recently begun attempts to trace the changes from one level to the next by incorporating aspects of information-processing theory into the Piagetian framework. In parallel developments in this country, researchers have attempted to outline the intervening rules or strategies employed in moving from one level to the next. Some of these attempts will be discussed in the next section of this chapter. One potential outcome of this research would be to resolve the apparent incompatibility between incremental and stage descriptions of intellectual growth.

Related to issues of theory are concerns with the process of measuring developmental level. At the present time, most attempts to place stages into a framework of assessment have employed some form of a simplex scale (Guttman 1955). Such measurement is based on the notion that one is capable of passing all items at and below one's developmental level and not those items above that level. A variant on this type of scaling has been used by Kohlberg (1969) as a demonstration of the validity of his moral judgment sequence (see Table 8-1). There are problems, however, with such scalogram analysis. Though the simplex scale will demonstrate that events occur in a given sequence, the technique is not designed to account for transitional events. Thus, the scale cannot account for decalage, which must be either treated as error or ignored. Despite the limits of Guttman scaling, attempts have been made recently to reconcile Piagetian and psychometric approaches. (See Modgil 1976 for a review.) Most ambitious are attempts to employ Rasch scaling (Elliot 1975, 1976; Pearson 1975) as a means of assessing the spread of abilities (decalage within a stage), as well as measuring movement to advanced levels with a series of subscales.

Controversies regarding the validity of Piaget's theory notwithstanding, there has been a trend in recent years to examine seriously the relationships between the Piagetian view of cognitive development and the process of educational growth. Assumptions regarding the potential for such a relationship stem from (a) interpretations of development in the Piagetian sense as an educational aim in itself, thus equating cognitive development (which includes social cognition, for example, moral development) with educational growth; (b) the notion that certain forms of academic content can only be fully understood when the appropriate cognitive structures have been developed; and (c) the notion that the rate of stage change cannot be increased beyond certain limits. Taken together, points (b) and (c) suggest that the process of cognitive development places constraints upon educational growth.

The relationship between the attainment of concrete operations and educational success has been estimated both for school readiness and for the attainment of skills in reading and mathematics in the elementary school. Piagetian measures appear to be good indexes of school readiness. Scott (1969) found that the reasoning level of kindergarten children (n = 356), as measured by a simple seriation task, correlated .69 with scores on the Metropolitan Readiness Test of arithmetic and .82 with scores for reading readiness. Most interesting is the finding that the seriation task measure proved to be a better predictor of later reading achievement than did the standardized readiness test. Kaufman and Kaufman (1972) reported that scores of kindergarten children on a battery of Piagetian tasks correlated .60 with first-grade reading achievement and .64 with arithmetic achievement. Again the Piagetian measure had greater predictive validity than standard readiness measures. Findings for studies investigating the relationship between cognitive level and reading achievement in school-age children are summarized in Table 8-2. The findings show a low or moderate correlation between operative level and reading achievement. Worth noting is the variance in size of correlation depending upon the cognitive task employed. A general trend in the data suggests that the development of class inclusion (knowing that members of one class, for example, cows, are also members of a larger class, that is, animals), and ordinal relations (placing things in order along a single dimension, for example, short to long) are more aligned with reading ability than is the ability to conserve amount (knowing that changes in shape do not change amount). If supported by future research, this trend would indicate that aspects of a given level of development operate independently with regard to the attainment of academic skill rather than as a coordinated structure. Similar moderate correlations are reported in studies investigating operative level and mathematics achievement (see Table 8-2). In sum, the correlations between traditional measures of academic achievement and cognitive development among elementary school children suggest a modest relationship between the two variables.

One factor reducing the size of the correlations is the small age range among subjects within each of the reported studies. Because of this, the possibility exists that the variance in scores of operative thinking among subjects would be quite low, thus reducing the overall correlation with measures estimating more refined quantitative differences in performance. This hypothesis is weakened, however, by findings relating scores on standardized achievement tests with the attainment of formal reasoning ability (Neimark 1975). Findings from several studies (Chiapetta 1976, Kuhn et al. 1977, Shayer et al. 1976) demonstrated that the spread of scores for the attainment of formal thought is quite high among adolescent subjects. Nonetheless, Neimark reports correlations between formal reasoning ability and achievement in mathematics and science of about the same magnitude ($r = .31$ to $.40$ for significant correlations) as those found with younger children (see Table 8-3).

Perhaps the best explanation for these moderate correlations comes from factor analysis (DeVries 1974), indicating that Piagetian measures of knowledge and standard psychometric measures (IQ and achievement tests) overlap to some degree but also measure different aspects of cognitive functioning. Piagetian theory makes a distinction

Table 8-2

Correlation between developmental level assessed
with concrete operations tasks and school achievement

Source	Piagetian task	N	Achievement Measure	r
		Reading achievement		
Almy et al. (1966)	Conservation	37 (kindergarten)	Stanford Achievement	.53
		23 (kindergarten)		.38
		38 (seven-year-olds)		.37
		22 (seven-year-olds)		.39
DeVries (1974)	Cons. liquid	122 (five- to seven-	MAT – Reading	.07
	Cons. mass	year-olds and low IQ		.20
	Cons. number	children six- to twelve-		.09
	Class inclusion	year-olds with MA		.24
	Cons. length	five to seven years)		.02
	Seriation			.22
	Seriation		MAT – word discrimination	.35
Kaufman and Kaufman (1972)	Piaget battery	80 (kindergarten)	Stanford Achievement at first grade	.60
Lunzer and Dolan (1976)	Conservation	210 (six- to seven-year-	Schonell	.31
	Operativity	210 olds)	(graded word)	.57
	Conservation	210	Neal (analytic	.17
	Operativity	210	reading comp.)	.38
Orpet et al. (1976)	Conservation of liquid	52	Stanford Achievement	.13
		Math achievement		
DeVries (1974)	Cons. mass	122 (five- to seven-	MAT, arithmetic subtest	.20
	Cons. number	year-olds and low IQ		.21
	Class inclusion	children six- to twelve-		.41
	Cons. liquid	year-olds with MA		.33
	Cons. length	five to seven years)		.02
	Seriation			.22
Dodwell (1961)	Conservation	34 (kindergarten)	Arithmetic test constructed by experimenter	.59
Kaufman and Kaufman (1972)	Piaget battery	80 (kindergarten)	Stanford Achievement at first grade	.64
Lunzer and Dolan (1976)	Conservation	210 (six-point-seven to	Math test	.48
	Operativity	seven-year-olds)	constructed by experimenters	.71

Table 8-3

Correlations between reasoning level assessed
with formal operations tasks and Stanford Achievement test scores (N=86)

Piagetian task	Language	Arithmetic concept	Arithmetic application	Science
Combination 1	.13	.24	.25	.17
Combination 2	.20	.27	.31*	.16
Permutation 1	.22	.31*	.31*	.19
Permutation 1, IMC	.22	.30	.38	.28
Permutation 2	.18	.40*	.34*	.29
Permutation 2, IMC	.20	.24	.35*	.31*
Correlations: probability notions	.23	.25	.28	.38*

Adapted from Neimark 1975.

*.05 level of significance.

between factual content, which can be acquired through learning, and the actively constructed forms of logic, which interrelate one's store of facts. Standard psychometric tests are heavily saturated with such content, since one function of schooling is to assess students' acquisition of culturally valued information, such as rules of grammar, vocabulary, scientific "facts." In addition, even those aspects of such tests that are interrelated with logic (for example, mathematical skills) may well be estimating a student's ability to apply memorized procedures rather than the student's understanding of the problems or their solutions. From this point of view, then, standard means of assessment play an important role in measuring acquistion of culturally valued facts and skills, but they provide only a rough estimate of the students' cognitive level.

Consistent with this interpretation are findings from studies (Collis 1973, Griffiths, 1976, Herron 1975, Lawson 1974) that have demonstrated more powerful relationships between cognitive level and school-related competencies when the achievement variable was defined in terms of problem-solving ability rather than content familiarity. As an example, Griffiths (1976) found that college students' familiarity with physics content had no relationship to their ability to solve a classic problem in physics; rather, the capacity for formal reasoning appeared to be a requisite for success with the task. Interestingly, Griffiths reports that a number of those subjects with formal reasoning ability and the capacity to master the physics problem were not admitted to a four-year college because of their low scores on standard achievement tests. While such low scores might well have a bearing on other aspects of the skills necessary for success in college, a clear implication of these results is that current measures of educational growth are not adequate measures of a student's cognitive level.

ATTEMPTS AT RECONCILIATION

In recent years there have been a number of attempts to bridge the differences between incremental growth models and Piagetian stage theory (Case 1978a, Céllerier 1972, Pascual-Leone 1970, Scandura 1977, Siegler 1978, Simon 1972). This development has stemmed on the one hand from an awareness of the inadequacy of traditional (S-R) learning theory as an account of the sorts of cognitive changes defined by Piaget and a dissatisfaction on the other hand with the perceived imprecision of Piaget's macroscopic analysis of cognitive structure and his description of stage change.

In the educational arena, these approaches were foreshadowed by Gagné's description (1977) of a cumulative learning hierarchy in which S-R associations are viewed as the basis for later more complex forms of learning such as concept formulation and problem solving. Gagné accounts for the changes in cognitive capacity described by Piaget in terms of the progressive acquisition of superordinate concepts, rules, and skills. To account for the emergence of novel solutions and conceptual abstractions, Gagné has included the possibility that movement from basic S-R learning to higher-order processes may occur through self-initiated cognitive activity. He does not make clear, however, how such self-initiated inductive and deductive processes can be accounted for in terms of S-R histories. Thus, Gagné's attempt to accommodate S-R theory to structuralism has been rigorously criticized as internally contradictory and unparsimonious (Achenbach 1978, Scandura 1973).

In contrast with Gagné, most recent approaches to a fine-grained analysis of cognitive growth have accepted two of Piaget's central notions as the starting point of their examination. First, the learner is viewed as actively processing information, rather than passively acquiring it. Second, the S-R bond has been replaced by the cognitive scheme (or its equivalent, for example, "rule," [Scandura 1973]) as the basic unit of learning. These accommodations with cognitive theory are not confined to models of intellectual growth but are evidenced in a shift in contemporary social learning theory away from its earlier mediation theory stance to its current alignment with cognitive information processing and attribution theories (Aronfreed 1976, Bandura 1977, Mischel and Mischel 1976. See Gordon 1978, for a more thorough discussion.)

Although each of the moves toward accommodating incremental and cognitive developmental theories is distinct, a clear sense of the general form taken by these approaches can be illustrated with brief reference to two models that make direct claims of educational applicability: structural behaviorism (Scandura 1973, 1976, 1977) and the neo-Piagetian approach (Case 1975, 1978a, 1978b, Pascual-Leone 1970).

In both structural behaviorism and the neo-Piagetian model, there is an acceptance of the basic sequence of stages outlined by Piaget as the framework for defining the general course of cognitive growth. Like other contemporary cognitive theorists, however, both Case and Scandura have attempted to add precision to Piaget's description. In Case's model this is achieved by defining the stages in terms of groups of executive strategies that can be modeled by computer simulation rather than in terms of symbolic logic. These executive strategies serve to coordinate the operations, or cognitive subprocesses, involved in the solution of specific problems. Scandura's description of cognitive structure is quite similar to Case's. While Case defines cognitive structure in terms of executive strategies and suboperations, however, Scandura (1977) talks of relational networks or sets of higher-order and lower-order rules (cognitive processes) that comprise the cognitive structures for a given content domain.

Despite these subtle differences in descriptive language, both structural behaviorism and the neo-Piagetian model employ similar procedures to move from global descriptions of overall cognitive organization to microanalysis of the rules or operations that skilled members of a given population employ to solve specific problems, such as long division, subtraction, class inclusion. The method as described by Case (1978b) contains elements from both artificial intelligence research (Klahr and Wallace 1976, Simon 1972) and Piaget's (1960) clinical method. Briefly, the technique combines observation, logical analysis, and experimentation to arrive at a description of the general strategy individuals use to solve a given problem. Once this general strategy has been determined, a detailed analysis of the operations needed to execute each step of the strategy is conducted. The resulting algorithm may then be refined by reading each step in the procedure to an adult who is asked to carry out each operation. If a given procedure results in behavior not observed in the target skilled population, that aspect of the algorithm is modified. By employing variants of this procedure, Case and Scandura claim to be able to identify the nature of shifts in cognitive ability or skill acquisition involved in the mastery of sequences of increasingly complex problems.

In addition to analyzing the progression of strategies or rules employed in comprehending increasingly complex content, any serious attempt to bridge the gap between incremental and Piagetian growth models has to account for the saltatory changes in cognitive capacity associated with Piagetian stage change. Nearly all contemporary models of cognitive growth (for example, Case 1978a, Farnham-Diggory 1972, Klahr and Wallace 1976, Pascual-Leone 1970, Scandura 1977) explain these shifts in cognitive ability in terms of an interrelationship between the complexity of the rules available to the learner and the processing capacity of the individual. This notion (included in structural behaviorism) is most clearly articulated in the neo-Piagetian models, in which the general level of "operativity" considered by Piaget to represent the underlying capacity associated with each developmental stage is redefined in terms of quantifiable levels (units) of working memory. Within the neo-Piagetian framework, the limits in cognitive capacity associated with younger children are explained in terms of restrictions in the complexity of cognitive strategies imposed by the number of available units of working memory. According to Case (1978a), development can be seen as a process of increasing one's units of working memory. Within the model, working memory increases from a biologically determined "functional memory" capacity as a product of the construction and use of increasingly more complex executive strategies. This development occurs progressively as the operations of a given substage are assembled in working memory out of components of the previous stage. Once these new operations become automatized (out of general experience), they add to the capacity of working memory. This increase in memory capacity in turn allows for the construction of more sophisticated executive strategies.

The teaching implications of structural behaviorism and neo-Piagetian theory are being explored (Case 1975, 1978b; Scandura 1973, 1976). We wish to underline several important features of these two contemporary approaches that make them attractive as models of educational growth. First, these models move toward a methodology that permits educators to integrate the step-wise shifts in learner strategy associated with learning culturally defined cognitive skills (for example, the rules of long division) with the series of step-wise changes in learner strategies (cognitive processes) that mark the transition from one level of development to the next. Further, Scandura (1977) has provided a cogent argument that even the construction of general logical abilities is a function of experience within a given content domain. That is, the rules one has available to execute higher-order rules or executive strategies can be effected only if one has the subrules or strategies particular to a given content domain. Thus the prospect exists that one can begin to explain and predict decalage (stage mixture) as the absence of rules or strategies needed to permit the generalization of previously learned procedures to a novel content domain.

With the approach to defining cognitive growth offered by these two models, one can begin to order educational tasks in a nonarbitrary hierarchy as a function of the position of the task in a particular skill algorithm and the position of that algorithm relative to superordinate rules or executive strategies. The ordering of tasks is not only along a vertical dimension of difficulty but also along a horizontal dimension of content. The precision with which task difficulty and corresponding learner capacity can be assessed is further enhanced by the inclusion of a quantitative measure of underlying cognitive capacity (units of working memory) that establishes the general parameters of the complexity of strategies available to the learner.

Evidence that the sort of analysis just described can be translated into practical assessment techniques has been provided in a series of studies conducted by Scandura and his associates. Their general procedure was to identify the algorithms that represent the sequence of rules used by skilled members of a target population to solve a given set of problems. The algorithms were then used to partial out the problems into tasks of equivalent difficulty. Next, an experimental group was tested with two items from each of the equivalence classes. Performance on one item from each equivalence class was used to predict success or failure on the second item. The rationale behind this procedure was that the presence or absence of a given rule set should relate directly to success or failure on problems of a given type. Conversely, success or failure on an item of a given type should be evidence of the presence or absence of the rule. In this fashion, overt behavior on an objective test should provide an accurate indication of whether or not the learner possesses specific rules or strategies that can be precisely located in a sequence of educational growth. When such testing was done under ordinary classroom conditions, the predictions were accurate in about 84 percent of the cases (Durnin and Scandura 1973).

It is a great leap to go from results of this sort to construction of assessment devices that can reliably and accurately index an individual's position on a growth function. However, the possibility that one can generate a sequence of test items that corresponds to a meaningful skill dimension integrated with a nonarbitrarily designated course of cognitive development offers an exciting prospect. Such a procedure has clear advantages over simplistic applications of Rasch scaling, in which the studied absence of theoretical assumptions about what one is measuring can lead to the ranking of tasks along trivial dimensions. Conjoining Rasch scaling with the sort of analytic procedures offered by neo-Piagetian and structural behaviorist models, however, may prove to be a formidable approach with which to define educational growth.

Although the models accommodating Piagetian and incremental views of cognitive growth offer education a set of new and exciting prospects, some words of caution are in order. Regarding Case's work, Flavell (1978) has remarked that it has yet to be demonstrated that the units of working memory can be reliably defined. Without such reliability, the utility of that aspect of the model is lost. In the same vein, one can reasonably ask whether the definition of operativity in terms of units of working memory constitutes an oversimplification of stage change by focusing upon one outcome (memory capacity) resulting from increases in the flexibility of thought associated with progressive transformations in cognitive structure.

A second problem faced by neo-Piagetian and structural-behaviorist accounts of cognitive growth is that the number of algorithms and their potential interrelations needed to account for a complete microanalysis of cognitive growth is staggering. Related to the problem posed by the sheer number of processes to be described is the probability that the algorithms defined will not accurately reflect the reasoning of all individuals. That is, while one can define a procedure *sufficient* to solve a given problem and perhaps even hit upon an approach used by many individuals, a given algorithm does not constitute a *necessary* approach to solving a given problem. Thus, one cannot assume that the steps outlined in one's analysis will necessarily hold for a given individual's approach to solving specific problems. In response to such issues, Scandura (1977) and similar theorists (Case 1975, 1978b, Klahr and Wallace 1976, Siegler 1978) present the view that there are in practice a finite number of ways in which a given population will solve problems within the bounds of a given content domain, and these procedures can be defined with sufficient precision to match the needs of the normal members of the population.

The issues raised regarding the number and form of the algorithms needed to account accurately for cognitive growth touch on the central problem area in attempts to conjoin incremental and cognitive developmental theories. As we have already noted, Piaget (1963) makes a distinction between knowledge (facts or procedures) that can be acquired through direct instruction and the process of logic underlying comprehension of those procedures. From a Piagetian perspective, the emergence of logical operations is a function of the individual's construction of knowledge out of the person's actions on the environment. The precise steps involved in the construction of knowledge are hence postulated as *unique* to each individual. From the cognitive-developmental stance, the psychologist can outline the procedures that emerge at substages representing points at which these individual constructions eventuate in common general strategies. In addition, one can outline in algorithmic form the culturally variable problem-solving strategies (procedures for adding columns of numbers) that depend upon certain minimal logical competencies represented by a given substage. One cannot hope, however, to apply a common algorithm to represent the paths that individuals take to reach those developmental plateaus. The differentiation between what can be instructed and that which must be constructed has never

Comparison of aspects emphasized in psychological models of educational growth

Growth models	Genetic determinants	Continuity	Qualitative transformation	Acquisition of information	Cognition	Affect	Theory	Measurement	Absolute criteria of growth
Psychometric	2	4	1	4	2	1	1	4	1
Psychoanalytic									
Freud	4	1	4	1	1	4	4	1	4
Erikson	3	2	4	2	2	4	4	2	3
Functional/Descriptive									
Gesell	4	1	3	1	1	2	1	3	3
Havighurst	2	2	3	3	1	3	1	1	2
Cognitive-Developmental									
Piaget	2	2	4	2	4	1	4	2	4
Kohlberg	2	2	4	2	4	2	4	2	4
Hierarchical behaviorism									
Gagné	1	3	3	4	2	1	2	3	2
Behavioral structuralism									
Scandura	1	3	3	4	3	1	4	4	3
Neo-Piagetian									
Case	2	3	3	3	4	1	4	3	4

1—Little emphasis.
2—Moderate emphasis.
3—Strong emphasis.
4—Very strong emphasis.

been clearly made in any of the existing attempts to link incremental and stage theories. Such a differentiation is necessary, however, if we hope to delineate general transindividual patterns of educational growth that can be defined and measured with general procedures from the idiographic shifts in cognitive strategy inherent in the individual's construction of knowledge.

SUMMARY AND CONCLUSIONS

In this chapter we have examined a number of psychological models of intellectual and affective development relevant to the definition of educational growth. As models of educational growth, each of the approaches has strengths and weaknesses stemming from the aspects they emphasize. As can be seen in Table 8-4 (constructed by the authors), psychometric approaches—emphasizing measurement, information acquisition, and continuity—provide excellent means of assessing incremental changes in the acquisition of facts. However, the relative lack of emphasis on qualitative changes in cognitive functioning makes them less useful than cognitive-developmental approaches for the assessment of transformations in students' ways of thinking. In addition, the cognitive-developmental approaches offer a set of absolute rather than normative measures of growth, thus increasing their utility. On the other hand, by not emphasizing measurement of the changes taking place between stages, current cognitive-developmental approaches reduce their power as general models of growth. Recent approaches to cognitive growth (as illustrated by the neo-Piagetian and structural-behaviorist models) offer the prospect of combining several of the best features of both the psychometric and cognitive-developmental approaches. As we saw earlier in the chapter, advances in statistical analysis (Bock 1975, Rasch 1966) open up the possibility that such a combination of cognitive-developmental and psychometric approaches can be achieved.

Even the marriage of psychometrics and cognitive-stage theory, however, cannot compensate for the historical lack of emphasis on affective growth in those models. At the present time there is no other approach that incorporates the descriptive richness of affective growth offered by the psychoanalytic models. Unfortunately, the lack of emphasis on measurement and cognitive development makes psychoanalytic approaches poor candidates as models of educational growth. Thus, there is a need for future research emphasizing the interaction between cognitive and affective growth processes if we are to develop a complete model of educational growth. Current trends in research on social cognition offer promise in this regard. (See Chapter 5 in this volume.)

REFERENCES

Achenbach, Thomas M. *Research in Developmental Psychology: Concepts, Strategies, Methods.* New York: Free Press, 1978.

Almy, Millie; Crittenden, Edward; and Miller, Paula. *Young Children's Thinking.* New York: Teachers College Press, 1966.

Ames, Louise B., and Ilg, Frances L. "Gesell Behavior Tests as Predictive of Later Grade Placement." *Perceptual and Motor Skills* 19 (December 1964): 719-22.

Anastasi, Anne. *Psychological Testing.* 4th ed. New York: Macmillan, 1976.

Aronfreed, Justin. "Moral Development from the Standpoint of a General Psychological Theory." In *Moral Development and Behavior: Theory, Research, and Social Issues,* edited by Thomas Lickona, pp. 54-69. New York: Holt, Rinehart and Winston, 1976.

Bandura, Albert. *Social Learning Theory.* Englewood Cliffs, N.J.: Prentice-Hall, 1977.

Barglow, Peter. "The Fate of the Feminine Self in Normative Adolescent Regression." Paper presented at the Second Annual Central States Conference, American Society for Adolescent Psychiatry, Dallas, Texas, 1977.

Bart, W.M. "The Factor Structure of Formal Operations." *British Journal of Educational Psychology* 41 (February 1971): 70-77.

Batschelet, Edward. *Introduction to Mathematics for Life Scientists.* New York: Springer-Verlag, 1971.

Bayley, Nancy. "Development of Mental Abilities." In *Carmichael's Manual of Child Psychology.* Vol. 2. Edited by Paul H. Mussen, pp. 1163-1210. New York: John Wiley, 1970.

Bettelheim, Bruno. "The Social-studies Teacher and the Emotional Needs of Adolescents." *School Review* 56 (December 1948): 585-92.

Binet, Alfred, and Simon, Th. *The Development of Intelligence in Children.* Baltimore: Williams and Wilkens, 1916.

Blum, Gerald S. "A Study of the Psychoanalytic Theory of Psychosexual Development." *Genetic Psychology Monographs* 39 (February 1949): 3-99.

Bock, R. Darrell. "Basic Issues in the Measurement of Change." Unpublished manuscript, University of Chicago, 1975.

Broughton, John. "The Development of Natural Epistemology in Adolescence and Early Adulthood." Ph.D. dissertation, Harvard University, 1975.

Brown, G., and Desforges, C. "Piagetian Psychology and Education: Time for Revision." *British Journal of Educational Psychology* 47 (February 1977): 7-17.

Case, Robbie. "Gearing the Demands of Instruction to the Developmental Capacities of the Learner." *Review of Educational Research* 45 (Winter 1975): 59-87.

————. "Intellectual Development from Birth to Adulthood: A Neo-Piagetian Interpretation." In *Children's Thinking: What Develops?* edited by Robert S. Siegler, pp. 37-71. Hillsdale, N.J.: Lawrence Erlbaum Associates, 1978(a).

————. "A Developmentally Based Theory and Technology of Instruction." *Review of Educational Research* 48 (Summer 1978b): 439-63.

Cellérier, Guy. "Information Processing Tendencies in Recent Experiments in Cognitive Learning: Theoretical Implications." In *Information Processing in Children,* edited by Sylvia Farnham-Diggory, pp. 115-23. New York: Academic Press, 1972.

Chiapetta, Eugene L. "A Review of Piagetian Studies Relevant to Science Instruction at the Secondary and College Level." *Science Education* 60 (April-June 1976): 253-61.

Ciaccio, N.V. "A Test of Erikson's Theory of Ego Epigenesis." *Developmental Psychology* 4 (May 1971): 306-311.

Collis, Kevin F. "A Study of Children's Ability to Work with Elementary Mathematical Systems." *Australian Journal of Psychology* 25 (August 1973): 121-30.

Constantinople, Anne. "An Eriksonian Measure of Personality Development in College Students." *Developmental Psychology* 1 (July 1969): 357-72.

Counsilman, James E. *The Science of Swimming.* Englewood Cliffs, N.J.: Prentice-Hall, 1968.

Dale, Edgar. "Vocabulary Measurement: Techniques and Major Findings." *Elementary English* 42 (December 1965): 895-948.

Dasen, Pierre R., ed. *Piagetian Psychology: Cross-Cultural Contributions.* New York: Gardner, 1977.

DeVries, Rheta. "Relationships among Piagetian, I.Q., and Achievement Assessments." *Child Development* 45 (September 1974): 746-56.

Dignan, Mary H. "Ego Identity, Maternal Identification, and Adjustment in College Women." Ph.D. dissertation, Fordham University, 1963.

Dodwell, P.C. "Children's Understanding of Number Concepts: Characteristics of an Individual and of a Group Test." *Canadian Journal of Psychology* 15 (March 1961): 29-36.

Douvan, Elizabeth, and Adelson, Joseph. *The Adolescent Experience.* New York: John Wiley, 1966.

Durnin, John, and Scandura, Joseph. "An Algorithmic Approach to Assessing Behavior Potential: Comparison with Item Forms and Hierarchical Technologies." *Journal of Educational Psychology* 65 (October 1973): 262-72.

Ekstein, Rudolf, and Motto, Rocco L. "Psychoanalysis and Education: Teachers Teaching Techniques and the Curriculum." *Reiss-David Clinic Bulletin* 3 (1966): 5-73.

Elliott, Colin. "The British Intelligence Scale: Final Report Before Standardization, 1975-76." Paper presented to the Annual Conference of the British Psychological Society, Nottingham, England, 1975.

————. "The Measurement of Development." In *Piaget, Psychology, and Education*, edited by Ved P. Varma and Phillip Williams, pp. 57-73. Itasca, Ill.: Peacock, 1976.

Erikson, Erik. *Childhood and Society*. New York: Norton, 1950.

Farnham-Diggory, Sylvia. "The Development of Equivalence Systems." In *Information Processing in Children*, edited by Sylvia Farnham-Diggory, pp. 43-64. New York: Academic Press, 1972.

Flavell, John H. "Comments." In *Children's Thinking: What Develops?* edited by Robert S. Siegler, pp. 97-105. Hillsdale, N.J.: Lawrence Erlbaum Associates, 1978.

Freud, Anna. *The Writings of Anna Freud*, vol. 2: *The Ego and the Mechanisms of Defense*. New York: International Universities, 1966.

————. "Adolescence as a Developmental Disturbance." In *Adolescence: Psychosocial Perspectives*, edited by Gerald Caplan and Serge Lebovici, pp. 5-10. New York: Basic Books, 1969.

Freud, Sigmund. *A General Introduction to Psychoanalysis*, translated by Joan Riviere. New York: Permabooks, 1953.

Gagné, Robert. *The Conditions of Learning*. New York: Holt, Rinehart and Winston, 1977.

Gallatin, Judith E. *Adolescence and Individuality: A Conceptual Approach to Adolescent Psychology*. New York: Harper & Row, 1975.

Gesell, Arnold. *Infancy and Human Growth*. New York: Macmillan, 1928.

Ginsburg, Herbert, and Opper, Sylvia. *Piaget's Theory of Intellectual Development*. Englewood Cliffs, N.J.: Prentice-Hall, 1969.

Gordon, Neal J. "A Review of Albert Bandura's *Social Learning Theory*." *International Journal of Political Education* 1 (September 1978): 292-95.

Griffiths, David H. "Physics Teaching: Does It Hinder Development?" *American Journal of Physics* 44 (January 1976): 81-86.

Guttman, Louis. "A Generalized Simplex for Factor Analysis." *Psychometrika* 20 (September 1955): 173-92.

Haan, Norma. *Coping and Defending*. San Francisco: Academic Press, 1977.

Hartmann, Heinz. *Ego Psychology and the Problem of Adaptation*, translated by David Rapaport. New York: International Universities, 1939.

Havighurst, Robert J. *Developmental Tasks and Education*. Chicago: University of Chicago Press, 1948.

————. *Human Development and Education*. New York: Longmans, 1953.

————. "Youth in Exploration and Man Emergent." In *Man in a World at Work*, edited by Henry Borow, pp. 237-56. Boston: Houghton Mifflin Co., 1964.

Herron, J. Dudley. "Piaget for Chemists: Explaining What Good Students Cannot Understand." *Journal of Chemical Education* 52 (March 1975): 146-50.

Ilg, Frances L., and Ames, Louise B. *School Readiness*. New York: Harper & Row, 1965.

Inhelder, Bärbel; Sinclair, Hermine; and Bovet, Magali. *Learning and the Development of Cognition.* Cambridge, Mass.: Harvard University Press, 1974.

Kamii, Constance, and Derman, Louise. "Comments on Engelmann's Paper: The Engelmann Approach to Teaching Logical Thinking. Findings from the Administration of Some Piagetian Tasks." In *Measurement and Piaget,* edited by Donald R. Green, Marguerite P. Ford, and George B. Flamer, pp. 127-46. New York: McGraw-Hill, 1971.

Kaufman, Alan S., and Kaufman, Nadeen L. "Tests Built from Piaget's and Gesell's Tasks and Predictors of First-grade Achievement." *Child Development* 43 (June 1972): 521-35.

Klahr, David, and Wallace, J.G. *Cognitive Development: An Information Processing View.* New York: John Wiley, 1976.

Kohlberg, Lawrence. "Stage and Sequence: The Cognitive-Developmental Approach to Socialization." In *Handbook of Socialization Theory and Research,* edited by David A. Goslin, pp. 347-480. Chicago: Rand McNally, 1969.

———. "Continuities in Childhood and Adult Moral Development Revisited." In *Life-span Developmental Psychology: Personality and Socialization,* edited by Paul B. Baltes and K. Warner Schaie, pp. 180-207. New York: Academic Press, 1973.

Kuhn, Deanna. "Mechanisms of Change in the Development of Cognitive Structures." *Child Development* 43 (September 1972): 833-44.

Kuhn, Deanna et al. "The Development of Formal Operations in Logical and Moral Judgment." *Genetic Psychology Monographs* 95 (February 1977): 97-188.

Lawson, A.E. "Relationship of Concrete and Formal Operational Science Subject Matter and the Developmental Level of the Learner." Paper presented at the National Association of Science Teaching Convention, April 1974.

Lenneberg, Eric H. *Biological Foundations of Language.* New York: John Wiley, 1967.

Linn, Robert L., and Slinde, Jeffrey A. "The Determination of the Significance of Change between Pre- and Posttesting Periods." *Review of Educational Research* 47 (Winter 1977): 121-50.

Loevinger, Jane. "The Meaning and Measurement of Ego Development." *American Psychologist* 21 (March 1966): 195-206.

Lorge, Irving, and Chall, Jeanne. "Estimating the Size of Vocabularies of Children and Adults: An Analysis of Methodological Issues." *Journal of Experimental Education* 32 (Winter 1963): 147-57.

Lumsden, James. "Test Theory." In *Annual Review of Psychology.* Vol. 27. Edited by Mark Rosenzweig and Lyman W. Porter, pp. 251-80. Palo Alto, Calif.: Annual Reviews, 1976.

Lunzer, E.A.; Dolan, T.; and Wilkinson, J.E. "The Effectiveness of Measures of Operativity, Language, and Short-term Memory in the Prediction of Reading and Mathematical Understanding." *British Journal of Educational Psychology* 46 (November 1976): 295-305.

Marcia, James E. "Development and Validation of Ego-Identity Status." *Journal of Personality and Social Psychology* 3 (May 1966): 551-58.

————. "Identity Six Years After: A Follow-up Study." *Journal of Youth and Adolescence* 5 (1976): 145-60.

————. "Studies in Ego-Identity." Unpublished monograph, Simon Fraser University, 1975.

Marcia, James E., and Friedman, Meredith L. "Ego-Identity Status in College Women." *Journal of Personality* 38 (June 1970): 249-63.

McLaughlin, Barry. "Second Language Learning in Children." *Psychological Bulletin* 84 (May 1977): 438-59.

Mischel, Walter, and Mischel, Harriet N. "A Cognitive Social-Learning Approach to Morality and Self-Regulation." In *Moral Development and Behavior: Theory, Research, and Social Issues*, edited by Thomas Lickona, pp. 84-107. New York: Holt, Rinehart and Winston, 1976.

Modgil, Sohan. *Piagetian Research: Compilation and Commentary*. Atlantic Highlands, N.J.: Humanities Press, 1976.

Neimark, Edith D. "A Preliminary Search for Formal Operations Structures." *Journal of Genetic Psychology* 116 (June 1970): 223-32.

————. "Longitudinal Development of Formal Operations Thought." *Genetic Psychology Monographs* 91 (November 1975): 171-225.

Nucci, Larry P. "Social Development: Personal, Conventional, and Moral Concepts." Ph.D. dissertation, University of California, Santa Cruz, 1977.

Nucci, Larry P., and Turiel, Elliot. "Social Interactions and the Development of Social Concepts in Preschool Children." *Child Development* 49 (June 1978): 400-407.

O'Connell, Agnes N. "The Relationship between Life Style and Identity Synthesis and Resynthesis in Traditional, Neotraditional, and Nontraditional Women." *Journal of Personality* 44 (December 1976): 675-88.

Orlofsky, Jacob L.; Marcia, James E.; and Lesser, Ira M. "Ego Identity Status and the Intimacy vs. Isolation Crisis of Young Adulthood." *Journal of Personality and Social Psychology* 27 (August 1973): 211-19.

Orpet, R.E.; Meyers, C.E.; and Grein, Susan, "Relationship between Performance on a Piagetian Liquid Conservation Task and Reading Achievement in Seven-Year-Old Children." *Educational and Psychological Measurement* 36 (Winter 1976): 1021-24.

Pascual-Leone, Juan. "A Mathematical Model for the Transition Rule in Piaget's Developmental Stages." *Acta Psychologica* 32 (August 1970): 301-45.

Pearson, L. "Developmental Scales in the British Intelligence Scale." Paper presented to the Annual Conference of the British Psychological Society, Nottingham, England, 1975.

Piaget, Jean. "The General Problems of the Psychobiological Development of the Child." In *Discussions on Child Development*. Vol. 4. Edited by James M. Tanner and Bärbel Inhelder, pp. 3-27. New York: International Universities Press, 1960.

————. *The Origins of Intelligence in Children*. New York: Norton, 1963.

————. *Six Psychological Studies*. New York: Random House, 1968.

————. "Piaget's Theory." In *Carmichael's Manual of Child Psychology*. Vol 2. Edited by Paul H. Mussen, pp. 703-732. New York: John Wiley, 1970.

Rasch, George. "An Item Analysis Which Takes Individual Differences into Account." *British Journal of Mathematical and Statistical Psychology* 19 (1966): 49-57.

Riegel, Klaus F. "Influences of Economic and Political Ideologies on the Development of Developmental Psychology." *Psychological Bulletin* 78 (August 1972): 129-41.

Scandura, Joseph M. *Structural Learning I: Theory and Research.* London: Gordon and Breach Science Publishers, 1973.

————. "A Deterministic Theory of Learning and Teaching." In *Structural Theories of Thinking and Learning and Their Implications for Science Instruction,* edited by Hans Spada and W.F. Kempf, pp. 345-382. Bern: Huber, 1976.

————. "Structural Approach to Instructional Problems." *American Psychologist* 32 (January 1977): 33-53.

Scott, Ralph. "Social Class, Race, Seriating and Reading Readiness: A Study of Their Relationship at the Kindergarten Level." *Journal of Genetic Psychology* 115 (September 1969): 86-96.

Shayer, M.; Kuchemann, D.E.; and Wylam, H. "The Distribution of Piagetian Stages of Thinking in British Middle and Secondary School Children." *British Journal of Educational Psychology* 46 (June 1976): 164-73.

Siegler, Robert S. "The Origins of Scientific Reasoning." In *Children's Thinking: What Develops?* edited by Robert S. Siegler, pp. 109-149. Hillsdale, N.J.: Lawrence Erlbaum Associates, 1978.

Simon, Herbert A. "On the Development of the Processor." In *Information Processing in Children,* edited by Sylvia Farnham-Diggory, pp. 5-22. New York: Academic Press, 1972.

Skinner, B.F. "Are Theories of Learning Necessary?" *Psychological Review* 57 (July 1950): 193-216.

Smedslund, Jan. "The Acquisition of Conservation of Substance and Weight in Children." *Scandinavian Journal of Psychology* 2, 1 (1961): 11-20.

Smith, Mary K. "Measurement of the Size of General English Vocabulary through the Elementary Grades and High School." *General Psychological Monographs* 24 (November 1941): 311-45.

Snow, Catherine E., and Hoefnagle-Höhle, Marian. "The Critical Period for Language Acquisition: Evidence from Second Language Learning." *Child Development* 49 (December 1978): 1114-28.

Strauss, Sidney. "Inducing Cognitive Development and Learning: A Review of Short-term Training Experiments: 1. The Organismic Approach." *Cognition* 1, 4 (1972): 329-57.

————. "A Reply to Brainerd." *Cognition* 3, 2 (1974/75): 155-85.

Strauss, Sidney, and Liberman, Dov. "The Empirical Violation of Conservation Laws and Its Relation to Structural Change." *Journal of Experimental Child Psychology* 18 (December 1974): 464-79.

Strauss, Sidney; Danziger, Josepha; and Ramati, Tsila. "University Students' Understanding of Nonconservation: Implications for Structural Reversion." *Developmental Psychology* 13 (July 1977): 359-63.

Thurstone, L.L. "The Absolute Zero in Intelligence Measurement." *Psychological Review* 35 (May 1929): 175-97.

Turiel, Elliot. "An Experimental Test of the Sequentiality of Developmental Stages in the Child's Moral Judgments." *Journal of Personality and Social Psychology* 3 (June 1966): 611-18.

————. "Conflict and Transition in Adolescent Moral Development." *Child Development* 45 (March 1974): 14-29.

————. "The Development of Concepts of Social Structure: Social Convention." In *The Development of Social Understanding*, edited by Joseph Glick and K. Alison Clarke-Stewart, pp. 25-108. New York: Gardner, 1978.

Walberg, Herbert J. "Psychological Theories of Educational Individualization." In *Systems of Individualized Education*, edited by Harriet Talmage, pp. 5-26. Berkeley, Calif.: McCutchan, 1975.

Walberg, H.J.; Keiko, Hase; and Rasher, Sue P. "English Acquisition as a Diminishing Function of Experience Rather Than Age." *TESOL Quarterly* 12 (December, 1978): 427-37.

Waterman, Alan S., and Goldman, Jeffrey A. "A Longitudinal Study of Ego Identity Development at a Liberal Arts College." *Journal of Youth and Adolescence* 5 (December 1976): 361-69.

Wright, Benjamin D. "Solving Measurement Problems with the Rasch Model." *Journal of Educational Measurement* 14 (Summer 1977): 97-116.

PART THREE
Learning and Instruction

Overview

Wittrock's chapter on learning and memory begins this section. It starts with a review of ideas from Plato, Socrates, and Aristotle. In the generative model that Wittrock proposes, one finds elements similar to the ideas of Aristotle. For example, two processes—memory and recollection—are fundamentally important to both men. In Wittrock's perspective, the emphasis in research on learning and memory should be on investigations of what learners do with the information they receive, what mental transformations they put upon it, what organizations they have for mental activity, and what previous experiences relate to current learning. Teaching should be the design and construction of educational activities that facilitate learners' active construction of verbal and imaginal mental processes. The research he reviews suggests several teaching implications for improving learning and memory, among them ideas focusing on having students attend to paragraph headings, summary sentences, underlining of words, note taking, imaging, and drawing pictures. In each of these suggestions, the focus is on the generative activity of the students.

The perspective Johnson takes argues that the transfer of knowledge is fundamentally a social process. Consequently, education results from interactions among the people. He believes that student-student interactions are perhaps the most important personal interactions, followed by teacher-student interactions and then the interactions among school personnel. In his emphasis on the importance of student-student interactions, Johnson is offering a perspective different from the traditional one which underscores the primary importance of teacher-student interactions. He brings to his argument a comprehensive review of empirical data suggesting the importance of student-student relationships. Among other areas, one finds that peer relations are important indicators of: future psychological health, illegal drug use, aggressive impulses, sex role identity, perspective-taking abilities, and educational aspirations and achievement. The mere quantity of student-student interactions is not the most fundamental ingredient for these outcomes; what matters is the quality of these social interactions. It appears from the data Johnson reviews that social interactions characterized as supportive and accepting are most effective for educational growth. Johnson's perspective is that the best classes have goals that are a mixture of cooperation, competition, and individual activities. He presents a model emphasizing the importance of controversy within educational settings. In this respect, his viewpoint is consonant with the Piagetian notion of cognitive conflict as an essential ingredient for development.

The final chapter in Part Three, prepared by Merrill, Kowallis, and Wilson, focuses on instructional design in transition. The chapter serves much the same capstone purpose as the Nucci-Walberg chapter at the end of Part Two. What Merrill, Kowallis, and Wilson accomplish is a thorough review of instructional design models from both behavioral-science and cognitive-science bases. They argue that the theoretical base that influences the kind of procedures to be researched in instructional design has shifted from a behavioral science to a cognitive science point of view. Rather than emphasizing instructional design materials, the focus is on procedures to direct student processing and interaction. In their review of instructional design programs based on behavioral science, they consider programmed instruction, military task analysis, categories of learning, and presentation theories. Their discussion also incorporates their own orientation—component display theory—which assumes that all instruction occurs through two modes, either telling or questioning. Underlying the behavioral-science approaches is the assumption that instruction leads directly to learning outcomes. On the other hand, in the cognitive-science-based orientations, the assumption is that instruction leads to memory structures, which in turn lead to learning. The consideration of cognitive-science-based instructional design moves from work on early cognitive influences (for example, Ausubel) to information processing, path analysis, structural learning theory, cybernetics, entailment meshes and conversation theory, elaboration theory, and learning strategies. As is apparent, their chapter incorporates an enormous range of material and provides a useful framework for conceptualizing instructional design research. They conclude with a plea for additional attention on how the research they have reviewed might be implemented in practice.

Together the three chapters in Part Three illustrate the state of the art of research and theory on learning, memory, and instructional design. From the perspectives of the authors in this part, it appears there is an increasing reliance on research and theory that emphasizes the student's constructions of material, student-student interaction, and the cognitive bases of learning and memory. The days in which the emphasis was on students as passive recipients of environmental influences seem to have passed. Instead one finds orientations stressing the active, constructive, and complex sets of influences on learning, memory, and instructional design.

9. Learning and Memory

M. C. Wittrock

Knowledge of human learning and memory influences what we know and do about teaching. In this chapter we will develop that theme, concentrating the discussion upon recent discoveries in research in educational psychology on the processes of learning and memory. We will begin with a brief look at the history of ideas about learning and memory, including research in educational psychology during the first half of the twentieth century. Then we will discuss some of the most recent findings that exemplify advances of the last few years of research in learning and memory. The research findings will be organized around the fundamental principles of learning that underlie them, unite them with one another, and convey their educational import.

A BRIEF LOOK AT HISTORY

Plato wrote that ideas and concepts are innate or inherited. We do not learn them, in the usual sense of that word. Instead, we only recollect them. In his model of learning, memory is a central process. A teacher helps a learner to remember concepts present in his or her mind since birth. In the *Meno,* Socrates could teach the Pythagorean theorem to the slave boy because he believed that all people have inherited that idea even though they may not be able to remember it. The Socratic method of teaching exemplifies an educational application of Plato's theory of learning and memory. In the Socratic method one does not teach in the sense of didactically imparting information. Instead, through questions and discussions a teacher stimulates the learner's memories and thought processes to interact with environmental events. From memory and reason it is the learner who recalls, discovers, or constructs the ideas that are taught. Here we see ties between Plato's beliefs about learning and memory and a method of teaching that has persevered for several thousand years.

Aristotle, the founder of the theory of associationism in memory, wrote that we remember or store information only by forming *images* of it (English translation 1964). We recollect or retrieve the stored information by forming *associations* among the memories and by placing them in *order* according to the principles of similarity, contrast, and contiguity. Although he did not believe that ideas are inherited, Aristotle emphasized the importance of memory in learning and teaching, as did Plato. In Aristotle's theory, two processes, memory (storage) and recollection (retrieval from memory), are fundamentally important. Imagery is the basis of memory, and association and order are the bases of recollection.

His model of learning and memory was highly influential in ancient times, in medieval times, and again in twentieth-century America. In ancient Greece and in ancient Rome, Aristotle's model of memory influenced teaching in practical ways. Without a ready supply of inexpensive writing materials and books, students learned to remember information from lectures and answers to examination questions, lawyers to recollect arguments, actors to recall lines, teachers to recite lessons, and statesmen to deliver long, organized speeches. In each case, Aristotle's theory of memory was used to teach the students and professionals to remember information without external memory aids. As described in several sources (for example, *Rhetorica ad Herrenium*), public speakers were often taught to form vivid, active images of the ideas they wished to remember and to arrange these images in the order they wished to recollect them. These same principles of imagery and association in memory underlie some of the techniques taught in medieval days and modern times in courses designed to facilitate memory.

In the middle ages, Thomas Aquinas and Albertus Magnus revived Aristotle's model of memory and taught it to clergymen to help them remember their talks and speeches. It is possible, though not proven, that Aristotle's model of memory influenced the elaborate use of beautiful paintings, frescos, friezes, statues, mosaics, and other artwork that decorated the medieval cathedrals of Europe. In addition to being beautiful, these works of art may also have functioned as aids in the teaching of abstract and difficult concepts according to Aristotle's model of imagery in memory. Conceived in this way, a cathedral is an impressive learning environment. It surrounded people, many of whom were illiterate, with memorable, organized, nonverbal representations and vivid examples of the principles they were to learn and to remember.

With the coming of the printing press and with the mass production of inexpensive materials and writing instruments, external aids to verbal learning came into widespread use. With them came a decline in the pedagogical application of imagery to facilitate memory.

However, the principles of association and order, the bases of the retrieval half of Aristotle's model of memory, continued to flourish in the study of learning and memory, perhaps because they were amenable to the study of verbal processes. In Europe in the eighteenth and nineteenth centuries, learning and memory were frequently described as associationistic processes that involved mental events. In the United States near the turn of the twentieth century, Edward L. Thorndike, the founder of educational psychology in America, described learning as a trial and error process of forming associations between stimuli and responses, rather than as a process of forming associations between mental events, such as images. Thorndike believed that the response of the learner that leads to a satisfying state of affairs increases the bond or association between the stimulus and the rewarded response. His model of learning later came to be called instrumental conditioning, because the response was instrumental in attaining the satisfying state of affairs and in the formation of the S-R association.

Thorndike's associationistic model of learning influenced American schools. Through his pioneering research studies in the teaching of school subjects, such as reading and arithmetic, many educators learned to teach according to Thorndike's theory of learning. In it he emphasized that the rewarded practice of the behavior to be learned was a way to form an association between a stimulus and a response.

During the first half of the twentieth century associationism flourished in America. However, the associations were between stimuli and behavioral responses, not between ideas or mental events. John Watson, the renowned behaviorist, eschewed mentalistic processes, such as images and thoughts, in the study of learning.

Contrary to popular belief, behaviorists are not distinguished from other researchers in learning by their interest in behavior. Nearly all modern-day researchers who study learning and memory study behavior. Rather, behaviorists maintain that it is more productive to study behavior as a direct product of observable stimuli than as a product of the learner's mental processes, such as attention, motivation, thinking, and imagery.

B.F. Skinner, a modern-day behaviorist, stated that any stimulus, such as a compliment, a piece of food, or even a shock that followed a response and that increased the probability of that response occurring again in the presence of the same or a highly similar contextual stimulus, was a reinforcer for that behavioral response. In other words, the environment controls learning, and associations are formed between stimuli and responses that are contingent upon the reinforcers, the stimuli which follow them and which increase their probability of future occurrence. From this powerful idea came extensive pedagogical implications and significant changes in American education. Teaching became the arranging of reinforcers contingent upon the behavior to be associated with an environmental stimulus. Teachers taught students by changing the environment of learning and by managing reinforcers, rather than by asking the learners to use their memories and thought processes to construct images or other mental representations for concepts and information.

Teaching machines and programmed instructional materials were derived from Skinner's model of learning, called operant conditioning. These machines and materials provided the many and frequent immediate and discriminative reinforcers needed to form each association, such as 2 + 2 to 4, or a printed word to its spoken counterpart. Behavioral objectives, behavior shaping, successive approximations, contingency management, positive and negative reinforcers, and schedules of reinforcement were terms that moved from discussions in the experimental psychological laboratory into the vernacular of elementary and secondary schoolteachers. Teachers were trained to

write behavioral objectives and carefully to reinforce student responses successively approximating those behaviors.

Within a behavioristic model of learning, the need to study memory declined. If environmental stimuli controlled behavior, then memory and images were no longer of central importance to learning and
the design of teaching. As introduced by Aristotle, the concept of
associations influenced modern-day behaviorism, although the associations were between stimuli and responses, not between thoughts or
images. Associations no longer involved retrieval from memory; instead they involved learning and the acquisition of behavior.

Learning became largely a problem of motivation and selection of
behavior, rather than the acquisition of new responses, the comprehension of concepts, or an interaction between memories and new
events. The educational implications of this model of learning are
widespread today in elementary and secondary schools. These implications scarcely need to be elaborated upon, except to note their
relationships with earlier conceptions of associations that date to
Aristotle's theory of learning and memory.

RECENT RESEARCH IN LEARNING AND MEMORY

The most recent research in educational psychology on learning
and memory reintroduces memory and related cognitive processes
that were not emphasized during the first half of the twentieth century in America. Many current researchers have found that it is more
productive to study learning as a result of the mental activities of
people, including images, motives, feelings, thoughts, attention, and
memory, than as a direct product of environmental stimuli. People
learn not only by taking action in the presence of environmental
stimuli, but also by imitating and observing other people, by listening, reading, and discussing issues, by forming images, plans, and
verbal analogies, by thinking, without the necessity of practice or
even of overt behavior. It seems that both halves of Aristotle's model
of memory have survived the twentieth century, although they are
changed and sometimes scarcely recognizable.

Today, the study of the learners' cognitive processes in learning
and memory is the central focus of research in instruction within
educational psychology. Many people who study learning and instruction find that it is more productive to study how instruction in-

fluences the learners' cognitive processes of attention, motivation, understanding, and memory, which in turn influence learning and behavior, than it is productive to study how instruction directly or automatically influences students' behavior. In this recent return to an ancient cognitive approach, learning is conceived as a result of the learners' active mental processes, rather than as a direct product of environmental conditions or teacher activities. We will now look at some of the findings that have been produced by recent cognitive approaches to the study of learning and memory instruction. We must be selective rather than comprehensive in the coverage of recent research and the ideas behind the studies. See Wittrock and Lumsdaine (1977) and Wittrock (1978a) for further discussion of cognition and instruction, and Wittrock (1978c, 1980) for further discussion of cognition and the brain.

Let us begin this discussion of recent research with two studies that indicate the importance in learning and memory of the learners' mental processing of environmental events. Kaufman, Baron, and Kopp (1966) gave learners in a concept formation study inaccurate information about how their responses would be reinforced. The information given the learners was designed to produce rates of responding different from those expected from the actual schedule of reinforcement given to the learners. The data from the learners were clear and unambiguous. The learners performed according to the schedule of reinforcement they were told was in effect, not according to the schedule actually used.

Delay of feedback during learning, another frequently studied environmental event, has usually been thought directly to reduce learning when the delayed feedback is compared with feedback given to learners immediately after they make their responses. However, if the learners' cognitive processes influence learning, then the effects of the delay of feedback could enhance, have no effect upon, or reduce learning, depending upon the learners' activity during the delay. Atkinson (1969) found that a delay of feedback produced those three different effects, depending upon the type of rehearsal activities performed by the learners during the delay. Most recently, Sturges (1978) also found that a delay of feedback increased memory when the delay followed an incorrect response. These studies indicate that learners construct their understanding of information, as developmental psychologists such as Jean Piaget and Lev Vygotsky maintain.

To understand learning and memory we should then study what learners do with the information they receive, what mental transformations they perform upon it, what organization they impose upon it, and what previous experience they relate to it. These topics will be discussed in the following sections on attention, encoding and memory, motivation, and cognitive styles. We will emphasize the studies of these cognitive processes that lead to educational implications regarding the facilitation of learning and understanding.

ATTENTION

One of the frequently studied cognitive processes involved in learning and memory is attention, or how one selects and directs mental activity and behavior. In educational psychology, the control of attention among learners is a focus of interest. Adjunct questions, which are questions inserted into a text, and objectives given to learners have been studied as ways to direct the learners' attention when they are reading or when they are learning from instruction.

If attention and possibly encoding as well are influenced by inserted questions and objectives, then the learning of the information indicated by the question or the objective should be increased while the learning of other information should be decreased. In the research on adjunct questions, a prequestion—one that the learner reads before reading the relevant text—should more narrowly focus attention to the cued information than should a postquestion, which is one that learners encounter after reading the relevant text. Sagaria and DiVesta (1978) found that prequestions narrowed learning more than did postquestions, which facilitated learning compared with a control group given no inserted questions. Attention and perhaps encoding were influenced according to the model outlined here. Boker (1974) found that prequestions facilitated the learning of information specifically mentioned in the question and reduced the learning of other information. Postquestions facilitated learning more broadly, again, as one would expect if attention is being influenced by the questions.

Similar results have been attained in other areas of educational research. Mayer (1975) found that the learning of mathematics could be facilitated with adjunct questions that directed the learners to the goals of the instruction. The breadth of the information cued by the question was related to the breadth of student learning. Felker and Dapra (1975) found a related result with adjunct questions that cued the broad application of a model facilitating comprehensive learning. Specific questions again narrowed learning.

These data on inserted questions agree with a selective attention model and exemplify the utility of a cognitive approach to instruction. In these studies, a cognitive approach predicts that it is more productive of explanations and understanding to study how inserted questions influence a cognitive process, in this case attention, than it is productive to study how inserted questions directly influence behavior. In the studies of inserted questions, a selective attention model helps to explain their complex and seemingly inconsistent findings.

In recent research on objectives given to learners either before or after reading a text, Kaplan and Simmons (1974) found that the information directly relevant to the objectives was learned well in both conditions, but other information representing a broader learning was learned better when the objectives were given after reading of the text. Again, these results fit a selective attention model. However, because of the limited number of related research studies, it is too early to reach a generalization about the cognitive effects of objectives given to learners.

With adjunct questions and with objectives, the educational utility of a cognitive approach is apparent. It promises to supply an understanding of how questions and objectives influence some types of learning and memory.

ENCODING AND MEMORY

In the process of learning and remembering, people organize stimuli, relate them to past experience and to schemata, elaborate their meanings, and transform their mode of presentation. The mental organizations, elaborations, and transformations performed upon stimuli in the process of understanding them and storing them in memory involve cognitive processes that are studied under the heading of *encoding*. In particular, verbal and imaginal encoding processes have been studied frequently in recent research in educational psychology.

Verbal Cognitive Processes in the Facilitation of Learning and Memory

Bower and Clark (1969) taught college students to improve their memory of serially ordered lists of words from an average of 14 percent to 94 percent of the words, simply by asking the college undergraduates to make a story out of the words. In another study, students were asked to take the perspective of either a burglar or a home buyer when they read a story about a house (Pichert and Anderson 1977). The perspective they were asked to take substantially influenced the type of information they learned and remembered. In these two studies, the way the information was processed or thought about influenced learning and memory.

In 1974 I introduced a model of learning as a generative process. In the model, the constructive processes used by the learner to relate stimuli to distinctive memories of experience or to concepts and schemata determine learning and memory (Wittrock 1974). In one study testing implications of the model, reading was viewed as a generative process (Wittrock, Marks, and Doctorow 1975). Children were given undefined vocabulary words inserted into a familiar story. Compared with a comparable procedure using an unfamiliar story, it was hypothesized and found that the familiar story helped the children to generate and remember the meanings of new, never-defined vocabulary words. In another application of the model of generative learning, Wittrock and Carter (1975) found that learners asked to generatively process hierarchies of words often doubled their retention of them, compared with students who read and copied them. In the generative processing groups, the learners were asked to construct relations among the words and to try to discover a hierarchy among them.

In a recently completed study (Doctorow, Wittrock, and Marks 1978), public school sixth graders were asked to read commercially published reading materials commonly used to teach reading. In the experimental groups the children were given paragraph headings or instructions to generate summary sentences for each paragraph after they had read it or a combination of both headings and generative processing instructions. From the generative model of learning, it was predicted and found that in the experimental group the paragraph headings enhanced learning compared with the control group who read the stories without any of the experimental procedures. The groups asked to generate summary sentences for each paragraph learned as much as did the group given the paragraph headings. As predicted, with time to learn held constant, the groups given both the headings and the generative processing instructions learned and remembered the most of any of the groups in the experiment, approximately doubling the scores of the control group.

The predictions were derived from the model as follows. Generative processing can involve either or both semantic or abstract memory and distinctive or episodic memory in interaction with the stimuli. The paragraph headings stimulate abstract concepts or schemata; the summary sentences primarily stimulate distinctive memories; and the combination of headings and generative instructions stimulate distinctive memories within semantically appropriate abstract areas.

Another way to stimulate verbal cognitive processes is to ask learners to underline words in sentences. In a study of the generative processes stimulated by the underlining of words as one reads stories, Rickards and August (1975) found that when students underline words that they decide are important their learning is greatest, greater than when structurally important words are underlined for them by a teacher. The third highest learning was obtained with the control group that read the stories with no underlining of words. The lowest amount of learning occurred when the learners underlined words that they decided were structurally unimportant to the story. In agreement with the generative model, the learners' cognitive processes engaged by the instructions produced large differences in learning.

Note taking is another way to facilitate constructive cognitive processes involved in learning and memory. Peper and Mayer (1978) studied note taking as a generative activity rather than as a memory aid. In support of the generative model of learning, the taking of notes was found to be a process of generating meaning that produces transfer to new concepts. They write, "The results provide consistent support for the predictions of the strict version of a generative theory, rather than attention or effort theories." The learners seem to assimilate the new information with their past experience and generate a representation of it. It is also clear that young children, second graders at least, often do not perceive reading as a process of constructing meaning involving the semantic dimensions of paragraphs (Myers and Paris 1978).

These studies on verbal cognitive processes in encoding and in the generation of meaning have implications for teaching. One implication is that the meaning of the story or the text involves more than the information on the printed page. The meaning also involves the learners' knowledge, memory, and beliefs in interaction with the story. For the teacher, one implication is that learners can, but often do not, relate texts and stories to their stores of information. Learning can sometimes be improved with simple and inexpensive instructions or other devices that actively involve the learner in generating relationships between memories and the stimuli.

Imagery in the Facilitation of Learning and Memory

Another cognitive process involved in encoding is imagery. In educational psychology, four methods of facilitating imagery have been studied: instructions to image, pictures, the drawing of pictures, and to a lesser extent, high-imagery words. Mischel and Baker (1975) asked hungry nursery schoolchildren to delay as long as possible eating the marshmallows and pretzels placed in front of them. One group of children was asked to imagine that the marshmallows were white clouds or that the pretzels were logs. These simple instructions to image food as inedible objects raised the interval of delay from about six minutes to about fourteen minutes. Levin, Davidson, Wolff, and Citron (1973) found that second and fifth graders can use either an image generation strategy or a sentence generation strategy to enhance their learning and memory of paired-associates. Educable mentally retarded elementary schoolchildren can sometimes increase their learning by training in the use of imagery elaboration or sentence elaboration (Taylor, Josberger, and Whitely 1973). Levin (1973) found that a visual imagery strategy facilitated reading comprehension among fourth graders, if they had an adequate vocabulary of words. Instructions to imagine, when used with kindergarten children learning verbally presented problems in addition, facilitated performance on the more difficult items (Grunau 1978). From these studies and related experiments, it seems that the ability to profit from instructions to image increases with mental ability and with age and is limited before ages five or six. Prior to about age eight, children do not seem to be able to generate images upon request unless the images are carefully described to them.

Pictures often facilitate learning and memory among children, although the effects of pictures upon reading are not always favorable. Lesgold, Levin, Shimron, and Guttman (1975) found that pictures given to six-year-old children facilitated recall of the text they had read. Bender and Levin (1978) found that pictures, but not instructions to construct images, sizably facilitated learning and memory of a story among ten- to sixteen-year-old educable mentally retarded boys and girls. Pictures enhance learning and memory at early mental ages, when instructions to construct unspecified images are not useful with many children. With children three to fifteen years old, age rather than experience correlates with the ability to generate interactive images (Levin and Pressley 1978).

Instructions to draw pictures of concepts or information have also been studied. Bull and Wittrock (1973) found a modest gain in the learning of definitions of vocabulary words among elementary schoolchildren who drew diagrams of the meanings of the terms. The drawing of the pictures is a useful way of insuring that the learners have constructed an image as requested in the instructions. The drawing of the picture may not be as important as the process of generating a mental image. To test the effects upon learning of instructions to image, it is important to establish that the learners have engaged in the cognitive processes mentioned in the directions.

High-imagery words also can facilitate learning and memory. Wittrock and Goldberg (1975) found that among college students, imagery and recall were enhanced more by words of high-imagery value than by instructions to image written words. Among elementary schoolchildren, both high-imagery words and imagery instructions increased recall.

The nature of the images children and adults construct is also a relevant issue. Since ancient times, interactive images, which involve the information to be remembered and a familiar object, have been used to facilitate memory. Whether noninteractive images are also facilitative of memory is not well known. However, recent research applying an ancient interactive imagery technique, the keyword method, shows large gains of about 83 percent in the retention of foreign vocabulary words (Pressley 1977a, 1977b).

Summary of Recent Research on Verbal Processes and Imagery

In research on verbal processes and imagery, the comprehension and retention of information ranging from paired-associates to arithmetic and reading has been facilitated, sometimes doubled, by use of inexpensive cognitive techniques. In these procedures, learners often are given pictures, stories, and high-imagery words or are asked to construct mental representations and elaborations of the information they are to learn. In the process, they seem to relate the concepts, stories, and information to their store of knowledge and their memories of experience. From these techniques, gains in learning and memory are frequently obtained, although it is not yet known when and under what conditions the different procedures are most useful with different learners and different materials. These findings imply that facilitating learning in schools involves inducing learners actively to construct their own mental representations of the information they are to learn.

MOTIVATION

Brief mention of some of the close ties between recent research in learning and memory and recent research in motivation can help to explain how affective processes and intellectual processes interact to increase learning and memory. In a cognitive approach, the teacher and the learner each has a distinct responsibility for teaching and for learning. The learners' perceptions of the causes of learning are important for teachers to know and understand. It may be possible to improve learning and memory by changing the learners' perceptions of their responsibility for learning, their probability of success at learning, and their ability to influence their destiny in school.

Without changing curriculum or instructional materials or encoding strategies, deCharms (1976) taught elementary schoolteachers to perceive themselves as origins, people who teach from personal commitment, who believe they cause their own actions. In turn, these teachers taught their elementary school students in an inner-city school to perceive themselves as origins, people who believe that they cause their own actions, rather than as pawns, that is, people who believe that someone else or something external to them causes their behavior. The data from the study indicated that after two years of training the motivation of the teachers and the students was changed in the direction of greater personal responsibility for achievement; that is, they tended to become origins. The students' achievement in language and arithmetic was also sizably improved, especially among the boys. One implication of the study is that achievement in schools can sometimes be facilitated by changing teachers' and learners' perceptions of their cognitive attributional processes.

Weiner (1979) elaborated an educationally relevant model of motivation based upon the perceived attributions for success and failure in school. In addition to the perceived internal or external locus studied by deCharms, Weiner includes the dimensions of control and stability. For example, he finds that learning attributed to effort—an internal and changeable motive—rather than to luck or ability, often leads students to believe that by increasing their effort they can increase their success in school in closely related tasks.

In motivation, as in learning and memory, the learners' cognitive elaborations and perceptions are important in determining behavior. Learning can be enhanced by a change in the learners' attribution of success to their own effort, by a change in belief about one's ability to learn, and by an assumption of responsibility by teachers for the improvement of their teaching. These close ties between motivation and learning evidence a variety of ways that instruction and teaching can be improved by the application of principles of cognitive psychology. Effort, individual responsibility for learning, and belief in people's ability to influence their own destiny are old ideas with newly found utility for educators. These old ideas call into question the long-term effects upon students of the belief, as in the movement for accountability of teachers and in behavioristic models of learning, that someone else is responsible for and controls their learning. Not only is learning likely to be reduced by that belief, but students' self-concepts are likely to be altered by it as well. Again, knowledge about learning and motivation influences teaching.

INDIVIDUAL DIFFERENCES IN COGNITIVE PROCESSES

Within the last several years, research in individual differences in learning and instruction has centered upon cognitive styles and strategies. These process-oriented individual differences offer promise for differentiating instruction according to the learning strategies employed by different students. Compared with ability differences, process-oriented individual differences promise to provide greater insight into the mental operations of learners. As used here, process refers to the changes, strategies, transformations, and organizations that people impose upon information to learn and remember it.

The study of cognitive styles is one educationally significant area of research on process-oriented individual differences. Cognitive styles are the characteristic ways people perceive, learn, and remember information. Witkin et al. (1977) extensively studied people with a differentiated, or field-independent, cognitive style and people with a global, or field-dependent, cognitive style. He finds that field-independent people tend to be interested in abstractions, to be individualistic, and to be intrinsically motivated. They tend not to need or to want reinforcement or approval from other people, nor are they sensitive to the feelings and the facial expressions of others. They tend to be analytic, to follow internalized values, and to disregard contextual cues. Field-independent teachers tend to organize curricula into small, tightly organized, logically ordered units. They prefer subject matter that is abstract and logically organized, such as the physical sciences. They teach without emphasis upon social interactions among students and without externally defined goals. They tend to feel that learning is intrinsically motivating, an intellectual rather than a social process.

Field-dependent people, on the other hand, tend to be interested in other people and proficient at discerning their feelings and their nonverbal expressions of those feelings. Field-dependent people tend to consider contextual cues in organizing their environment, which they tend to accept as it is presented. They are responsive to reinforcement from others and sensitive to other people in the definition of their values and in the regulation of their behavior. Field-dependent teachers organize course and lessons globally into large units or sections. They teach using group and project activities that facilitate social interactions among students and teachers. They prefer clearly stated, externally defined goals for instruction, explicit reinforcement, and subject matter, such as the social sciences, that deals with people and social processes.

One interesting educational application of research on articulated and global cognitive styles is the study of teachers and students who differ in cognitive styles. Packer and Bain (1978) found that field-independent teachers were more successful with field-independent students than with field-dependent students in obtaining achievement in mathetmatics. The field-dependent teachers were equally effective with field-dependent learners and with field-independent learners in the attainment of achievement in mathematics, which was below that obtained by the match between field-independent teachers and students but well above that obtained by the mismatch between field-independent teachers and field-dependent learners. In the subjective student ratings of the teachers they preferred, the field-dependent students much preferred the field-dependent teachers. The field-independent students also preferred the field-dependent teachers, although their difference in preference between the two cognitive styles of teachers was not large.

In the study by Packer and Bain, the relations between the cognitive styles of the teachers and the students were important in determining achievement and student liking of teachers. Contrary to intuition, a match between student and teacher cognitive styles did not always produce better learning or greater satisfaction than did a mismatch. Field-independent teachers apparently do not fare well in student ratings. None of the field-dependent students rated favorably any field-independent teacher.

Individual differences in attribution processes, which were discussed in the section on motivation, are recently becoming of interest to educational psychologists. Andrews and Debus (1978) successfully taught fifth and sixth graders to change their attribution for academic failures to lack of effort rather than to task difficulty. As a result of the attribution retraining programs, the students increased their persistence at learning and their achievement. Dweck (1975) found that children between the ages of eight and thirteen years who felt they were helpless in ability to succeed in school enhanced their achievement and their ability to respond favorably to failures after they had been in an attribution retraining program. In the program the children were taught to attribute failure to a lack of effort. A control condition, in which children experienced only success, produced no effect upon the children's deterioration in performance after failures given later. The control condition showed that treating only the outcomes of learning, by providing rewarding, successful experiences, was inadequate to improve learning or to improve reactions to later failures. The cognitive processes of learning, in this study the attributions of the learners, and not only the products of learning were important in the design of effective training procedures. As found by deCharms in his study of origins and pawns, it is sometimes important to attend to the learners' thought processes in addition to the environments in which children are placed in schools.

A third area of process-oriented individual differences is locus of control. Daniels and Stevens (1976) classified college undergraduates as internals or externals. In an introductory course in psychology, half of each group was taught by a contract plan and the other half was taught by a teacher-controlled plan. As the authors hypothesized, internals performed better with the contract plan than with the traditional method of instruction, the teacher-controlled plan. The externals performed better with the traditional, teacher-directed control than with the contract plan. Again, information about the cognitive processes of the learner was useful for the design and differentiation of instruction.

Das, Kirby, and Jarman (1975) compared retarded and nonretarded children in their information processing strategies, particularly their use of simultaneous processing, in which information from different sources is synthesized at the same time, versus their use of successive processing, in which information is organized in a linear sequence and treated one element at a time, as they matched a visual array of patterns to an auditorially presented sequence of taps. The nonretarded children characteristically used a successive strategy, while the retarded children used a mixture of simultaneous and successive processing that lowered their scores. One implication of their findings is that the retarded children can profit from training in the use of a successive processing strategy when it is appropriate for linearly organized information. Torgesen, Bowen, and Ivey (1978) found that the simultaneous or successive organization of a digit span task was more important than its visual or auditory mode of presentation among nine-year-old boys of average intelligence, half of whom were good readers and half of whom were poor readers. The good and poor readers differed in their ability to learn from simultaneous, visually presented digit tasks, with the good readers outperforming the poor readers. Differences between visual and auditory presentation did not evidence comparable differences across good and poor readers in learning. An implication of their finding is that task organization which parallels cognitive processes provides useful information about the individualization of instruction, perhaps more useful than information about the visual or auditory mode of the stimuli. DeBoth and Dominowski (1978) found that among the college students in their study, the differences between visual and auditory modes of presenting word lists were not important; individual differences among learners persisted across these two modes of stimuli. The students could not be classified as visual learners or auditory learners.

One important implication of these studies is that the mode of the instructional treatments is not as important in influencing learning as is the cognitive transformation performed by the learner upon the incoming information. Treatments mean different things to different learners. To understand what they will learn from them, we need to study how learners process treatments. Experiments that compare one mode of stimulus with another mode of stimulus, without comparing individual differences in cognitive processing of the stimulus modes, are not likely to be productive.

Another frequently studied cognitive style that has educational utility is reflectivity-impulsivity. Kagan, Moss, and Sigel (1963) found that children with an analytic conceptual style tend to be reflective, to use considerable time before making their responses, and to score well on analytic tasks that involve ignoring several irrelevant, distracting stimulus dimensions. Children with a global conceptual style tend to be impulsive and to make many errors in analytic tasks. Zelniker and Jeffrey (1976) found that on analytic or detailed tasks the reflective children performed better than the impulsive children, but on tasks involving global matches, that is, matches involving the overall configuration of the pictured forms, no difference in performance was found. Rollins and Genser (1977) found that when two dimensions of a task were involved, the reflective children scored better than the impulsive children. But when many distracting dimensions were involved in the task, the impulsive children performed better than the reflective children. It is not clear why an impulsive strategy should lead to more correct choices than should a reflective strategy when many dimensions are involved in the task, unless the correct choice was highly probable before the instruction began. In that case, reflecting upon all the rational bases for selecting a choice would not be as effective as selecting by intuition the most salient dimensions of the stimuli. The basis for all correct choices in this study was the number of the stimuli.

Another frequently studied process-oriented individual difference variable is emerging from research on the human brain. The recent research on the brain indicates that among the many cognitive processes of the brain there is an analytic, linear propositional strategy well suited to organize verbal information, such as printed words, and there is a holistic, nonlinear processing strategy well suited to organize spatial information, such as pictures or paintings. The educational implications of the recent research on the brain are just beginning to emerge (Wittrock 1978c, 1980). However, the research on the brain complements some of the research discussed in this chapter on learning and memory, and lends support to the recent research in cognitive psychology on process-oriented individual differences.

In a study testing a model for relating research in cognitive processes to instruction (Wittrock 1978b), the instruction that was best for teaching children to solve problems depended upon the developmental level of the children. Only when the instruction focused on a relevant but not yet well-learned dimension of the problem was performance facilitated, reducing the number of trials needed to solve a problem from about ten to one.

These studies all converge upon a model of instruction that relates process-oriented individual differences to teaching. In these studies, knowledge about the learners' cognitive processes leads to instruction that capitalizes upon and stimulates the learners' appropriate ways of processing information, or to instruction that compensates for the learners' inappropriate ways of processing information.

EDUCATIONAL IMPLICATIONS

In the recent research on learning and memory that we have discussed, the learners are active and responsible for attending to information, for organizing it, elaborating it, and encoding it into long-term memory. Learners use their cognitive information processing strategies to relate new information to their memories of experience and their schemata. Learning does not occur automatically when teachers dispense information or reinforcers. Instead, it is a constructive, effortful process influenced by the learners' background of information and cognitive information processing strategies, which interact with the task or the stimuli. In a cognitive approach, the learners' individual differences in previous relevant learning, in experience, and in cognitive processes and aptitudes, such as attention, motivation, and encoding, become centrally important in the design of instruction and in teaching.

Teachers also acquire new roles and responsibilities within cognitive models of learning and memory. Teaching becomes the art of facilitating the learners' construction of meaning, and enhancing the interaction between the learners' backgrounds and cognitive processes and the information to be learned. To teach according to a cognitive model, one should understand individual differences among the learners and adapt the methods and the materials to the learners' aptitudes and cognitive processes.

Teachers facilitate attention by using questions, objectives, and directions, and by presenting problems to be solved. Teachers influence motivation, including attributional processes, by showing that effort devoted to learning increases success in school.

Teachers enhance comprehension and memory by stimulating learners to relate relevant memories and schemata to the information they are to learn. Recent research in cognition implies that if the learners cannot construct relations between subject matter and their memories, then the teachers might try using verbal devices, such as directions, analogies, metaphors, stories, and examples, or imagery, such as is found in pictures, diagrams, and high-imagery words.

If the learners can but do not spontaneously construct relations between information and their experience, then teachers should discreetly direct the learners' attention to the important issues and to the subtle meanings that otherwise would be overlooked.

Within a cognitive approach one does not teach in the everyday sense of the word. Instead one designs and conducts the educational activities that facilitate the learners' active construction of verbal and imaginal mental processes that transfer or relate memories and knowledge to new information. From this interaction come the changes that we call learning and memory.

These pedagogical procedures for stimulating learning and memory remind me of the techniques used in ancient times in Greece and Rome to improve the memories of orators and students. Our new interest in cognitive priciples as old as Aristotle's model of memory promises to unite much of the twentieth century research on learning around the explanatory concepts discussed in this chapter. Cognitive principles also lead to a unity of interest among educators and researchers who study learning and memory. In keeping with the theme of this chapter, cognitive principles of learning and memory influence what we know and do about teaching. These principles imply that learning is an effortful constructive process that teachers facilitate by enhancing interactions between individual learner's aptitudes, experience, and schemata and the materials and concepts to be learned.

REFERENCES

Andrews, Gregory R., and Debus, Ray L. "Persistence and the Causal Perception of Failure: Modifying Cognitive Attributions." *Journal of Educational Psychology* 70 (April 1978): 154-66.

Aristotle. "On Memory and Recollection." Appendix to *On the soul (de Anima); Parva naturalia;* and *On breath.* Translated by W.S. Hett. Cambridge, Mass.: Harvard University Press, 1964.

Atkinson, Richard C. "Information Delay in Human Learning." *Journal of Verbal Learning and Verbal Behavior* 8 (August 1969): 507-511.

Bender, Bruce G., and Levin, Joel R. "Pictures, Imagery, and Retarded Children's Prose Learning." *Journal of Educational Psychology* 70 (August 1978): 583-88.

Boker, John R. "Immediate and Delayed Retention Effects of Interspersing Questions in Written Instructional Passages." *Journal of Educational Psychology* 66 (February 1974): 96-98.

Bower, Gordon H., and Clark, Michael C. "Narrative Stories as Mediators for Serial Learning." *Psychonomic Science* 14, 4 (1969): 181-2

Bull, Britta L., and Wittrock, M.C. "Imagery in the Learning of Verbal Definitions." *British Journal of Educational Psychology* 43 (November 1973): 289-93.

Caplan, Henry, trans. *Rhetorica ad herennium.* Cambridge, Mass.: Harvard University Press, Loeb Classical Library, 1967.

Daniels, Richard L., and Stevens, James P. "The Interaction between the Internal-External Locus of Control and Two Methods of College Instruction." *American Educational Research Journal* 13 (Spring 1976): 103-113.

Das, J. P.; Kirby, J.; and Jarman, R. F. "Simultaneous and Successive Syntheses: An Alternative Model for Cognitive Abilities." *Psychological Bulletin* 82 (January 1975): 87-103.

DeBoth, Carol J., and Dominowski, Roger L. "Individual Differences in Learning: Visual versus Auditory Presentation." *Journal of Educational Psychology* 70 (August 1978): 498-503.

deCharms, Richard. *Enhancing Motivation: Change in the Classroom.* New York: Irvington, 1976.

Doctorow, Marlene J.; Wittrock, M.C.; and Marks, Carolyn B. "Generative Processes in Reading Comprehension." *Journal of Educational Psychology* 70 (April 1978): 109-118.

Dweck, Carol S. "The Role of Expectations and Attributions in the Alleviation of Learned Helplessness." *Journal of Personality and Social Psychology* 31 (April 1975): 674-85.

Felker, Daniel B., and Dapra, Richard A. "Effects of Question Type and Question Placement on Problem-Solving Ability from Prose Material." *Journal of Educational Psychology* 67 (June 1975): 380-84.

Grunau, Ruth V. E. "Effects of Elaborative Prompt Condition and Developmental Level on the Performance of Addition Problems by Kindergarten Children." *Journal of Educational Psychology* 70 (June 1978): 422-32.

Kagan, Jerome; Moss, Howard A.; and Sigel, Irving E. "Psychological Significance of Styles of Conceptualization." In *Basic Cognitive Processing in Children*, edited by John C. Wright and Jerome Kagan. *Monographs of the Society for Research in Child Development* 28, 2 (1963): 73-112. Serial No. 86.

Kaplan, Robert, and Simmons, Francene G. "Effects of Instructional Objectives
Used as Orienting Stimuli or as Summary/Review upon Prose Learning."
Journal of Educational Psychology 66 (August 1974): 614-22.

Kaufman, Arnold; Baron, Alan; and Kopp, Rosemarie. "Some Effects of Instruction on Human Operant Behavior." *Psychonomic Monograph Supplements* 1
(1966): 243-50.

Lesgold, Alan M. et al. "Pictures and Young Children's Learning from Oral
Prose." *Journal of Educational Psychology* 67 (October 1975): 636-42.

Levin, Joel R. "Inducing Comprehension in Poor Readers: A Test of a Recent
Model." *Journal of Educational Psychology* 65 (August 1973): 19-24.

Levin, Joel R. et al. "A Comparison of Induced Imagery and Sentence Strategies
in Children's Paired-Associate Learning." *Journal of Educational Psychology*
64 (June 1973): 306-309.

Levin, Joel R., and Pressley, Michael. "A Test of the Developmental Imagery
Hypothesis in Children's Associative Learning." *Journal of Educational
Psychology* 70 (October 1978): 691-94.

Mayer, Richard E. "Different Problem-Solving Competencies Established in
Learning Computer Programming with and without Meaningful Models."
Journal of Educational Psychology 67 (December 1975): 725-34.

Mischel, Walter, and Baker, Nancy. "Cognitive Appraisals and Transformations
in Delay Behavior." *Journal of Personality and Social Psychology* 31 (February 1975): 254-61.

Myers, Meyer II, and Paris, Scott G. "Children's Metacognitive Knowledge about
Reading." *Journal of Educational Psychology* 70 (October 1978): 680-90.

Packer, James, and Bain, John D. "Cognitive Style and Teacher-Student Com-
patibility." *Journal of Educational Psychology* 70 (October 1978): 864-71.

Peper, Richard J., and Mayer, Richard E. "Note Taking as a Generative Activity."
Journal of Educational Psychology 70 (August 1978): 514-22.

Pichert, James W., and Anderson, R. C. "Taking Different Perspectives on a
Story." *Journal of Educational Psychology* 69 (August 1977): 309-15.

Pressley, G. Michael. "Children's Use of the Keyword Method to Learn Simple
Spanish Vocabulary Words." *Journal of Educational Psychology* 69 (October
1977a): 465-72.

―――. "Imagery and Children's Learning: Putting the Picture in Developmental
Perspective." *Review of Educational Research* 47 (Fall 1977b): 585-622.

Rickards, John P., and August, Gerald J. "Generative Underlining Strategies in
Prose Recall." *Journal of Educational Psychology* 67 (December 1975):
860-65.

Rollins, Jr., Howard A., and Genser, Lynn. "Role of Cognitive Style in a Cognitive Task: A Case Favoring the Impulsive Approach to Problem Solving."
Journal of Educational Psychology 69 (June 1977): 281-87.

Sagaria, Sabato D., and DiVesta, Francis J. "Learner Expectations Induced by Adjunct Questions and the Retrieval of Intentional and Incidental Information." *Journal of Educational Psychology* 70 (June 1978): 280-88.

Sturges, Persis T. "Delay of Informative Feedback in Computer-Assisted Testing." *Journal of Educational Psychology* 70 (June 1978): 378-87.

Taylor, Arthur M.; Josberger, M.; and Whitely, Susan E. "Elaboration Instruction and Verbalization as Factors Facilitating Retarded Children's Recall." *Journal of Educational Psychology* 64 (June 1973): 341-46.

Torgesen, Joseph K.; Bowen, C.; and Ivey, C. "Task Structure versus Modality of Presentation: A Study of the Construct Validity of the Visual-Aural Digit-Span Test." *Journal of Educational Psychology* 70 (August 1978): 451-56.

Weiner, Bernard. "A Theory of Motivation for Some Classroom Experiences." *Journal of Educational Psychology* 71 (February 1979): 3-25.

Witkin, H. A. et al. "Field-Dependent and Field-Independent Cognitive Styles and Their Educational Implications." *Review of Educational Research* 47 (Winter 1977): 1-64.

Wittrock, M. C. "Learning as a Generative Process." *Educational Psychologist* 11, 2 (1974): 87-95.

————. "The Cognitive Movement in Instruction." *Educational Psychologist* 13, 1 (1978a): 15-30.

————. "Developmental Processes in Learning from Instruction." *Journal of Genetic Psychology* 132 (March 1978b): 37-54.

————. "Education and the Cognitive Processes of the Brain." In *Education and the Brain*, edited by Jeanne S. Chall and Allan Mirsky, pp. 61-102. Seventy-seventh Yearbook of the National Society for the Study of Education, Part II. Chicago, Ill.: University of Chicago Press, 1978(c).

————. "Learning and the Brain." In *The Brain and Psychology*, edited by M.C. Wittrock, pp. 371-403. New York: Academic Press, 1980.

Wittrock, M. C., and Carter, John F. "Generative Processing of Hierarchically Organized Words." *American Journal of Psychology* 88 (September 1975): 489-501.

Wittrock, M. C., and Goldberg, Sheila M. "Imagery and Meaningfulness in Free Recall: Word Attributes and Instructional Sets." *Journal of General Psychology* 92 (January 1975): 137-51.

Wittrock, M. C.; Marks, Carolyn B.; and Doctorow, Marleen J. "Reading as a Generative Process." *Journal of Educational Psychology* 67 (August 1975): 484-89.

Wittrock, M.C., and Lumsdaine, Arthur A. "Instructional Psychology." *Annual Review of Psychology*, Vol. 28. Edited by Mark R. Rosenzweig and Lyman W. Porter, pp. 417-99. Palo Alto, Calif.: Annual Reviews, 1977.

Zelniker, Tamar, and Jeffrey, Wendell E. "Reflective and Impulsive Children: Strategies of Information Processing Underlying Differences in Problem Solving." *Monographs of the Society for Research in Child Development* 41, 5 (1976). Serial No. 168.

10. Social Psychology

David W. Johnson

EDUCATION AS A SOCIAL PROCESS

Education is primarily a social process that cannot occur except through structured interpersonal interaction within a classroom. In the classroom, teachers talk to students, students talk with one another, and students talk to teachers. Hands go up and down, questions are raised and answered, instructions are given and followed, misbehavior is corrected, students help and advise each other, teachers present material, disagreements arise and are resolved—all with a speed that is invariably surprising to those who have not recently witnessed it. Studies of the number of individual interchanges between teacher and students reveal that teachers in the middle grades typically engage in about two hundred interpersonal interchanges per hour (Jackson 1968). And when one extends an analysis of interpersonal interaction to the school or the school district as a whole, the amount of human interaction that is taking place during a school day is astronomical. Cohen (1979), furthermore, notes that most of the variance in student achievement (between 70 and 90 percent) actually occurs within schools and that classroom effects are more powerful than school effects. He concludes that the primary focus of educational researchers should be on the social organization of the classroom.

Like all social systems, the school (and the classroom) is made up of a network of interpersonal relationships structured to facilitate the achievement of educational goals (Johnson 1970, 1979). And similar to all other social systems, the school (and the classroom) can be described as an open system consisting of inputs, a transformational process, and outputs. The classroom inputs consist of students and teachers, other school personnel, materials, information, and so forth, which are used to *transform* students into outputs of more socialized, skilled, trained, and healthy individuals who will enter other classrooms the following year. In order to transform students successfully, the classroom (and school) must have:

1. clear, cooperative goals that school personnel and students are committed to achieve;
2. a network of interpersonal relationships structured by: (a) role definitions and (b) norms defining appropriate behavior;
3. technologies consisting of knowledge about the performance of instructional and organizational tasks and activities, which include teaching strategies, curriculum materials, collaborative skills, and so forth;
4. a management system that integrates human and material resources into a total system for achieving the goals of the classroom and school.

The basic dynamics of the school and the classroom are that educational goals are achieved through structured interpersonal relationships and the utilization of the technology of instruction under the supervision of a manager.

Educational *goals* are based on the fact that human beings are particularly adept at transferring knowledge and tradition from one generation to the next. Because we teach and learn, we accumulate a culture over many generations. The process of transferring accumulated knowledge, skills, and culture across generations is fundamentally a social process requiring communication and interaction among people who exchange ideas, skills, attitudes, and feelings. Schools have evolved to enhance and systematize this transfer, and educational goals focus on the short-term and long-term objectives for doing so. A discussion of educational goals can be found in Johnson (1979), but broadly they consist of transferring knowledge and skills; socializing children and adolescents into the perspectives, values, and attitudes they need to function effectively within our bureaucratic, technological society; and facilitating the cognitive, social, and physical development of each individual student.

Social systems function only as individuals interact, and schools are no exception. Education is primarily a social process that cannot occur except through *interpersonal interaction* and, therefore, the major concern of educators has to be the quality of relationships within the school and the classroom. Computers, teaching machines, textbooks, laboratory equipment, and so forth cannot educate or socialize a child; they are only aides to doing so. Teaching and learning take place only as people interact. Within the classroom the major sources of interpersonal interaction are between teachers and students and among the students themselves. The teacher and student role definitions carefully structure how individuals are to interact with each other, as do the general norms concerning appropriate and inappropriate behavior. Yet one has only to observe the difference between a substitute and a regular teacher in interacting with students to conclude that the quality of the relationship supercedes role definitions in determining how effective interpersonal interaction is in achieving educational goals. While educational psychology has traditionally emphasized the importance of adult-child interaction within the classroom, the aspects of student role definition and classroom norms concerning student-student interaction may be of equal or more importance. The other students in the class, and friendship groups in particular, serve as reference groups for students, providing role models, standards of comparison, and expectation systems that influence academic behavior and achievement of individual students. It is the interaction among students that is the forgotten, underemphasized, and underutilized relationship within American education and, therefore, it will be discussed at length within this chapter.

There are many important *instructional technologies* that facilitate the achievement of educational goals. Of central importance are the instructional strategies that directly facilitate the building of high quality adult-child and peer relationships which promote the achievement of educational goals and generally improve the quality of life within the classroom. These instructional strategies must take three important aspects of classroom life into account. The first is that it is within the classroom that social organization factors influence student achievement, socialization, and development. The second is that student attendance is compulsory, and since students are (at least in part) the involuntary clientele of the schools, their willingness to engage in the formally prescribed activities and to abide by the formal role definitions and social norms must be treated as problematic rather than taken for granted. The third is that classrooms are collective social settings. It is this collective character of classrooms that makes instruction much more than the simple application of the principles of learning psychology. Instruction must be viewed as the managing of behavior in groups. Student-student interaction is as powerful a fact of classroom life as teacher-student interactions, and it poses a source of influence that can either facilitate or obstruct the achievement of educational goals. Within this chapter, therefore, instructional strategies are discussed that are classroom based, directly affect students' acceptance of their roles and the classroom norms, and take into account the collective nature of the classroom by directly affecting the quality of the interpersonal relationships and student-student interaction within the classroom.

The *management system* generally consists of the authority hierarchy in the classroom, school, and school district and the degree to which students are involved in the ongoing, day-to-day decision making within the classroom. The management system has to take into account the compulsory attendance of students, the need to build student commitment to educational goals and to the reliable fulfillment of the student role, and the collective nature of the classroom. In the classroom the teacher has more authority than the students, but teachers can define their roles differently to share greater or lesser amounts of decision making about consequential or inconsequential academic and nonacademic matters with students. In this chapter, therefore, the effects of sharing authority and decision-making power with students are also discussed.

In summary, education is primarily a social process that cannot occur except through structured interpersonal interaction within a classroom. The basic dynamics of the classroom are that educational goals are achieved through structured interpersonal relationships and the utilization of the technology of instruction under the supervision of a manager. Educational goals are very broadly to promote the mastery of subject matter and the socialization and the cognitive, social, and physical development of each student. These goals are achieved as teachers and students interact and as students interact with each other. Generally, educational psychology has primarily focused on teacher-student interaction and the instructional technologies and management systems that facilitate teacher-student interaction. Student-student interaction and the instructional technologies and management systems that facilitate constructive peer relationships within the classroom have been less researched and less utilized in American schools and colleges. The purpose of this chapter, therefore, is to review the importance of peer relationships for the achievement of educational goals, to discuss two instructional strategies (the appropriate use of cooperative, competitive, and individualistic goal structures and structured academic controversies among students), and to discuss a management system that promotes constructive student-student interaction through involvement of students in classroom decision making.

IMPORTANCE OF STUDENT-STUDENT RELATIONSHIPS

The interaction between the teacher and the student has traditionally been viewed by educators and psychologists as the most important relationship for achieving the educational goals of mastering subject matter, socialization, and cognitive, social, and physical development. Three assumptions have supported this view: (a) students' learning is primarily dependent on the interaction with the teacher; (b) peer relationships have little impact on the student and, therefore, should be ignored; and (c) the infrequent and minor peer influences that do exist in the classroom are an unhealthy and bothersome influence on students' achievement, socialization, and development, discouraging academic achievement and encouraging off-task, disruptive behavior in the classroom.

These three assumptions have resulted in the suppression of student-student relationships in the classroom. Most legitimate peer interaction within schools has been limited to extracurricular activities that rarely deal with the basic issues of classroom life (McPartland 1977). In many classrooms a system of instruction is used that emphasizes lectures by teachers and individual seat work by students. In such a system, attempts by students to interact with each other are seen as off-task disruptiveness. Combs and Slaby (1977) note that educators systematically fail to train students in the most basic social skills necessary for interacting effectively with peers, as such social skills are not considered to be useful for learning. Without question, the dyadic, adult-child view of teaching and learning has led to a de-emphasis on student-student relationships and interaction within the classroom.

The assumption by educators and psychologists that the most important relationships children form are with adults such as parents and teachers is reflected in the considerable research that has focused on the teacher's (a) expectations of the student's ability to perform on academic tasks, (b) warmth, empathy, and democraticness in dealing with the student, (c) distribution of reinforcers to students for achievement and appropriate social behavior, and (d) feedback to students concerning achievement and appropriate behavior. This assumption has so dominated that between the 1930s and the 1970s relatively few studies have been conducted examining the impact of peer relationships on development and achievement. Lewis and Rosenblum (1975) note that from both a psychoanalytic and Piagetian point of view, peer relationships were thought to be unimportant, and the study of children's early social behavior was, therefore, directed toward parent-child interaction, especially mother-child relationships. Psychoanalytic theory emphasizes that children's early social experiences form the context for later social development, and their later social relationships, therefore, are all greatly influenced by their interaction with their mothers and fathers. The infant-mother dyad is considered so important that other social relationships are considered to be derivatives and are neglected or not considered at all. Piagetian theory views cognitive-structural capacities of the young child as restricting the child's social behavior. Thus, for complex social behavior to occur, a person old enough to be capable of controlling and manipulating the dynamics of the relationship (that is, an adult) needs to be present. The view that children lack the cognitive faculties necessary for social interaction results in the restriction of the study of early child-peer relationships. The aspects of psychoanalytic and Piagetian theories that deemphasize the importance of peer relationships, however, are now being vigorously questioned.

The adult-child dyadic view of teaching and learning is grossly oversimplified when the power of the social dynamics that occur regularly in the classroom among students is taken into consideration. Schmuck (1978) notes that while classroom teachers do interact frequently with individual students, virtually all of the teacher's classroom behaviors occur within the context of the student peer group. A student responding to a teacher's directive, for example, does so while being aware of and influenced by the feelings, attitudes, and relationships shared with the student peer group. Teacher statements and actions are responded to by students in the context of the students' relationships with other students.

Within educational psychology as well there has been an emphasis on adult-child dyadic relationships and a deemphasis on the constructive nature of student-student relationships. One of the purposes of this chapter is to provide evidence that experiences with peers are not a superficial luxury to be enjoyed by some students and not by others but rather an absolute necessity for maximal achievement, socialization, and healthy cognitive and social development. In fact, social interactions among peers may be the primary relationships within which development and socialization take place (Lewis and Rosenblum 1975). There are many important ways in which constructive student-student relationships can contribute to the achievement of the school's goals, such as by: contributing to the socialization of values, attitudes, competencies, and ways of perceiving the world; being prognostic indicators of future psychological health; teaching the social competencies necessary to reduce social isolation; influencing the occurrence or nonoccurrence of potential problem behaviors in adolescence such as the use of illegal drugs; providing the context in which children learn to master aggressive impulses; contributing to the development of sex role identity; contributing to the emergence of perspective-taking abilities; and influencing educational aspirations and achievement. Each of these correlates and consequences of peer relationships will be discussed below.

Socializing Influence

Students are effective socializing agents vis-à-vis each other. *Socialization* is the process of learning and internalizing the values, attitudes, roles, competencies, and ways of perceiving the world that are shared by one's family, community, and society (Johnson 1979). There are three important aspects of socialization: (a) the specific values, attitudes, roles, competencies, and perspectives that children and adolescents adopt are learned; (b) socialization has its origin in interaction with other people—it is within interpersonal relationships that children and adolescents are confronted with expectations as to what are appropriate values, attitudes, roles, competencies, and perspectives; (c) socialization is *not* a passive process—it is a dynamic process in which children and adolescents seek out and select alternatives for responding to the expectations of the people around them. Students learn and internalize the values, attitudes, roles, competencies, and perspectives of other people with whom they interact and whom they select to be influenced by.

Three of the most powerful processes through which socialization takes place are direct learning, identification, and role learning (Johnson 1979). Direct learning needs no definition. *Identification* occurs when children and adolescents try to incorporate the qualities and attributes of another person into themselves. Identification can be positive (that is, based on admiration of the other person or respect for the other person's competencies) or negative (that is, based on fear of or anger toward the other person). Identification often seems to take place without full awareness of the extent to which one is adopting the attributes of another person. Finally, through acquiring social roles, children and adolescents learn large integrated patterns of consistent behavior that they perform in relationships with other people. A *social role* is a set of expectations aimed at structuring interaction within a relationship. Examples of relationships in which social roles are learned are male-female, friend-friend, tutor-student, and student-teacher.

There is considerable evidence that peer relationships are of central importance in the socialization of the child—providing expectations, models, and reinforcements that shape a wide variety of social behaviors, attitudes, and perspectives (Hartup 1976, Johnson and Johnson 1978, Wahler 1967). Schmuck (1971) states that peers constitute the immediate environment as well as the environment of greatest impact for students in school. On the basis of his review of the literature, he states that compared to interactions with teachers, interactions with peers are more frequent, intense, and varied. In their interactions with peers, children and adolescents directly learn attitudes, values, and information unobtainable from adults, such as the nature of sexual relations and how they are to be developed and managed with peers. In their interactions with peers, children and adolescents imitate each other's actions and identify with friends who have admired competencies. The way in which in-group messages are phrased, the nature of clothes and hair styles, the music valued, what is defined as enjoyable and what is defined as distasteful, what competencies need to be practiced and developed, and so forth are all based on identification with and imitation of peers. In their interaction with peers, children and adolescents try out, practice, and perfect social roles. Young children may play house, fire department, and a variety of other adult career roles, older children may experiment with various ways in which to be a friend, and adolescents may practice social roles aimed at obtaining acceptance into desired peer groups. Through practicing social roles in their relationships with peers, students have the opportunity for paced, slowly elaborating enlargement of communicative, aggressive, defensive, and cooperative skills. The formation of relationships with peers, furthermore, not only promotes the values, attitudes, competencies, and perspectives needed to manage the challenges of adulthood productively, it also creates coalitions that may last into adulthood to the benefit of the children and their friends and/or partners.

The importance of socialization through interaction with peers does not end during adolescence. Several studies have demonstrated that peers greatly influence the adoption and internalization of values and attitudes by college students (Chickering 1969, Newcomb et al. 1970, 1971, Vreeland and Bidwell 1965, Wallace 1966). Lacy (1978) found that frequency of interaction with peers was not a sufficient factor to affect the values of college students. For peers to be an important influence on the internalization of values and attitudes, the content of the interaction had to be relevant to the value dimension, and students had to be generally satisfied with and responsive to their fellow students. Friends have an important impact on values throughout one's life. While much of the evidence indicating that peer relationships are vital and important for socialization is correlational, it is consistent in indicating considerable peer influence on socialization and development.

Indicator of Future Psychological Health

The ability to build and maintain interdependent, cooperative relationships is often cited as a primary manifestation of psychological health (Johnson and Matross 1977). It is no surprise, therefore, that several studies have found a relationship between (a) poor peer relations in children and (b) destructive social conduct in adolescence and psychological pathology in adulthood. Kohn and Clausen (1955) found among adults diagnosed as psychotic a much higher percentage who were socially isolated as children than was the case among adults in a normal control sample. In a study of servicemen who had formerly been patients at a child-guidance clinic, Roff (1961) found that men receiving "bad conduct" discharges were more frequently rated by their childhood counselors as having poor peer adjustment than were men with successful service records. In a study of adult males who were seen as children at child-guidance clinics, Roff (1963) found that poor peer relationships were predictive of adult neurotic and psychotic disturbances in a variety of types, as well as disturbances in sexual behavior and adjustment.

Cowen and his associates (1973) found that poor peer adjustment in the third grade was an excellent predictor of emotional difficulties in early adulthood. They accumulated a variety of measures on the children, including IQ scores, school grades, achievement test results, school attendance records, teacher ratings, and peer ratings. Eleven years later, community mental health registers were examined to determine which members of the sample were consulting a mental health professional. Of all the measures secured in the third grade, the best predictor of adult mental health status was the peer rating. Roff, Sells, and Golden (1972) found a significant correlation between childhood peer acceptance and delinquency in adolescence. Among upper-lower-class and middle-class males, delinquency rates were higher among children who were not accepted by their peers than among those who were. Among lower-class males, both highly accepted and highly rejected children had higher delinquency rates than did those who were moderately accepted by peers, but individual case records suggested that the ultimate social adjustment of the peer-accepted children would be better than the rejected ones.

Roff and his associates noted, furthermore, that no evidence exists to contradict the hypothesis that peer relations play a central role in psychological development. Finally, Johnson and Norem-Hebeisen (1977) found that adolescents oriented toward individualism and separation from peers displayed high levels of psychological pathology. There is considerable correlational evidence, therefore, that poor peer relationships in elementary school predict psychological disturbance in high school, and poor peer relationships in both elementary and high school predict adult psychological pathology.

Acquiring Social Competencies

There is some evidence that social isolation is related to a lack of social competencies and that constructive interaction with peers increases children's social skills. Children identified as social isolates in preschool situations tend to be deficient in leadership skills (Kohn and Rosman 1972) and tend not to elicit reactions from other children (Stanley and Gottman 1976). Koch (1935) identified seven distinctly unsocial children along with seven matched control children. For thirty minutes every day for twenty days, each "experimental" child was removed from the nursery along with one sociable child of the subject's own age and surrounded with play materials believed to stimulate cooperative play. The published reports are incomplete, but "changes in the direction of increased sociability were cumulative throughout the investigation" (Page 1936). Furman, Rahe, and Hartup (in press) conducted a similar study in which they identified preschool children who were social isolates, paired them with a same-age or younger peer, and placed them in a playroom with toys aimed at stimulating cooperative play for ten sessions. The socially withdrawn children were then observed in their regular classroom. The cooperative play significantly increased the frequency of social interaction of the withdrawn children, especially for those children who were paired with a younger peer. In addition, the withdrawn children positively reinforced their peers much more frequently, giving help and gifts, sharing, accepting guidance and suggestions, and engaging in cooperative play. The researchers concluded that the play sessions provided an opportunity for the isolates to have experiences that occurred infrequently in the regular classroom, such as being socially assertive by directing social activity.

Occurrence of Illegal Drug Use

Adolescents' peer groups and friends seem to have considerable influence on drug-use patterns as well as other problem or possible transition behaviors. There is considerable correlational evidence indicating that whether or not adolescents engage in the use of illegal drugs such as marihuana or engage in other problem or possible transition behaviors such as sexual intercourse and problem drinking is highly related to perceptions of one's friends as engaging in and being approving of the behaviors (Becker 1953, 1955; Elseroad and Goodman 1970; Goode 1970; Jessor 1975; Jessor, Jessor, and Finney 1973; Johnson 1973; Johnston 1973; Josephson 1974; Kandel 1975; Lavenhar et al. (1972). The correlational nature of this evidence supports the position that providing adolescents with peers and friends who do engage in or disapprove of problem behaviors such as the use of illegal drugs may have considerable influence on adolescents' behavior.

Managing Aggressive Impulses

Children learn to master aggressive impulses within the context of peer relations (Hartup 1978). Peer interaction provides an opportunity to experiment aggressively with coequals, and it is assumed that children who show generalized hostility and unusual modes of aggressive behavior or children who are unusually timid in the presence of aggressive attack may be lacking exposure to certain kinds of contacts with peers such as rough and tumble play. Rough and tumble play seems to promote the acquisition of a repertory of effective aggressive behaviors and also establishes necessary regulatory mechanisms for modulating aggressive affect. Aggression occurs more frequently in child-child interaction than in adult-child interaction in many different cultures (Whiting and Whiting 1975), and observational studies in the United States clearly show that feedback from peers escalates and deescalates rates of aggression among nursery schoolchildren (Patterson, Littman, and Bricker 1967, Patterson and Cobb 1971).

Socializing Sex Role Identity

Hartup (1978) notes that although gender typing first occurs in interactions between the child and its parents (Money and Ehrhardt 1972), the peer culture extends and elaborates this process. Fagot and Patterson (1969) found that social rewards are exchanged within the peer culture according to the gender appropriateness of the child's behavior, and Kobasigawa (1968) found that peer models also contribute to the formation of appropriate sexual attitudes. Kinsey, Pomeroy, and Martin (1948) noted that sexual experimentation is pervasive in child-child interactions and must be seen as contributing positively rather than negatively to socialization. Roff (1966) has shown that adults who are arrested for committing crimes of sexual assault or who have disturbances in sexual adjustment have histories of peer rejection and social isolation. As Hartup (1976) has so aptly stated, if parents were to be given sole responsibility for the socialization of sexuality, humans would not survive as a species.

Acquiring Perspective-taking Abilities

It is through interaction with peers that children develop the ability to view situations and problems from perspectives other than their own (Piaget 1932). Perspective taking is one of the most critical competencies for cognitive and social development, as it has been found to be related to effective presentation of information, effective comprehension of information, the constructive resolution of conflicts, willingness to disclose information on a personal level, effective group problem solving, cooperativeness, positive attitudes toward others within the same situation, autonomous moral judgment, intellectual and cognitive judgment, intellectual and cognitive development, and social adjustment (Johnson 1975, 1980a). *Social perspective taking* may be defined as the ability to understand how a situation appears to another person and how that person is reacting cognitively and emotionally to the situation. The opposite of perspective taking is *egocentrism*, the embeddedness in one's own viewpoint to the extent that one is unaware of other points of view and of the limitations in one's perspective.

Piaget (1932) views all psychological development as a progressive loss of egocentrism and an increase in ability to take wider and more complex perspectives. In discussing Piaget's theorizing, Flavell states:

In the course of this contact (and especially, his conflicts and arguments) with other children, the child increasingly finds himself forced to reexamine his own percepts and concepts in the light of others, and by so doing, gradually rids himself of cognitive egocentrism. [1963, p. 279.]

There is correlational and experimental evidence that the development of perspective-taking ability and the reduction of egocentrism are dependent upon interaction with peers. Gottman, Gonso, and Rasmussen (1975) found that children who were able to take the perspective of others were more socially active and more competent in social exchanges with other children than were less able perspective takers. Keasey (1973), in a study of fifth and sixth graders, found that those who belonged to many social organizations (and therefore interacted with peers more) had higher moral judgment scores (of which perspective taking is a major ingredient) than did children who belonged to few clubs. Johnson et al. (1976) found that individualistic learning experiences in which students were separated from each other and not allowed to interact promoted higher egocentrism and less perspective-taking ability than did learning in small cooperative groups.

Raising Educational Aspirations and Achievement

Peers have a great deal of influence on students' educational aspirations (Alexander and Campbell 1964, Coleman 1961, Coleman et al. 1966, Ramsøy 1961, Turner 1964, Wilson 1959). Alexander and Campbell (1964), for example, found that a student is more likely to aspire to higher education and actually get to college if his best friend also plans to go to college. There is also evidence that students' achievement is related to the educational and economic levels of other students in the school (Coleman et al. 1966, Crain and Weisman 1972). Freedman (1967) conducted an extensive review of the literature and concluded that educational aspirations and actual achievement were more affected by fellow students than by any other school influence.

Two studies dealing with primary age students in elementary schools servicing children from low-income families found consistent negative correlations between subject matter achievement and high frequencies of students studying alone; consistent positive correlations were found between time spent with peers in moderate size (three to seven) or large groups under the teacher's direction and subject matter achievement (Soar 1973, Stallings and Kaskowitz 1974). These studies imply that when students are young and when they have poor study skills, interaction with peers can significantly increase achievement.

QUALITY OF STUDENT-STUDENT RELATIONSHIPS

Interpersonal interaction is the basis for learning, socialization, and development. While there has been considerable emphasis on teacher-student interaction, the educational value of student-student interaction has largely been ignored. There is evidence indicating that among other things student-student interaction will contribute to general socialization, future psychological health, acquisition of social competencies, avoidance of engaging in antisocial or problem behaviors, mastery and control of impulses such as aggression, development of a sex role identity, emergence of perspective-taking ability, and development of high educational aspirations and achievement. *Simply placing students near each other and allowing interaction to take place does not mean, however, that these outcomes will appear.* The nature of the interaction is important. Some interaction leads to students rejecting each other and defensively avoiding being influenced by peers. When student-student interaction leads to relationships characterized by perceived support and acceptance, then the potential beneficial effects described in the previous section are likely to be found.

In order for peer relationships to be constructive influences, they must promote feelings of belonging, acceptance, support, and caring rather than feelings of hostility and rejection. Perceptions of being accepted by peers affect the following aspects of classroom life:

1. Peer acceptance is positively correlated with willingness to engage in social interaction (Furman 1977, Johnson and Ahlgren 1976, Johnson, Johnson, and Anderson 1978).
2. Peer acceptance is positively correlated with the extent to which students provide positive social rewards for peers (Hartup, Glazer, and Charlesworth 1967).
3. Isolation in the classroom is associated with high anxiety, low self-esteem, poor interpersonal skills, emotional handicaps, and psychological pathology (Bower 1960, Gronlund 1959, Horowitz 1962, Johnson and Norem-Hebeisen 1977, Mensh and Glidewell 1958, Schmuck 1963, 1966, Smith 1958, Van Egmond 1960).
4. Rejection by peers is related to disruptive classroom behavior (Lorber 1966), hostile behavior and negative affect (Lippitt and Gold 1959), and negative attitudes toward other students and school (Schmuck 1966).
5. Acceptance by peers is related to utilization of abilities in achievement situations (Schmuck 1963, 1966, Van Egmond 1960).

On the basis of this evidence it may be concluded that peer relationships will have constructive effects only when student-student interaction is characterized by support and acceptance. In order to promote constructive peer influences, therefore, teachers must ensure first that students interact with each other and second that the interaction takes place within a supportive and accepting context. In other words, teachers must control the major factors affecting student-student interaction, which include the way in which learning goals are structured and the way in which conflicts among ideas are managed. It is to these two areas that we now turn.

INSTRUCTIONAL STRATEGY 1: GOAL STRUCTURES

Given the importance of constructive peer relationships within the classroom, there is a need for validated instructional procedures that maximize constructive student-student interaction during academic activities. One such instructional strategy is the creation of appropriate goal interdependence among students as they learn. There are three types of goal interdependence among students that teachers can create during instruction (Deutsch 1962, Johnson and Johnson 1975): cooperative (positive goal interdependence), competitive (negative goal interdependence), and individualistic (no goal interdependence). A *cooperative* goal structure exists when there is a positive correlation among students' goal attainments; that is, when students perceive that they can obtain their goal if and only if the other students with whom they are cooperatively linked obtain their goals. A *competitive* goal structure exists when there is a negative correlation among students' goal attainments; that is, when students perceive that they can obtain their goal if and only if the other students with whom they are linked fail to obtain their goals. An *individualistic* goal structure exists when there is no correlation among students' goal attainments; that is, when students perceive that obtaining their goal is unrelated to the goal achievement of other students.

In the ideal classroom all three goal structures will be appropriately used. All students would learn how to work collaboratively with other students, compete for fun and enjoyment, and work autonomously on their own. Students would work on instructional tasks within the goal structure that is most productive for the type of task to be done and for the cognitive and affective outcomes desired. It is the teacher who decides which goal structure to implement within each instructional activity. The way in which teachers structure learning goals determines how students interact with each other and with the teacher. These interaction patterns, in turn, determine the cognitive and affective outcomes of instruction. There may possibly be no aspect of teaching more important than the appropriate use of goal structures.

Each goal structure promotes a different pattern of interaction among students. Cooperation provides opportunities for positive interaction among students; competition promotes cautious and defensive student-student interaction (except under limited conditions); while in individualistic situations, students work by themselves without interacting with other students. There is considerable research documenting the relative effects of the three goal structures on interaction patterns among students (Johnson and Johnson 1974, 1975, 1978). The evidence indicates that cooperation, compared with competitive and individualistic efforts, promotes more effective communication and exchange of information among students, greater facilitation of each other's achievement, more tutoring and sharing of resources among students, greater trust among students, greater emotional involvement in and commitment to learning by more students, higher utilization of the resources of other students, higher achievement motivation by more students, lower fear of failure by more students, greater acceptance and support by peers, more peer pressure toward achievement, and more divergent and risk-taking thinking. Of special interest are the findings that cooperative learning experiences result in stronger beliefs that one is liked, supported, and accepted by other students and that other students care about how much one learns and want to help one learn.

There has been a great deal of research on the instructional outcomes promoted by cooperative, competitive, and individualistic efforts (Johnson and Johnson 1974, 1975, 1978). According to the hundreds of research studies that have been conducted, dramatically different learning outcomes will result from the use of the different goal structures. While space is too short in this chapter to review all of the research, the evidence concerning achievement, perspective taking, self-esteem, psychological health, liking for other students, and positive attitudes toward school personnel such as teachers and principals will be discussed.

Achievement

Johnson et al. (in press) have recently completed a meta-analysis of 108 studies comparing the relative effects of cooperation, cooperation with intergroup competition, interpersonal competition, and individualistic efforts on achievement and productivity. These studies yielded 242 findings from which 352 comparisons among conditions were made. Three meta-analysis procedures were used: the voting method that counts the number of significant positive and negative as well as nonsignificant findings, Glass's (1977) effect-size method that calculates the average of the differences between the means of pairs of treatment conditions divided by the within-group standard deviation, and Stouffer's (1949) unweighted z-score method based on the sum of the z-scores computed from the probability of the finding being due to chance divided by the square root of the number of findings involved. All studies available to the authors comparing cooperative, competitive, and individualistic efforts (or any two of the three goal structures) on achievement and productivity and using North American samples were included. The results of the meta-analyses indicate that cooperative goal structures promote higher achievement than do either competitive or individualistic goal structures. The effect-size analysis, for example, indicated that the average student in the cooperative condition performed at the seventy-eighth percentile of the competitive condition (based on fifty-seven findings) and at the seventy-ninth percentile of the individualistic condition (based on ninety-eight findings). The average student in the cooperative-with-intergroup-competition condition performed at the sixty-fifth percentile of the interpersonal competition condition (based on sixteen findings) and at the sixty-ninth percentile of the individualistic condition (based on twenty findings). The results of the voting method and z-score method of meta-analysis are essentially the same. These results hold for all types of tasks other than rote decoding and correcting, for all age levels, and for all subject areas.

Development

There are a number of outcomes indicative of healthy cognitive, social, and physical development (for specific references, see Johnson and Johnson 1974, 1975, 1978). Cooperative learning experiences have been found to promote greater cognitive and emotional perspective-taking abilities than either competitive or individualistic learning experiences do. Cooperative learning experiences and attitudes are more related to high levels of self-esteem than are competitive and individualistic learning experiences and attitudes. Cooperative attitudes are highly related to psychological health, competitive attitudes are somewhat related to psychological health, and individualistic attitudes are related to psychological pathology.

Relationships

A number of studies have focused on the effects of the three goal structures on student-student and teacher-student relationships (Johnson and Johnson 1974, 1975, 1978, 1980). There is considerable evidence that cooperative learning experiences, compared with competitive and individualistic ones, result in more positive student-student relationships characterized by mutual liking, positive attitudes toward each other, mutual concern, friendliness, attentiveness, feelings of obligation to each other, and desire to win each other's respect. In competitive situations, there is a tendency for students to choose their friends on the basis of academic performance so that high-performance students in particular form a coherent and exclusive friendship group; while in cooperative situations, friendship circles tend to be more fluid and open and are formed on the basis of interests and other variables in addition to academic performance. There is evidence that cooperative learning experiences promote more positive attitudes toward heterogeneity among peers than do the other two goal structures and that more cross-ethnic, cross-social-class, cross-ability, and cross-sex friendships are formed in cooperative than in competitive or individualistic learning situations. Thus, cooperation promotes considerably more positive relationships and friendships among students than the other two goal structures do, and the friendships extend across the ethnic, social class, and ability dimensions that have traditionally separated students from each other.

Cooperative learning experiences, compared with competitive and individualistic ones, also promote more positive attitudes toward teachers and other school personnel. Students experiencing cooperative instruction like the teacher better and perceive the teacher as being more supportive and accepting, academically and personally. Such positive perceptions by students of their relationship with the teacher are important for many reasons, not the least of which is that the more positive the relationship between the teacher and the students, the less the teacher has to rely on direct power and coercion to motivate students to comply with the classroom regulations and the student role definition concerning participation in instructional activities. The above findings are consistent enough so that the more teachers use cooperative learning activities, the more they can expect to be better liked by their students.

Summary

The appropriate use of cooperative, competitive, and individualistic goal structures is an important instructional strategy allowing teachers to promote high achievement, effective socialization, and healthy development simultaneously. It is the cooperative goal structure that especially promotes the positive interaction among students (characterized by peer acceptance, support, and liking; student-student exchange of information; peer tutoring and encouragement for learning; and so forth) that is essential for educational success. The emphasis on positive goal interdependence among students not only creates the supportive, accepting, and caring relationships vital for socialization and healthy development, it also promotes achievement, perspective-taking ability, self-esteem, psychological health, liking for peers no matter how diverse they are, and positive attitudes toward school personnel. Despite the overwhelming research evidence, however, American schools are currently dominated by competitive and individualistic instruction that separates students and mitigates against constructive peer relationships.

INSTRUCTIONAL STRATEGY 2: CONTROVERSY

A second instructional strategy that promotes constructive student-student interaction and peer influences involves the management of conflicts among ideas during instructional activities. In any learning situation, conflicts among ideas and opinions are inevitable. They will occur no matter what the teacher does. And, like all conflicts, such controversies have the potential for producing highly constructive or highly destructive outcomes, depending on how they are managed. A *controversy* exists when one person's ideas, information, conclusions, theories, and opinions are incompatible with those of another, and the two seek to reach an agreement. The conflict resides in the two people's attempts to reach a common position. When two students, for example, must come to an agreement on the answer to a mathematics problem and they disagree as to what the answer should be, a controversy exists.

If managed constructively, controversies can increase student achievement, effective socialization, and healthy development. The process by which controversy does so is outlined in Figure 10-1. During a constructive controversy, a student will move from a conclusion based on current experiences and information to having that conclusion challenged by a peer or by the teacher to experiencing a state of internal conceptual conflict or disequilibrium to actively seeking more information, new experiences, or a more adequate cognitive

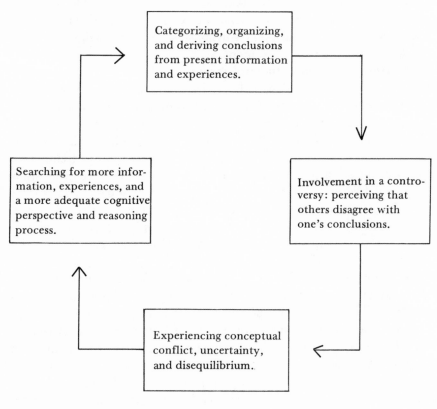

Figure 10-1

Process of controversy

perspective and reasoning process in hopes of resolving the uncertainty to reaching a new or reorganized conclusion that takes into account the perspective and reasoning of others. In this section both the outcomes of constructively managed controversy and the conditions determining whether controversy will be constructive or destructive will be reviewed.

Outcomes of Controversy

There is considerable evidence concerning the educational outcomes promoted by the constructive use of controversy. For a specific review of that evidence readers are referred to Johnson and Johnson (1979) and Johnson (1980b). For the most part, only a general summary of the evidence is given in this chapter. Effectively managed controversies promote epistemic curiosity, accuracy of cognitive perspective taking, transitions to higher stages of cognitive reasoning, increased quality of problem solving and decision making, greater creativity, and higher achievement.

Controversy among students creates conceptual conflict, which leads to epistemic curiosity or the active search for more information. Conceptual conflict exists when two ideas do not seem to be compatible or when information received does not seem to fit with what one already knows (Berlyne 1966). Disagreement with another person can be a source of conceptual conflict that provokes attempts to explore the other person's ideas. The research evidence indicates that conceptual conflict and epistemic curiosity are greater the greater the disagreement among students, the more frequently the disagreement occurs, the greater the number of people disagreeing with a student's position, and the more competitive the context of the controversy.

In resolving controversies, students need to be able both to comprehend the information being presented by their opposition and to understand the cognitive perspective their opposition is using to organize and interpret the information. A cognitive perspective consists of the cognitive organization being used to give meaning to a person's knowledge and the structure of a person's reasoning. The evidence indicates that controversy promotes greater understanding of another person's cognitive perspective than does discussion without controversy. Cognitive development theorists (Flavell 1963, Kohlberg 1969, Piaget 1948, 1950) have posited, furthermore, that it is repeated interpersonal controversies in which students are forced again and again to take cognizance of the perspective of others that promote *cognitive and moral development,* the ability to think logically, and the reduction of egocentric reasoning. Controversies are posited to create disequilibrium within students' cognitive structures, which motivates a search for a more adequate and mature process of reasoning. The evidence does indicate that controversies can promote transitions to higher stages of cognitive and moral reasoning. Finally, there is evidence that the presence of controversy promotes higher quality and more creative problem solving and decision making as well as higher achievement.

CONDITIONS AFFECTING THE CONSTRUCTIVENESS OF CONTROVERSY

Although controversy can operate in a beneficial way, it will not do so under all conditions. As with all conflict, the potential for either constructive or destructive outcomes is present. Whether positive or negative consequences result depends on the conditions within which the controversy occurs and the way in which it is managed. These conditions and procedures are discussed below. For a specific listing of the empirical support for the following statements, see Johnson and Johnson (1979) and Johnson (1980b).

1. The more cooperative (and less competitive) the context of the controversy, the more constructive it will be. The more cooperative the context, the more accurate and complete the communication of information; the more supportive the climate, the more disagreement is valued; the more open expression of feelings and ideas, the more disagreements are defined as problems to be jointly solved (as opposed to win-lose situations) and the easier it is to identify similarities between positions.

2. The more heterogenous the participants, the more likely the occurence of controversy. The more differences among students in terms of personality, sex, attitudes, background, social class, ethnic membership, ability levels, cognitive reasoning strategies, cognitive perspectives, information, and skills, the more likely controversy is to occur.

3. The more relevant information available and the more willing

and skilled students are in combining different items of information, the more constructive the controversy.

4. The higher students' skills in disagreeing with one another while confirming each other's competence (and without imputing incompetence on the part of the opposition), the more constructive the controversy.

5. The higher students' perspective-taking skills, the more constructive the controversy.

Summary

In order for accepting and supportive relationships to be developed and maintained among students, the controversies that arise as students study together must be managed constructively. Controversies spark conceptual conflict within students, creating curiosity and the motivation to find more information or to reorganize what they already know. Controversy also increases the accuracy of perspective taking, the transition to higher stages of cognitive and moral reasoning, higher quality and more creative problem solving, and higher achievement. Factors that influence whether controversies are managed constructively or destructively are a cooperative (as opposed to a competitive) context, heterogeneity among students, having relevant information and expertise available, having the necessary interpersonal skills, and being able to take others' perspectives.

Despite the importance of controversy as an instructional strategy, teachers and students generally avoid such conflict in most classrooms. It is not uncommon for teachers to suppress disagreement among students in American schools, and it is rare that controversy is actually utilized as an instructional strategy (Johnson 1979).

MANAGEMENT THROUGH SHARED DECISION MAKING

For instructional strategies to be effective, students must commit themselves to the achievement of the school's goals and accept the role definition and norms appropriate for doing so. Part of the teacher's role is to supervise students in ways that ensure that students behave appropriately. The management procedures teachers use need to take into account the compulsory attendance of students, the need to build student commitment to educational goals and to the reliable fulfillment of the student role, and the collective nature of the classroom. Some instructional strategies increase student commitment more than others. There is evidence that cooperative learning situations and constructively structured controversies promote students' liking for school, liking for the subject matter being studied, liking for current instructional activities, emotional involvement in and commitment to learning, and intrinsic motivation to learn (Johnson and Johnson 1974, 1975, 1978, Johnson 1980b). But there are additional direct management procedures teachers can use to maximize students' commitment to educational goals and reliable role performance.

In the classroom the teacher has more authority than the students do, but the teacher can involve students in decision making about the selection, organization, completion, presentation, evaluation, and continuation of activities (Epstein 1979). Students can help select elective subjects, text materials, or alternative learning activities; they can choose among alternative methods of instruction or among alternative tasks; they can participate in decisions about scheduling the order and the timing of projects as well as the person(s) or materials needed to help them complete a task; they can choose what information to share with others or how to present written and oral material to classmates; they can help set the criteria used to evaluate their work as well as the nature and timing of rewards received; and students can be given choices of more advanced or additional activities related to or extending from previous learning.

A collaborative or democratic involvement of students in classroom decision making is often contrasted to the more traditional authoritarian management system in which teachers make all of the decisions governing students' instructional and noninstructional life within the classroom. The more democratic the classroom, the more students like the teacher and feel committed to the student-teacher relationship, and the more students accept the teacher's influence (Epstein and McPartland 1978, Tjosvold 1979). Furthermore, there is reason to believe, on the basis of industrial research, that involvement in decision making will promote more commitment by students to educational goals and to the reliable performance of the student's role (Johnson 1970, Tjosvold 1979, Watson and Johnson 1972). Certainly student participation in classroom decision making will promote more constructive interaction with peers than will an authoritarian management system. Here again, however, classroom practice seems to lag behind educational research as it is somewhat rare in American schools to find classrooms where students are meaningfully involved in decision making.

SUMMARY AND CONCLUSIONS

Education is primarily a social process that cannot occur except through interpersonal interaction within a social system such as a school or classroom. Like all social systems, a classroom must have a clear set of goals, a network of interpersonal relationships structured by role definitions and social norms, technologies that promote the interpersonal interaction patterns needed to achieve the classroom's goals, and a management system that integrates human and material resources. Broadly educational goals consist of promoting mastery of subject matter and reasoning processes, effective socialization into the perspectives and attitudes needed to function within our society, and the healthy cognitive, social, and physical development of each student. Relationships between the teacher and the students and among the students are structured to achieve these goals. It is the quality of these relationships that largely determines the effectiveness of American education.

While the teacher-student relationship has traditionally been emphasized in American schools and colleges, there is considerable evidence that student-student relationships may be more important determinants of educational success. Peer relationships contribute to general socialization, future psychological health, acquisition of social competencies, avoidance of antisocial or problem behavioral patterns, mastery and control of impulses such as aggression, development of a healthy sex role identity, emergence of perspective-taking ability, and high levels of educational aspirations and achievement. These potential outcomes of peer relationships do not, however, automatically result from proximity to other students.

In order for student-student interaction to have a constructive impact on learning, socialization, and development, it must be characterized by acceptance, support, and liking. Two instructional strategies that directly affect the quality of peer relationships among students are the way in which teachers structure learning goals and the way in which teachers encourage and manage controversies within student learning groups. There are three ways in which learning goals may be structured: cooperative, competitive, and individualistic. It is the cooperative goal structure that is most effective in promoting supportive peer relationships as well as achievement, healthy development, and effective socialization. When students interact on instructional tasks, furthermore, disagreements or controversies are inevitable. Such conflicts can be highly constructive in promoting student achievement, socialization, and development if they are encouraged and properly managed. Both of these instructional strategies, furthermore, create student acceptance of educational goals and reliable student role performance. The management system that is most appropriate for promoting constructive peer relationships and successful education may be a collaborative or democratic system in which students are involved to varying degrees in classroom decision making.

This chapter highlights a series of contradictions in American education. Constructive student-student interaction is essential to learning, socialization, and development, yet most classrooms are dominated by teacher-student interaction to the exclusion of peer interaction. Two of the more empirically validated instructional strategies are cooperative learning and controversy, yet competition, individualistic learning, and the avoidance of conflict among ideas dominates most American classrooms. Given the need to induce student commitment to educational goals and the reliable performance of their student role, most American classrooms are dominated by authoritarian management systems that minimize student involvement in classroom decision making. Perhaps in the future there will be a greater correspondence between what social psychological research indicates and actual educational practice.

REFERENCES

Alexander, C. Norman, and Campbell, Ernest Q. "Peer Influences on Adolescent Aspirations and Attainments." *American Sociological Review* 29 (August 1964): 568-75.

Becker, Howard S. "Becoming a Marihuana User." *American Journal of Sociology* 57 (November 1953): 235-42.

———. "Marihuana Use and the Social Context." *Social Problems* 3 (July 1955): 35-44.

Berlyne, Daniel. "Notes on Intrinsic Motivation and Intrinsic Reward in Relation to Instruction." In *Learning about Learning*, Cooperative Research Monograph No. 15, edited by Jerome S. Bruner, pp. 105-110. Washington, D.C.: Office of Education, U.S. Department of Health, Education, and Welfare, 1966.

Bower, Eli M. *Early Identification of Emotionally Handicapped Children in School.* Springfield, Ill.: Charles C. Thomas, 1960.

Chickering, Arthur W. *Education and Identity.* San Francisco: Jossey-Bass, 1969.

Cohen, Michael. "Recent Advances in Our Understanding of School Effects Research." Paper presented at annual meeting of American Association of Colleges of Teacher Education, Chicago, March 1979.

Coleman, James S. *The Adolescent Society.* New York: Macmillan, 1961.

Coleman, James S. et al. *Equality of Educational Opportunity.* Washington, D.C.: U.S. Office of Health, Education, and Welfare, 1966.

Combs, Melinda L., and Slaby, Diana A. "Social Skills Training with Children." In *Advances in Clinical Child Psychology.* Vol. 1. Edited by Benjamin B. Lahey and Alan E. Kazdin. New York: Plenum Press, 1977.

Cowen, Emory L. et al. "Long-term Follow-up of Early Detected Vulnerable Children." *Journal of Consulting and Clinical Psychology* 41 (December 1973): 438-46.

Crain, Robert L., and Weisman, Carol S. *Discrimination, Personality, and Achievement: A Survey of Northern Blacks.* New York: Seminar Press, 1972.

Deutsch, Morton. "Cooperation and Trust: Some Theoretical Notes." In *Nebraska Symposium on Motivation,* edited by Marshall R. Jones, pp. 275-320. Lincoln, Neb.: University of Nebraska Press, 1962.

Elseroad, H., and Goodman, S. *A Survey of Secondary School Students' Perceptions and Attitudes toward Use of Drugs by Teenagers: Parts I, II, III.* Rockville, Md.: Montgomery County Public Schools, 1970.

Epstein, Joyce L. *Field Search: Practitioners Inform Research on Authority Structures*, Report No. 277. Baltimore: Center for Social Organization of Schools, Johns Hopkins University, 1979.

Epstein, Joyce L., and McPartland, James M. *Authority Structures and Student Development*, Report No. 246. Baltimore: Center for Social Organization of Schools, Johns Hopkins University, 1978.

Fagot, Beverly I., and Patterson, Gerald R. "An *in Vivo* Analysis of the Reinforcing Contingencies for Sex-Role Behaviors in the Preschool Child." *Developmental Psychology* 5 (September 1969): 563-68.

Flavell, John. *The Developmental Psychology of Jean Piaget.* Princeton, N.J.: D. Van Nostrand Co., 1963.

Freedman, Mervin B. *The Student and Campus Climates of Learning.* Washington, D.C.: U.S. Department of Health, Education, and Welfare, 1967.

Furman, Wyndol. "Friendship Selections and Individual Peer Interactions: A New Approach to Sociometric Research." Paper presented at Biennial meeting of the Society for Research in Child Development, New Orleans, 1977.

Furman, Wyndol; Rahe, Donald F.; and Hartup, Willard W. "Rehabilitation of Socially Withdrawn Children through Mixed-age and Same-age Socialization." *Child Development*, in press.

Glass, Gene V. "Integrating Findings: The Meta-analysis of Research." In *Review of Research in Education.* Vol. 5. Edited by Lee S. Shulman, pp. 351-79. Itasca, Ill.: Peacock, 1977.

Goode, Erich. *The Marihuana Smokers.* New York: Basic Books, 1970.

Gottman, John; Gonso, Jonni; and Rasmussen, Brian. "Social Interaction, Social Competence, and Friendship in Children." *Child Development* 46 (September 1975): 709-18.

Gronlund, Norman. *Sociometry in the Classroom.* New York: Harper & Row, 1959.

Hartup, Willard W. "Peer Interaction and the Behavioral Development of the Individual Child." In *Psychopathology and Child Development; Research and Treatment,* edited by Eric Schopler and Robert J. Reichler, pp. 203-218. New York: Plenum Press, 1976.

―――. "Children and Their Friends." In *Issues in Childhood Social Development,* edited by Harry McGurk. London: Methuen, 1978.

Hartup, Willard W.; Glazer, Jane A.; and Charlesworth, Rosalind. "Peer Reinforcement and Sociometric Status." *Child Development* 38 (December 1967): 1017-24.

Horowitz, Frances. "The Relationship of Anxiety, Self-Concept, and Sociometric Status among 4th, 5th, and 6th Grade Children." *Journal of Abnormal and Social Psychology* 65, 3 (1962): 212-14.

Jackson, Philip W. *Life in Classrooms.* New York: Holt, Rinehart and Winston, 1968.

Jessor, Richard. "Predicting Time of Onset of Marihuana Use: A Developmental Study of High School Youth." In *Predicting Adolescent Drug Abuse,* edited by Dan J. Lettieri, pp. 283-98. Washington, D.C.: National Institute of Drug Abuse, 1975.

Jessor, Richard; Jessor, Shirley; and Finney, John. "A Social Psychology of Marihuana Use: Longitudinal Studies of High School and College Youth." *Journal of Personality and Social Psychology* 26 (April 1973): 1-15.

Johnson, Bruce D. *Marihuana Users and Drug Subcultures.* New York: John Wiley, 1973.

Johnson, David W. *The Social Psychology of Education.* New York: Holt, Rinehart and Winston, 1970.

―――. "Cooperative Competencies and the Prevention and Treatment of Drug Abuse." *Research in Education* (November 1975). ERIC: ED 108 066.

―――. *Educational Psychology.* Englewood Cliffs, N.J.: Prentice-Hall, 1979.

―――. "Constructive Peer Relationships, Social Development, and Cooperative Learning Experiences: Implications for the Prevention of Drug Abuse." *Journal of Drug Education* 10 (February 1980a): 7-24.

―――. "Group Processes: Influences on Student-Student Interaction and School Outcomes." In *Social Psychology of School Learning,* edited by James McMillan. New York: Academic Press, 1980(b).

Johnson, David W., and Ahlgren, Andrew. "Relationship between Student Attitudes about Cooperation and Competition and Attitudes toward Schooling," *Journal of Educational Psychology* 68 (February 1976): 92-102.

Johnson, David W., and Johnson, Roger. "Instructional Goal Structure: Co-operative, Competitive, or Individualization." *Review of Educational Research* 44 (Spring 1974): 213-40.

————. *Learning Together and Alone: Cooperation, Competition, and Individualization.* Englewood Cliffs, N.J.: Prentice-Hall, 1975.

————. "Conflict in the Classroom: Controversy and Learning." *Review of Educational Research* 49 (Winter 1979): 51-70.

————. "Classroom Learning Structure and Attitudes toward Handicapped Children in Mainstream Settings: A Theoretical Model and Research Evidence." In *Attitudes and Attitude Change in Special Education*, edited by Reginald Jones. Reston, Va.: Council for Exceptional Children, 1980.

Johnson, David W., and Johnson, Roger, eds. "Social Interdependence in the Classroom: Cooperation, Competition, and Individualism." *Journal of Research and Development in Education* 12 (Fall 1978): 1-152.

Johnson, David W.; Johnson, Roger; and Anderson, Douglas. "Relationship between Student Cooperative, Competitive, and Individualistic Attitudes and Attitudes toward Schooling." *Journal of Psychology* 100 (November 1978): 183-99.

Johnson, David W. et al. "Effects of Cooperative vs. Individualized Instruction on Student Prosocial Behavior, Attitudes toward Learning, and Achievement," *Journal of Educational Psychology* 68 (August 1976): 446-52.

————. "The Effects of Cooperative, Competitive, and Individualistic Goal Structures on Achievement: A Meta-Analysis." *Psychological Bulletin*, in press.

Johnson, David W. and Matross, Ronald. "The Interpersonal Influence of the Psychotherapist: A Social Psychological View." In *Effective Psychotherapy: A Handbook of Research*, edited by Alan S. Gurman and Andrew M. Razin, pp. 395-432. Elmsford, N.Y.: Pergamon Press, 1977.

Johnson, David W., and Norem-Hebeisen, Ardyth. "Attitudes toward Interdependence among Persons and Psychological Health." *Psychological Reports* 40 (December 1977): 843-50.

Johnston, Lloyd. *Drugs and American Youth.* Ann Arbor, Mich.: Institute for Social Research, 1973.

Josephson, Eric. "Trends in Adolescent Marihuana Use." In *Drug Use: Epidemiological and Sociological Approaches*, edited by Eric Josephson and Eleanor Carroll, pp. 177-205. New York: Halsted Press, 1974.

Kandel, Denise. "Some Comments on the Relationship of Selected Criteria Variables to Adolescent Illicit Drug Use." In *Predicting Adolescent Drug Abuse*, edited by Dan J. Lettieri, pp. 243-361. Washington, D.C.: National Institute on Drug Abuse, 1975.

Keasey, Charles B. "Experimentally Induced Changes in Moral Opinions and Reasoning." *Journal of Personality and Social Psychology* 26 (April 1973): 30-38.

Kinsey, Alfred C.; Pomeroy, Wardell B.; and Martin, Clyde E. *Sexual Behavior in the Human Male.* Philadelphia: W. B. Saunders, 1948.

Kobasigawa, Akira. "Inhibitory and Disinhibitory Effects of Models on Sex-Inappropriate Behavior in Children." *Psychologia* 11 (June 1968): 86-96.

Koch, Lois. "The Modification of Unsocialness in Preschool Children." *Psychological Bulletin* 32 (November 1935): 700-701.

Kohlberg, Lawrence. "Stage and Sequence: The Cognitive-Developmental Approach to Socialization." In *Handbook of Socialization Theory and Research*, edited by David Goslin, pp. 347-480. Chicago: Rand McNally, 1969.

Kohn, Melvin, and Clausen, John A. "Social Isolation and Schizophrenia." *American Sociological Review* 20 (June 1955): 265-73.

Kohn, Martin, and Rosman, Bernice. "A Social Competence Scale and Symptom Checklist for the Preschool Child: Factor Dimensions, Their Cross-Instrument Generality, and Longitudinal Persistence." *Development Psychology* 6 (May 1972): 445-52.

Lacy, William B. "Interpersonal Relationships as Mediators of Structural Effects: College Student Socialization in a Traditional and Experimental University Environment." *Sociology of Education* 51 (July 1978): 201-211.

Lavenhar, M. et al. "A Survey of Drug Abuse in Six Suburban New Jersey High Schools: II, Characteristics of Drug Users and Nonusers." In *Student Drug Surveys*, edited by Stanley Ernstein and S. Allen. Farmingdale, N.Y.: Baywood, 1972.

Lewis, Michael, and Rosenblum, Leonard A., eds. *Friendship and Peer Relations.* New York: John Wiley, 1975.

Lippitt, Ronald, and Gold, Marvin. "Classroom Social Structure as a Mental Health Problem." *Journal of Social Issues* 15, 1 (1959): 40-58.

Lorber, N. M. "Inadequate Social Acceptance and Disruptive Classroom Behavior." *Journal of Educational Research* 59 (1966): 360-62.

McPartland, James M. "Social Authority Systems and Student Motivation." Paper presented at the annual meeting of the American Educational Research Association, New York, April 1977.

Mensh, Ivan, and Glidewell, John C. "Children's Perceptions of Relationships among Their Family and Friends." *Journal of Experimental Education* 27 (September 1958): 65-71.

Money, John, and Ehrhardt, Anke A. *Man and Woman, Boy and Girl.* Baltimore, Md.: Johns Hopkins University Press, 1972.

Newcomb, Theodore M. et al. "The University of Michigan's Residential College." In *The New Colleges: Toward an Appraisal*, edited by Paul Dressel. Monograph No. 7, American College Testing Program and the American Association for Higher Education, pp. 99-142. Iowa City, Iowa: American College Testing Program, 1971.

————. "Self-Selection and Change." In *The Cluster College*, edited by Jerry G. Gaff, pp. 137-60. San Francisco: Jossey-Bass, 1970.

Page, Marjorie L. "The Modification of Ascendant Behavior in Preschool Children," *University of Iowa Studies in Child Welfare* 12, 3 (1936), New Series no. 234.

Patterson, Gerald R., and Cobb, Joseph A. "A Dyadic Analysis of Aggressive Behaviors." In *Minnesota Symposia on Child Development.* Vol. 5. Edited by John Hill, pp. 72-129. Minneapolis: University of Minnesota Press, 1971.

Patterson, Gerald R.; Littman, Richard A.; and Bricker, William. "Assertive Behavior in Children: A Step toward a Theory of Aggression." *Monographs of the Society for Research in Child Development* 32, 5 (1967). Serial No. 113.

Piaget, Jean. *The Moral Judgment of the Child.* Glencoe, Ill.: Free Press, 1932, 1948.

————. *The Psychology of Intelligence.* New York: Harcourt, Brace, 1950.

Ramsøy, Natalie R. *American High Schools at Mid-Century.* New York: Bureau of Applied Social Research, Columbia University, 1961.

Roff, Merrill F. "Childhood Social Interaction and Young Adult Bad Conduct." *Journal of Abnormal and Social Psychology* 63 (September 1961): 333-37.

————. "Childhood Social Interaction and Young Adult Psychosis," *Journal of Clinical Psychology* 19 (January 1963): 152-57.

————. *Some Childhood and Adolescent Characteristics of Adult Homosexuals.* Report No. 66-5. Washington, D.C.: U.S. Army Medical Research and Development Command, May, 1966.

Roff, Merrill F.; Sells, S. B.; and Golden, Mary M. *Social Adjustment and Personality Development in Children.* Minneapolis: University of Minnesota Press, 1972.

Schmuck, Richard. "Applications of Social Psychology to Classroom Life." In *Social Psychology of Education: Theory and Research,* edited by Daniel Bar-Tal and Leonard Saxe. Washington, D.C.: Hemisphere, 1978.

————. "Some Relationships of Peer Liking Patterns in the Classroom to Pupil Attitudes and Achievement." *School Review* 71 (Autumn 1963): 337-59.

————. "Some Aspects of Classroom Social Climate." *Psychology in the School* 3 (January 1966): 59-65.

————. "Influence of the Peer Group." In *Psychology and Educational Practice,* edited by Gerald Lesser, pp. 502-29. Glenview, Ill: Scott, Foresman, 1971.

Smith, Louis M. "The Concurrent Validity of Six Personality and Adjustment Tests for Children." *Psychological Monographs: General and Applied* 72, 4 (1958), whole No. 457.

Soar, Robert S. *Follow-Through Classroom Process Measurement and Pupil Growth.* Final Report. Gainesville, Florida: College of Education, University of Florida, 1973.

Stallings, Jane, and Kaskowitz, David. *Follow-Through Classroom Observation Evaluation.* Menlo Park, Calif.: Stanford Research Institute, 1974.

Stanley, C. and Gottman, J. "Popularity, Social Structure, and Social Interaction in Children." Unpublished manuscript, 1976.

Stouffer, Samuel. *The American Soldier, vol. 1: Adjustment During Army Life.* Princeton, N.J.: Princeton University Press, 1949.

Tjosvold, Dean. "Alternative Organizations for Schools and Classrooms." In *Social Psychology of Education: Theory and Research,* edited by Daniel Bar-Tal and Leonard Saxe, pp. 275-98. Washington, D.C.: Hemisphere, 1979.

Turner, Ralph H. *The Social Context of Ambition.* San Francisco: Chandler Publishing, 1964.

Van Egmond, Elmer. "Social Interrelationship Skills and Effective Utilization of Intelligence in the Classroom." Ph.D. dissertation, University of Michigan, 1960.

Vreeland, Rebecca, and Bidwell, Charles E. "Organizational Effects in Students' Attitudes: A Study of the Harvard Houses." *Sociology of Education* 38 (Spring 1965): 233-50.

Wahler, Robert G. "Child-Child Interactions in Five Field Settings: Some Experimental Analyses." *Journal of Experimental Child Psychology* 5 (June 1967): 278-93.

Wallace, Walter L. *Student Culture: Social Structure and Continuity in a Liberal Arts College.* Chicago: Aldine, 1966.

Watson, Goodwin, B., and Johnson, David W. *Social Psychology: Issues and Insights.* Philadelphia: Lippincott, 1972.

Whiting, Beatrice B., and Whiting, John W. M. *Children of Six Cultures: A Psychocultural Analysis.* Cambridge, Mass.: Harvard University Press, 1975.

Wilson, Alan B. "Residential Segregation of Social Classes and Aspirations of High School Boys." *American Sociological Review* 24 (December 1959): 836-45.

11. Instructional Design in Transition

M. David Merrill, Trudy Kowallis, and *Brent G. Wilson*

   While education is almost as old as the human race, the systematic design of instructional materials is of rather recent origin. The purpose of this chapter is to present a brief review of some of the instructional design procedures developed during the past twenty years. We have emphasized those procedures that seem to have contemporary relevance. Furthermore, we have attempted to include those procedures that have received some empirical verification or are based on principles that have received some empirical verification. (See Reigeluth, Bunderson, and Merrill 1978.) We want to do more, however, than merely summarize the various procedures that have been advocated. We will also try to identify the philosophical origins of these procedures, and we will group related sets of procedures into families so that the reader has some sense of how these various procedures are related to one another.

   Our underlying thesis is that the metatheory (Snow 1973) influencing the kinds of principles and procedures that have been advocated has shifted from a behavioral science orientation (where the emphasis was to promote a student's overt performance by the manipulation of stimulus materials) to a cognitive science orientation

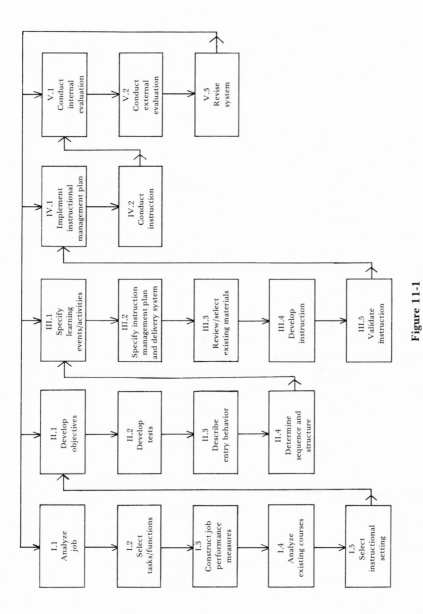

Figure 11-1

Interservice ISD model

(where the emphasis is to promote cognitive processing). With this shift in philosophy, there has also been a noticeable shift from procedures for manipulating the materials to be presented by an instructional system to procedures for directing student processing and interaction with the instructional system. We have attempted to review those prescriptions that are based primarily on behavioral science principles and show that some are in current use while others have been demonstrated as inadequate. We have also described the modifications that have occurred in recommended procedures as a result of an increased emphasis on cognitive theory, including some techniques presently in the formative stages of development.

During the past decade there has been an increased emphasis on the systematic development of instructional materials and programs (Baker 1973, Dick and Carey 1978, Briggs 1977, Gagné and Briggs 1979; see Andrews and Goodson 1979 for other references). Much of this literature has presented general models for instructional development which consist of a series of procedural steps. The interservice ISD model (*Interservice Procedures for Instructional Systems Development* 1975) is typical of these models. Figure 11-1 is a flow chart representing the principle phases in this model.

These systems models for the development of instruction are surprisingly lacking in prescriptions that suggest how to execute the various steps in the model. Although it would probably be unfair to say that the models contain empty boxes, the impressive-looking models do offer only limited help for the designer interested in principles of instruction. Our review will not attempt to summarize these general instructional development models but rather it will summarize procedures that may be used to execute some of the steps in such models.

Figure 11-2 is an attempt to identify the major families of instructional design procedures (the rectangles) and their metatheory base (the ovals) that we will consider in this chapter. This is a sort of conceptual genealogy chart in which the vertical connecting lines indicate the major threads of commonality between families of procedures and their metatheory orientations. Some of these conceptual threads have evolved with the shift in metatheory, while others have stayed relatively consistent with their origins. Ideas have multiple parenthood and are nurtured by many outside of their immediate family; consequently this genealogy of conceptual roots is oversimpli-

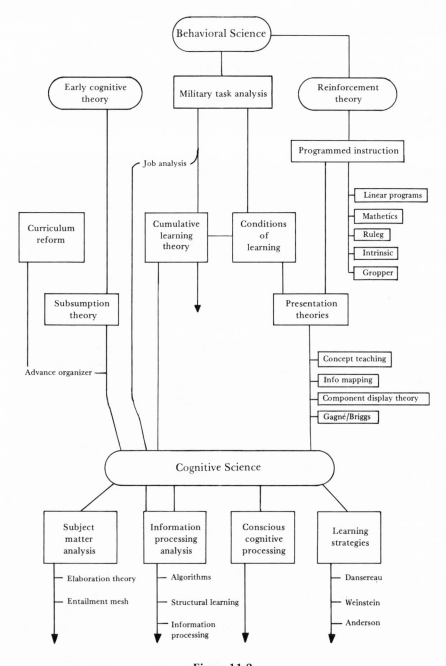

Figure 11-2

Conceptual roots of the major recommendations for instructional design

fied and subject to considerable disagreement. Nonetheless, we feel that it does help to put design procedures in some kind of context.

Figure 11-2 has been used to organize our chapter, and we will consider the various families of procedures moving in a rough chronological order from procedures oriented toward behavioral science to those oriented toward cognitive science. We have attempted to summarize the various procedures as concisely as possible, and in the process we have retained some of the technical vocabulary used by the particular theorists. Because of space limitations, it has not been possible to define all of these terms; hence some readers may find the presentation somewhat technical. Nevertheless, we feel the vocabulary that has been retained adequately reflects the procedures advocated. The purpose of our presentation is to put these various procedures in context rather than to present each position completely. The sources referenced should enable the reader to investigate more thoroughly the procedures we have summarized.

BEHAVIORAL SCIENCE BASE

The design of instruction is almost by definition a stimulus-based activity. Traditionally conceived, the problem of instruction is how to design the instructional presentation (stimulus) in such a way that it will elicit the desired behavior (response) from students. When viewed in historical perspective, this simple S-R approach to instruction had considerable support from the prevailing psychological climate during the formative years of instructional research. Behaviorism, particularly reinforcement theory, was firmly established as the predominant learning theory in the United States during the 1950s, when concern over instructional design received increased attention from psychologists.

Programmed Instruction

The programmed instruction movement of the 1950s and 1960s provided the historical backdrop for the development of modern instructional design principles. Skinner (1954) is credited with providing the impetus needed in applying psychological principles to the design of instruction. The programmed instruction movement began on this note: "There is a simple job to be done. The task can be

stated in concrete terms. The necessary techniques are known"
(Skinner 1954, p. 97).

Linear Programs. Confident that learning principles derived from
S-R research could be applied directly to school learning, programmed instructional principles included the following:

1. Instruction should require overt responses from the student.
2. Instruction should provide immediate reinforcement to student
   responses.
3. Instruction should contain small steps.
4. Instruction should elicit few or no errors in student response.
5. Instruction should be self-paced.

As the programmed instruction movement gained momentum, a
body of literature accumulated containing pragmatic, experience-
based prescriptions as well as scientific principles for the design of
instruction. Markle's *Good Frames and Bad* (1969) is one of the
best instructional grammars presenting some of these programming
principles.

Mathetics. Specific methods of programming instruction were a
natural consequence of the growth of the movement. Gilbert's
(1962) mathetics represented an attempt to apply reinforcement
theory directly in the form of a self-contained technology for the
design of instruction. Gilbert's main contribution to the field was his
method known as backward chaining in which procedural sequences
are taught starting at the end and gradually proceeding backward so
that the entire sequence is completed during each trial. Gilbert has
recently extended the backward chaining idea to form the rationale
for a five-stage model of instruction. The general sequence advocated
resembles a backward chaining approach: "First, show them where
things are going—the consequences of performance; next, provide the
mediating generalizations they need; and, finally, teach the discrimination skills" (Gilbert 1978, p. 267). Figure 11-3 presents a summary of the five-stage model. The students are first shown why the
content of the lesson is important and useful and how it will "fit in"
with what they already know. The second stage teaches any prerequisite skills needed to learn the new skills. The third stage teaches
the essential elements and generalizations of the task. The fourth
stage teaches the specific skills used in performing the task. Finally,
the fifth stage helps the student perform the skills in the appropriate context.

Stage of instruction	Description of stage	Function of stage	Illustration: How to troubleshoot and repair a turbine engine
1 Inductive stage	Teach the students the consequences	Motivate and familiarize	 Learns the analogy between a gas turbine and a percolator and also the importance of learning this new technology
2 Preparatory tools (propaedeutic stage)	Teaching students the basic prerequisite skills needed before they can learn the intended accomplishment	Teach prerequisite skills	1. Charles' law: $PV = kt$ 2. Turbine-fan, and so on
3 Theory stage	Teaching students those generalizations that characterize the task	Teach essentials	 Learns the essential elements of how the turbine works
4 Skill stage	Teaching students the discriminations required for performance	Teach skills	 Learns how to troubleshoot and repair the turbine
5 Application stage	Teach students to apply the training to real situations	Teach applications	 Gets on-the-job training

Figure 11-3

Gilbert's five-stage model of instruction and learning

Adapted from Gilbert 1978.

It is interesting that, although Gilbert's model relies on a strict S-R philosophy, in some respects it resembles other design prescriptions based on differing assumptions, such as Gagné's cumulative learning theory, Ausubel's subsumption theory, and Merrill and Reigeluth's elaboration theory, all described below. To some degree all of the design procedures described share similar principles that are independent of the underlying philosophies.

Ruleg. The ruleg system (Evans, Homme, and Glaser 1962) presented a generalization (the ru) followed by an instance of that generalization (the eg). Alternatives to ruleg switched the sequence of the components resulting in instance followed by generality (egrul) or instance followed by generality followed by a second instance (egruleg). When to apply one sequence over another depended on subject matter and target population variables, which are not fully explicated by the systems' proponents.

Intrinsic Programming. One important approach to programmed instruction differed significantly from linear programming. Crowder (1960) proposed intrinsic programming or branching programs, in which the error-free principle was loosened to allow for flexibility in the structure of the program. Depending on the initial response, the student was directed either to a remedial loop or to proceed with instruction. Student errors thus provided the basis for individualization in Crowder's branching programs. This challenge to basic S-R principles reflected the kind of growth in instructional design knowledge stimulated by programmed instruction.

Gropper. Although programmed instruction is no longer a dominant influence in instructional design theory, behavioristic techniques are still being promoted by a number of instructional designers. Gropper's *Instructional Strategies* (1974, 1976) addresses the question, "What should be the nature and extent of the . . . practice units . . . within each level of instruction?" (p. 7). He claims, "the aim of strategy formulation is to create the right number of stages, neither too many nor too few, and to create the right type of practice at each stage" (p. 20). Operating from this behavioristic framework, Gropper proceeds to present instructional strategies that in many ways resemble the work of Merrill, Markle, and other presentation theorists described below.

In its attempt at merging theory and practice, programmed instruction did much to stimulate the evolution of instructional science.

Programmed instruction stimulated researchers to think more seriously about instructional design questions. Research in programmed instruction became popular because of the highly replicable, controlled nature of the instructional presentations providing a testing ground for S-R applications to instruction. Lumsdaine, for example, first started talking about a "science of instruction" in 1961. Following his analysis, there was room for a science of instruction between a general theory of learning and a technology of application. This science of instruction—or "science of programmed instruction"—would entail "a series of contingent generalizations which take account of the interactions of variables . . . " (Lumsdaine 1961, p. 499). Lumsdaine particularly suggested that the development of a task taxonomy would contribute to a science of instruction, with task characteristics entering into contingent principles of instruction.

Another influence of programmed instruction that is widely felt today is the emphasis on individualizing instruction. Programmed instruction and teaching machines provided an operational method for self-paced instruction that contributed to the concern of educators and theorists for the possibilities of matching instruction to individual aptitude and preferences. Finally, the programmed instruction movement demonstrated that the application of theory to practice requires a prolonged sophisticated effort. Much of the research demonstrated that programmed instruction was not the panacea for the world's educational problems. While this knowledge shook the faith of some researchers and educators, it also provided a needed context for further productive inquiry into the instructional process.

Military Task Analysis

At approximately the same time as the interest in programmed instruction was taking place, a related but distinct movement was evolving in the military. During the early 1950s various branches of the military recognized the need to train personnel to shorten the lag in using newly developed equipment. Consequently, hundreds of psychologists were hired to develop these training materials (Lumsdaine and Glaser 1960). For many psychologists the shift from the learning laboratory to the exigencies of preparing military training materials prompted the need for immediate hands-on instructional prescriptions. Principles or methodologies carefully conceived in the laboratory would no longer suffice. Glaser (1964) notes that during this time one of the most significant changes in the tone of the published works of the psychologists involved in developing military training materials was a greater "emphasis on the characteristics of task variables and the implications of task characteristics on different learning variables" (p. 163).

Prompted by the need for results, psychologists began to develop procedures that would maximize the acquisition of training skills and knowledge. These procedures were generally devoid of any particular theoretical basis or unaccompanied by any well-organized body of supporting evidence (Gagné 1962). Nevertheless, the early developers of task analysis techniques (Miller 1962, Crawford 1962, Gagné 1962) found their methods to be very successful in developing training materials. In fact, the behavioral objective movement of the 1960s can in large part be attributed to task analysis techniques used in the military and elsewhere (Gagné 1965a, Mager 1962). The steps below offer a skeletal outline typical of many of the task analysis techniques originated in the context of military training (Crawford 1962):

1. Analysis of operational subsystem.
2. Analysis of the particular job.
3. Specification of knowledge and rules.
4. Determination of training objectives.
5. Construction of training program.
6. Development of measures of program proficiency.
7. Evaluation of training program.

The techniques of task analysis initiated by the military movement also extended into industrial training where they became known as job analysis (Holt and Shoemaker 1965). Task and job analysis in various forms continue to provide a viable and productive set of prescriptions for preparing instructional materials in performance-based environments such as industry and the military.

Cumulative Learning Theory

The seminal theory to evolve out of the military task analysis movement was Gagné's cumulative learning theory. Gagné asked, "What principles of learning would I look for to bring to bear on training problems?" (Gagné 1962, p. 83). He concluded that many of the well-known learning principles, such as reinforcement, distribution of practice, meaningfulness, distinctiveness of task elements, and so on, were of limited use in developing successful training programs. Consequently Gagné developed another set of principles based on his experience with military training. From his observations he reasoned that an individual has inherent capabilities that build on each other. "Thus it becomes possible to 'work backward' from any given objective of learning to determine what the prerequisite learnings must be; if necessary, all the way back to simple verbal associations and chains. When such an analysis is made, the result is a kind of map of what must be learned" (Gagné 1965b, pp. 172-73).

Based on this assumption about how we learn, Gagné (1962) suggested that a given terminal task can be divided into sets of component tasks. These tasks have a hierarchical arrangement representing a transfer structure where lower-level tasks must be mastered before higher-level tasks. The implications of these principles for designers are:

1. Identify terminal task or behavior.
2. Identify component tasks by asking, "What does the student need to be able to do to learn this task?"
3. Sequence component tasks to optimize transfer insuring that each of the component tasks is fully achieved before proceeding.

Today one of the most widely used instructional design procedures is learning hierarchy analysis, which is based on Gagné's cumulative learning theory. The learning hierarchy is "an arrangement of intellectual skills objectives into a pattern which shows the prerequisite relationships among them" (Gagné and Briggs 1974, p. 109). Learning hierarchies are constructed by approaching a target objective with the question: "What simpler skill(s) would a learner have to possess in order to learn this skill?" (Gagné and Briggs 1979, p. 110). This procedure is carried out on successively lower levels of component skills until the desired specificity is attained. Thus the lines of the hierarchy indicate learning prerequisite relationships; that is, before a learner can learn a superordinate skill, the skills directly below it must be in the student's repertory. Despite some criticism (Strike and Posner 1976, Reigeluth 1979), learning hierarchies are still widely used by many instructional design practitioners.

Categories of Learning

Bloom's Taxonomy. The development of taxonomies of human learning types marked another innovative departure from a strict adherence to S-R theory, and they play an inestimable role in the growth of instructional design theories. Operating within an educational framework, Bloom and associates (Bloom et al. 1956) developed a taxonomy of educational objectives that called attention to the wide array of learning types in education. One effect of Bloom's taxonomy was that higher-level cognitive objectives—for example, application and analysis—were acknowledged and emphasized. The taxonomy's major weakness lay in its largely atheoretical base. Little attempt was made to tie the objectives to an analysis of learning types or cognitive processing.

Conditions of Learning. Increased attention was given to the development of conceptual schemes for categorizing learning types in the early 1960s (see Melton 1964). Gagné (1965b) proposed a taxonomy of learning types reflective of his earlier work with task analysis and cumulative learning. In his first edition of *The Conditions of Learning*, Gagné (1965b) postulated a hierarchical arrangement of eight different learning types: signal learning, stimulus-response learning, chaining, verbal association, multiple-discrimination learning, concept learning, principle learning, and problem solving. He reasoned, "there are as many varieties of learning as there are distinguishable conditions for learning" (p. 22). The ability to perform at each level was contingent upon the individual's ability to perform successfully the prerequisite learning skills relevant to a given task. Thus, the taxonomy of learning types is closely related to the previously discussed cumulative learning theory.

Presentation Theories

Following *The Conditions of Learning,* instructional theorists proposed further specifications for instructional presentations (for example, Markle and Tiemann 1970; Gagné and Briggs 1974, 1979; Merrill, Olsen, and Coldeway 1976; Klausmeier, Ghatala, and Frayer 1974). These theorists accepted the notion of learning types; indeed, refinements of the Gagné taxonomy were suggested (Merrill 1971, Tiemann and Markle 1973). We will briefly review some of this work, including a somewhat fuller treatment for our own component display theory.

Gagné and Briggs. Gagné and Briggs have offered their own set of design recommendations for applying the eclectic learning theory of later editions of *The Conditions of Learning* (Gagné and Briggs 1974,

Effective learning conditions for cognitive strategies, information, attitudes, and motor skills

Type of lesson objective	Learning conditions
Cognitive strategy	Recall of relevant rules and concepts
	Successive presentation (usually over an extended time) of novel problem situations with class of solution unspecified
	Demonstration of solution by student
Information	
Names or labels	Recall of verbal chains
	Encoding (by student) by relating name to image or meaningful sentence
Facts	Recall of context of meaningful information
	Performance of reinstating fact in the larger context of information
Knowledge	Recall of context of related information
	Performance of reinstating new knowledge in the context of related information
Attitude	Recall of information and intellectual skills relevant to the targeted personal actions
	Establishment or recall of respect for "source" (usually a person)

Effective learning conditions for intellectual skill objectives

Type of lesson objective	Learning conditions
Discrimination	Recall of S-R connections ("responses")
	Repetition of situations presenting "same" and "different" stimuli, with feedback
	Emphasis on distinctive features
Concrete concept	Recall of discrimination of relevant object qualities
	Presentation of several concept instances, varying in irrelevant object qualities
	Identification of concept instances by student
Defined concept	Recall of component concepts
	Demonstration of the components of the concept or verbal statement of the definition
	Demonstration of concept by the student
Rule	Recall of component concepts or subordinate rules
	Demonstration or verbal statement of the rule
	Demonstration of rule-application by student

Category	Conditions of learning
	Reward for personal action either by direct experience or vicariously by observation of respected person
Higher-order rule	Recall of relevant subordinate rules Presentation of a novel problem Demonstration of new rule in achieving problem solution
Motor skill	Recall of component motor chains Establishment or recall of executive sub-routine (rules) Practice of total skill

Figure 11-4

Conditions of learning for various categories of learning types

From Gagné and Briggs 1979.

1979). The revised categories of learning are: (1) verbal information, (2) intellectual skills, (3) cognitive strategies, (4) attitudes, and (5) motor skills. Intellectual skills are subdivided into (a) discriminations, (b) concrete concepts, (c) defined concepts, (d) rules, and (c) higher-order rules. Figure 11-4 summarizes the conditions related to each of these learning types. Gagné and Briggs draw from a number of sources and theories in their effort to provide guidance for the design of instruction, but much is still left to the intuition of the individual designer.

Concept Teaching. Markel and Tiemann (1970) investigated ways to teach concepts. Of particular interest is their notion of a minimum rational set of examples and nonexamples presumed necessary for full understanding of a concept. A minimum rational set of nonexamples was equal to the number of "critical attributes" (the defining characteristics) of the concept and consisted of nonexamples of each of those attributes. For instance, if "chair" is defined as an object used for the seating of individuals, then a minimum rational set of nonexamples could include a love seat (two-person seat), a beach seat (not a rigid seat), and a stool (no back). A minimum rational set of examples was not restricted in number, the only requirement being that all "irrelevant attributes" (those nondefining characteristics) be varied across the examples.

Markle and Tiemann's work is an example of instructional theory that evolved from its programmed instruction roots. However, the idea of a rational set is derived primarily from an information-theory orientation; that is, instruction should contain all the elements of an adequate message. In teaching concepts, great care should be taken that adequate information is provided for the student to learn the boundaries, limitations, and extensions of the concept. This information-theory approach seems to be a middle ground between a strict behavioral and a cognitive approach to instruction. The presentation theories of this section were heavily influenced by the information requirements of instruction. Klausmeier proposes a number of instructional design prescriptions based on a developmental model of conceptual learning (Klausmeier and Goodwin 1975; Klausmeier, Ghatala, and Frayer 1974). Four levels of concept learning are hypothesized: concrete, identity, classification, and formal. These levels range from simply recognizing an object that has been previously encountered (concrete) to naming the concept, defining the concept in terms of its critical attributes, discriminating and naming its critical attributes, and classifying instances as examples or non-examples of that concept (formal level). As a concept is learned at progressively higher levels, the concept can be used in a wider variety of applications. At the classification and formal levels, for example, the concept can be used in classifying instances; in identifying structural relations between concepts such as superordinate, subordinate, and coordinate; in formulating and using principles; and in solving complex problems.

Klausmeier and Goodwin (1975) distill research and theory for various learning types into relevant principles and corresponding teacher behaviors. Figure 11-5 presents learning principles and design prescriptions for factual information and concepts. Other prescriptions are made for teaching problem solving, creativity, and psychomotor skills. These principles are general in nature and listed rather than tied together into a comprehensive theory. Indeed, these guidelines point out the limitations of much current design theory: explicit, direct prescriptions for the design of instruction are not easily formulated, and when they are attempted, research is often lacking to support the generalizability of the prescriptions.

Information Mapping. Horn (1976) has developed a set of prescriptive guidelines, known as information mapping, for designing instructional materials. These prescriptions were developed in order to make the training materials often found in business, government, and industrial settings more simple and efficient. Horn's guidelines consist of a system of procedures for identifying, categorizing, interrelating, sequencing, and graphically presenting instructional materials. Horn has attempted "the classification of all sentences and diagrams in a subject matter into a new unit of writing called the *Information Block*" (p. 5). An information block is one or more sentences and/or diagrams that represent a logically consistent and distinct segment of subject matter. All blocks of a given type are similar and modular. Horn has identified up to thirty-eight types of information blocks (for example, definition, diagram, example, parts, non-example, procedure, and so forth). Each block can be readily identified as a separate visual unit on a page and is accompanied by a label in the margin that describes its content.

An "information map" is the combination of these information blocks and several other special features. These are the main features

Factual Information

Learning principle	Design prescription
1. Organizing material into appropriate learning units facilitates the acquisition of knowledge	1. Organize material into appropriate learning units
2. Perceiving relationships between new information and what one already knows facilitates learning the new information	2. Help the individual to perceive meaningful relationships
3. Organizing complex material into sequential parts facilitates factual learning	3. Provide for proper sequencing of material
4. Making the correct response initially facilitates knowledge acquisition	4. Provide for correct responding on the first trial
5. Practicing, or using, is essential for attaining a high level of mastery of information and subsequent retention of it	5. Arrange for appropriate practice: a. practice in context b. provide informative feedback c. provide for distributed practice d. arrange study sessions of appropriate length
6. Evaluating the adequacy and accuracy of one's information is essential for attaining independence in learning factual information	6. Encourage independent evaluation

Figure 11-5, Part 1

Learning principles and corresponding design prescriptions for factual information

Concept Learning

Learning principles	Design principles
1. Being able to perform certain mental operations is essential to attaining a concept at any of the four levels	1. Identify the level at which the student can attain the concept(s)
2. Having a strategy for differentiating examples and non-examples promotes concept attainment	2. Teach a strategy for attaining the concept(s)
3. Identifying examples and nonexamples is essential for concept attainment at the classificatory level	3. Provide for properly sequenced sets of examples and nonexamples in teaching and testing
4. Discriminating and naming the attributes of a concept facilitates concept attainment at the two higher levels and also the uses of the concept	4. Define the concept in terms of its attributes
5. Acquiring the names of the concept and its attributes (and related word meanings) facilitates the attainment of concepts at the two higher levels: classificatory and formal	5. Establish the correct terminology for the concepts and attributes
6. Knowing whether one's responses are correct is essential for inferring a concept and also for differentiating newly encountered instances	6. Provide for feedback
7. Attaining a concept at the classificatory or formal level aids but does not assure use of the concept	7. Provide for use of the concept
8. Attaining independence in concept and principle learning requires self-initiated inquiry and evaluation	8. Encourage and guide student discovery and independent evaluation

Figure 11-5, Part 2

Learning principles and corresponding design prescriptions for concept learning

Adapted from Klausmeier and Goodwin 1975.

of an information map: (a) information is presented in blocks; (b) labels identify kind of information; (c) consistent format for each kind of information; (d) local index to provide quick location of prerequisite topics; (e) exercises and feedback questions located in close proximity to information (Horn 1976, p. 4). Horn also distinguishes among concept, structure, process, procedures, classification, and fact maps and provides procedures on how to construct each kind.

Horn's prescriptions indirectly draw from research findings in such areas as cuing (Glaser 1965), the use of diagrams and pictorial materials (Briggs 1968), sentence structures (Gagné and Rohwer 1969), and feedback. Horn's work has also been greatly influenced by basic task analysis techniques, programmed instruction, display technology, and communications principles including effective writing techniques. Information mapping is a comprehensive and explicit presentation technology. It is relatively easy to implement and is adaptable to a wide variety of subject matters. At this point, however, the authors know of no empirical research aimed at validating the claims of information mapping.

Component Display Theory. In our work we have attempted to provide a comprehensive design theory for instructional presentations (Merrill, Reigeluth, and Faust 1979, Merrill et al. 1977). Component display theory evolved from our earlier work on designing concept lessons (Merrill and Tennyson 1977) and from our attempts to clarify the categories specified by Gagné in *The Conditions of Learning* (see Merrill 1971).

A basic assumption of component display theory is that a given presentation can be segmented into a series of discrete displays. Component display theory assumes that all cognitive instruction occurs through two modes, telling or questioning, and that these modes can be used with two instructional elements, generalities or examples. Four primary presentation forms have been identified—generality, example, generality practice, and instance practice. (See Figure 11-6.)

The examples shown in Figure 11-6 illustrate the distinct function of each presentation form. Each of the these primary presentation forms can appear in a variety of formats and are not limited to those represented by the examples. For instance, a generality can be presented as a definition, as an algorithm, or as a diagram. Likewise each of the other primary presentation forms can be presented in a variety of formats while still serving the same function.

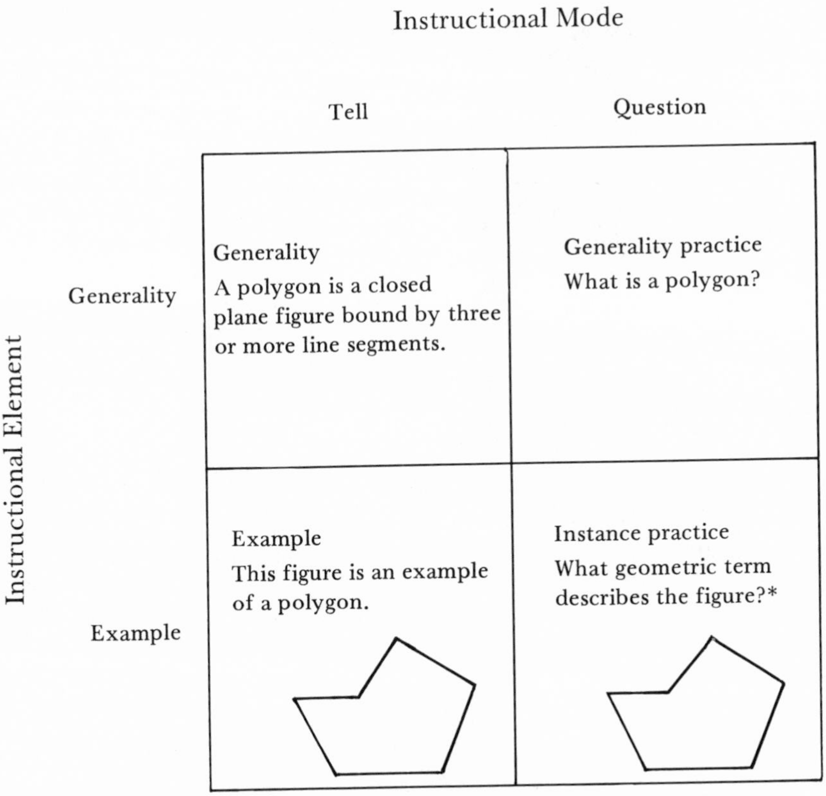

Instructional Mode

Figure 11-6

**Primary presentation form (PPF) matrix
with selected examples of each PPF form**

The second major assumption underlying component display theory is that learning outcomes can be classified on two dimensions: the type of content involved and the task level required of the student with respect to that content. The task/content matrix is illustrated in Figure 11-7.

Four types of content are indicated: facts, concepts, procedures and principles. A fact is a one-to-one association between objects, events, or symbols. A concept is a class of objects, events, or symbols that share critical attributes and that have discriminably different individual members. A procedure is a series of performances required to produce a specified outcome. A principle is some relationship

		Facts	Concepts	Procedures	Principles
Task*	Find	░░░	(Given a set of examples:) Describe what a circumference is.	(Given a set of examples:) Describe how you figure the circumference of a circle.	(Given a set of examples:) Describe the relationship between the radius and circumference of a circle.
	Use	░░░	If we measure how far it is around a tree, we have measured its _____ ?	Figure the circumference of a ball with a radius of 2 inches.	What happens to the circumference when you double the radius?
	Remember	What is the circumference of the earth?	What is a circumference?	How do you find the circumference of a circle?	What kind of relationship exists between the radius and circumference of a circle?

Content

*This dimension of the matrix has been collapsed for this paper. Task levels can be expanded to include: (1) remember instance verbatim; (2) remember instance alternate form; (3) remember generality verbatim; (4) remember generality paraphrase; (5) use generality; and (6) find generality. (Merrill, Reigeluth, and Faust 1978; Merrill, Richards, Schmidt, and Wood 1977.)

Figure 11-7

The task/content matrix assumed by component display theory

(usually cause and effect) between two or more concepts. Three levels of task are indicated: (1) a remember level where the student is required to remember an example or generality verbatim or in some alternate form; (2) a use level where the student is required to implement or apply a generality; and (3) a find level where the student is expected to discover a generality.

All the prescriptions of component display theory are described in terms of the components of two matrices outlined above. The theory includes three types of prescriptions: component specifications, consistency rules, and adequacy rules. Component specifications describe what is required to construct an adequate primary presentation form of each type for each cell of the task/content matrix. These specifications are necessary because the nature of primary presentation forms will differ across task levels. For instance, to remember an example verbatim requires the example and practice item to be identical, with practice consisting of repetition with the same instance. In contrast, to use a concept requires a divergent set of example and practice items, with practice consisting of previously unencountered instances. Thus a primary presentation form at one task level may not always be the same as the same type of primary presentation form at another task level.

Consistency rules indicate that for each cell in the task/content matrix there exists a combination of primary presentation forms that is optimal for producing the specified outcome. This means that to achieve the type of learning outcome corresponding with the use-concept cell, the instruction should include a generality, a set of examples, and a set of practice items. However, for the remember-principle cell, a generality and a generality-practice item would be the only primary presentation forms prescribed. Procedures for determining consistency in existing materials have been specified in several documents (Merrill, Reigeluth, and Faust 1979, Merrill et al. 1977).

Adequacy rules indicate what strategy components should be included for each primary presentation form and what characteristics each of those strategy components should have. Strategy components include feedback, isolation, mnemonic aids, attention-focusing devices, and algorithms. Some of the adequacy rules prescribed by component display theory are as follows:

1. Feedback: Instance-practice items or generality-practice items should be followed by immediate feedback as to whether or not the response is correct, what the correct response is, and why it is the correct response.
2. Isolation: The primary presentation forms and their elaborations should be separated and labeled in such a way that the student can easily skip over or turn to a display of a given type.

3. Attention-focusing devices such as color, underlining, arrows, or boxes should be used to direct the student's attention to critical information.

4. Divergence: The example and instance-practice sets should be divergent with respect to variable attributes or context.

5. Matching: Example displays should consist of example-nonexample pairs matched with respect to variable (irrelevant) attributes.

These prescriptions and others are outlined in more detail in several documents (Merrill, Reigeluth, and Faust 1979, Ellis and Wulfeck 1978, Merrill et al. 1977). Component display theory also includes specifications for test adequacy that differ somewhat from the prescriptions for presentation adequacy.

Component display theory has been used in a significant amount of applied instructional design. It was the rationale underlying the design of the TICCIT computer-based learning system (Merrill, Schneider, and Fletcher 1979). It forms a major foundation for the design of hundreds of hours of instruction designed by Courseware, Inc. These prescriptions have also received considerable research support in both laboratory and field experiments (Merrill, Olsen, and Coldeway 1976).

COGNITIVE SCIENCE BASE

The instructional design technologies discussed thus far are products of what Gagné and White (1978) have termed an "instruction → learning outcome" paradigm (p. 187). This two-element paradigm is indicative of the influence S-R learning theory has had on instructional design. However, within the past decade the dominant psychological influence has shifted from a behavioristic paradigm to a cognitive paradigm. Gagné and White (1978) have depicted this change by a three-element instructional paradigm—instruction → memory structure → learning outcome—to correspond with this cognitive view of learning (p. 187). They suggest that the effects of instruction can best be understood by exploring this new relation. The concern over finding instructional applications congruent with this view of learning is evidenced by numerous recent reviews discussing the implications of cognitive research for instruction (Klahr 1976, Lesgold et al. 1978, Wittrock 1978, Wittrock and Lumsdaine

1977, Anderson, Spiro, and Montague 1977). Nonetheless, Dansereau (1978) points out that "as is usually the case, application lags behind basic research" (p. 3). In the remainder of this chapter we will examine some of the design principles that have evolved so far from this new instructional paradigm and explore possible avenues for future instructional prescriptions formulated from a cognitive perspective.

Early Cognitive Influence

Pask. Some of the earliest work taking a cognitive orientation was done by Pask and associates using teaching machines in implementing adaptive instruction. Their first adaptive teaching machine was developed in 1953 (Lewis and Pask 1965).

Concept Strategies. On a somewhat different track, Bruner's (Bruner, Goodnow, and Austin 1956) pioneering research investigated the psychological conditions for concept learning, as well as specific problem-solving strategies followed by learners in discovering concepts.

Curriculum Reform. Bruner was also influential in the curriculum reform movement of the late 1950s and 1960s (Bruner 1960). Bruner and others (see Elam 1964) called for a different method of teaching traditional subject matters in which the central concepts and inquiry processes of the disciplines would be given pivotal roles in the curriculum. The "structure of the discipline" includes those principles from which other principles and concepts can be "derived" (see Schwab 1962, 1964). Bruner stated: "Grasping the structure of a subject is understanding it in a way that permits many other things to be related to it meaningfully. To learn structure, in short, is to learn how things are related" (Bruner 1960, p. 7).

Curriculum reform did not have a major impact on instructional design thinking partly because it was a values-based movement rather than a science-based movement. Concepts and recommendations were not rigorously defined and tested, and applications in the development of curricula (for example, *Man: A Course of Study* and *BSCS biology*) were not intended to be direct empirical tests of ideas for curriculum reform. Furthermore, as Ausubel (1964) pointed out out, curriculum designers need to consider both the logical structure of the subject matter and the psychological cognitive structure of the students. The curriculum reform theorists concentrated primarily on the logical structure of the subject matter.

Subsumption Theory. Ausubel's subsumption theory (Ausubel 1963, 1968) is an attempt to explicate some of the interrelationships between logical relations and psychological relations among concepts. According to Ausubel, meaningful verbal learning occurs when the instructional content is related to the student's cognitive structure in a nonarbitrary, substantive way. New material may be subsumed by an anchoring idea—a more inclusive, superordinate concept that provides ideational scaffolding for lower-level information. Thus, the context of learning becomes very important.

Instructional implications of subsumption theory include two principles stated by Ausubel:

1. Progressive differentiation: "The most general and inclusive ideas of the discipline (should be) presented first," which are "then progressively differentiated in terms of detail and specificity" (Ausubel 1968, p. 152).
2. Integrative reconciliation: "Instruction should explicitly point in what ways previously learned ideas (whether preexisting in cognitive structure or previously covered in instruction) are either similar to or different from new ideas and information in the learning task" (Ausubel 1968, p. 157).

Ausubel's theory has been criticized for lack of precision and for being difficult to make operational and test. However, many of Ausubel's principles are appealing and have considerable relevance for instructional design. Unfortunately, about the only enduring trace of Ausubel's work is the use of advance organizers, material presented prior to the primary instruction to which the student can relate the subsequent materials. Advance organizers are only one possible application of his underlying theory.

Information Processing Analysis

A variety of task analysis procedures have been developed over the past several years that attempt to identify mental operations carried out in the performance of a task.

Resnick. Resnick is one of the foremost instructional researchers investigating cognitive-task analytic techniques (Resnick 1973, Resnick, Wang, and Kaplan 1973, Resnick 1975, 1976). Her work has extended learning hierarchy analysis to include consideration of the psychological processes implicit in the task performance. (See Gagné and Briggs 1979, chap. 6.) To this end she has combined learning prerequisite relationships with performance prerequisite relationships (see Gropper 1974), resulting in hierarchies such as Figure 11-8. In this figure, the terminal objective forms the apex of the hierarchy; the second level represents operations carried out in performance; and the third level shows learning prerequisites for these performance operations.

Resnick's combined hierarchies hold the advantage of displaying cognitive operations while maintaining the learning-prerequisite relationships. Thus, for known cognitive operations, a procedure or algorithm can be developed, whereas for elements of the task that have not been so completely analyzed, learning-prerequisite relationships are still considered in the analysis.

Resnick advocates two mutually supportive methods of task analysis: rational and empirical analysis. Rational analysis is defined

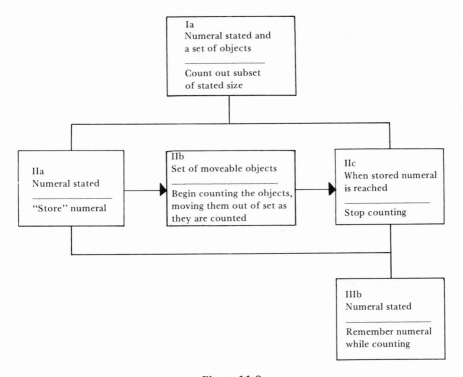

Figure 11-8

Analysis of the objective: "Given a numeral stated and a set of objects, the child can count out a subset of stated size"

From Resnick, Wang, and Kaplan 1973.

as "an attempt to specify processes or procedures that would be used in the highly efficient performance of some task" (Resnick 1976, p. 65). The result of rational analysis—an algorithmic routine or cognitive processing model—is derived primarily from the inferred cognitive and subject-matter structures. Empirical task analysis, on the other hand, is based on data collected during the actual perform-ance of the task. From the interpretation of these data, a bottom-up construction is made of the procedures (for examples, see Groen and Resnick 1977, Resnick 1976). Rational and empirical analyses are complementary. At present, due to costs and technological limita-tions, most analyses are rational. However, as efficient techniques are developed, empirical analysis will probably play a greater role in the cognitive analysis process.

Figure 11-9 illustrates the relationship between rational and empirical task analyses as they bear upon the choice of a teaching routine. Completing the three-way interaction is the transformation of the instruction made by the student. Groen and Resnick (1977) illustrate how children can adapt an explicitly taught algorithm into a more efficient algorithm over a period of time and practice. Based on this conceptualization, Resnick has offered three criteria in choosing a teaching routine or procedure: (a) it must adequately display the

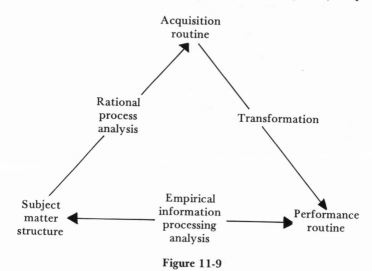

Figure 11-9

**Relation between acquisition routines, performance
routines, and the structure of subject matter**

Adapted from Resnick 1976.

underlying structure of the subject matter; (b) it must be easy to demonstrate or teach; (c) it must be capable of transformation into an efficient performance routine (Resnick 1976, p. 74).

Path Analysis. Paul Merrill is another cognitive information-processing analyst whose work grew out of the learning hierarchy tradition (P. F. Merrill 1976). Rather than combining learning-prerequisite relationships and performance-prerequisite relationships into a single figure, Merrill suggests that designers should perform both a learning hierarchy analysis and an information-processing analysis (P. F. Merrill 1978). As noted above, Gagné's latest design procedures (Gagné, 1977; Gagné and Briggs, 1979) advocate exactly that.

In comparing information-processing task analysis with learning-hierarchy analysis, Merrill utilizes the path analysis techniques of Scandura (1973) in producing a partial ordering of the different possible paths through an algorithm. Based on path analysis techniques (see Scandura 1973 and the discussion below), Merrill shows how analysis of the information-processing structure of a task (in the form of a branching algorithm) can clarify learning prerequisite relations, leading to a revised learning hierarchy (P. F. Merrill 1978). Through a path analysis of a simple subtraction algorithm, some boxes in a rationally determined learning hierarchy were shown to be trivial or ambiguous, while other important prerequisite relations were omitted. Merrill's work shows how learning-hierarchy analysis and information-processing analysis can complement one another. He points out, however, that information-processing analysis is most appropriate for tasks that are algorithmic in nature. Path analysis is only appropriate for branching algorithms (that is, algorithms containing decision points).

Structural Learning Theory. Scandura's work entails much more than instructional design principles and procedures. In a formally stated, axiomatic theoretical system, Scandura (1973) proposes a theory of knowledge and a theory of learning that naturally leads to direct instructional implications. Scandura summarizes his position as follows: "The present view rejects the idea that overt (and/or potentially overt) stimuli cause behavior. We assume instead that behavior is caused by rules, an underlying construct—in effect, that subjects actually do use rules. Stimuli simply provide the occasion for responding" (Scandura 1973, p. 15). Again, "two major assumptions are (1) all behavior is generated by rules, and (2) rules can be devised to account for all kinds of human behavior" (p. 41). Simply defined, rules may be thought of as procedures, represented in mathematical terms, containing a start step, a set of operating rules and decision points, and a halt step. For an example, see the subtraction routine presented in Figure 11-10. Scandura's rules and P. F. Merrill's algorithms are essentially equivalent.

The instructional relevance of Scandura's theory can be seen in his work in mathematics (Scandura 1971). Consider, for example, the report of a child who has developed his own system for adding decimals:

Given '.4 + .3' . . . the child would respond '.7.' Similarly, he could correctly add '.2 + .7.' His system works fine where the decimal point is to the left. But, when asked to add '3. + .2,' for instance, the child would respond '.5.' Why? . . . one must specify what rule would lead a child to respond correctly to the first two instances and incorrectly to the third. [1977, p. 21]

The subtraction task represented in Figure 11-10 illustrates how rules can be used in instructional design. A path analysis of the sort also advocated by P. F. Merrill reveals the different possible paths through the algorithm (not counting repeating loops through the same operations). In the case of this subtraction algorithm, twelve paths can be identified. These paths are essentially subrules contained within the general rule. Although the details of the path analysis are not shown here (compare Durnin and Scandura 1973 and P. F. Merrill 1978), exemplary instances of problems from each path are presented in the figure, showing the gradually increasing complexity required in performance.

The path analysis techniques advocated by P. F. Merrill (1973) and Scandura (1977) have promising applications for instructional design. For example, test construction can be made more effective and efficient. Scandura has shown that tests containing a single test item for each path can be highly reliable indicators of student achievement, while at the same time providing information that is far more useful diagnostically. These theory-based tests furnish information necessary to provide effective individualized instruction, depending on what parts of the task the student does or does not know.

Algorithms. The work of Landa (1974, 1976) offers yet another approach to analyzing supposed mental activity in task performance.

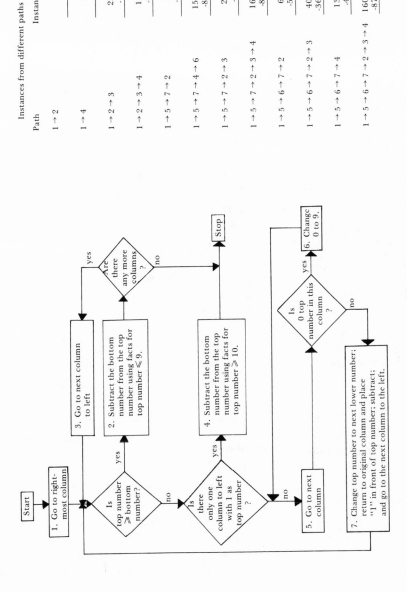

Figure 11-10

A subtraction rule with problems that require different paths through the rule

Different theories and research paradigms influenced Landa's work in the Soviet Union, but the degree of parallel between his work and others in the west (Scandura 1973, Pask 1975, 1976) is quite remarkable. Landa advocates viewing instruction from a cybernetic viewpoint (Landa 1977). A cybernetic system (in this case the learner) is one that receives feedback concerning the success of its actions in achieving a specified goal and using that feedback in adapting its future actions. In other words, a cybernetic system is a self-regulating, self-correcting, and goal-seeking system.

Instruction seen as a cybernetic system may be completely controlled (that is, instructional goals are achieved) or poorly controlled (goals are achieved only partially or not at all). The challenge of instructional design is to enable the student to gain control over the instructional process, that is, to achieve the instructional goals more effectively and efficiently. To clarify this distinct use of control, Landa states, "control . . . is defined not by the means used to influence the student (whether rigorous or not, dictatorial or nondictatorial), but by the attainment of a specific goal. Control occurs if the goal is achieved and fails to occur if it is not achieved" (Landa 1976, p. xii). The most important overall goal of instruction is to achieve self-control on the part of the learner, described by Landa as "the capacity for independent regulation of his own mental processes and behavior" (p. xii). Instruction should always be sensitive to that long-term goal.

A chief method proposed by Landa to bring instruction under control is through the formulation and instruction of explicit procedures to be carried out by the student in the course of performing a task. These procedures can be one of two general kinds: algorithms and heuristics. An algorithm is defined as "a precise, generally comprehensible prescription for carrying out a defined . . . sequence of elementary operations . . . in order to solve any problems belonging to a certain class (or type)" (Landa 1974, p. 11; italics deleted). While algorithms by definition are capable of always solving a class of problems, heuristic procedures cannot guarantee the solution of a problem; rather they provide useful strategies that will probably lead to a correct solution. Thus heuristics are more likely to utilize the feedback mechanisms of the cybernetic system (in this case, the student) in evaluating the effects of actions and adapting future actions.

Landa has devoted a great deal of attention to implementing his approach to specific subject matters, such as geometric proofs, foreign language instruction, and Russian grammar. He readily admits that not all subject-matter tasks can be represented algorithmically but defends the algorithmic-heuristic approach as a promising means toward gaining greater control over instruction. Although Landa's work differs somewhat from that of Scandura, Resnick, and P. F. Merrill, the general intent is the same: to represent the mental processes engaged in the performance of complex tasks and to use that representation in teaching, testing, and diagnosis to make learning more effective and efficient.

Having briefly reviewed different information processing theories for instructional design, we should consider some of the problems to be faced in implementing these procedures. First, as these theorists readily admit, not all tasks can be represented by algorithms. Scandura, for example, distinguished between deterministic and non-deterministic rules (roughly equivalent, we presume, to algorithms and heuristics), but he builds most of his theory around deterministic rules. Less is known about heuristics or nondeterministic rules, yet these seem to hold greater promise for complex problem solving tasks. Mathematics is a very highly developed sophisticated body of knowledge; consequently, most algorithmic analysis has been done in the areas of arithmetic and geometry. A number of fields, however, are not so well defined. How generally applicable are information processing procedures over a variety of tasks and subject matters? These are questions of interest that do not minimize the value of information processing approaches but merely attempt to define their scope and range of application.

Another problem in exteriorizing mental processes is the likelihood that mental processes vary from person to person, especially when ability and prior experience are taken into account. When a variety of possible algorithms may be intuitively implemented by students, how does the instructional designer determine which, if any, to use explicitly to teach the student? Is the loss in flexibility compensated for by increased control over the instructional process?

Finally, once a procedure is formulated that represents internal processes, what is the best way to go about teaching that procedure to the student? Path analysis can partially identify sequencing priorities, yet several questions are left unanswered. How do memory limitations of human processing affect the design strategy for teaching algorithms? Scandura and others have addressed these questions (Scandura 1973, chap. 10), yet clear instructional prescriptions have not been developed. Closely related to memory limitations is the question of developmental differences (see Kail and Hagen 1977; Case 1978a, 1978b). Much of the work is cognitive in the sense that it describes the task in structural/process terms, but many design questions remain concerning how to map the task structure onto the pre-existing cognitive structure of the learner.

Subject Matter Analysis

Entailment Meshes. Pask (1975, 1976) has devised a number of fairly elaborate techniques "to exteriorize cognitive operations" (Pask 1976, p. 1). He proposes that one way of doing this is through verbal conversations in which the learners explain how they learn while participating in the actual learning process. Pask has developed a conversational language so that an observer or mechanized system can interact with the learner to provide descriptions of conversational domains and map out the internal structure of a particular subject matter. Pask (1976) terms this approach "conversation theory" based on his proposition that the basic unit of psychological/educational observation is a conversation.

The products resulting from these interactions with learners are called entailment structures or meshes. These entailment meshes represent the interrelationships among the different components of a particular subject matter as viewed by the learner. The topic relations among a particular subject matter appear as nodes in the entailment mesh. These topic nodes are linked by derivation chains to still other nodes. Entailment meshes represent syntactic as well as semantic relationships. Each node in an entailment mesh is also attached through data links to another structure known as a task structure. This structure tells what may be done to bring about the topic relations represented at the corresponding node. In many respects, Pask's work represents an operationalized version of schema theory (Norman 1978, Rumelhart and Ortony 1977). One parallel is the notion suggested by Dorner (1978) of the coexistence of heuristical structures (parallel to the entailment mesh) and epistemical structures (parallel to the task structure) within a person's scheme.

Through a process known as pruning, a given entailment mesh can be reduced into component networks. Figure 11-11 illustrates sim-

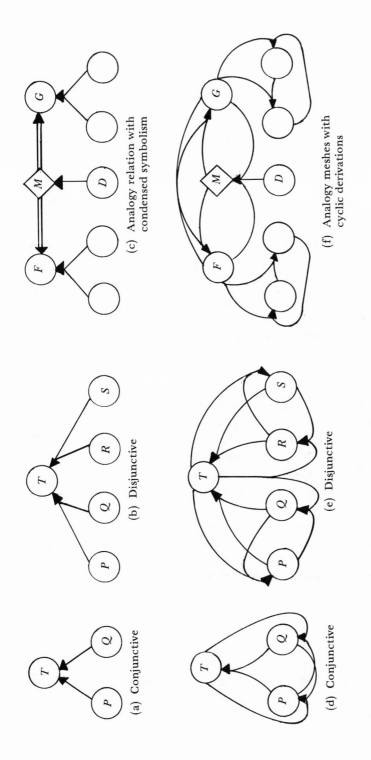

(a) Conjunctive

(b) Disjunctive

(c) Analogy relation with condensed symbolism

(d) Conjunctive

(e) Disjunctive

(f) Analogy meshes with cyclic derivations

Figure 11-11

Types of structural relationships in entailment mesh

plified representations of these structural relationships. They consist of conjunctive relationships, disjunctive relationships, and analogy relationships.

Pask (1976) claims that "any legitimate network is an analogy relation in its own right" (p. 53). In addition, he readily acknowledges the importance this construct plays in the instructional process.

We posit that the rate of learning is materially influenced by the number (or density) of analogies a learner can appreciate, the quality of learning by the number of valid analogies that the learner comes to understand. [p. 17]

Elaboration Theory. Elaboration theory (Reigeluth, Merrill, and Wilson in press, Reigeluth 1979) is based on the assumption that the task/content matrix of component display theory can be extended to include a structural dimension. Facts, concepts, procedures, and principles refer to single constructs; relationships between multiple constructs comprise content structures, or lists, taxonomies, parts hierarchies, procedures, and models. Figure 11-12 presents an overview of these structure types. Lists are the simplest and probably the most common type of structure. Components of a list may be ordered on some attribute, such as time, location, or color. Taxonomies are sets of concepts connected by superordinate, subordinate, and coordinate relationships constructed on the basis of class inclusion. Parts hierarchies are similar structures; however, the relationship is part to whole rather than class inclusion. Procedures are series of event concepts that specify the performances required to accomplish a given objective. Procedures may be highly or loosely sequenced, branching or linear, and algorithmic or heuristic. Finally, models may be of two kinds: physical or theoretical. Physical models attempt to represent real-world objects, physical systems, or processes. Theoretical models, on the other hand, connect concepts, both abstract and concrete, in an effort to explain the world through causal relationships.

This set of structures makes no pretense at being an exhaustive list of the kinds of relationships between concepts. Their worth, rather, should be judged on how they may be put to use in the design of effective, efficient instruction. Elaboration theory argues their usefulness from two grounds: (1) structural relations themselves should be explicitly taught and tested, resulting in more meaningful, stable learning, and (2) the instructional presentation should be

Type of structure	Description	Examples	Method of elaboration
Ordered list	Collection of things organized on some parameter of attribute	—chronology of Lincoln's life —alphabetical list of . . . —towns along highway 40	Provide overview and scope of subject Identify ordering parameter Teach list
Kinds taxonomy	"*A* is a kind of *B*" classification system	—botanical taxonomy —kinds of research reports —kinds of experimental designs —kinds of sailboats —kinds of furniture	Proceed from top down teaching discriminating attributes at each level
Parts taxonomy	"*A* is a part of *B*" classification system	—branches of mathematics —parts of a gasoline engine —subroutines of a computer program —parts of a research paper	Proceed from top down teaching relationship between parts at each level
Procedure	Series of steps required to attain some specified result	—tying a shoelace —solving a linear equation —laying out a rafter —addressing a microcomputer	Teach simplified form of the procedure gradually adding complexity
Model	Physical or casual representations of the world	—model of open education —Newtonian physics —cross section of a tree —precipitation cycle —map of New Hampshire	Teach fundamental relationship first adding on other concepts and principles that increase the precision of the model and that handle the complexity found in the real world

Figure 11-12

An overview of the structure types as proposed by elaboration theory

organized around these structures, following an elaboration model that proceeds from general to detailed, simple to complex.

A number of different methods could conceivably be employed to represent the relations between concepts of a subject matter. The point of elaboration theory is that teaching these interrelationships should be a primary concern of instruction, and these interrelationships should be explicitly taught rather than left to the discovery of the learner. The use of diagrams, tables, graphs, and figures is hypothesized to have an important beneficial effect and can serve as a useful alternative to standard forms of prose instruction. It is hypothesized that when structural relations are taught explicitly, learning will be more meaningful, leading to greater retention and transfer. Wilcox (1979), in a preliminary study, found that presentation of a taxonomy structure increased posttest scores for concept classification of seven interrelated concepts.

The elaboration model for organizing instruction is based on the identification of structures in the subject matter. Depending on the goals of the instruction, the designer formulates an organizing structure for the course. For example, is the course intended to teach "how to" skills, provide a conceptual overview, or teach the underlying principles? This organizing structure could be of any type for any subject matter, again depending on the goals of instruction. After specifying the organizing structure, an epitome is extracted from the structure that presents the core features of the complete organizing structure. The epitome is usually the most general or structurally simple portion of the organizing structure that can be taught in an introductory lesson. The epitome for a taxonomy might be the first two levels of generality, leaving lower levels to be elaborated in subsequent lessons. For a complex theoretical model, the epitome might entail the basic principle, leaving out the host of qualifiers, refinements, and contingent principles that would be elaborated in later instruction.

Once the organizing structure (and other supporting structures) have been formulated and an epitome extracted from the organizing structure, the elaboration principle can be implemented. The epitome is first presented, followed by a level of elaboration. An expanded epitome follows that includes the portion of the organizing structure immediately elaborated upon. The cycle of *elaborate → synthesize → elaborate → synthesize* is followed until instruction is complete. The elaboration model is often represented as a zoom lens approach to instruction: instruction begins with a wide-angle view of the material to be covered, zooming in on levels of detail, periodically returning to a wide-angle view to keep the detail in context. Typically the zooming is presequenced by the instructional system. Instruction could be designed to accommodate student control of the level of detail (Reigeluth 1979).

A simple example may clarify the elaborative process. If a course were designed in economics and the goals of instruction were theoretical in nature, the epitome might be a presentation of the basic laws of supply and demand. The first level of elaboration could extend these principles to macroeconomics, a second level could introduce factors and principles relating to imperfect markets, and so on. Each level of elaboration reiterates the basic concepts of previous levels, building upon the foundation laid by previous elaborations.

Although both cumulative learning theory and elaboration theory build on previously presented material, the two approaches differ in their perspective. Cumulative learning theory seeks to analyze the whole task into its parts, teaching each part until the whole is learned. In contrast, elaboration theory seeks to present an overview of the whole (the epitome) first, followed by elaboration of the parts that relate to the whole (Wilson 1979).

The principles underlying elaboration theory are relatively simple. Yet to be demonstrated, however, is how easily and effectively the method can be made operational in the design of real instruction. Also, recent developments (Merrill and Wilson 1979) have suggested an increasing emphasis on the cognitive structure as well as subject matter structure by introducing a working analogy or model at the onset of instruction. Undoubtedly the model will be refined as experimentation and field testing demonstrate strengths and weaknesses.

Learning Strategies

The study of learning strategies is another area of particular interest for instructional design that has evolved out of the cognitive science movement. Many precedents in this area originated from early research on problem solving and artificial intelligence (Newell, Shaw, and Simon 1958; Miller, Galanter, and Pribram 1960). More recently, in their work using a computer to model short-term memory processes, Gilmarten, Newell, and Simon (1976) claim that the different behaviors humans show in a task environment are due in part to the differences in the strategies they use to process the information. They maintain that knowledge about the correspondence between tasks and optimal strategies could allow researchers to decompose tasks into basic information processing requirements and predict strategies that allow for the best performance. Likewise, Resnick and Glaser (1977) argue that processes involved in certain problem solving situations may be similar to those used when learning in the absence of direct or complete instruction. They submit that directly teaching these processes might be a means of increasing students' general learning-to-learn abilities.

Craik and Tulving (1975) articulated the need for learning strategies by pointing out that "people do not necessarily learn best when they are merely given 'learn' instructions" (p. 292). Dansereau (1978) administered an extensive learning strategy inventory and found that even good college students have very little knowledge of alternative learning techniques. Weinstein (1978) reports findings from a series of protocols administered across a wide variety of students to determine what types of elaboration strategies successful students use. Results indicated that more successful learners and those with more years of schooling used meaningful elaboration strategies more frequently than rote or superficial strategies.

In Figure 11-13, Rigney (1978) provides a helpful conceptualization of the various categories of learning strategies (cognitive strategies). He has devised a matrix that categorizes these strategies according to the control of the orienting task and the explicitness of the cognitive strategy. He suggests that orienting tasks (for example, underlining, asking questions, following instructions) can be either student assigned or instructional system assigned. Furthermore, a cognitive strategy can be either detached, described independently from the subject matter, or it can be embedded in the instructional system, where the student is required to use processing resources to accomplish the orienting task for that particular subject matter. In the future, it may be advantageous to determine the relative usefulness of using learning strategies in each of these contexts with different student populations and using different tasks.

Some of the most current research with respect to learning strategies is being conducted as part of a program of research in learning strategies initiated by the Defense Advance Research Projects Agency

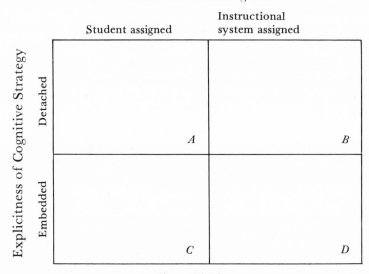

Control of orienting task

Figure 11-13

Alternative approaches to teaching and using cognitive strategies

From Rigney 1978.

(DARPA) in 1976. Much of the research and findings of those in-volved with this project is reported in O'Neil (1978). Dansereau (1978) reports the development of a learning strategies curriculum based on a theoretical framework where it was assumed that effective learning requires: (a) identification of important, unfamiliar, and difficult material; (b) the application of techniques for the compre-hension and retention of this identified material; (c) the efficient retrieval of this information under appropriate circumstances; and (d) the effective coping with internal and external distractions while the other processes are being employed (p. 8).

Dansereau (1978) and others devised a training curriculum corre-sponding to these assumptions and based on strategies derived from the literature. The results of their study showed no significant differ-ence on the immediate training assessment test. On the delayed test, however, the group effects were significant. The learning strategies used in this study (paraphrase-imagery, networking, and analysis of key ideas) seem to correspond with categories A, C, and D, respec-tively, of Rigney's strategy matrix.

Logan (1978) suggests that we should be particularly concerned about integrating findings regarding learning strategies with instructional design theory and research. Obviously, the orientating tasks identified by Rigney (1978) are principally communicated through instructional materials or through especially designed instructional management procedures. The compelling need for instructional designers at the moment was summarized by Weinstein (1978):

Although many educators and psychologists agree that successful learners use a variety of effective elaboration strategies to organize and execute any particular learning act, the type and essential components of these strategies have not been systematically identified or classified. [p. 49]

Weinstein (1978) reports a study investigating the effects of a diversified elaboration-skill training program on the learning outcomes of ninth graders. This study focused primarily on the effects of different elaboration strategies on student performance. The cognitive strategies included sentence elaboration, imaginal elaboration, analysis drawing implications, creative relationships, and paraphrasing. The treatment groups consisted of an experimental training group, a control group, and a posttest only group. Stimulus materials represented a variety of content areas and the learning tasks included paired associate, free recall, serial learning, and reading comprehension tasks.

The results showed significant performance differences for the training group only on the free recall measure on the immediate posttest. For the delayed posttest, the data showed significant differences on reading comprehension and trial 1 of the serial learning task. Other comparisons failed to reach significance. Although the findings were not conclusive, Weinstein (1978) suggests that this study provided evidence that a generalizable learning strategy program could be successfully developed and implemented. More recently, in conjunction with the learning strategies project sponsored by DARPA, Weinstein (1978) has been doing descriptive/protocol work in order to provide a data base for further investigations.

Recently another team of researchers (Anderson 1979) have designed a comprehensive set of learning strategies for studying textbook materials in preparation for taking an examination. They have outlined procedural guidelines for the three stages of studying: (a) prereading activities, (b) during reading activities, and (c) postreading

activities. Of significance in this approach is the use of mapping techniques as part of the third stage of studying. Anderson et al. have
designed a set of mapping techniques that allows students to visually
record the primary components and relationships of text materials.
The maps themselves take on different shapes depending on the
kinds of questions they answer. Figure 11-14a illustrates the type of
map associated with questions concerned with the relationships between a concept and examples of that concept (type I), a concept
and properties of that concept (type II), and a concept and its definition (type III). Figure 11-14b illustrates the mapping techniques
associated with questions concerning the comparison and contrast
of two concepts (type IV). Finally, a third type of map, shown
in Figure 11-14c, represents questions involving the relationship of
events in time (type V) and the relationships of events to their causes
and effects.

The procedures outlined by Anderson are an attempt to provide
students with a set of visually oriented elaboration algorithms. These
techniques seem to correspond most closely with category C of
Rigney's learning strategy matrix. Although these techniques seem
theoretically sound, they have yet to be extensively field tested and
proven effective. One criticism that might arise with regard to this
type of approach to studying is the motivation and implementation
problems inherent in a technique that requires considerable training,
effort, and time on the part of the students.

Conscious Cognitive Processing

Component display theory indicated that for each task/content
category, there was a particular combination of primary presentation
forms believed to be optimal for promoting acquisition of the specified outcome. We would like to expand this model to suggest that for
each category of the task/content matrix, there is not only an optimal combination of primary presentation forms but also an optimal
combination of processing activities associated with each of these displays. For example, if a student is learning to classify unencountered
instances of a concept, component display theory would prescribe a
strategy consisting of a generality display, a set of example displays,
and a set of divergent practice displays. It might be advantageous if,
given the generality display, the students were instructed to attempt
to paraphrase the definition and to try to think of an example from

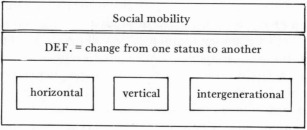

(a) Concept and examples

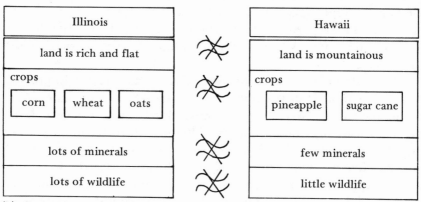

(b) Comparing two concepts

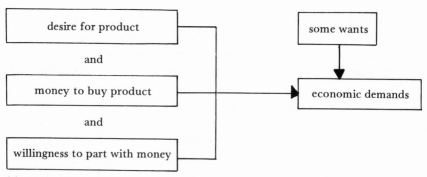

(c) Events in time

Figure 11-14

Mapping as a study strategy

F. Anderson et al. 1979.

their own experience prior to going to the example displays. A complete set of such prescriptions is not yet available, but the above should suggest the direction in which we are moving.

A related idea is compensating strategies. Much of the available instructional material is inadequate judged against the prescriptions of component display theory. One way to increase student learning is to redesign the instruction using the applications of component display theory, such as the Instructional Strategy Diagnostic Profile (Merrill et al. 1977), or the Instructional Quality Inventory (Ellis and Wulfeck 1978) as a guide. However, it may ultimately be more profitable to train the student in specific processing strategies that will help compensate for the incomplete instruction. For example, if instruction does not include alternative forms of the generality, the student can be directed to search her or his memory for a possible example or to search for a nonexample when one is not provided by the material. If practice is not included, the student can turn some of the provided examples into practice items. Our preliminary investigations of compensating strategies indicate that processing displays added to less than adequate instructional materials do indeed facilitate student performance (Callahan 1979).

This model of processing strategies has the advantage of taking into account parameters of the instructional presentation hypothesized by component display theory to affect learning outcomes. Rather than responding in the same way to all instructional presentations, student processing depends on the characteristics of instruction. The student in a sense becomes a sort of instructional analyst, analyzing the instructional presentation and, based on that analysis, determining the processing strategies that will help achieve the goals of instruction.

Implementing these processing strategies may take two forms. Processing displays can be incorporated into the instructional presentation by processing displays that direct the student to process portions of instruction in different ways. This built-in approach to processing strategies corresponds to the system assigned-embedded cell of Rigney's matrix of processing strategies (see Fig. 11-13). To achieve a greater degree of learner independence, students could be taught the strategies independently of instruction in much the same way as Anderson, Dansereau, and Weinstein's strategy instruction. This independent approach matches the student assigned-detached cell of Rigney's matrix. The student would then be able to approach a wider variety of instructional types and apply the strategies independent of processing displays. Perhaps a combination of both types of implementation would prove most useful.

SUMMARY

In this chapter we have attempted to summarize the areas of investigation that have resulted in some form of prescriptions for the design of instruction. While much of what is done in instructional development is based on tradition and intuition, a body of systematic knowledge has been accumulating that enables the instructional design process to be more scientific and data based. It is clear that the fads that often surround a given type of approach seem to come and go, yet there remains a residual of data-based prescriptions that can be useful in the design of instructional materials.

Perhaps the greatest need in the development of a scientific approach to instructional design is in the transition from theory to practice. Many of the data-based prescriptions that have been developed as a result of the efforts we have summarized have been reported in scholarly publications. The investigators have not taken the next step, that is, to translate their ideas into procedures easily used by practicing instructional designers. Those who are on the firing line of developing products often do not have the time, nor the inclination, to read scholarly publications and develop their own operational procedures. Hence, much of the excellent work described here has not found its way into widespread practice. To those investigating the instructional process and to those who are funding these investigations, we would end our presentation with a plea that more emphasis be placed on the translation of theoretical data-based techniques into practical usable instructional design guides. In this way the *art* of instructional design can move toward the *science* of instructional design.

REFERENCES

Anderson, Richard C.; Spiro, Rand J.; and Montague, William E. *Schooling and the Acquisition of Knowledge.* New York: John Wiley, 1977.

Anderson, T.H. *Studying Textbook Materials in Preparation for Taking an Examination.* Final Report, Project No. N00123-77-C-0622. San Diego, Calif.: Navy Personnel Research and Development Center, January 1979.

Andrews, Dee H., and Goodson, L.A. "Models of Instructional Design: Origins, Purposes, and Uses." Paper presented at the annual meeting of the American Educational Research Association, San Francisco, 1979.

Ausubel, David P. *The Psychology of Meaningful Verbal Learning.* New York: Grune and Stratton, 1963.

————. "Some Psychological Aspects of the Structure of Knowledge." In *Education and the Structure of Knowledge,* edited by Stanley Elam, pp. 221-49. Chicago: Rand McNally, 1964.

————. *Educational Psychology: A Cognitive View.* New York: Holt, Rinehart and Winston, 1968.

Baker, Eva L. "The Technology of Instructional Development." In *Second Handbook of Research on Teaching,* edited by Robert M.W. Travers, pp. 245-85. Chicago: Rand McNally, 1973.

Bloom, Benjamin S. et al. *Taxonomy of Educational Objectives: The Classification of Educational Goals. Handbook 1: Cognitive Domain.* New York: David McKay, 1956.

Briggs, Leslie J. "Learner Variables and Educational Media." *Review of Educational Research* 38 (April 1968): 160-76.

————. *Instructional Design.* Englewood Cliffs, N.J.: Educational Technology Publications, 1977.

Bruner, Jerome S. *The Process of Education.* New York: Random House, 1960.

Bruner, Jerome S.; Goodnow, Jacqueline J.; and Austin, George A. *A Study of Thinking.* New York: John Wiley, 1956.

Callahan, Edward. "The Effects of Objectives and Cognitive Compensating Strategy on Impoverished Instructional Materials in a Concept Task." Ph.D. dissertation, Brigham Young University, 1979.

Case, Robbie. "A Developmentally Based Theory and Technology of Instruction." *Review of Educational Research* 48 (Summer 1978a): 439-63.

————. "Implications of Developmental Psychology for Design of Effective Instruction." In *Cognitive Psychology and Instruction,* edited by Alan M. Lesgold et al., pp. 441-63. New York, Plenum Press, 1978(b).

Craik, Fergus I. M., and Tulving, Endel. "Depth of Processing and the Retention of Words in Episodic Memory." *Journal of Experimental Psychology: General* 104 (September 1975): 268-94.

Crawford, M.P. "Concepts of Training." In *Psychological Principles in System Development,* edited by Robert M. Gagné, pp. 301-41. New York: Holt, Rinehart and Winston, 1962.

Crowder, Norman A. "Automatic Tutoring by Intrinsic Programming." In *Teaching Machines and Programmed Learning,* edited by Arthur A. Lumsdaine and Robert Glaser, pp. 286-98. Washington, D.C.: National Education Association, 1960.

Dansereau, Donald. "The Development of a Learning Strategies Curriculum." In *Learning Strategies,* edited by Harold F. O'Neil, Jr., pp. 1-29. New York: Academic Press, 1978.

Dick, Walter, and Carey, Lou. *The Systematic Design of Instruction.* Glenview, Ill.: Scott, Foresman, 1978.

Dörner, Dietrich. "Theoretical Advances of Cognitive Psychology Relevant to Instruction." In *Cognitive Psychology and Instruction,* edited by Alan M. Lesgold et al., pp. 231-52. New York: Plenum Press, 1978.

Durnin, John H., and Scandura, Joseph M. "An Algorithmic Approach to Assessing Behavior Potential: Comparison with Item Forms and Hierarchical Technologies." *Journal of Educational Psychology* 65 (October 1973): 262-72.

Elam, Stanley, ed. *Education and the Structure of Knowledge.* Chicago: Rand McNally, 1964.

Ellis, John A., and Wulfeck II, W.H. *Interim Training Manual for the Instructional Quality Inventory.* NPROC TN 78-5. San Diego, Calif.: Navy Personnel Research and Development Center, 1978.

Evans, James L.; Homme, Lloyd E.; and Glaser, Robert. "The Ruleg System for the Construction of Programmed Verbal Learning Sequences." *Journal of Educational Research* 55 (June-July 1962): 513-18.

Gagné, Robert M. "Military Training and Principles of Learning." *American Psychologist* 17 (January 1962): 83-91.

————. "The Analysis of Instructional Objectives for the Design of Instruction." *Teaching Machines and Programmed Learning, II: Data and Directions,* edited by Robert Glaser, pp. 21-65. Washington, D.C.: National Education Association, 1965(a).

————. *The Conditions of Learning.* New York: Holt, Rinehart and Winston, 1965(b).

————. "Analysis of Objectives." In *Instructional Design,* edited by Leslie J. Briggs, pp. 115-48. Englewood Cliffs, N.J.: Educational Technology Publications, 1977.

Gagné, Robert M., and Briggs, Leslie J. *Principles of Instructional Design.* New York: Holt, Rinehart and Winston, 1974; 2d ed., 1979.

Gagné, Robert M., and Rohwer, Jr., William D. "Instructional Psychology." *Annual Review of Psychology.* Vol. 20. Edited by Paul H. Mussen and Mark R. Rosenzweig, pp. 381-418. Palo Alto, Calif.: Annual Reviews, 1969.

Gagné, Robert M., and White, Richard T. "Memory Structures and Learning Outcomes." *Review of Educational Research* 48 (Spring 1978): 187-222.

Gilbert, Thomas F. "Mathetics: The Technology of Education." *Journal of Mathetics* 1 (January 1962): 7-73. Reprinted in *Instructional Design: Readings,* edited by M. David Merrill, pp. 214-63. Englewood Cliffs, N.J.: Prentice-Hall, 1971.

————. *Human Competence.* New York: McGraw-Hill, 1978.

Gilmartin, Kevin J.; Newell, Allen; and Simon, Herbert A. "A Program Modeling Short-term Memory under Strategy Control." In *The Structure of Human Memory,* edited by C.N. Cofer, pp. 16-30. San Francisco: W.H. Freeman, 1976.

Glaser, Robert. "Implications of Training Research for Education." In *Theories of Learning and Instruction,* edited by Ernest R. Hilgard, pp. 153-81. Sixty-third Yearbook of the National Society for the Study of Education, Part I. Chicago, Ill.: University of Chicago Press, 1964.

————. *Training Research and Education.* New York: John Wiley, 1965.

Groen, Guy, and Resnick, Lauren B. "Can Preschool Children Invent Addition Algorithms?" *Journal of Educational Psychology* 69 (December 1977): 645-52.

Gropper, George L. *Instructional Strategies.* Englewood Cliffs, N.J.: Educational Technology Publications, 1974.

————. *Diagnosis and Revision in the Development of Instructional Materials.* Englewood Cliffs, N.J.: Educational Technology Publications, 1976.

Holt, H.O., and Shoemaker, H.A. "The Use of Programmed Instruction in Industry." In *Teaching Machines and Programmed Learning, II: Data and Directions,* edited by Robert Glaser, pp. 685-742. Washington, D.C.: National Education Association, 1965.

Horn, Robert E. *How to Write Information Mapping.* Lexington, Mass.: Information Resources, Inc., 1976.

Interservice Procedures for Instructional Systems Development. Prepared under Contract Number N-61339-73-C-1050 between the Center for Educational Technology at Florida State University and the U.S. Army Combat Arms Training Board, Ft. Benning, Georgia, 1975.

Kail, Robert V., and Hagen, John W. *Perspectives on the Development of Memory and Cognition.* Hillsdale, N.J.: Lawrence Erlbaum Associates, 1977.

Klahr, David. *Cognition and Instruction.* Hillsdale, N.J.: Lawrence Erlbaum Associates, 1976.

Klausmeier, Herbert J.; Ghatala, Elizabeth S.; and Frayer, Dorothy A. *Conceptual Learning and Development: A Cognitive View.* New York: Academic Press, 1974.

Klausmeier, Herbert J., and Goodwin, William. *Learning and Human Abilities: Educational Psychology,* 4th ed. New York: Harper & Row, 1975.

Landa, Lev N. *Algorithmization in Learning and Instruction.* Englewood Cliffs, N.J.: Educational Technology Publications, 1974.

————. *Instructional Regulation and Control.* Englewood Cliffs, N.J.: Educational Technology Publications, 1976.

————. "Cybernetics Methods in Education." *Educational Technology* 17 (October 1977): 7-13.

Lesgold, Alan M. et al., eds. *Cognitive Psychology and Instruction.* New York: Plenum Press, 1978.

Lewis, Brian N., and Pask, Gordon. "The Theory and Practice of Adaptive Teaching Machines." In *Teaching Machines and Programmed Learning, II: Data and Directions,* edited by Robert Glaser, pp. 213-66. Washington, D.C.: National Education Association, 1965.

Logan, Robert S. "An Instructional Systems Development Approach for Learning Strategies." In *Learning Strategies,* edited by Harold F. O'Neil, Jr., pp. 141-63. New York: Academic Press, 1978.

Lumsdaine, Arthur A. "Some Conclusions Concerning Student Responses and a Science of Instruction." In *Student Response in Programmed Instruction,* edited by Arthur A. Lumsdaine, pp. 471-500. Washington, D.C.: National Academy of Sciences—National Research Council Publications 943, 1961.

Lumsdaine, Arthur A., and Glaser, Robert. *Teaching Machines and Programmed Learning: A Source Book.* Washington, D.C.: National Education Association, 1960.

Mager, Robert F. *Preparing Instructional Objectives.* Belmont, Calif.: Fearon Publishers, 1962.

Markle, Susan M. *Good Frames and Bad.* 2d ed. New York: John Wiley, 1969.

Markle, Susan M., and Tiemann, Philip W. *Really Understanding Concepts: Or in Frumious Pursuit of the Jabberwock.* 3d ed. Champaign, Ill.: Stipes Publishing Co., 1970.

Melton, Arthur W., ed. *Categories of Human Learning.* New York: Academic Press, 1964.

Merrill, M. David. "Necessary Psychological Conditions for Defining Instructional Outcomes." In *Instructional Design: Readings,* edited by M. David Merrill, pp. 173-84. Englewood Cliffs, N.J.: Prentice-Hall, 1971.

Merrill, M. David; Olsen, J. B.; and Coldeway, Nancy S. *Research Support for the Instructional Strategy Diagnostic Profile.* Technical Report, Series No. 3 San Diego, Calif.: Courseware, Inc., 1976.

Merrill, M. David; Reigeluth, Charles M.; and Faust, Gerald W. "The Instructional Quality Profile: A Curriculum Evaluation and Design Tool." In *Instructional Systems Developments: Tools and Methodologies,* edited by Harold F. O'Neil, Jr., pp. 165-204. New York: Academic Press, 1979.

Merrill, M. David et al. *The Instructional Strategy Diagnostic Profile Training Manual.* San Diego, Calif.: Courseware, Inc., 1977.

Merrill, M. David, and Tennyson, Robert D. *Teaching Concepts: An Instructional Design Guide.* Englewood Cliffs, N.J.: Educational Technology Publications, 1977.

Merrill, M. David; Schneider, E.; and Fletcher, K. *TICCIT.* Englewood Cliffs, N.J.: Educational Technology Publications, 1979.

Merrill, M. David, and Wilson, Brent G. "Elaboration Theory and Cognitive Psychology." Paper presented at the Annual Convention of the Association for Educational Communications and Technology, March 1979.

Merrill, Paul F. "Task Analysis—An Information Processing Approach." *NSPI Journal* 15, 2 (1976): 7-11.

————. "Hierarchical and Informational Processing Task Analysis: A Comparison." *Journal of Instructional Development* 1, 2 (1978): 35-40.

Miller, George A.; Galanter, Eugene; and Pribram, Karl H. *Plans and the Structure of Behaviors.* New York: Holt, Rinehart and Winston, 1960.

Miller, R. B. "Analysis and Specification of Behavior for Training." In *Psychological Principles in System Development,* edited by Robert M. Gagné, pp. 31-62. New York: Holt, Rinehart and Winston, 1962.

Newell, Allen; Shaw, J.C.; and Simon, Herbert A. "Elements of a Theory of Human Problem Solving." *Psychological Review* 65 (May 1958): 151-66.

Norman, Donald A. "Notes toward a Theory of Complex Learning." In *Cognitive Psychology and Instruction,* edited by Alan M. Lesgold et al., pp. 39-48. New York: Plenum Press, 1978.

O'Neil, Harold F., Jr. *Learning Strategies.* New York: Academic Press, 1978.

Pask, Gordon. *The Cybernetics of Human Learning and Performance: A Guide to Theory and Research*. London: Hutchinson and Co., 1975.

————. *Conversation Theory: Applications in Education and Epistemology*. New York: Elsevier Scientific Publishing Co., 1976.

Reigeluth, Charles M. "In Search of a Better Way to Organize Instruction: The Elaboration Theory." Paper presented at the annual convention of the Association for Educational Communications and Technology, March 1979.

Reigeluth, Charles M.; Bunderson, C. Victor; and Merrill, M. David. "What is the Design Science of Instruction?" *Journal of Instructional Development* 1, 2 (1978): 11-16.

Reigeluth, Charles M.; Merrill, M. David; and Wilson, Brent G. "The Elaboration Theory of Instruction: A Model for Sequencing and Synthesizing Instruction." *Instructional Science* 2 (November 1973): 311-62.

Resnick, Lauren B., "Hierarchies in Children's Learning: A Symposium," *Instructional Science* (in press).

————. *The Science and Art of Curriculum and Design*. Publication No. 1975/79. Pittsburgh: University of Pittsburgh, Learning Research and Dev

————. *The Science and Art of Curriculum and Design*. Publication No. 1975/79. Pittsburgh: University of Pittsburgh, Learning Research and Development Center, 1975.

————. "Task Analysis in Instructional Design: Some Cases from Mathematics." In *Cognition and Instruction*, edited by David Klahr, pp. 51-80. Hillsdale, N.J.: Lawrence Erlbaum Associates, 1976.

Resnick, Lauren B., and Glaser, Robert. "Problem Solving and Intelligence." In *The Nature of Intelligence*, edited by Lauren B. Resnick, pp. 205-230. Hillsdale, N.J.: Lawrence Erlbaum Associates, 1977.

Resnick, Lauren B.; Wang, M.C.; and Kaplan, J. "Task Analysis in Curriculum Design: A Hierarchically Sequenced Introductory Mathematics Curriculum." *Journal of Applied Behavior Analysis* 6 (Winter 1973): 710.

Rigney, Joseph W. "Learning Strategies: A Theoretical Perspective." In *Learning Strategies*, edited by Harold F. O'Neil, Jr., pp. 165-205. New York: Academic Press, 1978.

Rumelhart, David E., and Ortony, Andrew. "The Representation of Knowledge in Memory." In *Schooling and the Acquisition of Knowledge*, edited by Richard C. Anderson, Rand J. Spiro, and William E. Montague, pp. 99-135. Hillsdale, N.J.: Lawrence Erlbaum Associates, 1977.

Scandura, Joseph M. *Mathematics: Concrete Behavioral Foundations*. New York: Harper and Row, 1971.

————. *Structural Learning I: Theory and Research*. London: Gordon and Breach Science Publishers, 1973.

————. "Structural Approach to Behavioral Objectives and Criterion-referenced Testing." *Educational Technology* 17 (October 1977): 20-25.

Schwab, Joseph J. "The Concept of the Structure of a Discipline." *Educational Record* 43 (July 1962): 197-205.

————. "Problems, Topics, and Issues." In *Education and the Structure of Knowledge*, edited by Stanley Elam, pp. 4-42. Chicago: Rand McNally, 1964.

Skinner, B.F. "The Science of Learning and the Art of Teaching." *Harvard Educational Review* 24, 2 (1954): 86-97.

Snow, Richard E. "Theory Construction for Research on Teaching." In *Second Handbook of Research on Teaching*, edited by Robert M.W. Travers, pp. 77-112. Chicago: Rand McNally, 1973.

Strike, Kenneth A., and Posner, George J. "Epistemological Perspectives on Conceptions of Curriculum Organization and Learning." In *Review of Research in Education*. Vol. 4. Edited by Lee S. Shulman, pp. 106-141. Itasca, Ill.: Peacock Publishers, 1976.

Tiemann, Philip W., and Markle, Susan M. "Remodeling a Model: An Elaborated Hierarchy of Types of Learning." *Educational Psychologist* 10 (Fall 1973): 147-58.

Weinstein, Claire E. "Elaboration Skills as a Learning Strategy." In *Learning Strategies*, edited by Harold F. O'Neil, Jr., pp. 31-55. New York: Academic Press, 1978.

Wilcox, Wayne C. "Effect of Teaching a Conceptual Hierarchy on Concept Classification Performance." Ph.D. dissertation, Brigham Young University, 1979.

Wilson, Brent G. "Elaboration Theory and Cumulative Learning Theory: A Comparison." Paper presented at the annual convention of the Association for Educational Communications and Technology, March 1979.

Wittrock, M. C., "The Cognitive Movement in Instruction." *Educational Psychologist* 13, 1 (1978): 15-30.

Wittrock, M. C., and Lumsdaine, Arthur A. "Instructional Psychology." *Annual Review of Psychology*. Vol. 28. Edited by Mark R. Rosenzweig and Lyman W. Porter, pp. 417-99. Palo Alto, Calif.: Annual Reviews, 1977.

PART FOUR
The Past, Present, and Promise of the Union

Overview

The final part of the book encompasses three chapters, one on the history of educational psychology, one on its current status and future directions, and one on its potential. All of these chapters give indications not only of the state of the art within educational psychology but also of its etiology and evolution.

Grinder's survey of educational psychology from a historical perspective emphasizes the importance of Edward Thorndike, whose impact is also referred to in several other chapters of this volume. Grinder reviews three major obstacles that Thorndike overcame in the formulation of a science of educational psychology, indicates why Thorndike fell short in efforts to foster a common ideology and purpose among educational psychologists, and considers briefly how educational psychology may become more significant in the wider field of education.

Thorndike's view of educational psychologists posited them as "middlemen" in mediating between the science of psychology and the art of teaching. In Grinder's perspective, the survival of educational psychology depends on educational psychologists becoming authentic intermediaries, mediating and bridging the hiatus between exact science and educational practice. He believes that the future of educational psychology will turn on whether researchers choose to be both relevant in the laboratory and responsive in the classroom.

This notion is also incorporated in "Current Status and Future Directions of Educational Psychology as a Discipline." This chapter, prepared by Joseph Scandura, Lawrence Frase, Robert Gagné, Kay Stolurow, Lawrence Stolurow, and Guy Groen, presents the results of an inquiry to assess educational psychology as a discipline. The chapter is based on their considered opinions and on data collected from 590 educational psychologists. The authors identify several national needs that educational psychology could address. These include the need to understand the teaching-learning process better; to work directly with school personnel; to implement the ideas of educational psychology in industry, higher education, and government; and to reevaluate existing educational psychology programs on the university level. While there have been some promising advances in the field (principles of reinforcement, behavioral objectives, learning hierarchies, developmental stages, mastery and criterion-referenced testing), research funds are required for future work. Suggestions are offered on how professional organizations and editors of publications may work to improve theoretical perspectives and to stress their practical implications. The authors call for increased attention to the ways in which educational psychologists can increase our understanding of instructional science. Research ideas with direct relevance for teaching are encouraged as is increased attention to "quality control" in the training of educational psychologists. School-based educational psychologists who assist teachers in improving students' cognitive abilities to process schoolwork are envisioned. These educational psychologists would be the direct counterparts to school psychologists, who traditionally attend more to affective and abnormal behavior problems. In short, the chapter provides readers with a clear perception of national needs in education, the current status of educational psychology, promising advances in the discipline, and future recommendations for educational psychologists.

Philip Jackson's chapter again calls to mind the memory of E.L. Thorndike; Jackson believes Thorndike had naive and exaggerated expectations about "The Promise of Educational Psychology." The progress made in the last eighty years has been disappointing and modest, especially in comparison to the expectations of our early practitioners. Nevertheless, in Jackson's view, we have learned one fact for certain: People are more complex than our early views led us to believe. Consequently, the promise that educational psychology has is its ability to help us sketch in some of that complexity. If the union of psychology and education will contribute to that sketch, then that promise will be fulfilled.

In terms of fulfillment, what we have seen in our preparation for this volume is a concerted effort on the part of our contributors to appreciate not only research and theory but also educational practice. Movement to largely cognitive orientations is also reflected in these chapters. Emphases on active constructions by students, complex cognitive and affective interactions, and social activity have been identified. We have seen that educational psychology and its practitioners offer much to those interested in psychology and education. The state of the union suggests that considerable development has taken place in the discipline and that images of a scientifically based, philosophically sound, and educationally relevant series of hypotheses, prescriptions, and logical frameworks are available.

12. The "New" Science of Education: Educational Psychology in Search of a Mission

Robert E. Grinder

About the time of the American Revolution, schooling took place in one-room settings. Teachers were poorly paid, pupil attendance was voluntary, and age grading was unheard of. In colonial America, the elementary school was the dame school, so called because instruction in beginning reading or writing was often given by a woman in her own home for a small fee per pupil. Children were driven to learn by corporal punishment, and the dame schools became renowned for a particular disciplinary technique—the dames would rap the heads of disorderly pupils with their thimbles, which were usually handy because the dames often engaged in knitting or sewing during the time that they were teaching. Colonial educators disdained teaching youngsters to read and write, and they left these onerous tasks to the dames while they taught in the more prestigious Latin grammar schools and academies, preparing boys—but not girls—for such professions as the ministry, law, and medicine. Students learned their lessons individually. The curriculum content changed hardly at all

Revised version of paper entitled: "What 200 Years Tells Us about Professional Priorities in Educational Psychology. *Educational Psychologist,* 12 (1978): 284-89.

from year to year. A body of knowledge had been gathered for each purpose, and pupils were expected to recite whatever the teacher and textbook gave them. No one thought that teachers needed any special preparation prior to entering the classroom. Educational psychology, obviously, had nothing to do with schooling practices two hundred years ago.

The trends toward sequenced classes, age grading, and small homogeneous classes had begun by the mid nineteenth century. The recognition of the need for pedagogical training led to the establishment of the first normal schools for the training of teachers. The core of early teacher training was a course entitled Mental Philosophy, Intellectual Physics, or Physiology of the Soul (Joncich 1968). When the Englishman James Sully wrote, in 1885, *Outlines of Psychology with Special Reference to the Theory of Education,* courses in psycology oriented toward science were beginning to supplant those derived from philosophy. During the 1890s, the psychological content of teacher training was identified as "child study" or genetic psychology. The term "educational psychology" began to attain widespread use with the publication, in 1903, of the first edition of E.L. Thorndike's *Educational Psychology* and the founding of the *Journal of Educational Psychology* in 1910.

Schooling had become primarily a public enterprise by the late nineteenth century. The rise of industrialism and the need for an enlightened citizenry had led to compulsory attendance laws and public demand that *all* children learn to read, write, add, subtract, and become socially and morally responsible for their actions. Financial expenditures accelerated as educators redoubled efforts to meet societal expectations. Pedagogy, however, was in the hands of practitioners. Principles of educational practice fostered in the normal schools were based on the random experiences of professors and the deductive speculations of earlier philosophers—Comenius, Froebel, Pestalozzi, and Rousseau. School objectives swiftly became too numerous and too complex for the available ideologies and forms of measurement. Such pedagogical resources were too primitive. The times demanded a radically new approach, and to many influential early twentieth-century educators, only one qualified: Pedagogy should become an exact science.

The traditional disciplines in the natural and physical sciences had acquired strong theoretical and applied systems through painstaking observation, data collection, and analysis. Distinguished universities had risen to foster scientific activity. Hence, a new science of education would be created via the methodologies of exact science—controlled experimentation, measurement, analysis, codified laws, and application of systematic theory. The new science would integrate principles of mental, moral, and social development. It would link sophisticated scales of learning, intellect, motivation, and so forth with empirically valid and reliable school tests. It would connect strategies of instruction with individual differences in children's capacity to learn; it would identify how children should learn; and it would demonstrate precisely whether or not children learned whatever they were expected to learn. The budding discipline would become educational psychology; it would apply principles of psychology to education, but more importantly it would lead to the development of unique new principles of behavior whose application would contribute directly to the betterment of humankind.

Edward L. Thorndike emerged as the man of the hour. A brilliant young psychologist on the professional horizon, he had earned a Ph.D. at Harvard in 1898 under William James and had accepted a post at Teachers College, Columbia University. He surfaced as a titan among those who sought to weave together theory and research to create educational psychology as a compelling inductive science. Thorndike rode the crest of enthusiasm to introduce the methods of exact science to education, and he successfully bulwarked his views against conflicting humanistic ideologies to establish educational psychology as a citadel of scientific rigor and methodology. Thorndike attacked speculation at every turn. The preface of the first edition of *Educational Psychology,* for example, carried the following proclamation:

This book attempts to apply to a number of educational problems the methods of exact science. I have therefore paid no attention to speculative opinions and very little attention to the conclusions of students who present data in so rough and incomplete a form that accurate quantitative treatment is impossible. [1903, p. v.]

When Thorndike was subsequently invited to contribute the lead essay in the first issue of the *Journal of Educational Psychology,* he seized upon the opportunity as an occasion to promote the new science. He said that "a complete science of psychology would tell every fact about everyone's intellect and character and behavior, would tell the cause of every change in human nature, would tell the result which every educational force—every act of every person that changed any other or the agent himself—would have." He insisted, too, that psychology contributes to knowledge of methods of teaching by explaining the characteristics of human learning, by indicating why certain teaching methods succeed better than others, and by suggesting means to test and verify or refute the claims of any method. The magnitude of Thorndike's effort to employ the reductionist methods of science to construct a grand, irrefutable theory of learning and development was quickly apparent. A host of standardized tests became available to practitioners between 1905 and 1915, among them the Hillegas Composition Scale, the Woody Arithmetic Test, the Thorn Reading Test, the Burgess Test of Silent Reading, the Woody-McCall Arithmetic Test, the Courtis Standard Practice Test in Arithmetic, the Thorndike-McCall Reading Scale, and the Morrison-McCall Spelling Scale. Further, Hall-Quest (1915) made a nationwide survey of instruction in educational psychology around 1915, and he reported that the trend in teaching was toward the "purely scientific."

Emphasis and methodology led educational psychology to the brink of scientific respectability, but this approach has brought neither unity within educational psychology nor integration with other disciplines. A divisive fissure runs through the entire history of the discipline. Educational psychologists have never agreed upon who they are or what they are about. Their history is marked, on the one hand, by struggles with metaphysicians and philosophers for academic esteem and, on the other, by an increasingly restrictive methodological posture in respect to social engineering and applied psychology. Thorndike performed a pivotal role in the sequence of frays. He led the vanguard that helped purge metaphysics from educational psychology, and he set in motion a rush of educational research that even now continues to accelerate. But the methodological trajectory on which he launched it was so narrow that the danger today of educational psychology passing into oblivion is more real than apparent. To appreciate the significance and current implications of the internecine battles, let us review three major obstacles that Thorndike overcame in deriving a science of educational psychology, indicate why Thorndike fell short in his effort to foster common ideology and purpose among educational psychologists, and finally consider briefly how hindsight suggests that the significance of educational psychology may be enhanced in the wider field of education. The three obstacles may be identified as the child-study movement, armchair theorizing, and faculty psychology.

Wringing the Sentiment from the Child-Study Movement. Rousseau had argued convincingly more than a century earlier that children's growth was a function of natural propensities expressed during different stages. G. Stanley Hall grafted Rousseau's descriptive categories to his belief that growth recapitulated biological evolution, and he divined himself to be a "Darwin of the mind." Although he professed a scientific approach to child study, his analyses were consummately deductive. His myopic adherence to recapitulation theory led him to ask absurd questions and to draw fantastic conclusions. But Hall was brilliant, enthusiastic, and charismatic; his followers were devoted, and their output was prodigious. Hall was a giant among intellects, and one took him on with trepidation. Nonetheless, his excesses had rendered him vulnerable; at the 1895 meeting of the National Educational Association, Hall lost face in a debate with Hugo Munsterberg. "This seductive but rude and untrained and untechnical gathering of cheap and vulgar material," Munsterberg said, "means a caricature and not an improvement of psychology" (Joncich 1968). Thorndike followed the lead and, from the time of his earliest publications, unhesitatingly attacked the atheoretical, unscientific aspects of the child-study movement.

Stamping out Armchair Theorizing—Bringing Herbartianism into the Scientific Fold. Herbart, who was born in 1776, nearly one hundred years before Thorndike, formulated John Locke's views on the association of ideas into a theory of learning known as "apperception." He started with the metaphysical assumption that the psyche or soul possessed one original tendency—to preserve itself. It began as a colorless void, without qualities, but as it attempted to assimilate experiences, ideas collided with one another, giving rise to a sense of consciousness. The ideas and sensations that entered the mind remained there to influence later learning, and those that maintained themselves in consciousness exerted the most influence on the psyche. These ideas, Herbart said, constituted an "apperceptive mass." His theory of learning emphasized the influence of past experience, and it directed the attention of teachers to the importance of commencing the learning process at a point commensurate with a child's readiness. The doctrine of apperception led to the idea of curriculum as a succession of presentations of closely related content.

Herbart also contributed to early educational psychology by offering an explanation of how interest and motivation affect learning. He said that ideas precede action. Interest develops when strong and vivid ideas are hospitable toward new ones, since a pleasant feeling arises from the association of old and new ideas. Herbart thus observed that interest was a source of motivation, since past associations could be used to facilitate the apperception of current ones. Herbartianism, in predicting that learning follows from building up a sequence of ideas important to the individual, gave teachers a semblance of motivational theory. It also led to the belief that development of interest was more effective than threat of punishment in fostering learning. Late in the nineteenth century, the two psychologies most commonly taught in pedagogical courses were Herbartianism and child study. The former was criticized as being insufficiently empirical and the latter as too sentimental (Joncich 1968). Perspectives began to change in 1885 with the founding of the National Herbart Society (to be renamed in 1902 the National Society for the Scientific Study of Education). In the early debates of the Herbart Society, it was impossible to separate the psychology of education from the philosophy of education. The gradual modification of metaphysical doctrines occurred in the early history of educational psychology "by the insistently intruding and unanswerable facts of classroom experience, plus, finally and characteristically modern, a new attempt at generalizations and ultimate theories" (Leary 1924, pp. 94-95). Thorndike participated in the demise of armchair theories by giving Herbartianism structure. He integrated concepts of association in terms of psychological reactions involving not only ideas but attitudinal, emotional, and motor expressions, and he specified the laws by which learning occurred.

Putting the Screws to Faculty Psychology. From the time of Plato and Aristotle, the psyche or soul had been described in terms of what it would do, that is, its functions or faculties. Philosophers subsequently reified the presumed functions, holding each of them to possess independent psychic energy. Discussion in the nineteenth century centered on determining the number and types of faculties and on improving them. The phrenologists, for example, insisted that there were upwards of two dozen. Educators, however, were mainly interested in the mental faculties—memory, judgment, imagination, and attention. Schooling consisted largely of efforts to mature the memory faculty. Latin, Greek, and mathematics were believed to be especially well suited for this purpose, but because it was important to exercise as many faculties as possible during a given school period and to convey worthwhile subject matter for memorization, educators spent considerable time debating the curricular appropriateness of competing subjects.

When Thorndike wrote *Educational Psychology,* a new interpretation of faculties had risen in American psychology. William James was now describing them not as faculties but as instincts. He acknowledged the functional significance of native capacities, but he concentrated on the biological and social factors that affected adjustment to the environment. He emphasized a long list of biological categories—fear, love, curiosity, imitation, pride, ambition, pugnacity, and so on. Whereas the faculty psychologists stressed learning through exercise, James anticipated subsequent developments in conditioning and instrumental learning when he said: "Every acquired reaction is, as a rule, either a complication grafted on a native reaction, or a substitute for a native reaction, which the same object originally tended to provoke" (James 1899). Thorndike was James's most ardent disciple in promoting functional psychology. Every individual, he said, is a product of an "original nature" and the "environment." We appreciate Thorndike for his contributions to learning theory so much that we forget that he placed special emphasis on the tendencies or instincts comprising original nature. He called for description and classification of their anatomy and physiology, source of origin, and order and dates of appearance and disappearance. The purpose or aim of eductaion was to perpetuate some of them, eliminate some, and modify or redirect others. Thorndike developed laws of learning consonant with both Herbart's and James's theories of association to account for the interaction of nature and nurture, and importantly, he supported these laws with findings drawn from replicable, relatively precise studies of animal learning.

Given the majesty of Thorndike's success in bringing scientific respectability to educational psychology, why did he fall short of also establishing unity in the profession? Thorndike himself provides a clue in his lead article for the *Journal of Educational Psychology.*

He described the future educational psychologist as a "middleman" who would mediate the science of psychology and the art of teaching. The middleman concept was reinforced at midcentury when a 1948 committee of the Division of Educational Psychology, Division 15 of the American Psychological Association, reiterated that "the educational psychologist functions as a scientist among teachers of education and acts, both in psychology and education, as an intermediary between 'pure' research and its application." Hindsight reveals today, however, that while Thorndike shared this view, the trends given impetus by his version of original nature and by his awesome emphasis upon scientific reductionism may actually have impeded the development of educational psychology as a profession.

First, Thorndike was only somewhat less metaphysical than his predecessors in describing original nature, and when he presented a long list of original tendencies, his critics contended that he erroneously classified many acquired behaviors as instinctive. Starch, a leading competitor of Thorndike in the textbook market, insisted for example that "the chief education doctrine based upon instincts . . . has very little justification in verified fact. This is a sane view, and we hope that it will tend to neutralize the overemphasis of instincts prevalent in educational discussion since James" (Remmers and Knight 1922). And John B. Watson threw out nearly all the instincts in establishing behaviorism. Watson emphasized nurture rather than nature, recognized only three original propensities—love, fear, and rage—and assumed virtually the entire range of human behavior to be subject to laws of learning. When Thorndike built educational psychology around original tendencies, he fueled a pseudo aspect of the nature-nurture controversy that swiftly found its way into the textbooks, and very soon not even the more astute educational psychologists could decipher any conceptual coherence in the discipline. For example, Hall-Quest (1915) said that "there is no general agreement on terminology or on the structure of courses in educational psychology." Remmers and Knight (1922) attempted an analysis of the leading textbooks, but they found that the texts diverged so markedly in "viewpoint, organization, and content" that they abandoned the project. Worcester (1927) actually reviewed the five leading textbooks in use in 1927 and said, "One would be somewhat put to it to discover five texts on supposedly the same subject which vary more than do these." He went on to say, "The fact that the books mentioned are those most commonly used as texts might be interpreted, then, not as a consensus but as a chaos of opinion."

Second, Thorndike and his adherents endeavored to deal with the conceptual shambles in educational psychology by advancing the discipline as an exact science and thereby promoted it solely as a body of principles to be induced from findings derived from educational research. They have indeed enjoyed a great deal of success, but they have also bred in themselves a strong tendency toward isolationism. In 1948, a report of a Division 15 committee on the contributions of educational psychology to education, for example, noted that for several years educational psychologists had disavowed responsibility for the value or direction of education. In brief, the report identified educational psychologists as interested only in the laws of learning, as unable to understand or be understood by others in education, and to be in the process of breaking down their areas of research even more minutely. An APA committee on relations between psychology and education chaired by Donald Snygg in 1954 pointed out that more and more of the influential theorists in educational psychology were withdrawing from the general problems of education and human relations into more limited fields of experimental psychology.

The long-term consequences of turning inward, of course, have led to considerable attrition in the number of topics considered to be issues in educational psychology and in the number of persons identified as educational psychologists. Hall-Quest noted in 1915 that courses in educational psychology included such topics as development from infancy to adolescence; mental inheritance; original nature of man; psychology and treatment of retarded, affective, and exceptional children; applications of experimental and physiological psychology to education; statistical methods; psychology of elementary school subjects; psychology of secondary school subjects; and clinical psychology. What has happened? The psychology of school subjects—language arts, reading, social studies, and science—have migrated to elementary and secondary curriculum courses. Departments of special education have risen to take over all aspects of exceptionality. Departments of counselor education have wiped most clinical and counseling considerations from educational psychology courses. Woodruff pointed out in 1950 that "we have no fundamental field which is our own to a greater extent than it belongs to anyone else." The APA "divisions of Evaluation and Measurement, Childhood and Adolescence, Personality and Social, School Psychologists, and Maturity and Old Age," he said, "have as much claim as we on such functions as learning, adjusting, individual differences, tests and measurement, statistics, and growth and development."

In the face of this fractionalization, members of the educational psychology profession tend to be held together by a common commitment to scientific rigor in their teaching and research, which today pertains mainly to human development, learning, school psychology, and statistics, since nearly everything else has been preempted by others. Faculty members in educational psychology look admiringly, however, upon their disciplined methods of inquiry and their accumulation of "hard facts." The faculties in the other colleges of the university, namely liberal arts, respect them as equals and often proclaim that the doctoral theses of educational psychology students are the only ones in education worth reading. But what is the real significance of such prestige? Educational psychologists stand today not on a middle ground but in a no man's land. Their existence is justified and their salaries are paid on the expectation that their work will be applicable to teacher training and school learning, but often their allegiance is Thorndikian—to advance principles and theories in accord with the highest standards of science. How, then, can educational psychologists reclaim a dynamic role for themselves in education? Long ago, Charles Judd (1915), a relentless critic of Thorndike, said that "If teachers could be induced to begin systematic observation in their special lines and to report their findings, the science of educational psychology would flourish." He also said such an approach might ameliorate "an acrimonious dispute that has been carried on in some quarters between practical school people and the so-called scientific experts . . . many a teacher is alienated and refuses to become a party to the scientific study of education because he does not sympathize with the expert's demand for rigid, scientific exactness." The answer, however, lies not in convincing educational psychologists to begin compiling scrapbooks illustrating outstanding events in teaching or to deliver homilies before throngs of teachers. No, the survival of educational psychology depends on bridging the hiatus between exact science and educational practice—on becoming authentic middle-persons.

The task may be accomplished by placing greater emphasis on the implications of constructs and by giving recognition to the epistemological pluralism that underlies them. The professional activities of educational psychologists require that they agree that theoretical unity is impossible at ethereal levels of abstraction. Educational psychology involves inquiry into the deepest complexities of human nature. What has been seen in studies of human behavior has been so intricate and so complex that educational psychologists have been unable to unite on a common theory of what takes place. Whatever the epistemological basis of the system each educational psychologist prefers—whether it be behaviorism, humanism, or something else— viewpoints are derived from diverse assumptions. Sigmund Koch (1976) refers to Skinner's latest treatise on science in human behavior, *About Behaviorism* (1974), as an illustration of "Skinnerian Cosmology" and "Skinnerian Theology." Perhaps he is right. Every scientific system is a product of implicit assumptions about human nature. Educational psychology is thus based partly on philosophical assumptions and partly on empirical data. The circumstances require that educational psychologists mitigate the intensity of their efforts to reduce concepts of human nature to exact measurement. They must recognize the merit of hunches, guesses, expectations, unintegrated principles, and partial theories and thereby assist educators in applying psychological lore to the wide range of instructional practices and learning activities that actually exists.

In this volume Jackson (Chapter 14) observes that Thorndike ignored "the art of education" in his influential 1910 essay. In stressing methodology, Jackson notes, Thorndike neglected the goals of the physical and social sciences, disregarded historical and cultural contexts, professed unwarranted faith in the social benefits to be derived from scientific investigations, and overlooked the aesthetic dimensions of the scientists' work. Jackson suggests that late twentieth-century perspective reveals Thorndike's approach to have been too simplistic. He appears to have rejected conceptions of psychology that lead to "the examination of reasons, explanations, and other expressions of human intentionality and purpose."

Jackson asserts, further, that "we must allow for the appropriateness of different conceptions for different *scientific* purposes," and he draws support for his view from a paper written by the prominent Harvard philosopher, Josiah Royce (1891), nineteen years before Thorndike appeared in the *Journal of Educational Psychology*.

Royce asked rhetorically, "Is there a science of education?" He insisted, however, that "human nature cannot be adequately described through any abstract formulation of its traits." "Hence," he explained, "the educator cannot hope to have defined for him, with abstract universality, neither the material upon which he must always work—namely human nature—nor the end toward which he must always aim—namely the highest moral perfection of his pupil. Both these matters are modified for him by the course of evolution and by the actual social environment." Royce thus concluded, "questions of science will always contain elements of uncertainty, will always require answers that will vary with time and occasion."

Who, then, are the forerunners of educational psychology—Thorndike and those dedicated to the methods of exact science or Royce, Judd, and other pluralists who attempted to construct multiple bridges between, on the one hand, philosophy and science and, on the other, diverse educational practices? Educational psychology indeed presents a philosophical reality of irreconcilable differences. If teachers and instructors are to be assisted in organizing developmental learning activities, educational psychologists cannot turn their backs on them while toiling in their laboratories to construct a grand theory that will account for all the educational practices of tomorrow. On the contrary, the times demand that educational psychologists set forth the assumptions and implications of the different theoretical and technological systems teachers are dealing with, indicate which laws of learning apply, and specify the probable outcomes of adopting them. These systems must be both comprehensive and comprehensible—teachers must be able to understand their philosophical and empirical origins and appreciate the ways in which they are applicable to ordinary instructional environments. The future of educational psychology turns on whether researchers choose to be both relevant in the laboratory and responsive in the classroom.

REFERENCES

Hall-Quest, Alfred L. "Present Tendencies in Educational Psychology." *Journal of Educational Psychology* 6 (December 1915): 601-14.

Jackson, Philip W. "The Promise of Educational Psychology." Chapter 14 in this volume.

James, William. *Talks to Teachers.* New York: Holt, 1899. P. 38.

Joncich, Geraldine. *The Sane Positivist: A Biography of Edward L. Thorndike.* Middleton, Conn.: Wesleyan University Press, 1968.

Judd, Charles H. *Psychology of High-School Subjects.* Boston: Ginn and Co., 1915.

Koch, Sigmund. "More Verbal Behavior from Dr. Skinner." *Contemporary Psychology* 21 (July 1976): 453-57.

Leary, Daniel P. "Development of Educational Psychology." In *Twenty-five Years of American Education*, edited by I. L. Kandel, pp. 91-114. New York: Macmillan, 1924.

Remmers, H. H., and Knight, F. B. "The Teaching of Educational Psychology in the United States." *Journal of Educational Psychology* 13 (October 1922): 399-407.

Royce, Josiah. "Is There a Science of Education?" *Educational Review* 1 (January 1891): 15-25; (February 1891): 121-32.

Skinner, B. F. *About Behaviorism.* New York: Knopf, 1974.

Thorndike, Edward L. *Educational Psychology.* New York: Lemcke and Buechner, 1903.

————. "The Contribution of Psychology to Education." *Journal of Educational Psychology* 1 (January 1910): 5-12.

Woodruff, Asahel D. See *Division 15 Newsletter* (February 1950). American Psychological Association.

Worcester, D.A. "The Wide Diversities of Practice in First Courses in Educational Psychology." *Journal of Educational Psychology* 18 (1927): 11-17.

13. Current Status and Future Directions of Educational Psychology as a Discipline

*Joseph M. Scandura, Lawrence T. Frase, Robert M. Gagné,
Kay A. Stolurow, Lawrence M. Stolurow,* and *Guy J. Groen*

Over the years, educational psychology has done perhaps more than its share of self-evaluation. As noted in 1967 by Robert E. Grinder, "educational psychology is unlike any other subspecialty in psychology. It has been treated most often as a leftover. It has provoked such vigorous pecks at its apparent oddity that, except for the resourcefulness of a hardy few, it would have disappeared in the 1950s."

Since that time, the field has grown considerably in both size and influence. Yet educational psychology still has not developed a well-defined image. The duties of Ph.D.-level educational psychologists

This chapter is based on a report prepared by Joseph M. Scandura, Lawrence T. Frase, Robert M. Gagné, Kay A. Stolurow, Lawrence M. Stolurow, and Guy J. Groen on behalf of an ad hoc committee of Division 15, American Psychological Association on the "Current Status and Future Directions of Educational Psychology as a Discipline." Membership of the committee included the above plus Kent Davis, John DeCecco, Frank Farley, and Ellis B. Page. Joseph M. Scandura served as chairman. Very helpful and detailed comments were also provided by John F. Feldhusen. The original report was published in the *Educational Psychologist* 13 (1978): 43-56. This slightly revised version is reproduced here with permission.

are highly varied and are as likely to involve general administrative responsibilities as scholarship or professional activities. Research in the field sometimes lacks focus; it often blindly follows a Fisherian research methodology designed for agriculture without asking what the basic problems are and how they might best be answered.

Fortunately, however, educational psychology is currently undergoing a renaissance of sorts. Consequently, there has been a growing conviction on the part of many educational psychologists that the field must begin to redefine its image as a discipline if it is to contribute significantly to the solution of educational problems and must divorce itself from the view that educational psychology is just "psychology applied to education."

Given this background, a group of mostly distinguished educational psychologists (the authors themselves making no claims in this regard), with the support of the preeminent organization in the field, was charged with the task of conducting an inquiry to clarify and reassess the role of educational psychology as a discipline. Our group recognized almost immediately that in order to achieve its goals, the scope of its activities would have to be limited. Indeed, any such undertaking poses serious dilemmas. On the one hand, we felt that our report should be as specific as possible and should avoid banalities. On the other hand, we did not want to take an unconstructive, critical approach. We wanted to encourage educational psychologists to think about both the good and the bad in the field and, even more important, to do something about making the discipline better. (Considerable evidence might be cited to justify the conclusion that all is well with the field, that educational psychologists are good, and that our only major problem is that the rest of the world does not sufficiently recognize our contributions. It is doubtful, however, that such conclusions would be in the best interests of educational psychology.)

We are well aware, of course, that no group of educational psychologists, no matter how eminent its composition, has all of the answers. In an attempt to broaden our input, we sought and received opinions from a large sample of the educational psychology community. Nonetheless, the report almost certainly does not represent a universal consensus among educational psychologists. Rather, it represents our considered views based on an honest attempt to determine the facts tempered by the "outside" input we have received. Whatever reaction follows from the specific recommendations contained herein, we shall consider our efforts worthwhile if the report stimulates thought and helps to bring about an improved discipline of educational psychology.

Our report is organized as follows:

1. National needs relevant to the disciplinary aspects of educational psychology. We wanted to identify some of the things that the nation and the world need and that educational psychology might provide.

2. The current status of educational psychology as a discipline. We wanted to find out how things are at present, especially relative to the above needs.

3. Promising advances in educational psychology. We wanted to know what we are doing well and what things look promising. Reward is more effective than punishment in shaping behavior; anyway, we all like to be told how good we are.

4. Recommendations for the future of educational psychology as a discipline. We hoped that these recommendations would bear some relationship to the prior analyses.

NATIONAL NEEDS RELEVANT TO THE DISCIPLINARY ASPECTS OF EDUCATIONAL PSYCHOLOGY

We begin with the basic premise that the discipline of educational psychology is concerned primarily with improving understanding of and providing means for improving the teaching-learning process—in all of its facets and in schools and training institutions of all types. Given this basic premise, national needs are classified according to disciplinary goals and the needs of relevant institutions.

Disciplinary Goals

The Need to Understand the Teaching-Learning Process. We list below some basic areas together with illustrative problems associated with each. This selection is neither exhaustive nor exclusive. Nonetheless, several members of the committee gave considerable attention to its formulation in the hope that it might be suggestive.

1. The need to better understand what there is to teach: What does it mean to know something? (a) How can subject-matter knowledge best be represented? Underlying competence? (b) How are heuristics and higher-level strategies (processes, rules) and intellectual skills related to more specific subject-

matter knowledge? How can they be identified and taught? (c) Exactly what is it that must be learned in such hard-to-define areas as reading, moral development, and reasoning? Relationships among different domains of learning outcomes? (d) What is the nature of the relationship between task analysis, learning hierarchy analysis, content analysis, algorithmic structural analysis, and so forth? More generally, how can one identify underlying competence? Structure?

2. The need to better understand how to find out what individuals do and do not know: (a) Are normative and criterion-referenced testing incompatible or is reconciliation possible? Criterion-referenced measurement and cognitive processes? What form should a performance test theory take? (b) How can one measure higher-level intellectual skills (processes, rules)? Reading-related skills?

3. The need to understand how people learn real subject matters: (a) What role do heuristics and other higher-level processes play in learning? What is the nature and role of motivation? Early development? Are behavioral and information-processing views of motivation incompatible or is reconciliation possible? (b) How do processing capacity and constraints on human receptors and effectors influence school learning? Are they innate? Determined via physical maturation? What about higher-level processes?

4. The need to understand the general properties of teaching and learning systems: (a) What is the nature of the ongoing teaching-learning interaction? Can dynamic relationships of this sort be spelled out in precise terms that lend themselves to scientific explanation, prediction, and control? What are the proper roles of cybernetics, systems theory, operations research, and so forth in spelling out these relationships? (b) How do the general requirements of instructional systems influence research in specific areas related to teaching and learning (such as problem areas 1-3)?

The Need to Identify Critical Problems in Real Teaching and Learning and to Be Able to Deal with Them Effectively and Efficiently. Among other things, instructional methods, design principles, and technologies are needed to:

1. Identify what must be learned concerning the various types of

educational objectives. (Included among these types of objectives, for example, are subject-matter knowledge; basic intellectual and physical skills such as those involved in reading, mathematics, sports, and so forth; higher-level skills such as reasoning, attitudes, and values.)

2. Develop effective and efficient tests that are appropriate for testing all types of educational objectives.

3. Develop effective and efficient instructional strategies that can be used to achieve predetermined kinds of educational goals.

4. In addition, there is a need to identify significant educational problems that can be solved on the basis of existing technologies and/or for which new technologies are needed. (Implicit in the above is the need for a deeper understanding of the relationship between basic research and the solution of educational problems. Implicit also are such things as reliable methods for distinguishing between bona fide educational problems and the educational views of special interests.)

In interpreting the above, it is important to recognize that the educational psychologist, generally speaking, will not be an expert in specialized subject matter areas such as linguistics and mathematics. It is important, therefore, that effective mechanisms also be developed for articulating instructional know-how with the views of experts in various fields. This need becomes increasingly important as the level of instruction shifts from elementary to secondary to university and to specialized technical training.

To summarize, answers are needed to such questions as: (a) How do people learn school subjects? (b) What are the basic causes of learning problems and what can be done to overcome them? (c) How can one identify and operationally specify educational objectives and "what is (to be) learned" in such hard-to-define areas as reading, child development, reasoning? (d) Can we develop new, more efficient, and more general technologies for educational design? Specific needs include more general methods for performance testing, content analysis, building in transfer potential, and instructional sequencing.

Needs of Recipient Institutions

The above needs are purposefully general and refer to traditional problem areas that have in the past and undoubtedly will in the future continue to have basic relevance. They all refer to the basic "need to understand," a general objective that remains the same even though specific questions and emphases may change as advances are made. Given their general and relatively permanent significance, it also seems useful to identify the more specific present needs of institutions in which educational psychology plays an important role.

Schools. When one considers the large variety of curriculum materials, methodologies, and educational fads that are being promoted today, it is not surprising that the classroom teacher often becomes confused and is unable to deal adequately with student needs. Take, for example, the emphasis on open or individualized education, which in some school systems is being imposed "from above," irrespective of whether the teachers are able to utilize the techniques properly or whether the students have the necessary self-initiative and independence.

Part of the problem derives from tradition and legalistic realities. While school systems and legislatures have generally recognized the value of such specialists as counselors and school psychologists in dealing with career and affective needs of students and, to a lesser extent, the value of subject-matter specialists, there has been very little awareness of the role that educational psychologists might play in improving everyday instruction. We hear much, for example, about counselors and school psychologists in school settings, but—with the exception of hardware experts in educational media and a few "educational researchers"—intensive involvement of educational psychologists has been limited. This is unfortunate, we feel, because specially trained masters-level and doctoral-level educational psychologists, by working directly with classroom teachers, might help them to improve their everyday teaching and to avoid obvious pitfalls. (These needs were traditionally met by school administrators, but few have the necessary expertise, and their other duties typically preclude giving the kind of help we feel is needed.) By stressing the everyday cognitive-motivational aspects of school learning, such specialists could complement the more traditional role played by school psychologists in the affective and abnormal domains.

Industry/Government/Higher Education. There also is a need for educational design specialists and technologists who are able to deal effectively with the vast and growing training needs of industry, higher education (including the medical area), and government (including the military). A somewhat different but important need in government is for personnel who are able to identify appropriate national needs and the possible role of educational psychology in solving them and to develop realistic, workable, and sound programs of support designed to meet these needs.

College Training. While some of the above needs are being met to some extent, especially in schools, there is an apparent need to revamp, update, or at least reevaluate existing courses and programs in educational psychology at both the undergraduate and graduate level. Since colleges provide the breeding ground for future educational psychologists, training programs in educational psychology must be designed to meet the various disciplinary and institutional needs identified above. In particular, graduate programs should be designed to train: (a) higher-caliber research workers and theorists who are able to identify and to deal creatively and productively with open questions pertaining to teaching and learning; (b) technological experts who are capable of developing new and better instructional technologies and/or of using them to design efficient learning systems; (c) specialists who are thoroughly familiar with the latest knowledge and technologies in educational psychology and who have had supervised clinical training in assisting classroom teachers to improve their instruction; and (d) educational psychologists who are thoroughly familiar with the latest knowledge and technologies in educational psychology and who plan to specialize in teaching educational psychology at the undergraduate and in-service levels. (Because continuing involvement in the discipline and intimate familiarity with school curricula are an indispensible part of such a role, the committee feels that doctoral education in this specialty should include experience in research and development and/or training in some special curriculum area.)

THE CURRENT STATUS OF EDUCATIONAL PSYCHOLOGY AS A DISCIPLINE

In this section, we review the current status of educational psychology as a discipline with particular reference to: (a) views and interests of educational psychologists as determined by a survey of the field; (b) kinds of research in which educational psychologists engage; (c) professional organizations relevant to the disciplinary aspects of educational psychology; (d) federal funding for educational psychology; (e) educational psychology in the university; and (f) the employment situation in educational psychology.

Views and Interests of Educational Psychologists

We conducted an extensive survey of educational psychologists to determine their views and interests. A questionnaire including sixteen rating scales and four open-ended questions (1. What statistical techniques do you use most in your research? 2. What has been the most significant advance in educational psychology during the past ten years? 3. What has been its greatest fault? 4. Other comments) was mailed to over 3000 educational psychologists during fall 1974. Responses were received from 590. Among other things, it was found that on the average the respondents spend less than half of their time on educational psychology. (Much time was spent in administration.) This survey also confirmed our expectation that educational psychology has lacked a well-defined identity and is ambivalent about splitting away from its parent discipline of psychology.

A significant number of respondents voiced either the opinion that there is currently not enough emphasis on theory or that recent theoretical work represents a positive advance. Only a third as many disapproved of theory in educational psychology. On the other hand, a significant number of respondents felt that current theory was too abstract and that they did not see its relevance to practice. Interestingly, an even larger number of respondents felt that current research was fragmented into narrow specialties, also presumably with little relevance. Apparently, most educational psychologists feel that we need comprehensive yet scientifically rigorous theories that have direct relevance to education—something that is not always the case with the contemporary theories in psychology and other disciplines.

The Content of Educational Psychology

As noted above, educational psychologists engage in a wide variety of activities and utilize a wide variety of techniques. Nonetheless, since educational psychology is in large part a problem-oriented discipline, the general content of the field can be reasonably well defined by areas of application. With this in mind we have listed in Table 13-1 those applied activities in which educational psychologists typically engage, together with some of their major disciplinary components.

Table 13-1

Content of educational psychology

Problem area	Disciplinary components
The identification of educational goals (needs analysis, goal definition, and so on.	Management science, opinion sampling, questionnaire and interview design, attitude measurement, operations research.
Analysis/determination of what must be learned (for example, job, task, and learning task analysis).	Personnel psychology, military psychology, instructional psychology.
Delivery/designing instructional systems (for example, designing instruction, media selection, instructional delivery).	Growing technical literature and the beginnings of theory on designing instruction, also many relations with contemporary learning theory, considerable literature but less theory on media selection, research at various levels (for example, individualized instruction, ATI research).
Readiness/evaluation of student behavior and course effectiveness (for example, developmental stages and readiness, assessment of student performance, evaluation of instructional programs).	Developmental psychology, test theory and interpretation, criterion-referenced testing, techniques of evaluation.

Whereas the components in Table 13-1 have attracted considerable attention, relatively little attention has been given to the interrelationships among these various problem areas. Nonetheless, although most educational psychologists have been trained to work within one or another of the above problem areas, it is not at all clear whether these areas may be usefully separated if one seeks a comprehensive understanding of teaching and learning. Presumably what are needed are comprehensive yet rigorous systems that could provide the necessary integration.

Professional Organizations Relevant to Educational Psychology

In recent years, initially at the instigation of one of the present committee members, questions have been raised about how the profession of educational psychology is organized. Informal surveys and discussions with numerous members and potential members suggest that a large portion of productive educational psychologists are *not* members of the American Psychological Association (APA). Many educational psychologists, for example, belong to the American Educational Research Association (AERA) but not to APA. A large number of high-caliber academics who are researching the problems of teaching and learning belong to neither organization. Many of them belong to more specialized societies such as the National Society for Performance and Instruction (NSPI), the Structural Learning Society, or other specialized interest groups of larger organizations such as AERA.

Federal Funds for Educational Psychology

The major types of research and development activities in which educational psychologists participate and the extent of support by various federal agencies are shown in Table 13-2. In this table, each agency is classified according to budget and emphasis. A budget is considered high if over 100 million dollars is allocated annually to activities in education and psychology. Educational emphasis refers to what might be called the principal mission of the agency as far as education is concerned. This refers to applied research and development rather than to basic research and to education rather than psychology. It is important to note that the research and development activities of an agency are not necessarily limited to this mission (thus, the National Institute of Health supports research on learning disabilities and in various areas of psychology as well as in medical education).

Of the various types of research and development activities, basic research includes both psychology and education. Teacher training refers to the "research on teaching" so highly visible in the literature, but it may include projects for training teachers in a specific curriculum. Evaluation includes the area of "tests and measurement." Technology mainly means computer-assisted instruction (CAI) and other efforts with a strong instructional design component. It does not include educational television curriculum projects such as "Sesame Street."

Table 13-2 suggests that stronger support seems likely in two areas of research and weaker support likely in one. Thus, limited support is available for teacher education. In the case of the National Institute of Education (NIE), major changes are currently underway. The

Table 13-2

Types of Research and Development Activities

Agency	Budget	Educational emphasis	Basic research	Teacher training	Curriculum	Evaluation	Technology	Special education
NSF	High	Science education	Yes	No	Yes	Yes	Yes	No
Defense (DOD)	High	Armed Forces personnel training	Mission-oriented	Limited	Yes	Yes	Yes	No
NIH	?	Medical education	Yes	Limited	Yes	Yes	Yes	Yes
NIMH	Low	Mental health	Yes	No	No	?	No	Yes
NIE	Low	Public education K to 12	Limited	Limited	Yes	Yes	Limited	?
OE	High	Public education K to 12	No	?	Yes	Yes	No	Yes

expectation, however, is that most support will continue to go to existing and possibly a few new laboratories and centers. In the case of NIH and the Department of Defense (DOD), it is limited to highly specific postsecondary areas. The winners seem to be evaluation and curriculum. Some qualifications need to be made regarding curriculum, however. Support is currently weak and may soon be nonexistent in areas related to the social sciences. Also, of all areas considered, curriculum is probably the one in which educational psychologists now play the least significant role. On the other hand, evaluation is likely to remain a high-priority activity, if only because of its close relationship to policy analysis. Policy is an important activity in which agencies engage. At the present time at the NIE, political realities tend to favor the educational research and development centers and laboratories. The amount of money going to unsolicited projects is unbelievably small in a country of this size. (Even small countries such as Holland devote considerably more money annually to educational research.)

Of the three remaining research and development activities, special education is stronger than Table 13-2 would indicate. This activity includes many aspects of the Office of Education (OE) compensatory education programs. Support may also increase for basic research. All agencies except OE have some kind of basic research program. DOD and NIE currently emphasize certain areas. DOD tends to fund research relevant to personnel training or human-factors engineering. NIE has emphasized reading and under its current priorities is moving into mathematics. NIH and the National Institute of Mental Health (NIMH) fund a broad range of research but tend toward basic research in traditional areas of psychology only. One major hope comes from the National Science Foundation (NSF), whose budget beginning with fiscal year 1977 included a significant amount for basic research in education.

The case of technology is considerably more ambiguous. It is weak at the elementary and secondary level but strong at the postsecondary level, especially in specific areas such as armed forces training and medical education. This support comes from agencies that have had more or less stable funding.

Educational Psychology in the University

This section represents an attempt to describe educational psychology as it exists in universities at the present time and the problems it faces both as a discipline and a curriculum in this setting. Although the views presented are necessarily limited, they seem fairly representative of the situations that exist at several major state and private universities.

Formal Status. Educational psychology exhibits a variety of individual patterns in different universities. In some, it is simply a part of a department of psychology, responsible for courses in educational psychology and school psychology and functioning within a college of liberal arts. In most, educational psychology is a separate department in a school or college of education. In that setting, it may be a section of a department, such as a department of education or a department of educational foundations. It is our impression that there has been a trend in public institutions over the past ten years to establish separate departments of educational psychology in schools of education.

Academic Responsibilities. Usually an educational psychology faculty is responsible for offering one or more undergraduate courses in educational psychology, often required for teacher certification. In addition, when separate departments exist, graduate degrees may be offered in this speciality. Typically, the content of educational psychology at both undergraduate and graduate levels includes the core areas of human development, human learning, and psychological measurement. Adjunct areas frequently occur, such as statistics, counseling, and some aspects of social psychology.

Quality of Academic Programs. At the undergraduate level, educational psychology has not always been distinguished by excellence. On the one hand, it is often criticized by students and former students as being "too theoretical" and/or "too remote from the problems of the classroom." On the other hand, it has long been plagued by inadequate texts that give the impression of "warmed-over" elementary psychology. The first of these criticisms is a genuine expression of dissatisfaction, but it probably does not capture the true difficulty. Educational psychology, after all, must be largely theoretical, unless it is to focus on the level of simply describing routine classroom procedures. It should be a course that broadens horizons of thought, not one that is restricted just to the learning of practical skills. The second criticism is actually more accurate and more serious. It means that because of the influence of social and economic factors, textbooks in educational psychology have been developed and produced in the image of the "comprehensive" and "eclectic" elementary text in psychology. For example, they often report the results of traditional psychological experiments without adequate explanation of what practical significance or relevance such findings have for school learning.

As for graduate programs in educational psychology, they appear to vary from barely adequate to quite good. Some still emphasize concerns adopted from "academic" psychology such as the learning of paired associates. Others avoid research altogether, with the exception of occasional dissertations that collect dust on library shelves. The best ones would appear to be those organized and administered by a separate faculty (either a separate department or a separately organized section of a larger department), although many of the weaker programs fall into this category too.

The situation in major private research universities is somewhat different. In such universities, education generally has been held in modest esteem, and the situation of educational psychology is only slightly better. In this context, it has often been essential to adopt a different strategy, one that purposefully draws upon the strengths of individual faculty members in other departments including, but not limited to, psychology. It must be said, however, that the success of such undertakings, as in most ad hoc arrangements, depends largely on the intellectual power and strengths of the personalities involved.

Effects of the Title. From the standpoint of what educational psychology ought to be, the effects of the word *psychology* in its title have been negative as often as positive.

1. The title has led to domination in an internal political sense by academic psychology. This means restrictions are placed upon educational psychology offerings by considerations of conflict with psychology's "turf."

2. Educational psychology is dominated by the larger social forces (within and without the university) that determine the content of psychology. As previous examples have indicated, this means that content tends to be included because it represents traditional psychology, not because it is needed.

3. Educational psychology is viewed as a strictly applied subject without a disciplinary content of its own. Thus, courses in educational psychology have the status of "service" courses in the larger field of psychology and are not encouraged to develop their own conceptual structure.

4. Educational psychology is not helped, and is probably hindered, by the common misconception that it is only a psychological specialty comparable to clinical psychology. This is deeply disturbing to its "self-concept," because educational psychology in its core meaning is not a professional specialty intended for service to the individual public.

Relations with Departments of Psychology. When educational psychology is a part of a department of psychology, it is subject to the domination of the latter discipline, as previously noted, and frequently holds the status of "service courses." Where separate departments exist, relations between the two are not always positive. Psychology (usually in liberal arts), for example, is frequently able to block the establishment of needed courses (on the grounds that they are "psychology") or to otherwise impose modifications on the development of separate course offerings. (Why should educational psychology teach a course on learning when psychology already offers one?)

Cooperative relationships sometimes exist between individual faculty members of psychology and educational psychology. These are scarcely more frequent than the cooperation of individual faculty members in other departments. At the graduate level, members of the psychology faculty are sometimes involved in graduate student committees, although again, this is not a highly frequent occurrence. Cooperative arrangements for seminars, colloquia, and the like are relatively rare, although exceptions do exist. Joint appointments in educational psychology and psychology also exist, but they tend to be nominal or of the "courtesy" variety.

One major belief is that educational psychology receives relatively little intellectual sustenance from departments of psychology. Psychology courses in such fields as learning, perception, motivation, and developmental psychology often do not serve the needs of students in educational psychology. Similarly, with some notable exceptions, the research done by psychologists in psychology departments often has little relevance to educational psychology. When members of departments of psychology work with schools, they are frequently concerned with imposing a doctrine (such as contingency management) rather than with attempting to solve school problems. (This is not always true, but there are many instances of it nonetheless.) It is quite possible that the development of a disciplinary structure may proceed best when educational psychology is independent of psychology and is unhampered by its name. The labels instructional science/research/design/evaluation have come to connote much of what is most promising about the field.

Employment Situation in Educational Psychology

In a word, the employment situation for educational psychologists, particularly at the doctoral level, has been dismal. Job opportunities for generalists have been few in number and very rarely provide opportunities for the sort of professional and intellectual growth implied throughout this report. On the brighter side, there are growing signs to indicate that the educational community at large is beginning to recognize the value of instructional design. (There are also some opportunities for test and evaluation specialists and school psychologists, but graduate training in these areas often takes place in separate programs.) Although the general level of recognition is relatively low in comparison with rather sophisticated recent advances, it appears to this committee that this is a positive development that should be promoted. See our recommendations concerning this below.

PROMISING ADVANCES IN EDUCATIONAL PSYCHOLOGY

Disciplinary Advances

The large amount of research and theory development on teaching and learning that is currently underway precludes any complete description or even listing of all the potentially promising advances. The list that follows is simply illustrative.

1. Advances that have penetrated through to the practitioner: principles of reinforcement (Skinner); behavioral objectives (Mager, Popham, Glaser); learning hierarchies (Gagné); developmental stages (Piaget).
2. Advances that have been widely understood and recognized by

the research community in educational psychology but that have not yet filtered through to most school practitioners: mastery and criterion-referenced testing (recognition is fairly widespread and is becoming more so); the paradigm shift from S-R to cognitive/information processing in psychology, particularly as this involves education; artificial intelligence and simulation models of complex human performance and instruction.

3. Promising advances that have not yet been fully evaluated, accepted, and/or understood by many educational psychologists: relatively formal structural, systems, and cybernetic theories of teaching and learning that incorporate ideas relevant to content analysis, cognitive psychology, and criterion-referenced testing, for example, but that transcend them by emphasizing their interaction in ongoing systems of teaching/learning as they change dynamically over time (for example, structural learning theory, conversation theory, algorithmic approaches to instruction).

Professional Organizations Relevant to Educational Psychology

At the present time, the interests of educational psychology must compete with those of a large number of influential divisions and special interests within the APA and AERA. As a result of such competing interests, the best interests of the vast majority of educational psychologists have not always been represented as fully as might be desired. In recent years, a number of alternative organizational models (for example, the Psychonomic Society) have been considered as a means of increasing the impact of educational psychology. During our committee deliberations, in fact, one such model was considered by Division 15 (Educational Psychology) of the APA but was voluntarily withdrawn after discussion of the pros and cons. This model was designed to maintain Division 15 much as it is while opening up the division to non-APA members. The committee takes no position on this particular proposal but does feel that educational psychologists should remain alert to alternatives that might broaden the base of support for educational psychology.

Federal Funding for Educational Psychology

In spite of the generally bleak picture in the funding of educational research, there are a few bright spots. Although hardly realized in terms of dollar commitments, the growing recognition of the potential value of instructional design is a positive advance that should be reinforced at NIE, NSF, and other relevant agencies. The same should be said about positions at universities, medical training institutions, and the like, where the role of instructional consultant has become increasingly common.

Educational Psychology in the University

With the diminution or abolition of educational psychology programs at some major universities, it is hard to be optimistic. Nonetheless, there are several encouraging signs, and educational psychologists should be cognizant of them in future planning. One promising advance concerns the growing acceptance of instructional design and evaluation. This has led to a number of new university programs that in some places have replaced and in other cases have complemented existing educational psychology programs. It would appear that the relatively well-defined focus such programs represent stands in stark contrast to the rather ill-defined image of traditional educational psychology.

Another promising development has been the increasing tendency of "academic" scholars to become involved in instructional problems, as evidenced by the growing number of effective working relationships between such individuals and educational psychologists. We believe that such cooperation should be encouraged, for it is only by developing a stronger interdisciplinary foundation for the study of teaching and learning that educational psychology will obtain acceptability in the broader community of scholars. A major problem for educational psychology, of course, will be gaining such acceptability while at the same time ensuring that the work retains a close relationship to educational reality.

Development of New Positions in Educational Psychology

We find few reasons for optimism in the employment picture. Teacher training programs, for example, which traditionally have been heavily serviced by educational psychologists, are diminishing in size all over the country. Although a variety of steps have been and are being taken to help maintain enrollments (for example, by emphasizing continuing education, attending to "fads"), these changes in emphasis have not augured well for the disciplinary aspects of educational psychology.

Again, one positive hope seems to be to capitalize on the increasing acceptance of educational/instructional design and evaluation by administrators in public schools, institutions of higher learning (for example, universities, medical schools), and businesses and organizations (for example, the military) where specialized training is required. More generally, educational psychologists must do a better job of public relations; we believe that this can only be accomplished over time, as a result of continuing substantive accomplishments by individuals and groups who are perceived as educational psychologists. We believe further that research and theory which contribute to both the disciplinary foundations and the practice of teaching and learning are most badly needed and will have the greatest impact.

RECOMMENDATIONS

As a general overall conclusion, we strongly recommend that educational psychologists take an active role in promoting the interests and identity of educational psychology as a discipline (although not necessarily by that name) at all levels and in as many ways as seems practical. APA's Division 15, especially modified as recommended (see below), should provide the central moving force for such activities. In order to accomplish this, we believe that the division, in addition to its traditional activities, must not only remain open to but must actively encourage promising new ideas, whether they involve theory and research, federal funding, university programs, or the job market. The following suggestions are directed toward these ends.

Disciplinary Foundations

Educational psychologists should take steps to encourage the development of a stronger disciplinary base within the field, while at the same time remaining open to advances in psychology and other disciplines that hold promise for the study and/or improvement of the educational process. Specifically, we feel at this time that the paradigm shift from S-R to information processing should be encouraged in the study of educational problems. Similarly, encouragement should be given to basic research on language and reading.

Nonetheless, one of the reasons that educational measurement and normative testing generally has been not only respected but closely identified with education over the years (as well as with psychology) is that the field was motivated initially and developed throughout its long history in large part by educational researchers. Educational psychology, we think, has a similar opportunity today. Such concerns as criterion-referenced testing, evaluation, instructional design, and algorithmic/structural approaches to instruction all fall within the rubric of "instructional science," an area that appears equally promising. Especially important, we think, are instructional systems and theories that serve to integrate and to define the field and that have a significant practical value.

In addition, we believe that such development should be actively promoted—not so much in terms of personalities but by the worthiness of the ideas. Since they most properly belong to educational psychology per se, broader recognition by other scientists of the contributions they make toward understanding the teaching/learning process can only serve to increase the esteem with which educational psychology is held.

In this regard, we make the following specific recommendations. **Recommendation 1**: Relevant journals, such as *The Journal of Educational Psychology, The Educational Psychologist, The American Educational Research Journal, Instructional Science, Contemporary Educational Psychology,* and so on, should be encouraged to solicit theoretical articles that deal with promising theoretical perspectives for instructional problems. (It should be noted that in 1973, under the editorship of Frank Farley, this became one of the stated goals of the *Educational Psychologist*). **Recommendation 2**: Division 15 and other relevant organizations should solicit symposia presentations that emphasize methodological and theoretical advances that have direct relevance for teaching and learning. **Recommendation 3**: Relevant organizations should explore the possibility of cosponsoring special conferences having direct relevance for the disciplinary foundations of educational psychology. Such groups might also explore the possibility of mutually beneficial liaison relationships with complementary societies and organizations, especially those that emphasize problems of direct relevance to educational psychology (for example, NSPI, Division C, and interest groups in AERA).

Research Support

Given the contraction of funding for educational research over the past several years, funds for new initiatives in educational psychology have been extremely limited. (Funding in the late 1960s was lush in comparison.) As a result, individual investigators, irrespective of their qualifications, have been at a serious disadvantage in competing with the highly organized, larger research institutions. The situation has been made even more difficult by the fact that AERA, a major political pressure group for educational research funding, has been heavily influenced by the interests of these same institutions, which in many cases compete with the interests of individual scientists at universities and smaller organizations.

In view of the above, the committee proposes **Recommendation 4:** Organizations in educational psychology should not only maintain but should also expand their current initiatives in promoting liaisons with federal funding agencies. Particular attention should be given to the needs of individual research scientists.

Educational Psychology in the University

In view of the state of uncertainty that currently exists, special attention should be given to defining alternative roles that educational psychology might usefully play and organizational structures within which it might properly exist in the university context. Attention should also be given to the task of identifying and evaluating the various disciplinary facets of educational psychology. The desirability of proposing minimum standards for training within each of these facets should also be considered, particularly at the doctoral level. Only by maintaining appropriate "quality control," we think, will educational psychology and educational psychologists gain the stature they deserve.

Recommendation 5: A committee should be set up to study the nature of educational psychology and its relationship within the university community more closely. Its primary function might be to identify the various major facets of educational psychology and to develop appropriate standards for graduate training programs with respect to these facets. In effect, the committee should consider the question of quality control, particularly at the graduate levels, and the desirability of Division 15 of APA exercising appropriate responsibility in the area.

Positions in Educational Psychology

If allowed to continue, the scarcity of positions for qualified Ph.D.'s in educational psychology can only hinder the development of the field. We urge that steps be taken to broaden the range of positions in which educational psychologists might contribute as educational psychologists. Particularly promising, we think, is the possibility of preparing educational psychologists who can work effectively and in an ongoing manner with teachers and principals in schools to promote more efficient cognitive learning and motivation. The school-based educational psychologist would thus be a direct cognitive counterpart of the school psychologist who tends to specialize in affective and abnormal behavior problems. Similar relationships might be developed in the medical areas where research support has traditionally been available in larger quantities. The specialized nature of the medical fields suggests that joint training and/or employment relationships with medical, dental, and nursing schools might be encouraged.

Recommendation 6: Relevant organizations should explore the possibility of "creating a need' and standards for training programs that prepare educational psychologists to work in schools, using evolving principles of instructional design, to promote more efficient cognitive learning and motivation. In addition to the strictly academic implications, these organizations should look into political and legal ramifications.

14. The Promise of Educational Psychology

Philip W. Jackson

Once I was an educational psychologist, or at least I professed to be. These days I am less certain about what to call myself. But no matter, for the truth is I no longer care as I once did whether this or that label accurately denotes what I do. Such, I suppose, is one of the benefits of middle age. Past forty, or thereabouts, I am pleased to report, worries about rank, titles, and other designations of status begin to taper off markedly. To be honest, however, I must confess that my occupational ambivalence, if it may be so labeled, bespeaks more than the normal decline of status anxiety or whatever you want to call the youthful affliction that causes our thoughts to center on what others think of us. It is as much an indictment of educational psychology as it is a confession of personal indifference. For when I think about the field's accomplishments to date and when I try to envision the promise it holds for the future, I do not come away cheered. At such moments I am keenly aware of the truth contained in Jack Carroll's observation of a few years back. Speaking of what educational psychology might do for teachers, he said:

Presented as an invited address before Division 15 of the American Psychological Association, August 26, 1977.

Until we have more research testimony concerning the operational effectiveness of educational psychology in training teachers to handle practical educational problems, we shall have to be content to regard it as a discipline with a large but by no means wholly realized potential for effective application, and we shall continue to teach educational psychology to teachers with a mixture of pious optimism and subdued embarrassment. [1963, p. 119]

"Pious optimism and subdued embarrassment"—I know the mixture well. And I dislike it.

More recently than Carroll, other psychologists prominent in the field of educational psychology have expressed equally disturbing sentiments. Lee J. Cronbach, for example, in his 1974 address to the American Psychological Association (APA) following his receipt of the Distinguished Scientific Contribution Award, spoke of the difficulties he had encountered in his search for attribute-treatment interactions, those elusive linkages that—if ever found—would enable us to arrange a proper match between student characteristics and instructional strategies. Cronbach and his coworkers were, as he put it, "thwarted by inconsistent findings." The trouble? Unidentified interactions. Moreover, having begun that identification process, there seemed to be no end in sight. "Once we attend to interactions," Cronbach complained, "we enter a hall of mirrors that extends to infinity" (Cronbach 1975, p. 119).

Further along in his talk Cronbach went on to despair of ever arriving at generalizations that will withstand the test of time long enough to be woven into an enduring theory. To dramatize his point he resorted again to metaphor. "It is as if we needed a gross of dry cells to power an engine," he said, "and could only make one a month. The energy would leak out of the first cells before we had half the battery completed. So it is with the potency of our generalizations" (p. 123). His speech did end on an optimistic note, I hasten to say; whether pious or not is a question to which we shall return, but the hall of mirrors imagery and the mental picture of the modern-day Sisyphus hard at work on the leaky battery are disquieting, to say the least.

In his presidential address to the APA convention last September, Wilbert McKeachie both began and ended more optimistically than had Cronbach two years earlier. It was, after all, the Bicentennial Year, a time for being pleased with our accomplishments and cheerful about the future. McKeachie wisely used the opportunity to celebrate the advancement of American psychology as a science from the days of William James forward. He ended by looking toward the future with high hopes.

Yet when he spoke specifically about educational psychology, his own specialty, McKeachie's optimism faltered. After reviewing the kind of pedagogical advice that William James gave in his famous *Talks to Teachers,* McKeachie acknowledged that with very minor changes we would say much the same thing today. Moreover, he went on to point out that most of James's basic ideas did not originate with him but, rather, "are the result of wisdom accumulated by teachers going back at least to the time of Socrates" (McKeachie 1976, p. 822). Thus, McKeachie warns, "[w]e should not expect that psychology in James's day or our own day will easily improve upon the wisdom built up over many generations."

Lest this warning be taken as an admission that psychology has not contributed much to our pedagogical wisdom, McKeachie hastened to add a corrective. Great teachers over the ages may indeed have discovered the bulk of today's teaching lore, "but," he insisted, "this does not mean that we have not made progress. The progress we have made in learning and educational psychology," he continued, "is not marked by the dramatic breakthroughs that have occurred in other areas of psychology. Rather, what we have learned is that learning is *more complex* than we had earlier believed" (p. 822). The bad news about this greater complexity "is that the work is much more descriptive than practical" (p. 826). The good news, we are informed, "is that we have models that seem more realistic in their level of complexity and seem more in touch with the wisdom of teachers, parents, and others who apply learning principles" (p. 826). Now I suppose we should take heart over the prospect of educational psychology catching up with the wisdom of the ages, but somehow I remain uninspired by such a vision.

Thus, try as I might, I fail to be cheered by McKeachie's bicentennial optimism, preferring instead, as a match for my mood, the discomforting truth of Carroll's subdued embarrassment and Cronbach's troubling symbols of disillusionment and futility. Yet whenever I allow my thoughts to darken in this way, they invariably trigger memories of brighter days; for, as hinted at the start, I was not always troubled by misgivings about the promise of educational psychology. As a graduate student in the early fifties I was uncommonly eager to join the ranks of what I then perceived to be a noble lineage of scholars and researchers who had pioneered in the development of standardized tests and measurements, who had contributed significantly to our understanding of the learning process, and who—before my very eyes—were hard at work developing techniques of research design and statistical analysis capable of teasing out the subtle strands of causality that lay entangled in the flux of everyday life. Educational psychologists all, and I could hardly wait to be numbered among them.

There are moments even now, a quarter century later, when I can with effort rekindle that earlier feeling, times when I still experience a stirring of pride at the thought of being a part of the research tradition into which I was initiated back then. But for the most part, I reluctantly admit, that earlier enthusiasm has waned and has been replaced by the gnawing doubt and uncertainty that several of my contemporaries seem to share. What went wrong?

Part of the answer to that question must surely be developmental. Disappointment and disillusionment may not be inevitable outcomes of the aging process, but they do seem to characterize a phase of development that few of us escape entirely. Educational psychologists, of course, are not its only victims. Jacques Barzun, writing about historians, introduces yet another metaphor to capture the essence of the phenomenon. "The task," he writes, "is to make bricks with the straw supplied to the willing workers. Every age presents its new talents with an enormous amount of fresh stubble, expecting to see it all turned into bricks. These talents go to work and find too late that they are somehow deceived" (Barzun, 1974, p. x).

The stubble and the bricks are a bit anachronistic, to be sure, but Barzun's depiction of the subjective reaction to the situation rings true. "Somehow deceived"—that's the feeling all right. Those two words epitomize my own sense of puzzlement mixed with disappointment. And both words are important, for it is not a case of open deception in which the culprit becomes known but rather a feeling of having *somehow* been led astray, directed off course by forces whose workings are poorly understood. Barzun refers to this feeling and our urge to cope with it as "the permanent cultural predicament." If he is right, and I suspect he is, then each new crop of us is destined to experience in greater or lesser degree that sense of having inherited a faulty guidance system, intellectual outlook, even a way of life that does not function as we were led to believe it would. Eventually, it would seem, we all find ourselves with Barzun's pile of stubble that dries out before the job of brick making is done. Each new generation of workers is left, caked earth in hand, to puzzle out for itself what went wrong.

But though the problem is surely developmental in part, chances are that it is not entirely so. And even if it were, we would still be left with the question of how to solve it. One solution, though extreme, is to abandon the field entirely and invest our energies elsewhere. The trouble with this remedy as applied to educational psychology is that the need to advance our understanding of educational matters is quite obviously great, and psychologists seem like such a logically appropriate group to help in the process. Thus, to leave the field is to desert a worthy cause, and I, for one, cannot bring myself to do it. Another alternative, less extreme than the first, is to discard as much of the past as possible and begin afresh. Something like this is suggested by my friend and former colleague, Lawrence Kohlberg, who advocates that we turn away from the historically dominant traditions of educational psychology and adopt instead a new and revolutionary outlook. Kohlberg's candidate for this new look is what he calls "a cognitive-developmental" point of view.

In one of the papers summarizing his argument, Kohlberg traces what he takes to be "the three broad streams of educational psychology." The first of these, which he calls "maturationist," commences with the writings of Rousseau and flows into modern thought through the teachings of Freud, Arnold Gesell, and their followers. In essence, Kohlberg tells us, "it holds that what is most important in the development of the child is that which comes from within him" (Kohlberg 1971, p. 2). The second stream is seen as stemming from John Locke, extending through the work of J.B. Watson, and culminating in the most recent pronouncements of B.F. Skinner. Kohlberg calls this line of thought "environmentalist." He claims that it assumes "that what is important in the child's development is the learning of cognitive and moral knowledge and the rules of the culture" (p. 3).

Kohlberg's third stream of thought in educational psychology and the one that he himself prefers is, as has been said, the cognitive-developmental or "interactional" view. It begins with the writings of

John Dewey, takes a transatlantic leap to Switzerland where it is enriched by the investigations of Claparede and Piaget, then returns to this country to be carried forward by the experimental work of a veritable army of cognitive and developmental psychologists, including of course Kohlberg himself. This third view, as Kohlberg describes it, "is based on the premise that the cognitive and affective structures, which education should nourish, emerge naturally from the *interaction* between child and the environment under conditions that allow or foster such interaction" (p. 3). This view, we are told, is in fact "revolutionary" because it redefines the school's aims and its methods for reaching those aims.

Now I admit to being deeply sympathetic with the argument that Kohlberg sets forth. Like him, I have been an admirer of John Dewey for some time and believe that his writings have been unduly neglected by psychologists. I, too, would like to see the emergence of an educational psychology that will help us to think constructively about the aims and ends of education. I, too, share the hope that Piaget and his followers will deliver us from evil. And yet, and yet— something holds me back, prevents me from becoming an enthusiastic enlistee in Kohlberg's crusade. What is it?

Perhaps Kohlberg's own evaluation of his three-stream theory holds the key. During the discussion of his paper at the conference where it was first delivered, he was quick to admit that the view he had presented was, in his own words, "oversimple." Oversimple— that's the problem. The world of educational psychology cannot be divided up that neatly. Three streams, indeed! The psychological landscape, as I view it, looks more like a swamp crosscut with intersecting channels, stagnant pools, and brackish backwaters. Clouds cover the moon, owls hoot in the distance, and a loon cries from across the lake. Out of the encircling mist a bark emerges carrying Jacques Barzun, who again offers a helping hand. "Yet on closer look," he counsels, "the actual choice for serious minds is never between an old unsatisfactory mode and a new exciting one. That is mere appearance. The choice is not *between*—it is *among* a multiplicity of tendencies, hopes, pretensions, routines, verbalisms, misrepresentations, fads, discoveries, and genuine new thought" (p. x).

Additional words of warning are contained in the writings of the philosopher of science, Stephen Toulmin, who decries efforts to compress into a nutshell statements about what science is or should be. "A nutshell definition of science—as of anything else," Toulmin cautions, "inevitably floats around on the surface. An investigation of any depth forces us to recognize that the truth is much more complex. To understand the ways in which meritorious scientific ideas differ in any age from their less deserving rivals calls for a painstaking and laborious study; only in this way shall we bring to light the manifold functions that science has performed, performs now, and *might* perform in the future within our whole intellectual economy" (Toulmin 1961, p. 15).

A painstaking and laborious study of a multiplicity of tendencies, hopes, pretentions, routines, and what have you. Fair enough, if that is what is required. But where do we begin? A good place is obviously the beginning, but to trace *ab initio* the thought and human activity that culminates in our current confusion about where educational psychology is or is not going would take us, I fear, back to antiquity. For the ancients, as we all know, were far from silent on the topic of man's mind, its nature and nurturance. Lacking both the time and talent for such a historical search, I am forced to move in considerably closer to the present day to initiate my own foraging into the roots of our present discomfort. What is wanted, then, is not the true beginning in a historical sense but merely a convenient jumping-off place from which to plunge into what both Barzun and Toulmin forewarn will turn out to be a thicket of controversy and confusion.

Though any such choice of a document to examine or a set of ideas to criticize is bound to be somewhat arbitrary, some choices are clearly more logically appealing than others. One historical event that has such logical appeal, because it signals—if not the coming of age of our subspeciality of psychology—at least a christening of sorts, is the appearance in January 1910 of the very first issue of the *Journal of Educational Psychology*. The lead article of that issue seems as good a place as any to anchor our thoughts. It was entitled, "The Contribution of Psychology to Education." Its author, as one could guess, was Edward L. Thorndike.

As might be expected, given the occasion and given what we know about the man himself, Thorndike's essay exudes an aura of bouyant optimism. The times were good and psychology, through its contribution to education, was going to make them even better. Just how much better quickly becomes evident as Thorndike sketches in bold strokes an outline of what he earnestly believes lies ahead for this budding young science. "A complete science of psychology," he writes, "would tell every fact about everyone's intellect and character and behavior, would tell the cause of every change in human nature, would tell the result which every educational force—every act of every person that changed any other or the agent himself—would have. It would aid us to use human begins for the world's welfare with the same surety of the result that we now have when we use falling bodies or chemical elements. In proportion as we get such a science we shall become masters of our own souls as we now are masters of heat and light. Progress toward such a science," Thorndike assures his readers, "is being made" (Thorndike 1910, p. 6).

This new psychology, which was portrayed as being a radical departure from the armchair theorizing and commonsense deductions of the past, was to be of help to educators in a variety of ways. It was to contribute to a better understanding of the *aims* of education "by defining them, making them clearer; by limiting them, showing us what can be done and what cannot; and by suggesting new features that should be made part of them" (p. 5). It was to contribute to an understanding of the *materials* of education by providing practitioners with knowledge of man's bodily or mental nature, the raw stuff, as it were, with which we work. It was to contribute to an understanding of the *means* of education, first, by telling us about the intellects and characters of the pupil's "parents, teachers, and friends" who are the important means of educating him and, second, by studying the influence of other means, such as "books, maps, or apparatus" as they act upon human nature. Finally, this new psychology was to contribute to our understanding of the *methods* of teaching in three ways.

First, Thorndike explained, some methods "may be deduced outright from the laws of human nature" (p. 7). Second, for those methods whose value has already been revealed by experience, psychology may provide an explanation of why they work as well as they do. Third, for both new and old practices psychology, through methods of measuring knowledge and skill, "may suggest means to test and verify or refute the claims of any method." Thus, Thorndike concludes, "Psychology, which teaches us how to measure changes in human nature, teaches us how to decide just what the results of any method of teaching are" (p. 8). This glowing portrayal of the promise of educational psychology is followed by some brief comment on a few current lines of investigation that seemed to be of special relevance to education, such as the measurement of intellectual functions, lines of work, that as Thorndike put it, "do extend and economize" the practical control of human nature.

Finally, in his closing paragraph, Thorndike apologizes to his readers for having belabored the obvious, which is "that action in the world should be guided by the truth about the world and that any truth about it will directly or indirectly, soon or late, benefit action" (p. 12). Thus ends the opening salvo from one of eduational psychology's biggest guns, announcing to the world that a new journal, and with it a new psychological discipline, had been born.

Now what are we to make of this curio from the archives of our profession—this essay, now yellowed with age, that comes so close to epitomizing Barzun's mind-boggling tangle of "tendencies, hopes, pretentions, routines, verbalisms, misrepresentations, fads, discoveries, and genuine new thought"? How can it help us as we try to make sense of where educational psychology is today and where it might be tomorrow? To begin with, we must avoid exaggerating the significance of Thorndike's brief essay. He did not offer it as a manifesto to be pasted in the hatbands of educational psychologists from that day to this. It was a journal article—nothing more, nothing less. Knowing Thorndike's love of the laboratory and his wide-ranging involvement in empirical studies of all sorts, we might even suspect that he did not take great care in its composition. There were, after all, more important or at least more interesting activities in which to invest his energies.

At the same time, even though the article may have been hastily written, it does provide us with a glimpse of the dominant ideology that was to shape and guide the thinking and practice of educational psychologists for decades to come. Portions of that ideology are still with us today. I have no quarrel with the spirit of empiricism that pervades Thorndike's essay. I share his assumption that there is a world of reality external to the sense about which reliable knowledge can be gained. I further share his conviction that knowledge about that world, including its human inhabitants, may prove to be of value to the actors themselves. I can even go along with the experimental temper of his view, with his insistence that we must patiently and ingeniously prod and poke external reality in order to divulge its secrets. I find the lure of "hard data" as appealing as Thorndike did.

Beyond these areas of agreement, however, lies disagreement as well. In my view, which has both the advantage and the disadvantage of being sixty-seven years distant from the object viewed, Thorndike's prolegomena to the maiden issue of the *Journal of Educational Psychology* has at least four shortcomings. It does not distinguish adequately between both the goals and the methods of the physical and the social sciences. It does not pay sufficient attention to the historical and cultural context within which humans live and learn and schools operate. It proffers a blind faith in the social benefits to be derived from scientific investigation. And, finally, it overlooks the aesthetic dimension of the scientist's work, ignoring what I choose to think of as the art of educational psychology. Each of these four assertions requires a brief elaboration.

Thorndike, like many of his contemporaries, was awed by the scientific advances that had taken place within his own lifetime. Unprecedented progress had been made in physics, chemistry, and biology. The technological spin-offs of those advances in the basic disciplines had literally transformed society. Small wonder, then, that Thorndike should seek to fashion his view of psychology in the image of what he believed to be true about these better established and visibly successful sciences. In this view, people—like rocks and stars and trees—are natural objects inhabiting a lawful universe. Therefore, they too—like falling stones—behave lawfully. Each human event, like each physical motion, must be caused. Simply stated, the goal of psychology is to seek those causes, to reveal the laws that govern human nature. The social use of that revelation is prediction and control in the interest of the common weal. Because advances in the physical sciences seemed to wait upon instrumentation—the development of measuring devices, such as the thermometer, the galvanometer, and the spectroscope—it followed that psychology, if it were to enjoy similar advances, needed its own instruments with which to measure the properties of human nature. In Thorndike's view the mental test was one of the first and most important of such badly needed yardsticks.

This view of human affairs, with its deterministic, positivistic, and behavioristic leanings, comprises one side of the great debate that has raged within the social sciences throughout this century. Indeed, the debate was already under way long before Thorndike put pen to paper. Its contemporary form was foreshadowed in the writings of

nineteenth-century continental philsosophers and is not the place to
join that debate, but it is important to point out that Thorndike's
fundamental premises about both the goals and methods of psychology are indeed debatable. There are alternative conceptions to the
ones he put forward, conceptions in which the examination of
reasons, explanations, and other expressions of human intentionality
and purpose replace the search for causes and effects, in which the
goals of understanding and interpretation substitute for prediction
and control.

In choosing among these competing conceptions of how best to
proceed in our scientific endeavor, as Barzun and Toulmin remind
us, the issue is not which is right and which is wrong. That is far too
simple-minded. Rather, we must allow for the appropriateness of different conceptions for different *scientific* purposes. As Toulmin puts
it, speaking of science in general:

Science has not one aim but many, and its development has passed through
many contrasted stages. It is therefore fruitless to look for a single, all-purpose
"scientific method": the growth and evolution of scientific ideas depends on no
one method and will always call for a broad range of different enquiries. Science
as a whole—the activity, its aims, its methods and ideas—evolves by variation and
selection." [p. 17.]

Exactly nineteen years before the first issue of the *Journal of Educational Psychology* was published, another educational journal, *The
Educational Review*, made its debut. It too began with a lead essay
by a prominent educator. The essayist was the Harvard philosopher
Josiah Royce. The title of his remarks posed the question: "Is There
a Science of Education?" One cannot help wondering whether or not
Thorndike ever read that essay, and, if he did, what he thought of it,
for it contains an argument that is in many ways diametrically opposed to the one Thorndike put forth.

In the beginning of his essay Royce borrows heavily from a paper
by the German philosopher Wilhelm Dilthey read before the Academy of Sciences in Berlin in 1888. In essence Dilthey argues, and
Royce agrees, that a universally valid science of pedagogy is impossible precisely because "human nature cannot be adequately described
through any abstract formulation of its traits" (Royce 1891, p. 17).
"Hence," Royce explains, "the educator cannot hope to have defined
for him, with abstract universality, either the material upon which

he must always work—namely human nature—nor the end toward which he must always aim—namely the highest moral perfection of his pupil. Both these matters are modified for him by the course of evolution and by the actual social environment" (p. 17). "And 'therefore,'" Royce again quotes from Dilthey, "'no concrete educational questions can be solved in terms of a universally valid science.'" "Such questions," Royce concludes, "will always contain elements of uncertainty, will always require the practical skill of the individual educator, and will always receive answers that will vary with time and occasion" (p. 20).

In a strange way Royce's and Dilthey's conclusions have a more modern ring than do Thorndike's, which were written almost twenty years later. The latter seem almost completely lacking in a sense of historicity and cultural relativity. As Thorndike describes human beings, they seem not to be inhabitants of cultures or even of historical epochs; rather, they seem to exist in culture-free and time-free "environments" where they are bombarded by stimuli as unchanging and universal as the sun's rays. Though not a religious man in the conventional sense, Thorndike did have a deep and abiding faith in the benefits that were to flow from scientific work. Twice in his brief essay he affirms his conviction that, as he first puts it, "directly or indirectly, soon or late, every advance in the science of human behavior will contribute to our success in controlling human nature and changing it to the advantage of the common weal" (p. 8). At the close of his remarks, almost in the manner of a benediction, he reiterates the same tenet. "Any truth about [the world]," his parting words tell us, "will directly or indirectly, soon or late, benefit action" (p. 12).

Now it is easy to understand how comforting such a faith would be to the person holding it. Imagine believing that everything you did in the way of uncovering truth, no matter how minor, inched the world toward a utopian future, an earthly paradise in which scientific knowledge had succeeded in overcoming all ignorance and eliminating all human suffering and folly. And one of the nicest things about this is that there is no wastage in the process. Every scrap of truth, the tiniest shard of knowledge will work its way, soon or late, into the grand design. Shades of Newton and the Enlightenment! At the same time it is easy to envision how such a faith might also be used by the scientist as a dodge to ward off pressure from the practical world. Faced with the impatient practitioner who questioned the value of some of his work, Thorndike was armed with the perfect rejoinder: "Just you wait, soon or late, all truth benefits action." With that reassurance given, he could return with a clear conscience to his laboratory studies of mental fatigue.

But, alas, times have changed and the "sea of faith," even secular faith of the type Thorndike espoused, no longer lays about us "like the folds of a bright girdle furled." Contrast, as against Thorndike's optimism, the following statement from a recent book on educational research edited by Cronbach and Suppes:

. . . it is not our assumption that social benefits will automatically come from any increase in the amount of inquiry. . . . Investigation of social processes is difficult at best, and it is possible for a costly inquiry to yield nothing of value. [1969, p. 141.]

It would be wrong to conclude from this quotation, however, that all traces of the old Thorndikean faith have been expurgated from the modern view. Cronbach and Suppes manage to keep old hopes alive in two ways. First, they point out that fundamental research, which they call "conclusion-oriented inquiry" to differentiate it from the more practical "decision-oriented inquiry," rarely feeds directly into human affairs. Rather, it alters, in a manner that is as yet poorly understood, the total belief system of our society, that diffuse complex of shared ideas that Cronbach and Suppes label "the prevailing view." Second, though they acknowledge that not every investigation will leave its mark even in this indirect way, they are confident that some will. As they put it:

The faith is that with a good many studies in progress, some of them will generate conceptual advances significant enough to offset the cost of the whole enterprise. [p. 23.]

So we still have faith, though it is more diluted and probabilistic than in Thorndike's day. It is, in a way that Thorndike himself might have found satisfying, a faith in numbers.

But even this remnant of an earlier utopian vision requires qualification. For it is not at all as clear as it once was that incremental additions, direct or indirect, to public understanding will eventuate in the kind of complete knowledge that Thorndike seemed to forecast. In his 1974 address Cronbach brings in "the eternal note of sadness" with these words:

As time passes, the prevailing view will not necessarily progress from hazy vision to crude sketch to articulate blueprint. . . . Though our sketch of man may become more elaborate, it will remain a sketch. [p. 126.]

The question is whether we can be content with this eroded faith. Does it leave us with sufficient will to carry on our efforts? Is a pessimistic educational psychology a contradiction in terms? Can a person who has begun to entertain a tragic vision of Man continue to give a damn about regression coefficients? And back we go to the hall of mirrors, the leaky battery, and the pile of stubble.

I mentioned at the start that Cronbach ended his speech on an optimistic note. It is time now to consider the source of his optimism. In essence, Cronbach believes that psychologists can be most helpful if they keep their sights lowered and do not aim too high. His plea is for what he calls "short-run empiricism" and "intensive local observation." He concludes that "the special task of the social scientist in each generation is to pin down the contemporary facts." But then he quickly adds, "Beyond that, he shares with the humanistic scholar and artist in the effort to gain insight into contemporary relationships and to realign the culture's view of man with present realities." "To know man as he is," Cronbach declares at the close, "is no mean aspiration" (p. 127).

Rousing though it may be, there is something about Cronbach's concluding thoughts that jars the sensibilities. Pinning down the contemporary facts sounds so humble, but joining with scholars and artists in realigning the culture's view of man sounds so noble. Can we have it both ways? As I was puzzling over this apparent paradox, I began to get picky about Cronbach's choice of words. He calls for us to "pin down the contemporary facts." Now I know the expression is common enough; I have used it many times myself. But are facts ever pinned down? In what sense? Does it mean pin to the mat, as might a wrestler? Or is it rather to affix with a pin, as might a seamstress? Trivial questions, to be sure, and more than a bit smart alecky perhaps, but they do bring me back to Thorndike and to my fourth and final complaint about his vision: its failure to take into account the aesthetic dimension of the scientist's work.

Thorndike, I fear, was not much given to self-reflection. In fact, he seems to have been naively unself-conscious, at least when it came to the contribution of his own imagination to his scientific work. He believed that the world of reality was simply out there, awaiting exploration. To him, facts were simply descriptive statements about that out-there world, something to be "pinned down." But the word *fact*, as its etymology reminds us, refers not simply to something discovered but to something made, a thing done, a deed. Thus in his search for facts, the scientist—like the artist—may be said to be actively engaged in the creation of meaning. He abides by different rules, of course, but he is nonetheless guided by his own vision of what is out there to be found. F.R. Leavis, the renowned literary critic, makes the point forcefully with these words:

It is a disastrous illusion that we can attain to the real by any abstracting process, or that perception is a matter of passive exposure to an objective world of which science gives a true report. The eye is part of the brain, and the brain is a representative of the living whole, an agent of the psyche: perception is creative. [Leavis, in Coveney 1967, p. 16.]

Oddly enough, however, this tendency to overlook the role of the mind in apprehending is not at all uncommon. It is part of what Whitehead called "the fallacy of misplaced concreteness" (Whitehead 1925, p. 72). Indeed, this blindness to his own contribution to discovery may be a condition of the scientist's success, for as the philosopher Michael Polanyi puts it:

The most daring feats of originality . . . must be performed on the assumption that they originate nothing, but merely reveal what is there. And their triumph confirms this assumption, for what has been found bears the mark of reality in being pregnant with yet unforeseeable implications . . . The whole process of discovery and confirmation ultimately relies on our own accrediting of our own vision of reality. [1958, p. 130.]

Thus, had Thorndike been more aware of his own artistry, perhaps he would not have been as inventive as he was; at the same time he might have been more cautious in his claims, recognizing that his vision of reality—even though meeting an acceptable standard of objectivity—would not be fully shared in other times and other places. He might also have been less slavishly dependent on the model of the physical sciences, more willing to have probed the metaphorical significance of words like "cause" and "measurement" and even "science" itself as applied to human affairs. He might, too, have been somewhat more patient with his forebearers—those so-called "prescientific" psychologists such as Herbart and Bain—whose writings, like the art of the Incas, contain messages worthy of preservation. A more finely honed aesthetic sense might also have made Thorndike more sensitive to the underlying rhetoric of what he himself said, cognizant that the obligation of the scientist is not merely to tell the truth but to tell it in a way that will persuade others. But all this is mere conjecture whose chief value is to remind us of the hard work that lies ahead.

Finally, returning to contemporary thought about what we should be doing, I find it intriguing that Cronbach himself, even while insisting on the primacy of facts, could not completely avoid all reference to the artistic side of the psychologist's work. The outcome of that work, he tells us, is to be a *sketch* of man. Not a bad metaphor on which to close; for even though that sketch may never be complete, the thought of penciling in a few lines is not at all unattractive. Nor does it matter if, sooner or later, others with fresher vision and surer hands should chance to squint critically at our wiggly tracings and try to do us one better. In fact, that would be a stroke of good fortune. For, to paraphrase Cronbach—while at the same time offering a parting salute to Thorndike—even to be known by man as he will become is no mean aspiration.

REFERENCES

Barzun, Jacques. *Clio and the Doctors.* Chicago: University of Chicago Press, 1974.

Carroll, John B. "The Place of Educational Psychology in the Study of Education." In *The Discipline of Education*, edited by John Walton and James L. Kuethe, pp. 101-19. Madison: University of Wisconsin Press, 1963.

Coveney, Peter. *The Image of Childhood*, with introduction by R. R. Leavis. Baltimore: Penguin Books, 1967.

Cronbach, Lee J. "Beyond the Two Disciplines of Scientific Psychology." *American Psychologist* 30 (February 1975): 116-27.

Cronbach, Lee J. and Suppes, Patrick. *Research for Tomorrow's Schools.* New York: Macmillan Co., 1969.

Kohlberg, Lawrence. "The Concepts of Developmental Psychology as the Central Guide to Education: Examples from Cognitive, Moral, and Psychological Education." In *Proceedings of the Conference on Psychology and the Process of Schooling in the Next Decade*, edited by Maynard Reynolds, pp. 1-55. Minneapolis: Department of Audio Visual Extension, University of Minnesota, 1971.

McKeachie, Wilbert J. "Psychology in America's Bicentennial Year." *American Psychologist* 31 (December 1976): 819-33.

Polanyi, Michael. *Personal Knowledge.* Chicago: University of Chicago Press, 1958.

Royce, Josiah. "Is There a Science of Education?" *Educational Review* 1 (January 1891): 15-25; (February 1891): 121-32.

Thorndike, Edward L. "The Contribution of Psychology to Education." *Journal of Educational Psychology* 1 (January 1910): 5-12.

Toulmin, Stephen. *Foresight and Understanding.* New York: Harper & Row, 1961.

Walton, John, and Kuethe, James L. *The Discipline of Education.* Madison: University of Wisconsin Press, 1963.

Whitehead, Alfred North. *Science and the Modern World.* New York: Macmillan, 1925.